THE TWELVE GENERATIONS OF THE CREATION

With Biblical Timelines from Adam to Christ

A Physician's Perspective of the Book of Genesis

Larry D. Edwards, M.D

xulon PRESS

The Twelve Generations of the Creation
By Larry D. Edwards, M.D.

Printed in the United States of America

Registration Number TXu1-295-864
October 13, 2006

ISBN 978-1-60034-913-3

www.xulonpress.com

AUTHOR'S NOTES

When helpful to clarify the meaning of a word or passage, the author uses NASB margin translations or his own translation from the Hebrew or Greek text. When using a NASB margin translation, NASB margin follows the Scripture reference.

In Hebrew, the name reflects the character. Fourteen different names of God are found in the book of Genesis. Each one enriches our understanding of the character of God. When it aids in understanding the Biblical text, the translations of the various Hebrew names of God into English occur throughout the manuscript (pages 50-54).

The English meaning of Hebrew words can often be translated several ways. In most circumstances, the chosen English translation is enclosed in quotation marks followed in parentheses by the English pronunciation and the Hebrew word, e.g., "expanse" (*raq̂îya'*, רקיע). Sometimes all three are enclosed in parentheses. English translations of a few Greek words from the New Testament are depicted in the same manner.

The author uses bold letters for his emphasis throughout the manuscript.

Repetition occasionally occurs for the purpose of emphasis and/or to maintain the flow of the discussion.

A map on page 160 details the sites encountered by the patriarchs during their journeys. The first time a site on the map appears in the text, brackets draw attention to its location, e.g., Ur [map site 1].

"I know that You can do all things, and that no purpose of Yours can be thwarted" (Job 42:2).

"There is no wisdom and no understanding and no counsel against the LORD" (Prov. 21:30).

DEDICATION

The effort invested in a commentary on the book of Genesis is a laborious but gratifying task.

My wife Ann, my co-laborer over the years, and our three children: Elliott, Sharon, and Beth have all shared in this work in one way or another. I love and respect them and am appreciative of each one's contribution.

My original intent was to prepare a manuscript just for the family's perusal. However, several individuals who attended our Bible studies over the years encouraged publication of the material as a book. As any teacher knows, one learns from the questions asked by students. I am thankful for all our friends who attended these Bible studies for their many contributions.

In addition, I am indebted to many friends and family members for suggestions. I owe a special debt of gratitude to several people who took time to proofread the text.

My sincere desire is for this book to honor the name of the One Triune God, the author of the Bible, and His message of eternal salvation for those who turn to Him in faith.

TABLE OF CONTENTS

TABLE OF CONTENTS—CONTINUED

TABLE OF CONTENTS—CONTINUED

TABLES, BAR GRAPH, MAP, AND CHARTS

TABLES, BAR GRAPH, MAP, AND CHARTS

CONTINUED

PROLOGUE

The creation account in the book of Genesis is more than the account of the heavens and earth. The book records different epochs of the creation. The Genesis account includes the progeny of the first humans and their successes and failures. It finishes with a family destined to become the nation of Israel. Abraham, the spiritual father of that nation, was to bless the nations of the earth through his progeny. The commission to Israel was to take the truth of God to the nations. Subsequent Biblical history tells of their failure to accomplish the task until the Messiah came and commissioned the church, the Israel of God, composed of believing Hebrews and Gentiles, to fulfill the task.

In the book of Genesis, two different Hebrew nouns are translated into English as generations, account, birth, genealogies, order, or time. The Hebrew noun, *toledot* (*toledot*, תולדות), is used to describe ten specific generations, ten spiritual epochs.

The Hebrew noun, *dor* (*dor̂*, דור), generally refers to generations in the sense of a lifetime. For example, it is used in the prophecy of the children of Israel's return to the Promised Land after spending 400 years plus in Egypt (Gen. 15:13-16, Exod. 12:40). After that time in Egypt, *Yahweh* stated that the nation of Israel would return to the Promised Land in the fourth "generation" (*dor̂,* דור), i.e., four lifetimes (pages 398-399):

"Then in the fourth generation they will return here, for the iniquity of the Amorite is not yet complete" (Gen. 15:16).

Dor is used alone in the description of two specific generations, the generations after the flood and Abraham's generations. In both of these circumstances, *dor* refers to the successive generations of the progeny of Shem, Ham, and Japheth and the progeny of Abraham, respectively. However, these two generations are also spiritual epochs. The first describes the covenant with all of mankind after the flood that will continue until the end of the present age. The second describes the progeny of Abraham (after his change from Abram) that would engender the nation of Israel, the church, and the Israel of God that will continue forever. Thus, *dor* has a secondary meaning in these two instances; both are spiritual epochs equal in significance to the other ten where the word, *toledot*, is used.

Both words describe the generations of Noah.

Therefore, the focus of this commentary is on 12 different beginnings, 12 different generations, 12 different spiritual epochs recorded in the book of Genesis.

1. The generations of the heavens and the earth—an account of the creation, the first couple, their temptation, and the Fall (Gen. 2:4).

2. The generations of Adam—a description of the righteous line after the Fall (Gen. 5:1).

3. The generations of Noah—the last family in the righteous line before the flood (Gen. 6:9, 7:1).

4. The generations after the flood—the Noahic covenant given to mankind, the earth, and all living creatures after the flood (Gen. 9:12).

5. The generations of Shem, Ham, and Japheth—the development of three people-groups from the three sons of Noah after the flood (Gen. 10:1, 32).

6. The generations of Shem—the record of the further development of the righteous line from the flood until the time of Abram (Gen. 11:10).

7. The generations of Terah—a split occurred within Terah's family. Most continued in the unrighteous line, but one man, Abram, continued the righteous line (Gen. 11:27).

8. The generations of Abraham—Abram's character (name) change resulted in a blessing to all the earth through the seed of the

promised son, Isaac, and eventually, the Seed of the promised Son, the LORD-Jesus-Christ/*YHWH-Yeshua-Mashiach* (page 51). The progeny of the other sons of Abraham, Ishmael from Hagar and the six sons from Keturah, became perpetual enemies of the nation of Israel. However, some became believers in *Yahweh* (LORD) and were among the multitude from the nations to whom blessing came through Abraham (Gen. 17:7, 9, 12).

9. The generations of Ishmael—Ishmael was the son obtained by Abram's own potency. Abram, not Abraham, was the father of Ishmael. Eventually this would result in enmity between Muslims who claim that Ishmael, the son of the flesh, is the promised son, and all Hebrews and Christians who claim that Isaac, the son of faith, is the promised son (Gen. 25:12-13).

10. The generations of Isaac—a further split occurred between Isaac's two sons. Esau continued in the unrighteous line; Jacob's seed continued in the righteous line (Gen. 25:19).

11. The generations of Esau—Esau became a godless, immoral man who furthered the enmity against Israel through his dominion of Mount Seir/Edom and through his progeny (Gen. 36:1, 9).

12. The generations of Jacob—Jacob became Israel, a changed man. He engendered the nation of Israel through his 12 sons (Gen. 37:2).

Therefore, in Hebrew, the definition of "generations" (*toledot* or *dor*) is a spiritual epoch of variable duration. In Greek, the same definition for a "generation" (*genea,* γενεά) applies in the New Testament:

"Truly I say to you, this generation will not pass away until all these things take place" (Matt. 24:34).

The present generation, the present spiritual epoch, is the one between the first and second coming of the LORD Jesus Christ.

The author has scrutinized several books written by biological and physical scientists on the creation. The authors of most of these books are deficient in their understanding of the Genesis account. In addition, evidence about the creation occurs throughout the Bible, not just in the book of Genesis. Many of these books are woefully inaccurate in their evaluation of the Biblical statements about the creation.

The comments on the creation herein are not an apologetic dissertation. There are several excellent books already written in defense of the creation account as stated in the Bible. However, since the thinking of many people is biased from reading the extra-Biblical literature about the creation, comparative remarks and references are given where the interested reader can pursue the subject further.

The author is a physician, not a theologian. Herein you will find the perspective of a physician with no special training other than that which comes from personal study. The author writes with the belief that the Bible is not a theological treatise for only those trained in seminaries and Bible schools. It is a book for all people to understand and apply to their lives.

Many commentaries do not discuss the numerous medical issues in the book of Genesis. It is the author's hope that the medical insights contained herein will be helpful to the reader.

The author believes that it is unwise to place human understanding above the One who is omniscient and created our minds. A person may benefit, or be harmed, by only intellectual truth found in the Bible. By itself, intellectual understanding is insufficient for gleaning spiritual truth. The Bible proclaims the condition necessary to gain its full meaning.

The Holy Spirit renews the minds of those that seek God, so His truth can become real to each person (Rom. 12:1-2). The Bible states that spiritual discernment is necessary. One must submit to the Holy Spirit as Teacher before the complete truth can be ascertained (John 7:17, 14:16). To gain such wisdom, one must come to God by faith, believing that He exists, and that He will reward those who seek Him (Heb. 11:6):

"You will seek Me and find Me when you search for Me with all your heart" (Jer. 29:13).

God has communicated to us through the Bible, the Word of God; our goal should be to understand what it says. Those who do not understand the statement that the Bible is the Word of God will benefit by reading Appendix I (pages 391-393).

This is not a commentary that dwells on all the possible interpretations of a passage. In the majority of circumstances, the author has sifted the contextual and linguistic issues and related Scriptures to arrive at a conclusion. If the reader wishes to read multiple possibilities for interpretation of a passage, many commentaries are available that relate the same.

During the author's attempt to understand the original languages versus the various English translations, it became clear that translators, instead of letting the text speak for itself, have sometimes given their theological bias in translation of some passages. Instead of using the linguistic idiom and changing cultural mores of the West, the author believes that it is more accurate to state the original meaning of a word, phrase, idiom, or sentence in the ancient language and culture of the people who originally received the message. Principles of interpretation are discussed in Appendix II (page 394).

Those who are not conversant with the Biblical languages can still benefit from the language notations and discussions on the culture that give additional illumination to the text.

The ages and times of the patriarchs are important in studying the spiritual epochs in Genesis and the rest of the Bible. There is significant variation in published Old Testament timelines. The author's commentary and calculations of the Biblical Timelines from Adam to Christ appear in Tables 10-12 (Appendix III, pages 395-410).

CHAPTER 1

THE GENERATIONS OF THE HEAVENS AND EARTH

INTRODUCTION

The title, Genesis (Γένεσις), comes from the Greek translation of the Old Testament, the Septuagint (η Μετάφραση των Εβδομήκοντα). The title in the Hebrew Bible, the *Tanakh*, is "In the Beginning," the three English words that translate the Hebrew preposition and word (*bre'shiŷth,* בראשית) that begin the book. It is the initial book of the first five called the Torah (תורה) in Hebrew and the Pentateuch (Πεντάτευχος) in Greek. The Hebrew manuscripts are the most reliable of all the ancient manuscripts.

Tanakh is an acronym—**T**orah (the first five books), ***N**evi'im* (the prophets), and the ***K**'tuvim* (the writings, the rest of the Old Testament).

The Bible reveals that God is Triune: God the Father is Creator; God the Son is Creator; God the Holy Spirit is Creator (Gen. 1:2, 5:1-5; John 1:1-3; Col. 1:15-17; Heb. 1:2, 11:3; Rev. 4:10-11). This may mean that the Trinity, in concert, commanded the creation:

"The earth was formless and void, and darkness was over the surface of the deep, and the Spirit of God was moving over the surface of the waters" (Gen. 1:2).

"By faith we understand that the worlds were prepared by the word of God, so that what is seen was not made out of things which are visible" (Heb. 11:3).

"In the beginning was the Word, and the Word was with God, and the Word was God. He was in the beginning with God. All things came into being through Him, and apart from Him nothing came into being that has come into being" (John 1:1-3).

"He is the image of the invisible God, the firstborn of all creation. For by Him all things were created, both in the heavens and on earth, visible and invisible, whether thrones or dominions or rulers or authorities—all things have been created through Him and for Him. He is before all things, and in Him all things hold together" (Col. 1:15-17).

The first quoted verse refers to the Holy Spirit. The second tells how God, by His word, commanded the creation. The last two passages refer to the LORD Jesus Christ, the Word, the person of the Godhead who fully expresses the character of God in human form.

The Hebrew word for God in the first chapter of Genesis is *Elohim*, a plural masculine noun. In this first chapter of Genesis, *Elohim* always refers to the One Triune God, the Creator. *Elohim* may refer to men or multiple gods in other parts of the Bible. In Hebrew, the verbs and/or related pronouns are plural in those references that refer to men or to many false gods (Psa. 82:6, 86:8; Jer. 16:11, 13). When the Trinity is referenced, i.e., *Elohim*, a singular verb or singular pronoun is used in Genesis and the rest of the Bible.

God commanded the creation into being. The phrase, "let there be," or a similar one, refers to His command of *de novo* creation. The creation required the conversion of God's energy to matter. Sometimes this was followed by the use of God's creative energy to change one type of matter into another, i.e., to make something. In Hebrew, the initial description of the creation closes with the words, "which God had created to make" (Gen. 2:3 NASB margin).

Four Different Verbs Describe the Creation

1. **To create** (*bara*, ברא) is to bring something material and/or spiritual forth that was not there prior to the creative act; energy is converted to some other form or material substance (Gen. 1:1).

God **created** the darkness and then **formed** the light that antedated the creation:

"I am the LORD, and there is no other, the One forming light and creating darkness" (Isa. 45:6b-7a).

God is light; His physical light represents His spiritual light (John 3:19-21, 8:12). He **formed** the light of creation; it was pre-existent. He **created** the darkness; it was a new creation:

"Then God said, 'Let there be light'; and there was light" (Gen. 1:3).

Since He is light, and He antedated the creation, His pre-existent light will continue in the new creation:

"And the city has no need of the sun or of the moon to shine on it, for the glory of God has illumined it, and its lamp is the Lamb" (Rev. 21:23).

God's creative power commanded there to be an "expanse" (*raq̂iŷa'*, רקיע) between the waters:

"Then God said, 'Let there be an expanse in the midst of the waters, and let it separate the waters from the waters'" (Gen. 1:6).

The expanse contains "two heavens," a dual noun in Hebrew (*sham̂ayim*, שׁמים) (Gen. 1:8).

God commanded and **created** the sea creatures and birds:

"Then God said, 'Let the waters teem with swarms of living creatures, and let birds fly above the earth in the open expanse of the heavens.' God created the great sea monsters and every living creature that moves, with which the waters swarmed after their kind, and every winged bird after its kind; and God saw that it was good" (Gen. 1:20-21).

Man became a spiritual being within a physical body, a trinity-in-unity, **created** in the *imago Dei*, the image of God:

"God created man in His own image, in the image of God He created him; male and female He created them" (Gen. 1:27).

2. The infinitive, **"to make"** (*asah*, עשׂה), is used when creatively changing one form of matter into another:

"Then God said, 'Let Us make man in Our image, according to Our likeness; and let them rule over the fish of the sea and over the birds of the sky and over the cattle and over all the earth, and over every creeping thing that creeps on the earth'" (Gen. 1:26).

God commanded the earth to produce:

"Then God said, 'Let the earth sprout vegetation: plants yielding seed, and fruit trees on the earth bearing fruit after their kind with seed in them; and it was so'" (Gen. 1:11).

The formed light came on the first day; on the fourth day, the light itself was the substance that was concentrated in specific light-bearing bodies:

"Then God said, 'Let there be lights in the expanse of the heavens to separate the day from the night, and let them be for signs and for season and for days and years; and let them be for lights in the expanse of the heavens to give light on the earth'; and it was so. God made the two great lights, the greater light to govern the day, and the lesser light to govern the night, the stars also" (Gen. 1:14-16).

God **made** all types of beasts and insects from the substance of the earth:

"Then God said, 'Let the earth bring forth living creatures after their kind: cattle and creeping things and beast of the earth after their kind.' God made the beasts of the earth; and it was so" (Gen. 1:24).

The past tense of the infinitive, "to make" (*asah*, עשׂה), is used as a summary statement for the six days. The reason for using this verb may have been that all the creation was now in some type of material substance:

"God saw all that He had made" (Gen. 1:31a).

Amplification of the verbs occurs at the close of the seventh day of creation, i.e., **"created to make"**:

"Then God blessed the seventh day and sanctified it, because in it He rested from all His work which God had created to make" (Gen. 2:3 NASB margin).

3. God also **"formed"** (*yatsar*, יצר) different parts of the creation:

"I am the LORD, and there is no other, the One forming light and creating darkness" (Isa. 45:6b-7a).

In addition, the LORD God (*Yahweh 'ĕlôhîym,* יהוה אלהים) **"formed"** (*yatsar*, יצר) man of dust from the ground (Gen. 2:7).

4. *Banah* (*bânâh*, בנה) means **"to build."** The woman was "built" (fashioned) from the rib of the man:

"The LORD God fashioned into a woman the rib which He had taken from the man, and brought her to the man" (Gen. 2:22).

THE *ELOHIM* ACCOUNT OF CREATION

Genesis 1:1-31

Gen. 1:1: The first verse of the Bible introduces the subject matter, the creation of the heavens and the earth.

The Hebrew word for "heavens" is a dual noun that denotes the fact that there is more than one heaven. Dual forms in Hebrew may have the meaning of two or more. Here the dual aspect may refer to the physical heaven as being separate from the spiritual heaven.

Solomon indicated this in his prayer for the nation: “Behold, heaven and the heaven of heavens cannot contain You” (2 Chr. 6:18b). The first part of heaven is the physical realm, “heaven,” and the latter, “heaven of heavens,” is the spiritual realm. The physical heaven has two parts, the immediate atmosphere and outer space. Therefore, it is possible to refer to three heavens, one spiritual and two physical ones. The Apostle Paul spoke of third heaven, the spiritual abode of God (2 Cor. 12:2).

Hebrew is read from right to left. In Hebrew, the fourth and sixth words of the first seven words of Genesis that occur just before heavens and before earth are composed of the *alef* and *tau* (**את**), the first and last letters of the Hebrew alphabet:

“In the beginning God created the heavens and the earth” (בראשית ברא אלהים **את** השמים ו**את** הארץ) (Gen. 1:1).

In the current use of the Hebrew language, this two-lettered word is the Defined Direct Object (DDO) that emphasizes its following object, and when used as such, it is absent from the English translation. Sometimes, את functions as a preposition, but not in this verse (pages 93-94).

Here the meaning of the DDO is much greater than this linguistic understanding. Originally, this two-lettered word meant “the essence of being.” In the context of this first verse, the DDO (**את**) refers to “the essence of being,” the eternal God, the One who contains the heavens and earth and all of time within His being. All will come to fear God and give Him glory as Creator:

“And he said with a loud voice, ‘Fear God, and give Him glory, because the hour of His judgment has come; worship Him who made the heaven and the earth and sea and springs of waters’” (Rev. 14:7).

Since this Hebrew word contains the first and last letters of the Hebrew alphabet, it symbolizes the fact that God is the beginning and the ending, the first and last (Rev. 1:17-18). In this first verse of Genesis, its placement indicates He is the first and last of the creation of the earth and the first and last of the creation of the heavens. God contains all within Himself (Acts 17:24-28): "The heaven of heavens cannot contain You" (1 Kin. 8:27a NASB margin).

Gen. 1:2: "The deep" (*tehôm*, תהום) can refer to the waters that cover Sheol. The likely meaning of Sheol in the Old Testament is the same as Hades, the abyss, and the bottomless pit in the New Testament (Rom. 10:7; 1 Pet. 3:18-19; Rev. 9:1-2, 20:1). Ezekiel spoke of the fate of Assyria in Sheol and the deep:

"Thus says the Lord GOD, 'On the day when it went down to Sheol I caused lamentations; I closed the deep over it and held back its rivers'" (Ezek. 31:15a).

Gehenna is the place of destruction of the body and the soul in the New Testament; Abaddon, "destruction" (*'aḇaddôn*, אבדון), has the same meaning in the Old Testament. Both words refer to Hell (page 322) (Job 31:12; Matt. 5:22, 10:28; Rev. 9:11):

"Naked is Sheol before Him, and Abaddon has no covering" (Job 26:6).

The creation of the darkness and the waters occurred **prior to the account** of the six days of creation (Genesis 1):

"I am the LORD, and there is no other, the One forming light and creating darkness" (Isa. 45:6b-7a).

"I clothe the heavens with blackness and make sackcloth their covering" (Isa. 50:3).

The Hebrew preposition translated as "in" can be translated as with, by, at, or above. Therefore, in the following verse, one possible translation of "in" is "above". Water was the substance already present at the beginning of the creation from which the earth was formed (Gen. 1:1, 7):

"He lays the beams of His upper chambers in the waters; He makes the clouds His chariot; He walks upon the wings of the wind" (Psa. 104:3).

"Praise Him, highest heavens, and the waters that are above the heavens." (Psa. 148:4).

"He has inscribed a circle on the surface of the waters at the boundary of light and darkness" (Job 26:10).

"For when they maintain this, it escapes their notice that by the word of God the heavens existed long ago and the earth was formed out of water and by water" (2 Pet. 3:5).

TOHU AND *BOHU*

The earth was "formless" (*tohu,* תהו) and "empty" (*bohu,* בהו). Some authors have suggested that *tohu* should be translated as "chaos"; they further suggest that Satan interfered with the creation at this time. Other authors have suggested there was a protracted period of time (gap theory) between the second and third verses.

It seems unlikely that the Creator would set out to create the heavens and the earth and then leave off the creative act for a long time. There are several reasons why the aforementioned are improbable interpretations:

1. The Holy Spirit was "hovering, moving gently (*rachaphat,* רחפת) over the surface of the waters." *Rachaphat* occurs just after the phrase that contains *tohu* and *bohu*. It seems unlikely that such a gentle movement would have occurred in the face of chaos.

2. The corresponding *bohu*, which is translated as "void," or "empty," does not suggest a chaotic scene. Isaiah and Jeremiah prophesied of a reversal to the state of *tohu* (*tohu,* תהו) and *bohu*

(*bohu,̂* בֹּהוּ) that will occur during the time of the end of the present age (Isa. 34:11, Jer. 4:1-28):

"I looked on the earth, and behold, it was formless and void; and to the heavens, and they had no light" (Jer. 4:23).

This suggests that God will remake the heavens and earth during the time of His wrath, another creative act. This will occur just prior to the millennial period, the thousand-year reign of the LORD Jesus Christ (Hag. 2:6, 21; Rev. 6:12-17).

The final destruction of the first earth and heavens will not occur until the end of the millennium (Rev. 20:11, 21:1).

3. *Yahweh* was **alone** during the initial creation, when He brought forth the heavens and the earth:

"Thus says the LORD your Redeemer, and the one who formed you from the womb, I, the LORD, am the maker of all things, stretching out the heavens by Myself, and spreading out the earth, who was with me? Causing the omens of boasters to fail, making fools out of diviners, causing wise men to draw back, and turning their knowledge into foolishness" (Isa. 44:24-25 NASB margin).

4. It is unthinkable that Lucifer, a created angel, could usurp *Yahweh Elohim* in His creative act.

5. The creation of Lucifer and the other angels did not occur until the second day, after the heavens were created (page 46).

The idea of formless, *tohu* (*tohu,̂* תֹּהוּ), and emptiness, *bohu* (*bohu,̂* בֹּהוּ), is a prelude to form and fullness. One can visualize this as the way an artist first paints the background of a painting and then fills in the details. The background is the creation of form; the fullness is the placement of detail within the form.

THE RELATIONSHIP BETWEEN THE DAYS OF CREATION

As the following table depicts, the first three days describe the form added to *tohu*, and the next three days describe the fullness added to *bohu*. There is a definite relationship between the first and fourth days, the second and fifth days, and the third and sixth days.

TABLE 1: THE DAYS OF CREATION	
***TOHU*—FORMLESS**	***BOHU*—EMPTINESS**
ADDED FORM	**ADDED FULLNESS**
Day 1: Light and Darkness	Day 4: Planetary Lights
Day 2: Heavens and Waters	Day 5: Birds and Sea Creatures
Day 3: Earth and Vegetation	Day 6: Animals and Man
Day 7: Sabbath Day of Rest	

The Hebrew word, *yom* (*yôm*, יום), describes the entire seven days of creation as well as each individual day (Gen. 2:4). Therefore, this word may apply to differing periods; the meaning must be ascertained from the context.

The cardinal, "one day" (*yôm 'echad̂*, יום אחד), not its ordinal, describes the initial day. However, ordinals describe the second, third, fourth, and fifth days. These days have no article before them in Hebrew; this is equivalent to the English article, **a**.

Calling the initial day by its cardinal may have been for the purpose of defining the period of one day, 24 hours. God who is limitless and timeless told how He established the duration of one day. On the fourth day, He made the heavenly bodies that determine time as currently understood: seasons, days, and years. Thus, the fourth day is pivotal for understanding time as determined by the heavenly bodies.

The use of the Hebrew article, **the** (ה), occurs only with the sixth (*shishshiŷ*, הששי) and seventh (*shebiŷ'iy̆*, השביעי) days. Adam and Eve were created on the sixth day. The creation of the heavenly bodies on the fourth day allowed the first couple to understand that each day contained 24 hours.

The seventh day was a day of rest. Since it is not possible to conceive of God as needing physical, mental, or spiritual rest, the Sabbath celebrated God's satisfaction with His work; His soul was "refreshed" (*naphash,* נפש) (Exod. 31:17). Because of his need for physical, mental, and spiritual rest, He set aside a day for man, a day for "soul refreshment" (Exod. 20:9-11, Mark 2:27-28).

Because of His labor in making the heavens and earth in six days, *Yahweh* commanded the observation of the Sabbath day.

"Six days you shall labor and do all your work, but the seventh day is a Sabbath of the LORD your God; in it you shall not do any work, you or your son or your daughter, your male or your female servant or your cattle or your sojourner who stays with you. For in six days the LORD made the heavens and the earth, the sea and all that is in them, and rested on the seventh day; therefore the LORD blessed the Sabbath day and made it holy" (Exod. 20:9-11).

It is inconceivable that these verses in Exodus mean anything other than 24-hour days. As previously discussed, day one is described by its cardinal. Each of the seven days started with an evening followed by a morning. Thus, each of the seven days of creation was a literal 24-hour day.

THE CREATION AND SCIENCE

The primary purpose of this discussion is to declare what the Bible says about the creation of the universe, its eventual destruction, and finally, the new creation. Discussion of current scientific theory relative to the creation account given in the Bible is important for understanding what scientists **believe** about the creation. Unfortunately, in the present age most people, including scientists, are Biblically illiterate. Therefore, declaration of Biblical truth is a necessity before one can compare the Biblical account with that of science.

The scientist who studies creation has a dilemma; he can only study the creation after it was completed. All scientific data and formulae are a study of data projected back to the beginning. The scientist can only infer how things began. In addition, one must understand that scientific theories continually undergo modification; the Biblical account is unchanging. When the scientist speculates about the beginning, he is expressing his faith in his data. That belief may, or may not, be justified. One must ascertain whether the scientist's **faith** in his data is as reliable as **faith** in God and His Word, the Bible (Appendix I, pages 391-393).

Most people in our society accept what science says, or what the media says about science, as truth without critical examination of the same. Some of the current scientific theories have validity, some partial validity, and some are false. Many people act as though scientific theories never change; only God is changeless.

The Bible is the revelation of the Creator; science is an effort by man to try to understand the creation. The former is perfect; the latter is speculative and based on incomplete data.

All valid scientific evidence will be supportive of the One who is the source of all knowledge. The Bible provides an understanding of the beginning as revealed by the Creator. Therefore, the Bible, the declaration of the Creator, judges science. Science, finite man's effort to understand the creation, will ultimately undergo His judgment.

Most of the scientific writers who have argued against the Biblical account of creation, and for a great age of the universe, reveal a casual, simplistic interpretation of the Bible. They often assume that the first two chapters of Genesis account for the total revelation about the creation given in the Bible. The Genesis account is merely the beginning of the creation account. Indeed, the LORD revealed many details about the creation in the prophets, the book of Job, and other books of the Bible. If one wishes to analyze the Bible's account of creation, it is necessary to examine carefully all the material that applies to the same.

Anything less is shoddy analysis. It is difficult to understand why many scientists read their literature with great care but are superficial in their evaluation of the contents of the Bible. If scientists would carefully examine all the comments on the creation in the Bible, they would be more circumspect in the comparison of their data with the Scriptures.

The LORD Jesus Christ proclaimed the Scriptures to be His word, His truth (Matt. 5:18, 24:35). That truth will judge science:

"The scholar has a vitally important task to perform within a carefully prescribed precinct. His task is to guarantee the purity of the text, to get as close as possible to the Word as originally given. He may compare Scripture with Scripture until he has discovered the true meaning of the text. But right there his authority ends. He must never sit in judgment upon what is written. He dare not bring the meaning of the Word before the bar of his reason. He dare not commend or condemn the Word as reasonable or unreasonable, scientific, or unscientific. After the meaning is discovered, that meaning judges him; never does he judge it."[1]

Yahweh Elohim's Description of the Creation of the Universe

God has deigned to tell us how He created and continues the creation. He emphasized the same by stating it at least 17 times over many centuries through different individuals. Different Hebrew verbs, translated into English in past, present, and future tenses for "stretch" and "spread," give an indication of how *Yahweh Elohim* initiated and continues the creation.

In the first 14 references, the Hebrew verb for "stretch" (*natah*, נטה) is found in its various tenses.

1. "Who alone stretches out the heavens and tramples down the waves of the sea" (Job 9:8).

2. "He stretches out the north over empty space, and hangs the earth on nothing" (Job 26:7).

3. “Where were you when I laid the foundation of the earth? Tell Me, if you have understanding, Who set its measurements? Since you know. Or who stretched the line on it?” (Job 38:4-5).

4. “Covering Yourself with light as with a cloak, stretching out heaven like a tent curtain” (Psa. 104:2).

5. “It is He who sits above the circle of the earth, and its inhabitants are like grasshoppers, Who stretches out the heavens like a curtain and spreads them out like a tent to dwell in” (Isa. 40:22).

6. “Thus says God the LORD, Who created the heavens and stretched them out, Who spread out the earth and its offspring, Who gives breath to the people on it and spirit to those who walk in it” (Isa. 42:5).

7. “Thus says the LORD, your Redeemer, and the one who formed you from the womb, ‘I, the LORD, am the maker of all things, stretching out the heavens by Myself and spreading out the earth all alone’” (Isa. 44:24).

8. “It is I who made the earth, and created man upon it. I stretched out the heavens with My hands and I ordained all their host” (Isa. 45:12).

9. “That you have forgotten the LORD your Maker, Who stretched out the heavens and laid the foundations of the earth, that you fear continually all day long because of the fury of the oppressor as he makes ready to destroy? But where is the fury of the oppressor?” (Isa. 51:13).

10. “It is He who made the earth by His power, Who established the world by His wisdom; and by His understanding He has stretched out the heavens” (Jer. 10:12).

11. “I have made the earth, the men and the beasts which are on the face of the earth by My great power and by My outstretched

arm, and I will give it to the one who is pleasing in My sight" (Jer. 27:5).

12. "Ah, Lord GOD. Behold, You have made the heavens and the earth by Your great power and by Your outstretched arm. Nothing is too difficult for You" (Jer. 32:17).

13. "It is He who made the earth by His power, Who established the world by His wisdom, and by His understanding He stretched out the heavens" (Jer. 51:15).

14. "The burden of the word of the LORD concerning Israel. Thus declares the LORD Who stretches out the heavens, lays the foundation of the earth, and forms the spirit of man within him" (Zech. 12:1).

Three Hebrew verbs mean "spread" (*raq̂a',* רקע) (*mat̂hach,* מתח) (*tap̂hach,* טפח) and have a similar meaning to *natah*. Three of the above quoted verses (Isa. 40:22, 42:5, 44:24) and the three following verses contain one of these verbs in their various tenses:

15. "Can you, with Him, spread out the skies, strong as a molten mirror?" (Job 37:18).

16. "To Him who spread out the earth above the waters, for His lovingkindness is everlasting" (Psa. 136:6).

17. "Surely My hand founded the earth, and My right hand spread out the heavens; When I call to them, they stand together" (Isa. 48:13).

In these 17 declarations, God gives us an understanding of the way He created the heavens and the earth. The remarkable consistency between these verses is self-evident. These verses confirm that God created by an initial burst of energy that stretched (spread), stretches (spreads), and is stretching (spreading) out the heavens. The Hebrew verbs, in their various tenses, indicate this was an initial act that continues (Acts 17:24-28).

Some scientists have come to similar conclusions with their observation that the universe started abruptly and continues to expand.[2] Some have referred to this observation as the "Big Bang Theory"; others have contested the same and offered other suggestions.[3]

Rapid Cooling of Initial Heat

After its initial rapid expansion, many scientists believe it took billions of years for the universe to cool down.[4] The initial development of great distances that occurred with the rapid stretching out of the heavens would have had a cooling effect on the matter created as heat dissipated. Temperature decline depends on the nature of the substance. For radiant heat the temperature decline (cooling) is proportionate to the distance involved. The doubling of the size of the expansion of radiant heat halves the temperature. The heat of hydrogen gas cools faster than radiant heat according to the square of the size.[5] The rapid stretching out of the heavens would have resulted in rapid cooling. Two benefits come from this observation.

1. It is an error to assume that it took billions of years to cool the heat dissipated by the original burst of creative energy. The rapid expansion of the universe would have resulted in the cooling of matter and made feasible the development of life on the earth. It is possible that this contributed to an initial ice age in the northern and southern regions of the earth.

2. The uncoupling of hydrogen gas from radiant heat produced a temperature differential that provided the energy necessary to give order to the universe.[6]

God has no limitations; the Creator knew how to control the temperature of His creation within the microsecond of its initiation.

Time and Distance in Space

Light travels at 186,282 miles per second on earth. A light-year is defined as the distance light travels in a vacuum in a calendar year, about six trillion miles. However, it is unlikely that space is a vacuum, so there is no way to be sure that such measurements are valid in space. Time distortion occurs in space.[7]

Einstein's general theory of relativity declares that time is dependent on the relative motion of an observer measuring the time. This theory indicates that gravity distorts space-time geometry, so that space is curved or warped. This gives rise to the terms, "space warp" and "time warp." One practical effect of this theory is the belief that time runs faster in space.[8]

Einstein's mass-energy equation, $e=mc^2$, where e is energy, m is mass, and c is the speed of light is well known. To create the mass of the heavens and the earth would require a source of energy beyond human comprehension. This equation raises the question of whether time would stand still when the creation of matter reached the square of the speed of light with an initial burst of energy (if $m = 1$ and $c^2 = 1$, then $e = 1$). In that particle-second of creation, light-years may have been a way to measure initial distance, but not time. Since a great distance occurred in the fraction of a second in which the release of energy produced the expansion, it precludes the possibility of determining the age of the creation of the universe based on distance. The very idea of an expanding universe (stretches, and stretching out the heavens) further precludes determining the age of the universe by attempting to measure current distances in space. The LORD says it cannot be done:

"Thus says the LORD, 'If the heavens above can be measured and the foundations of the earth searched out below, then I will also cast off all the offspring of Israel for all that they have done,' declares the LORD" (Jer. 31:37).

Recent discoveries reveal stars calculated to be twelve billion light-years away from the earth. Such calculations may simply be recognizing the distances associated with the original burst of energy and the continuation of that creative burst. In other words, the present calculation of the distance of planets and stars is a reflection of the receipt of light at our point in history that occurred during the original—and continuing—creative burst of energy from God. Therefore, it is futile to determine time by attempting to measure the distance of heavenly objects from the earth.

As quoted above, God states that such a measurement is impossible (Jer. 31:37). Time is contained within the Eternal One; God contains all of the creation within Himself (2 Chr. 2:6, 6:18; Psa. 24:1, 50:12, 89:11; 1 Cor. 10:26):

"Am I a God who is near,' declares the LORD, 'And not a God far off? Can a man hide himself in hiding places so I do not see him?' declares the LORD. 'Do I not fill the heavens and the earth?' declares the LORD" (Jer. 23:23-24).

"But will God indeed dwell on the earth? Behold, heaven and the highest heaven cannot contain You" (1 Kin. 8:27a).

"For in Him we live and move and exist as even some of your own poets have said, 'For we also are His children'" (Acts 17:28).

Changes in the Universe

If God stretched out the universe, and continues to do so, will it go on forever? The Bible teaches a time of destruction of the universe during the pouring out of God's wrath at the end of the present age:

"And all the host of heaven will wear away, and the sky will be rolled up like a scroll; all their hosts will also wither away as a leaf withers from the vine, or as one withers from the fig tree" (Isa. 34:4).

"I looked when He broke the sixth seal, and there was a great earthquake; and the sun became black as sackcloth made of hair, and the whole moon became like blood; and the stars of the sky fell to the earth as a fig tree casts its unripe figs when shaken by a great wind. The sky was split apart like a scroll when it is rolled up, and every mountain and island were moved out of their places. Then the kings of the earth and the great men and the commanders and the rich and the strong and every slave and free man hid themselves in the caves and among the rocks of the mountains; and they say to the mountains and to the rocks, 'Fall on us and hide us from the presence of Him who sits on the throne, and from the wrath of the Lamb; for the great day of their wrath has come, and who is able to stand?'" (Rev. 6:12-17).

Since most stars would obliterate the earth due to their size, the "stars" must be parts of disintegrating ones.

A contributing factor to the prophesied damage is the use of weapons of mass destruction (WMD) initiated by humans as part of the judgment decreed by the LORD:

"Now this will be the plague with which the LORD will strike all the peoples who have gone to war against Jerusalem; their flesh will rot while they stand on their feet, and their eyes will rot in their sockets, and their tongue will rot in their mouth...So also like this plague will be the plague on the horse, the mule, the camel, the donkey and all the cattle that will be in those camps" (Zech. 14:12, 15).

The Bible states that heat will be the means of destruction in the current heavens and earth (Zep. 1:18, 2:1-3):

"The heavens will pass away with a roar and the elements will be destroyed with intense heat, and the earth and its works will be burned up" (2 Peter 3:10b).

This destruction in the universe precedes a thousand-year reign of the LORD Jesus Christ on the earth (Rev. 20:1-6). Since the first heaven and earth will continue until the Great White Throne Judgment, the present heavens and earth will exist in a new form during the millennium (Rev. 20:11, 21:1). During the wrath of God, the earth will be "devoured by fire" (Zep. 3:8). This will be followed by the re-creation of the present heavens and earth. The following verses are a literal description of the Creator's plans for the earth during the millennial reign of the LORD Jesus Christ:

"For behold, I create new heavens and a new earth; and the former things will not be remembered or come to mind. But be glad and rejoice forever in what I create; for behold, I create Jerusalem for rejoicing and her people for gladness. I will also rejoice in Jerusalem and be glad in My people; and there will no longer be heard in her the voice of weeping and the sound of crying. No longer will there be in it an infant who lives but a few days, or an old man who does not live out his days; for the youth will die at the age of one hundred and the one who does not reach the age of one hundred will be thought accursed" (Isa. 65:17-20).

At the conclusion of the LORD's millennial reign, there will be a final judgment with the dissolution of the first heavens and earth. These will be replaced by a new heaven and earth (Rev. 20:11-15, 21:1).

Comparison Between These Scriptures and the Second Law of Thermodynamics

Thermodynamics is the science of the relationship between heat and work and the conversion of one into the other. The science of thermodynamics deals with the properties of systems for which the description of temperature is a necessary coordinate.

The laws of thermodynamics can only operate within a system. Since the universe is a system in which these mathematical laws apply, the universe had to be started at some point in history. These laws of physics argue for such a starting point, the creation of the universe.

The second law of thermodynamics is the major concern here—no cyclic process is possible in which heat is absorbed from a reservoir at a single temperature and converted completely into mechanical work. Entropy is a measure of the energy that is not available for work during a thermodynamic process. Entropy is a function of the following thermodynamic variables: temperature, pressure, and composition.

Thus, because of this loss of energy, the second law of thermodynamics states that there is disorder in the universe. Entropy is the mathematical method devised to quantify this disorder. Based on this observation, once thermodynamic equilibrium occurs, the universe will undergo a "heat death."[9] Note the similarity between this projection and the statement by the Apostle Peter quoted above (2 Pet. 3:10b).

The LORD's communication through His written Word, the Bible, gives more details and reveals more about the changes in the universe at the end of the present age, followed a thousand years later by its destruction, than current scientific theory does. The Bible foretells a new era that will follow the present one:

"For the anxious longing of the creation waits eagerly for the revealing of the sons of God. For the creation was subjected to futility, not willingly, but because of Him who subjected it, in hope that the creation itself also will be set free from its slavery to corruption into the freedom of the glory of the children of God. For we know that the whole creation groans and suffers the pains of childbirth together until now. And not only this, but also we ourselves, having the first fruits of the Spirit, even we ourselves groan within ourselves, waiting eagerly for our adoption as sons, the redemption of our body" (Rom. 8:19-23).

Time, the Flood, and Radioisotopes

The separation of the original landmass, Pangaea, probably occurred at the time of the flood. The changes produced by the generalized flood obfuscate estimates of age based on geological estimates.[10]

Radioisotope testing is an inexact science. Results of seven paired samples of Hawaiian lava rock from the same specimen, sent to different laboratories, varied from zero to seven million years in their estimated age.[11] Time projection, by the use of radioisotopes of uranium-238 and carbon-14, has its basis in the belief that such decay will continue over eons because of a constant half-life. Since there are no possible experimental controls for such extended periods, there is no way of being sure that this is a valid assumption.

The assumption about radioisotope decay, the distortion of geological specimens by the worldwide flood, and laboratory variability in testing the same specimen preclude accurately determining the age of the earth by current scientific methodology.

The Creator's Design

Where there is design, there must be a designer.[12] There is a common pattern by the Designer in all the creation, whether one considers DNA (deoxyribonucleic acid), data from astrophysics, or the human genome.

The DNA in the genome determines and maintains the unique qualities of all species. Scientists once thought that only three percent of the total genome was functional. The rest, **they believed**, was "junk DNA." But there is no "junk DNA," only incomplete data. Recent genetic studies have found significance in 50 percent or more of DNA.[13]

The force that binds an electron to a proton in a hydrogen atom is described by a physical law known as the inverse square law. If the separation between a proton and an electron is doubled, the force falls by one-fourth. This same inverse square law applies to the spatial relationship between heavenly bodies in the solar system.[14] The inverse square law (in its simplest form, $E=1/r^2$) is also relevant to radiation, sound, gravity, and light—all formulae result in a similar equation.

Furthermore, there is a precise matching relationship between the original explosive power of creation and the power of gravity within the solar system. If there had been too much explosive power, everything would have disintegrated; if gravity force dominated, everything would have collapsed upon itself.[15]

Calculation of the extent of the observable universe gives a result of twenty billion light-years across it. Assuming this to be correct (Jer. 31:37), the matching of these two forces, explosive and gravitating powers, would have to have been accurate to one in 10^{60} in order to avoid either disintegration or collapse at Planck time, 10^{-43} seconds, the earliest measurement of space and time in the creation. The specificity of the initial creative burst would have been such that a bullet fired twenty billion light-years across the universe at Planck time would have to have been accurate to one in 1,000,000,000,000,000,000,000,000,000,000,000,000,000,000,000, 000,000,000,000,000 times in order to hit a one inch target.[16]

THE THEORY OF EVOLUTION

The theory of evolution teaches that human beings came from primordial forms to evolve as biological entities with a gradual increase in intellectual ability. Those who subscribe to the theory of evolution are at a loss to explain the source of light and the initial creation of darkness and water.

Many who subscribe to the theory of evolution do not accept that man has a spirit. If man is simply a biologic creature without a Creator, he determines his own destiny and functions as his own god. That is a heavy responsibility for any individual—particularly when people disagree on matters. When people disagree on subjects ranging from religion (man's search for God) to politics, they often resort to violent behavior to resolve conflict. According to the theory, "the most fit" will survive and rule. In many situations, this has resulted in mental, spiritual, familial, and social disruption and destruction throughout history.

Anthropological studies of presumed primitive man, all debunked, include: Peking woman, based on a few teeth only; Java man, a hoax; Nebraska man, based on a tooth shown to be from a pig; Piltdown man, a hoax; and Neanderthal man, now recognized as a large *homo sapiens*. Forming entire skeletons out of one or a few bones and projecting the culture on the same is fraught with error. The place of the origin of early man shifts from continent to continent based on the most recent "specimen" reported.[17]

It is important to note that the basis of these scientific theories was faulty data, fabricated data, and/or misinterpretation of the available data. There is no new, improved theory on the identity of humans. The available data indicates humans have always had the same physical, mental, and spiritual attributes.

The primary axiom of biological evolution, based on random mutation within the genome, assumes selection of beneficial mutants to evolve to higher biological states. This belies the fact that mutations have been proven to be almost uniformly deleterious or "neutral," i.e., not beneficial. A few beneficial mutations observed to be helpful have resulted in less information in the genome, never more information, and are a sign of deterioration. Neutral mutations, which are astronomically high in number, have a deleterious effect on the genome. Recent data on the genome challenges the evolutionary theory of random, beneficial selection.[18]

Scientists once thought there was a one percent difference in the DNA of chimpanzees and humans. Current studies indicate a five percent difference.[19] With further studies on so-called "junk DNA," one can anticipate that the difference will increase to greater than five percent.[20]

As the Genesis account details, God made creatures after their own kind (1 Cor. 15:39). There is no scientific evidence that documents evolution between species. Horses can crossbreed with donkeys to produce mules, but the mules cannot reproduce. This is an example of regression, not evolution. The observed data indicates that changes can occur within, not between, species.

Science's effort to explain man in biological terms has contributed to a decline in understanding other human characteristics: mind, soul, and spirit. These basic errors arise, when man defines himself, instead of accepting his Creator's definition. This error can be corrected only by accepting the definition of man provided in the Bible, God's written communication to man.

Adam, the first man, was made in the image of God as a living soul with a mind, a body, and a spirit (Gen. 1:26-27, 2:7). Adam was intelligent with the ability to name and classify all the birds and animals. He supervised the Garden of Eden with an understanding of plant life. He was capable of classifying and ruling over the animal kingdom and the plant kingdom, even as he was charged by his Creator (Gen. 2:19-20).

Intelligence in Animals

No transitional forms have been found that would substantiate changes between species, e.g., chimpanzees to man, nor is there definitive evidence for a common ancestor.

Studies at Stanford University on Koko, a gorilla, revealed that she understood a vocabulary of more than two thousand words and had an expressive vocabulary of a thousand words with the use of sign language. This is compatible with the average vocabulary of a human.[21] Even if Koko was more intelligent than other gorillas, all the data that has emerged on primates is compatible with intelligent primates, not sub-human primates evolving to intelligent humans through a common ancestor. Similar results have been obtained in intelligence studies done on canines, felines, dolphins, and others.

Testing Darwin's Theory by His Own Standards

According to Darwin's own comments, the sudden appearance of major types of life forms without any evidence for origin from earlier progenitors would seriously damage his theory. That is precisely what occurred in the Cambrian explosion. The latter was the period when the sudden appearance of virtually every modern phylum of animals in one geological stratum occurred without evidence of prior ancestors.[22] If the theory of evolution is correct, the evidence from the Cambrian explosion is inexplicable. These findings have been an embarrassment to evolutionists who have attempted to explain this finding by sudden bursts after long lag times, a revision of the theory. However, the Cambrian explosion is an expected finding for the sudden death of animals during a worldwide flood (page 130) (Genesis 6–8).

In addition, Darwin made the following statement in *The Origin of the Species*: "If it could be demonstrated that any complex organ existed which could not possibly have been formed by numerous, successive, slight modifications, my theory would absolutely break down."[23]

The human cell is irreducibly complex in it chemical machinery.[24] The cell is a complex "organ" that could not possibly have been formed by numerous, successive, slight modifications. The irreducibly complex cell and its complicated genetic code refute Darwin's theory of evolution using his own criteria.

Furthermore, Darwin and subsequent evolutionists have found it difficult to explain the complexity of the human eye. Although objects appear upside down on the retina, the brain converts the images to right side up. The evolutionists have criticized the upside down effect of vision on the human retina. Investigation on the complexities of the retina of the human eye refute such criticisms by Darwin and subsequent evolutionists.[25]

"Darwin's Bulldog"—Thomas H. Huxley, M.D.

Many in the academic community took up the Darwinian worldview of evolution between the species, because they wanted an alternative to the creationists' position as stated in the Bible. This came from their prejudicial view of the Bible that was often based on poor analysis of the same. Their wish was for man to determine his own destiny, i.e., become his own god. Instead of making idols of creatures to worship, as was done in many ancient cultures, evolutionists idolize creatures by making them part of their ancestry:

"For since the creation of the world His invisible attributes, His eternal power and divine nature, have been clearly seen, being understood through what has been made, so that they are without excuse. For even though they knew God, they did not honor Him as God or give thanks, but they became futile in their speculations, and their foolish heart was darkened. Professing to be wise, they became fools, and exchanged the glory of the incorruptible God for an image in the form of corruptible man and of birds and four-footed animals and crawling creatures" (Rom. 1:20-23).

Thomas Henry Huxley, a physician who styled himself "Darwin's Bulldog," was the most noteworthy historical defender of Darwin's theory during his generation. Huxley believed that the question of God's existence was problematic. He coined the terms, agnostic and agnosticism. Today, one notes the same agnostic (but dogmatic) search, in the name of "humanism," by many in the academic community. The "bulldog approach" continues.[26]

A liberal media continues to quote the academicians who espouse the theory and refuses to examine all the scientific data that refutes the theory.

The Creation Account in the Book of Job

The LORD paid tribute to Noah, Daniel, and Job as righteous men (Ezek. 14:14). Thus, Job was an actual person, and the book of Job describes actual events. The contents of the book of Job suggest that it is a book of great antiquity. Job's age may have been as long as many of those in the righteous line during the first millennium (Table 10, page 397) (Job 32:6-7, 42:16-17).

Yahweh gave Job a description of many aspects of the creation. As He communicated directly with Job, He used poetic language, imagery, and literal descriptions (Job 38–41). Perhaps *Yahweh* used these different forms of communication, because the scientific aspects of the creation were beyond Job's ability to comprehend. In spite of the increased knowledge that has accrued through scientific investigation, it would behoove those in the scientific community to view with wonder the creation that they study and learn humility from the same:

"Who among all these does not know that the hand of the LORD has done this, in whose hand is the life of every living thing, and the breath of all mankind" (Job 12:9-10).

Job was from the land of Uz. Uz was Shem's grandson, Aram's son (Gen. 10:22-23). This would suggest that Uz was on the east side of the Fertile Crescent near the location of Paddan-Aram at the top of the Fertile Crescent.

Nahor's firstborn son and Dishan's firstborn son from Seir's line were also named Uz (Gen. 22:21, 36:28). Nahar settled in Paddan-Aram. Seir was from Mount Seir, which became Edom [map site 21]. Later in history, Edom was declared to be within a land of Uz (Lam. 4:21). The latter was located near Egypt [map site 20] and the land of the Philistines (Jer. 25:19-21). Its location was south of the land of Israel.

However, Job was "the greatest of all the men of the east" (Job 1:3b). Since Job was from the area east of Israel, the first description of the land of Uz is likely to have been the place of his residence (Gen. 10:22). It also suggests that Job lived during ancient times.

Since the book of Job is of great antiquity, and Job was from the east, it is likely that Job was a Gentile who had come to personal belief in *Yahweh* as his LORD (Job 1:21).

How did Job discover the name of God, *Yahweh*, and develop a personal faith in Him? In all probability, Job antedated the time of Moses to whom God told the full meaning of *Yahweh* (Exod. 3:14). *Yahweh's* personal interaction with Job and the antiquity of the book suggest personal revelation to him. From the beginning, God intended salvation to be available for Hebrews and Gentiles.

Revelation of God's message of salvation, made available to all mankind, was to come through the Hebrews after Abram became the first Hebrew (Gen. 14:13, John 4:22). However, Abram was a Gentile when he received personal revelation from *Yahweh*. Thus, these two patriarchs, Job and Abram, were originally Gentiles who came to faith in *Yahweh* following personal revelation.

Job could not understand why he was suffering from a disease. In the medical specialty of Infectious Diseases, "Job's Disease" is due to an immune aberration that predisposes to certain types of infections. It is as though *Yahweh* said to Job, "You do not understand my purpose in the creation, so how can you understand my purpose in allowing Satan to induce disease and suffering in you and others?"

Yahweh's conversation with Job about the creation is important, because it is His personal view. *Yahweh* proceeded to describe to Job the creation. He described a creature compatible with dinosaurs who were vegetarians, sauropods, whose skeletal remains suggest lengths that varied from 30 to 140 feet and weight that varied from 50 to 225 tons (Job 40:15-24). These creatures were "the first of the ways of God" (Job 40:19a).

God created these creatures that were subsequently "uncovered," not "discovered." Job knew about dinosaurs. The description of the dinosaur in Job is compatible with recovered skeletons of the same.[27]

Recent data on dinosaur bones have shown that the marrow is soft. If the skeletons had been around for eons, the marrow should have calcified and hardened.[28] The soft marrow suggests rapid death of the dinosaurs during the Cambrian explosion. This is compatible with their death at the time of the worldwide flood (Genesis 6–8).

There is a description of a fire-breathing dragon in the book of Job (Job 41:1-34). Since there is no way of knowing for sure the type of skin that covered bones from various ancient creatures, and whether or not they could breathe fire, some of them may have been dragons. The creature described was an aquatic one that may have been capable of flight (Job 41:5). How did the idea of a dragon occur, if not from this record? Such knowledge is dependent on revelation (Deut. 29:29).

Summary Points on the Bible and Science

The majority of academicians have a surfeit of ego. Men pride themselves on their theories, their golden idols of understanding. Many do not marvel at a Creator who by His nature is multivariate, far above and beyond the trite conceptions of our minds. The immensity of the detail of creation is all around us. One can observe it in all the variety of marine life, bird life, animal life, human life, the environment, in brief, all of creation (Psa. 8:1-9).

Man's pseudointellectual pride about his accomplishments makes him unwilling to accept his failures that have damaged the creation. In spite of that fact, the Creator maintains it every fraction of a second, and one day, will reclaim it and set it right.

The major aim herein has been to declare what the Bible says about the creation. The secondary aim has been to indicate that there is nothing in the more substantial scientific theories that is contrary to the Bible. At its best, science is a search for truth about the creation. Since the Bible is the inspired word of the Creator, it will be impossible to find conflict between the Bible and accurate information gained from science (2 Tim. 3:14-17, 1 Pet. 1:19-21).

No one can answer the question of exactly how the creation occurred and fathom the mystery of time and space. Revealed truth about the creation can be found in God's written word, the Bible (Deut. 29:29, Heb. 11:3).

God Is God of the Literate and the Illiterate

The Creator is God of all His creation. Education and literacy are variable commodities in the history of mankind. God is God of the illiterate and the literate. Just as God gave personal revelation to Job, He has done the same through several folk religions. These tribal cultures have handed down ancient teachings testifying to a high and holy God from whom they departed and to whom many desire to return (pages 150-151).[29]

In the Bible, there is enough revealed truth that the most simple, illiterate person who hears the message, and the most erudite, literate person who reads the message, can understand and worship the Creator. We are the created; He is our Creator. Our minds are not capable of grasping the full spectrum of His truth:

"For My thoughts are not your thoughts, nor are your ways My ways, declares the LORD. For as the heavens are higher than the earth, so are My ways higher than your ways and My thoughts than your thoughts" (Isa. 55:8-9).

A god who cannot communicate with all his creation is no god at all. The intellectual elite seem to desire a god compatible with only their view of the creation and/or to be their own god. The religious leaders of Israel during the time of Christ took the same position and disdained the uneducated (John 7:47-49). If each person reads and/or hears the message of the Bible and trusts what it says, literate or illiterate, each one can come to faith in the LORD Jesus Christ and know God as a person (John 17:3):

"For the word of the cross is foolishness to those who are perishing, but to us who are being saved it is the power of God. For it is written, 'I WILL DESTROY THE WISDOM OF THE WISE, AND THE CLEVERNESS OF THE CLEVER I WILL SET ASIDE.' Where is the wise man? Where is the scribe? Where is the debater of this age? Has not God made foolish the wisdom of the world? For since in the wisdom of God the world through its wisdom did not come to know God, God was well pleased through the foolishness of the message preached to save those who believe. For indeed Jews ask for signs and Greeks search for wisdom; but we preach Christ crucified, to Jews a stumbling block and to Gentiles foolishness, but to those who are the called, both Jews and Greeks, Christ the power of God and the wisdom of God. Because the foolishness of God is wiser than men, and the weakness of God is stronger than men. For consider your calling, brethren, that there were not many wise according to the flesh, not many mighty, not many noble; God has chosen the foolish things of the world to shame the wise, and God has chosen the weak things of the world to shame the things which are strong, and the base things of the world and the despised God has chosen, the things that are not, so that He may nullify the things that are, so that no man may boast before God. But by His doing you are in Christ Jesus, who became to us wisdom from God, and righteousness and sanctification, and redemption, so that, just as it is written, 'LET HIM WHO BOASTS, BOAST IN THE LORD'" (1 Cor. 1:18-31).

The Seven Days of Creation

The First and Fourth Days

Gen. 1:3-5, 14-19: On the first day, light was the form that lighted the darkness (Table 1, page 22). The heavens were not in existence yet, so there were no sun, moon, and stars. Our best understanding of the source of light comes in the New Testament description of the new city of God where the glory of God will illumine it, and its lamp is the Lamb (Rev. 21:22-25). It is likely that the original light was the *Shekhinah* glory of God that illumined the darkness; He will be the Light in the New Jerusalem. Note *Yahweh*'s statement to Job:

"Where is the way to the dwelling of light? And darkness, where is its place, that you may take it to its territory And that you may discern the paths to its home?...Where is the way that the light is divided?" (Job 38:19-20, 24a).

God determined that a day would be from evening to evening, not morning to morning. The Biblical day goes from the setting of the sun on one day to the setting of the sun on the following day. Two periods, from dusk to dawn and dawn to dusk, made up the day. In most books of the Bible, the day starts and finishes in the evening. A notable exception is the Gospel of John where the day is ascertained according to Roman time, i.e., two twelve-hour periods from midnight to noon and noon to midnight.

"Do you know the ordinances of the heavens, or fix their rule over the earth?" (Job 38:33).

The creation of the sun, moon, and stars occurred on the fourth day and separated light from darkness. The heavenly bodies were for signs, seasons, days, and years. The Hebrew word for the sources of light from these heavenly bodies can be translated as "light-bearers" (*me'orot̂*, מאורת). The source of light ultimately comes from God; the light-bearers merely receive His light as given to them in the form of energy, e.g., the sun, or reflect the light from one body to another, e.g., sun to moon. Since they are not the original source of light and energy, but a burst from that source, their light and energy should decline over time. This is what happens to dying stars.

The LORD Jesus Christ described Himself as the light of the world, certainly spiritual light, but also the source of all physical light (Gen. 1:3, John 3:12, Rev. 21:23-25). Since all His attributes are eternal, His light continues throughout eternity.

The Second and Fifth Days

Gen. 1:6-8, 20-23: In Hebrew, the word, "waters," is a dual noun. Two different bodies of waters were formed above and below the heavens (Psa. 148:4). The waters below the heavens were the seas. *Yahweh* described the formation of the seas to Job:

"Or who enclosed the sea with doors when, bursting forth, it went out from the womb; when I made a cloud its garment and thick darkness its swaddling band, and I placed boundaries on it and set a bolt and doors, and I said, 'Thus far you shall come, but no farther; and here shall your proud waves stop?'" (Job 38:8-11).

The psalmist proclaims, "He lays the beam of His upper chambers in the waters" (Psa. 104:3a). There are waters above the heavens. Third heaven, referred to previously in the discussion on the first verse of chapter one, is the spiritual abode of God and the holy angels.

The "heavens" were derived from an "expanse" or a "firmament." The latter Hebrew noun is related to a verb that means "to hammer" (*raq̂iŷa'*, רקיע). A massive release of energy occurred, when the heavens were "hammered out" between the waters.

The angels were present at the creation of the earth (Job 38:7). There is no Biblical evidence that they were present before the heavens. *Elohim* stated that the creation of the hosts of heaven occurred during this first week (Gen. 2:1). It is likely that the creation of the angels occurred after the heavens were "hammered out" on the second day (Neh. 9:6). Just as He created the earth before placing Adam and Eve on the earth, He created the heavens before He created the angels.

Note that the second day is the only day in which God does not call it good at its completion. Since Satan's rebellion would be in the future, this means the omniscient God, in His foreknowledge, was aware of the upcoming rebellion. This is supportive evidence that Lucifer, the highest angel who became Satan, was created at this time (Isa. 14:12, Luke 10:18). Therefore, if the creation of angels occurred on the second day, Satan could not have been in existence at the initiation of the creation (page 21).

The fifth day describes the creation of the sea creatures and the birds. They received a blessing by *Elohim* who told them to multiply. After the Fall, the destiny of all life forms, including the sea creatures, is to return to dust (Psa. 104:24-30).

The Third and Sixth Days

Gen. 1:9-13, 24-31: In His initial conversation with Job, *Yahweh* told of laying the foundation of the earth in the presence of the angels:

"Where were you when I laid the foundation of the earth? Tell Me, if you have understanding, Who set its measurements? Since you know. Or who stretched the line on it? On what were its bases sunk? Or who laid its cornerstone, when the morning stars sang together and all the sons of God shouted for joy?" (Job 38:4-7).

This sequence recorded in Job is the same as that in this first chapter of Genesis. The creation of the angels (sons of God) occurred on the second day before the earth and seas on the third day.

The gathering of the waters formed the seas and the dry land followed (Psa. 104:6). The formation of the land was from the waters; there was one landmass. This is compatible with Pangaea, the name given to the original single landmass of the earth. The disturbances brought about by a worldwide flood must have separated this original landmass into the present continents (Genesis 6-8).

The division of vegetation into plants and fruit trees occurred next. *Elohim* decreed that plants, fruit trees, birds, animals, and man could only reproduce after their kind.

On the sixth day, the creation of animals, insects, and man occurred. The earth brought forth the animals from the dust. Then followed the division of animals into "wild beasts of the field" (*chaŷyat̂,* את־חית) and "domestic animals" (*behêmaĥ*, את־הבהמה). Thus, domesticated animals were present from the initial creation. The "creepers" were the insects and similar life forms that were created from the dust.

In this first chapter, the Hebrew word for man is Adam. The One Triune God, *Elohim*, both **created** and **made** Adam. In ancient Hebrew, it is difficult to be sure of the meaning of the words, "image" and "likeness." In modern Hebrew, "image" can refer to a photograph and "likeness" to a portrait. To create means to bring forth something *de novo*. Here it refers to the creation of the nonphysical aspects of man. To make is to change something from one kind of matter into another kind; Adam's body came from the dust of the ground (Gen. 2:7).

Note the use of "Us" and "Our" in these sentences. God reveals Himself as Father, Son, and Holy Spirit (Psa. 2:7, 51:11; John 3:16, 15:26). He is Trinity-in-Unity, Three-in-One; the seraphim and cherubim cry, "Holy! Holy! Holy!" as they express His holiness in three Persons (Isa. 6:3, Rev. 4:8).

The creation of Adam in the *imago Dei* resulted in a trinity-in-unity also. Adam's body, mind, and spirit became active, when God breathed into him the breath of life, and he became a living soul (Gen. 2:7, 7:22).

God the Son became a man, and by so doing, demonstrated His blessing on the physical and the spiritual aspects of man made in the image and likeness of God.

"God created man in His own image, in the image of God He created him; male and female He created them" (Gen. 1:27).

The word, "man,' is a mistranslation (Gen. 1:27). In Hebrew, the word is Adam. In this verse, Adam is a plural noun denoting male and female. Therefore, the composite of male and female is in the *imago Dei*. Male and female together more exactly represent the image of God than either male or female separately.

Man, birds, animals, and insects are described by two consecutive words, "soul" and "life" (*nephesh chayyah*, נפש חיה); all living creatures have soul and life.

Man was a vegetarian; he ate green plants and fruit. Birds, animals, and insects were also vegetarians.

Man was to multiply and subdue the earth and have dominion over all the other creatures in the pre-Fall condition.

The third and sixth days are the only ones on which *Elohim* twice pronounced the benediction, "good." On the third day, He stated this after two separate creations, the creation of the earth and the creation of the plants and trees (Gen. 1:10, 12). On the sixth day, He stated the same after the creation of the animals and insects (Gen. 1:25). In addition, after creating man, *Elohim* saw that all the creation was "very good" (Gen. 1:31).

The Seventh Day

Genesis 2:1-25

Gen. 2:1-3: The first three verses of the second chapter belong to the *Elohim* account of creation. It would have been reasonable to extend the first chapter to end after the third verse of the second chapter.

Since "heavens" is a dual noun in Hebrew, the word refers to one physical heaven consisting of two parts and one spiritual heaven, the abode of God. The creation of all the hosts of the heavens and earth occurred during the seven days of creation.

Elohim completed His work on the seventh day and "was refreshed" (Exod. 31:17). *Shabbath* means "to cease from activity" (*shabbaṯh,* שׁבת). The Sabbath became the day of rest and was blessed and sanctified. It was the final day of the week and lasted from sundown to sundown (Lev. 23:32).

Seven is the number of perfection in that God finished His perfect work on the seventh day and was refreshed. The days of the week repeat in a non-ending cycle. In the Bible, seven and multiples thereof, are symbols of perfection and eternity.

Since *Elohim* used the terms, evening and morning, to describe each of the days of creation, the time period must have been literal 24-hour days. Substantiation occurs in the language used about the Sabbath in the law:

"For in six days the Lord made the heavens and the earth, the sea and all that is in them, and rested on the seventh day; therefore the Lord blessed the Sabbath day and made it holy" (Exod. 20:11).

In the Bible, the Hebrew day started at sundown and the evening was divided into two parts, "between the two evenings" (בין הערבים) (Exod. 29:39, 41 NASB margin). The first part of the evening occurred, when the globe of the sun first touched the horizon; the second part of the evening occurred, when the last vestige of the sun disappeared from sight (Deut. 23:11).

The Names of God in Genesis

As God interacted with man, He revealed Himself through a sequential revelation of His name. The names of God are a revelation of His character and His actions. In the book of Genesis, God revealed Himself by at least 14 different single and compound names:

1. *Elohim*, "the Creator" (*'ĕlôhîym,* אלהים)—The description of the One Triune God (Gen. 1:1-2:3). *El* (*el,* אל)—The singular form of *Elohim* (Gen. 33:20).

2. *Yahweh Elohim*, "the LORD and Creator" (*YHWH 'ĕlôhîym,* יהוה אלהים)—The covenant relationship with Adam and Eve (Gen. 2:4-3:24). *Yahweh*, "the Tetragrammaton" (*YHWH,* יהוה)—God is LORD of all His creation (Gen. 4:1).

3. *El Elyon*, "God Most High" (*'ĕl elyon,* אל עליון)—The name spoken by Melchizedek, priest of *El Elyon* (Gen. 14:18-20).

4. "Possessor" (*qânâh,* קנה) of heaven and earth—Melchizedek and Abram's affirmation that God owns all of creation (Gen. 14:19, 22).

5. *Adonai Yahweh*, "Sovereign and LORD" (*'âdônai YHWH,* אדני יהוה)—Abram's prayer for an heir from his body at a time he feared that Sarai might be nearing menopause (Gen. 15:2). *Adonai*, "Lord," i.e., "Sovereign" (*'âdônai,* אדני)—Abraham implored his Lord, his Sovereign, not to pass him by (Gen. 18:3).

6. "Angel of *Yahweh*" (*mal'âk YHWH,* מלאך יהוה)—A Christophany, the pre-incarnate Christ (Gen. 16:7).

7. *Elroi*, "God, the Living One who sees me" (*'êl ro'îy,* אל ראי)—His revelation to Hagar at *Beer-Lahai-Roi* (Gen. 16:13-14).

8. *El Shaddai*, "God, the All-Bountiful" (*'êl shaddai,* אל שדי)—God would supply all that Abraham needed (Gen. 17:1). *Shaddai,* "The All-Bountiful" (*shaddai,*)—One of the names of God used in the blessing of the progeny of Joseph (Gen. 49:25).

9. *Elohim Yireh*, "the One Triune God sees" (*'ĕlôhîym y'râ'âh,* אלהים יראה)—When he spoke to Isaac about the sacrifice, Abraham rightly discerned that *Elohim* was the One Triune God who sees the need (Gen. 22:8).

10. *Yahweh Yireh*, "the LORD sees" (*YHWH y'râ'âh,* יהוה יראה)—Abraham's assessment was correct; *Elohim* was *Yahweh* who saw the need for a sacrifice for sin and saw Himself as that Sacrifice (Gen. 22:14).

11. "The Fear of Isaac" (*hapachad yitschâq,* הפחד יצחק)—At Mount Moriah, Isaac learned to fear God (Gen. 22:10, 31:53).

12. "The Mighty One" (*'âbîyr,* אביר) of Jacob—One of the names of God used in the blessing of Joseph (Gen. 49:24).

13. "Shepherd" (*raah,* רעה) of Israel—Israel's Shepherd and a picture of Joseph as a prototype of the Messiah (Gen. 48:15, 49:24).

14. "Stone" (*'eben,* אבן) of Israel—A picture of Joseph as a prototype of the Messiah (Gen. 49:24).

The following are translations of the Old and New Testament names for the LORD-Jesus-Christ/*YHWH-Yeshua-Maschiach.*

YHWH—"LORD"; *Yehoshua* (*yehôshuâ,* ישׁוּעה) or *Yeshua* (*yeshu'âh,* ישׁוּעה)—"*Yahweh* is salvation" and Jesus (*Iēsous,* Ἰησοῦς)—"Jehovah is salvation"; *Mashiach* (*mâshîyach,* משיח) and Christ (*Christos,* Χριστός)—the Messiah, "the Anointed One"

The Hebrew name for Savior is *Mosheea* (*moshee'a`,* מוֹשִׁיע).

The names of God reveal His attributes. Those who follow Him are to reflect these attributes in their own lives (Matt.5:48).

The Special Name of God, the Tetragrammaton;
***El Shaddai*, the Name of God for the Patriarchs**

Moses was the first one to whom the significance of God's name, *YHWH*, was revealed (Exod. 3:13-15). The patriarchs did not understand the full meaning of the name:

"I appeared to Abraham, Isaac, and Jacob as God Almighty, but by My name, LORD, I did not make Myself known to them" (Exod. 6:3).

One can use a name of God and not know its full meaning. The patriarchs' relationship was to *Yahweh* as Creator and LORD in covenant with man but without a full appreciation for the meaning of the latter name (Gen. 14:22).

To know a name of God means to understand something of the fullness of that particular name and experience it in one's life. It is likely that Moses penned the name *Yahweh* in the Torah (Pentateuch) based on his complete understanding of the meaning of the name as it applied to each individual and his circumstances.

The patriarchs knew, i.e., understood and experienced God as *El Shaddai* (אל שׁדי). In most English translations, *El Shaddai* is translated as God Almighty (Gen. 17:1, 28:3, 48:3).

In Hebrew, *shad* (*shad* שׁד), is the masculine singular noun for "breast." Other dual anatomical appendages are feminine nouns. Since *Shaddai* refers to God (*El*), *shad* is a masculine noun. Its plural is *shaddim* (*shaddim*, שׁדים). *Shaddai* (*shaddai*, שׁדי) has a possessive, personal pronoun suffix; it means "My breast." Using the breast to refer to God suggests the One with bountiful supply to nourish and care for His children. The word translated as "Almighty" in the following verse is "*Shaddai*." Note the relationship between it and the blessings of the "breasts" (*shaddim*, שׁדים) and the "womb" (*rechem,* רחם):

"From the God of your father who helps you, and by the Almighty who blesses you with blessings of heaven above, blessings of the deep that lies beneath, blessings of the breasts and of the womb" (Gen. 49:25).

When God says He revealed Himself as *El Shaddai* to Abraham, Isaac, and Jacob, He bountifully supplied all their physical and spiritual needs (Exod. 6:3).

Yahweh Tza'vot (*Yahweh tsebȃʾot*, יהוה צבאות), LORD of Hosts or Armies, a name that occurs later in Scripture, is more descriptive of the might of God when it refers to the time of His wrath (Jer. 42:18) and to a time of battle:

"Then David said to the Philistine, 'You come to me with a sword, a spear, and a javelin, but I come to you in the name of the LORD of hosts, the God of the armies of Israel, whom you have taunted'" (1 Sam. 17:45).

The name, *YHWH*, the four letters known as the Tetragrammaton in Hebrew, "I AM WHO I AM (*'hay̑ah̑ 'asher 'hay̑ah̑*, אהיה אשר אהיה) (Exod. 3:14), describes the eternal God who is pre-existent and beyond any human's ability to fully comprehend Him:

"Manoah said to the angel of the LORD, "What is your name, so that when your words come to pass we may honor you?" But the angel of the LORD said to him, 'Why do you ask my name, seeing it is wonderful?'" (Jdg. 13:17-18).

"Wonderful" can be translated as "incomprehensible" (*paliy̑'*, פלאי) (Jdg. 13:18). *Yahweh* described Himself to Moses in terms that transcend time—the God of the eternal present, and language—unable for full expression in human language by nouns and/or verbs:

"God said to Moses, 'I AM WHO I AM'; and He said, 'Thus you shall say to the sons of Israel, 'I AM has sent me to you'" (Exod. 3:14).

In the latter part of the first millennium A.D., Jewish scribes, the Masoretes, transcribed the Hebrew manuscripts and added vowels around the consonants on which the language is based. They omitted the present tense of the infinitive, "to be," to avoid saying, "I AM," out of respect for this special name of God. They took the vowels of *Adonai* and added them to *YHWH* to form *Yehovah* or Jehovah. Whenever they read *Yahweh* in the text, pious Jews say *Adonai* (Sovereign) or *Elohim* (the One Triune Creator).

Nevertheless, God chose to reveal Himself through His names. Therefore, it is proper to use each of these names reverentially and with understanding of the meaning of each one.

THE *YAHWEH ELOHIM* ACCOUNT OF CREATION

Gen. 2:4: A second account of the creation occurs in the rest of the second chapter. It provides details not available in the first chapter and the first three verses of the second chapter. The name of God changes to *Yahweh Elohim.*

In the Old Testament, the name, *Yahweh*, often applies to the pre-incarnate LORD Jesus Christ. However, it can apply to God the Father. The application of the name can often be determined from the context. In the following verse, *Yahweh* refers to God the Father and *Adoni* (my Lord) refers to God the Son:

"The LORD says to my Lord: 'Sit at My right hand until I make Your enemies a footstool for Your feet'" (Psa. 110:1).

The name, *Yahweh Elohim*, speaks of the covenantal relationship between man and his Creator as his LORD. The remainder of this second chapter is a personal account of the relationship between "the first Adam," the first man, and "the last Adam," the LORD Jesus Christ (Exod. 3:13-14, Psa. 105:7-8, 1 Cor. 15:45, Rom. 5:12-14, Col. 1:15-20).

Gen. 2:5-6: Until a man was available to till the soil, there were no shrubs and plant life did not grow or "sprout" (*tsâmach*, צמח). The noun form of this verb refers to the "Branch" or "Sprout" (*tsemach*, צמח) that is one of the names of the Messiah, the Christ. His temple, His body (the church), sprouts and grows:

"Then say to him, 'Thus says the LORD of hosts, 'Behold, a man whose name is Branch, for He will branch out from where He is; and He will build the temple of the LORD'" (Zech. 6:12).

A mist, arising from the surface of the ground, watered the earth until rain came. Man's assignment in the garden was to till the soil; plant life could then sprout and rain could come on the earth:

"Now no shrub of the field was yet in the earth, and no plant of the field had yet sprouted, for the LORD God had not sent rain upon the earth, and there was no man to cultivate the ground" (Gen. 2:5).

"Yet" is a translation of the Hebrew word, *terem* (*terem,* טרם); it occurs twice in this verse (Gen. 2:5). It means that rain was contingent on man being available to cultivate the ground. When man came to the garden, the mist would abate and rain would come.

Adam, and subsequently Cain, became tillers of the soil. Since Cain brought his offering from the produce of the ground that was dependent on rain for growth, it is reasonable to conclude that rain did come to the earth after man tilled the soil (Gen. 2:5, 4:2-3).

The flood did not occur until 1,656 Biblical years AA (After Adam's creation) (Table 10, page 397). Some have speculated that a canopy existed over the entire earth. When the windows of the heavens opened at the time of the flood, they believe the canopy was destroyed, and then rain came for the first time (Gen. 7:11).

The windows of the heavens will appear again during the time of the pouring out of God's wrath (Isa. 24:18). Therefore, since they will reappear, the disruption of the windows of the heavens at the time of the flood did not destroy them (Genesis 6-8).

After Adam and Eve were banished from Eden, they wore garments from animal skins to cloth their nakedness. The animal skins would have been too warm for them to wear, unless there was a climate change after they left the Garden of Eden. Hence, it is improbable that there was a canopy that covered the entire earth until the time of the flood. Otherwise, there would have been no need for using animal skins for clothing to protect Adam and Eve from the elements.

The Garden of Eden must have had a suitable temperature so that man could be comfortable when naked. Whether an enclosed environment with an overhead canopy was present only in Eden is problematic. Protection from the elements may have come from some type of "shelter" (*suk̂kah̑,* סכה). A localized "canopy" (*chuppah*, חפה), restricted to Mount Zion, will occur at the time of the millennial reign of the Messiah:

"When the Lord has washed away the filth of the daughters of Zion and purged the bloodshed of Jerusalem from her midst, by the spirit of judgment and the spirit of burning, then the LORD will create over the whole area of Mount Zion and over her assemblies a cloud by day, even smoke, and the brightness of a flaming fire by night; for over all the glory will be a canopy. There will be a shelter to give shade from the heat by day, and refuge and protection from the storm and the rain" (Isa. 4:4-6).

The future canopy will replicate God's *Shekhinah* glory. His presence and guidance were represented by cloud and by fire as He led Israel (Exod. 13:21). "A canopy and a shelter" (חפה וסכה) will be present in the millennium (Isa. 4:5-6). The construct of the Hebrew sentence does not make clear whether the canopy will function as the shelter, or the shelter will be a separate entity.

This Hebrew word for "canopy" (*chuppah,* חפה) occurs in two other places in the Old Testament. King David compared the sun to the bridegroom coming out of his "chamber" (*chuppah,* חפה), and the prophet Joel spoke of the bride coming forth from her bridal "chamber" (*chuppah,* חפה):

"Their line has gone out through all the earth and their utterances to the end of the world. In them He has placed a tent for the sun, which is as a bridegroom coming out of his chamber; it rejoices as a strong man to run his course" (Psa. 19:4-5).

"Gather the people, sanctify the congregation, assemble the elders, gather the children and the nursing infants. Let the bridegroom come out of his room and the bride out of her bridal chamber" (Joel 2:16).

The Hebrew name of the Jewish bridal canopy is the *chuppah* (חפה). The King's coming to Mount Zion with its canopy speaks of His wedding with His bride. Similarly, their Creator and LORD communicated regularly with the first couple in the Garden of Eden (Gen. 3:8).

The Totality of a Person

Gen. 2:7: The substance of man's body was the dust of the ground and water. The Hebrew word for earth is *adamah* (*'ădâmâh*, האדמה). The Hebrew word for the first man is Adam (*'Adâm*, אדם). Adam came from the *adamah*.

Yahweh Elohim breathed the breath of life into the first man, and he became a living soul. The Hebrew word for soul is *nephesh* (*nephesh*, נפש). The Hebrew word for "breath" (*neshâmâṯ*, נשמת) is different from the one for "spirit" (*rûach*, רוח). The breath from *Yahweh Elohim* animated the body of Adam to become a living soul. Since that breath came from *Yahweh Elohim* who is Spirit, man became a living soul by the life giving breath that came from the Spirit. Adam received "breath" (*neshâmâṯ*, נשמת) from the "Spirit" (*rûach*, רוח) and became a "living soul" (*nephesh chayah*, נפש חיה).

The first Adam became a living soul from *Yahweh Elohim's* breath. The last Adam is a life-giving Spirit (1 Cor. 15:45). Because He is perfect and does not fail, the LORD Jesus Christ is the "last Adam"; there is no need for another. The first Adam failed and was condemned to death. At the time of the flood, all men died, except Noah and his family. Death is the absence of the "breath" (*neshamat̂*, נשמת) of the "spirit" (*ruâch*, רוח) of "life" (*chayim,* חיים):

"All flesh that moved on the earth perished, birds and cattle and beasts and every swarming thing that swarms upon the earth, and all mankind; of all that was on the dry land, all in whose nostrils was the breath of the spirit of life, died" (Gen. 7:21-22).

Before the Fall, the spirit of man was dominant over the mind and gave direction to it. Since the Fall, man needs to reestablish this balance between the spirit and the mind:

"Be renewed in the spirit of your mind" (Eph. 4:23).

"Therefore I urge you, brethren, by the mercies of God, to present your bodies a living and holy sacrifice, acceptable to God, which is your spiritual service of worship. And do not be conformed to this world, but be transformed by the renewing of your mind, so that you may prove what the will of God is, that which is good and acceptable and perfect" (Rom. 12:1-2).

"Who has put wisdom in the innermost being or given understanding to the mind?" (Job 38:36).

God seeks people who will worship Him in "spirit" (*pneuma*, πνεῦμα) and "truth" (*aletheia*, ἀλήθεια) (John 4:24). Truth comes through the mind, the intellect. Therefore, in order to worship God, man's spirit and mind must be subject to the Holy Spirit who teaches the intellect and brings new life into the person:

"But an hour is coming, and now is, when the true worshipers will worship the Father in spirit and truth; for such people the Father seeks to be His worshipers. God is spirit, and those who worship Him must worship in spirit and truth" (John 4:23-24).

Man is a spirit with a mind inside a body. Man can lose his "soul" (*psuche,* ψυχή) and "body" (*soma*, σῶμα) in "Hell," Gehenna (*geenna*, γέεννα), not his mind and spirit:

"Do not fear those who kill the body but are unable to kill the soul, but rather fear Him who is able to destroy both soul and body in hell" (Matt. 10:28).

After death, unredeemed man will become less than a soul and body; redeemed man will receive an incorruptible body and will become higher than the angels (1 Cor. 15:42-45, Heb. 2:5-9). Redemption will bring about a new, perfect unity with God:

"I do not ask on behalf of these alone, but for those also who believe in Me through their word; that they may all be one; even as You, Father, are in Me and I in You, that they also may be in Us, so that the world may believe that You sent Me. The glory which You have given Me I have given to them, that they may be one, just as We are one; I in them and You in Me, that they may be perfected in unity, so that the world may know that You sent Me, and loved them, even as You have loved Me" (John 17:20-23).

Thus, each person is a living soul with a body, a mind, and a spirit (Gen. 2:7, 41:8; Prov. 16:9; John 4:23; Rom. 12:1-2; 1 Thess. 5:23; Heb. 4:12). The body is self-evident. The mind operates inside our body through the brain; it is intangible and not found on examination of the brain. The spirit is designed as the dominant part that can communicate internally with the mind and body and externally with God and others (John 4:23, Eph. 4:23, Job 7:11). The spirit is intangible and not found by examination of any anatomical organ. When redeemed, the spirit of the mind is renewed through the indwelling Holy Spirit (Job 38:36, Eph. 4:23).

The Garden of Eden

Gen. 2:8-9: *Yahweh Elohim* planted the Garden of Eden, "the garden of delight." Since fruit was on the trees, rapid growth to maturity occurred (Gen. 1:11). Trees were "pleasing to the sight and good for food." Pleasure from their beauty and the taste of their produce emanated from the trees in the garden.

The tree of life placed in the middle of the garden may have borne fruit that could have sustained man in eternal health. The tree of life in the New Jerusalem will have similar properties. It will bear fruit monthly. This suggests a need for its life-sustaining fruit and healing leaves. Time continues as part of eternal life in the New Jerusalem:

"On either side of the river was the tree of life, bearing twelve kinds of fruit, yielding its fruit every month; and the leaves of the tree were for the healing of the nations" (Rev. 22:2).

The tree of the knowledge of good and evil was also present in the middle of the garden. It was a fruit-bearing tree, but the type of fruit is not stated. Whether the fruit had the ability to trigger the knowledge of good and evil, and/or it was restricted only to ascertain if man would obey or disobey *Yahweh Elohim,* is problematic.

Gen. 2:10-14: Since the four described rivers came out of Eden, its location can be suggested based on an understanding of the geography of the two rivers that are still present. The Tigris and Euphrates have known locations on the eastern arm of the Fertile Crescent. The Tigris, "rapid" (*chiddeqel*, חדקל), is east of the Euphrates, "to break forth with fruitfulness" (*perat̂h*, פרת).

The other two rivers would have been located on the western arm of the Fertile Crescent. Gihon, "bursting forth" (*giŷchon̂*, גיחון), was the river that surrounded the whole land of Cush on the western arm of the Fertile Crescent. It was farther to the west than Pishon, "increase" (*piŷshon̂*, פישון). The Pishon would have gone through present day Israel; perhaps that is why its description came first (page 246).

There is Biblical and geologic evidence that Africa and Arabia were originally one landmass; Cush would have originally occupied the land that was contiguous to both of these locations. It is likely that the flood altered the location of the Pishon and Gihon, either sending them subsurface or obliterating them.

The Pishon surrounded the whole land of Havilah, "circle" (*chav̆iŷlaĥ*, חוילה). Its precious metals: gold, bdellium, and onyx stone would have enriched the people of Israel. God's original design was to bless Israel with abundance.

The great earthquake that will end the present generation and initiate the millennium will alter the landscape as it currently exists (Matt. 24:34, Rev. 16:18-20). Since there will be a river flowing east and west out of Jerusalem, the topography will be different from that suggested by the original positions of the Pishon and Gihon (Ezek. 47:1-12, Zech. 14:8).

Gen. 2:15-17: *Yahweh Elohim* placed Adam in the garden to work it. The Hebrew word for this "placement" (*yanach,* ינח) comes from the Hebrew root for "rest" (*nuach*, נוח). The same root is used for the name of Noah (*noach*, נח) who was to bring partial rest from the distortion of work that was produced by the Fall (Gen. 5:29).

Before the Fall, the Garden of Eden was to be a place of rest for Adam. For Adam to work in the garden and care for its plant life and animal life would have brought satisfaction and rest to his soul. There was a relationship between the growth of plant life on the third day (form from "formless," *tohu,* תֹּהוּ) and the creation of animals, insects, and man (fullness from "emptiness," *bohu,* בֹּהוּ) on the sixth day (Table 1, page 22). Man's assignment was to care for the plant life of the earth and to supervise the animals. Thus, the blessing of God was upon work; man needed work for his development and pleasure.

Adam received explicit instructions not to eat of the tree of the knowledge of good and evil. God's intent was for man to only know and experience the good. God is the source of all that is good. In English, the addition of one "o" changes the word, God, into the word, good. Rebellion against God results in the experience of anti-God, anti-good, evil. God wanted only "the good" for all His creation.

The Hebrew phrase made up of the infinitive absolute, "dying," followed by the imperfect ("future") tense of the verb, "you will die," is usually translated, "you will surely die." This is a traditional way of emphasizing the action involved. However, the literal translation for failure to obey *Yahweh Elohim's* instruction is, "dying, you will die" (*muṯh temuṯh*, מות תמו). This provides a better theological understanding of the sentence of death. If Adam became disobedient, he would immediately suffer spiritual death, spiritual separation from *Yahweh Elohim*, and start dying physically. Spiritual and physical restoration would require a substitute to take his place for his sin.

Gen. 2:18-25: *Yahweh Elohim* introduced the need of a helper for Adam.

HUSBAND AND WIFE IN THE *IMAGO DEI*

"God created man in His own image, in the image of God He created him; male and female He created them" (Gen. 1:27).

"He created them male and female, and blessed them and named them Man in the day when they were created" (Gen. 5:2).

The word, "Adam," is translated as "man" in both of these verses. The combination of male and female are called "Adam," and together they represent the *imago Dei*. Therefore, a second meaning of Adam in Genesis is husband and wife together in the *imago Dei*. The husband and wife together become greater than the sum of the two added together. In the *imago Dei*, the relationship becomes a synergistic one (page 90) (Gen. 2:24).

According to the first chapter, the bird and animal life antedated the creation of Adam; the creation of the birds occurred on the fifth day and the animals on the sixth day (Gen. 1:20-26). Part of the purpose of the second chapter was to describe the relationship between the first man, Adam, and these creatures.

Yahweh Elohim recognized the need for Adam to have a companion. After announcing this, *Yahweh Elohim* proceeded to bring all the birds, domestic animals, and wild animals to Adam to name (Gen. 2:19-20).

It seems evident that God had Adam review all creatures to ascertain that there was none suitable for him as a partner. As he reviewed each creature, Adam demonstrated his great intellectual capacity by naming and classifying them. Since the name in the Bible refers to the character or nature of the one named, the names given to animals were representative of their nature.

Yahweh Elohim placed Adam in a deep sleep (anesthesia) and took a rib "to build" (*bân̂aĥ*, בנה) a woman. Indirectly, she came from the dust of the earth. In order to demonstrate the intimate relationship between Adam and his wife, God took a part from Adam to build the woman. Adam contributed to her creation by giving part of himself. Thus, all husbands are required to give of themselves to their wives (Eph. 5:25-33).

The Hebrew phrase describing the relationship of the woman to Adam is difficult to translate. One Hebrew language authority translates it as "a help over against" (*'eẑer khnegedo*, עזר כנגדו). The woman was to be complementary to Adam in body, mind, and spirit with her own unique personhood, her soul.

The ribs cover and protect the heart, lungs, and part of the abdominal organs. The heart is the centerpiece of the cardiovascular system. The cardiovascular system provides sustenance to the brain and other organs via the blood. The brain is the anatomical organ through which the mind works. The liver, kidneys, and gallbladder help keep the chemicals of the body in balance.

The words for heart, kidneys, and gall (bile from the liver and gallbladder) in the Hebrew language describe different aspects of the spiritual and emotional balance of man. The "heart" (*leb̂,* לב) sustains the intellectual and emotional centers. The "kidneys" (*kilyot*, כליות) and the "gall" (*merer̂aĥ*, מררה) refer to the emotions, visceral responses that need to be kept in balance with the rest of the body:

"I will give heed to the blameless way. When will You come to me? I will walk within my house in the integrity of my heart" (Psa. 101:2).

"His arrows surround me. Without mercy He splits my kidneys open; He pours out my gall on the ground" (Job 16:13).

It was necessary for Adam to have his side wounded to contribute to his bride. He became vulnerable in order to provide for her wellbeing. Adam, the first man, represented the last Adam (1 Cor. 15:45), the LORD Jesus Christ, who had His side wounded when He provided salvation for His bride, the church. The spear pierced His pericardium (John 19:34-35). Since the picture of Adam's rib is a picture of Christ's sacrifice for His bride, the rib that God took must have been one from over Adam's heart.

If God had taken the bone from the skull, it would have been symbolic of Adam ruling the woman in a predominantly cerebral relationship. If He had taken it from the foot, it would have been symbolic of the woman submitting to Adam in a predominantly slavish relationship. Since it was a rib from over the heart, the woman was coequal with him as a person in a sharing and complementary relationship.

Symbolically, the heart keeps the intellectual and emotional components of a person in balance. Adam and his wife were in tune with their intellectual and emotional parts, complementary copies to each other. Before the Fall, they represented the *imago Dei* without the blight of sin.

The Trinity and the First Man and Woman

There is holy mystery in the Trinity. Before the creation of the heavenly and earthly hosts, if God were only One as opposed to Three-in-One, how would He have expressed His love? Since God is love, He must love Himself; the three Persons of the Trinity love each other (1 John 4:8). Since the Trinity is holy perfection, this self-love is a perfect love. Islam's book, the Koran, and its single god, Allah, do not teach or exhibit love.[30]

The names in the Trinity: Father, Son, and Holy Spirit, exemplify family relationships. Each is coequal as a person, but each has different functions (John 3:16, 10:29, 16:13-15). This expression of love between the three persons of the Trinity is a model for love within the nuclear family and the family of God.

The original plan was for Adam and his wife to be perfect in love for their LORD and Creator, each other, and self. They were equal as persons but different in function. The woman, created after Adam, was to follow Adam as her leader. They were to complement each other, and thus, become complete, a joined unity created in the image of the One Triune God (Gen. 1:27).

Yahweh Elohim's gift of a wife to Adam evoked his euphoric and poetic (musical?) response. New Hebrew words were used for "man" (*'îŷsh*, איש) and "wife" (*'ishshaĥ,* אשה):

"This is now bone of my bones, and flesh of my flesh; she shall be called woman, because she was taken out of man" (Gen. 2:23).

The basis for marriage is stated next. The marriage ceremony concludes with, "I now pronounce you man and wife." That statement comes from this Biblical understanding of *ish* and *ishshah*, "man and wife." A man is to leave his father and mother, so that he can cleave to his wife. They are to become one flesh. The word for "joined" (*daƀaq*, דבק) means "to cling, to adhere, and to stick close to each other" (Gen. 2:24).

Sexual intercourse instructs in the difference and coequality of the design of God for marital partners. If a husband and wife try to do the same thing while attempting sexual intercourse, they will not be able to join and complete the act. They have opposite functions that give pleasure to both. Each person is necessary, but each person has a different function. Husbands and wives are not to compete with each other but to recognize their differing physical, mental, and spiritual makeup that allows them to complement each other and become truly one. True complementary activity will evoke compliments to each other.

The man and his wife were both naked and were not ashamed (Gen. 2:20-25). It is possible that they responded physically when they saw each other. Therefore, they may have consummated their sexual union before the Fall. If so, this may have been the only time in all of history that a couple had sexual intercourse with perfect union of body, mind, and spirit without the baggage of sexual distortion brought to the relationship that occurs secondary to psychosexual, and/or physical, and/or spiritual sin.

Adam and his wife became one. Before the Fall, there was no shame associated with sexual intercourse. A joyous union was celebrated between the first couple within the bonds of marriage (Gen. 1:27-28).

Since the next recorded event is the temptation by the Serpent, the first physical union of Adam and his wife may have been delayed until after the Fall (Gen. 3:1, 4:1). Satan may have sought immediately to spoil what God created as good; he feared the strength of this union.

The Hebrew language denotes the designed sexual union in marriage by use of the infinitive, "to know" (*yaďa'*, ידע) (Gen. 4:1). *Yada* implies knowledge in all aspects of the human being: body, mind, spirit, and emotions—all of one's soul. As a husband and wife repeatedly unite as complementary copies in each of these dimensions, they develop a union of two bodies, minds, and spirits that become one. This relationship was meant to mirror the *imago Dei* (Gen. 1:27, 5:2; John 17:20-23).

In a loving marriage, sexual intercourse becomes better with experience as a husband and wife successfully become one through years of joint adventures in the vicissitudes of life. The Hollywood model of "best sex" at the peak of one's youth with the emphasis on the physical attributes of the couple is not the Biblical model.

NEPHESH, THE HEBREW WORD FOR SOUL

Nephesh (*nephesh*, נפשׁ) means "soul." It appears 35 times in 32 verses in the book of Genesis to describe all life forms: marine, bird, animal, insect, and human. The translators chose eight different English words for *nephesh*: lifeblood [Gen. 9:5], wish [Gen. 23:8], soul, life, living being, person(s), people, and creature(s) (Gen. 1:20-21, 24, 30; 2:7, 19; 9:4-5, 10, 12, 15-16; 12:5; 14:21; 17:14; 19:17, 19-20; 23:8; 27:4; 32:30; 34:8; 35:18; 37:21; 42:21; 44:30; 46:18, 22, 25-27; 49:6).

Nephesh appears in both the creation and flood accounts to describe all life forms other than plant life. It is unfortunate that many translators choose to use different English words for the translation of *nephesh*. It is erroneous, based on the Biblical text, to say that creatures other than man do not possess a soul. Any creature that the Creator made possesses a soul. Many children and adults would rejoice to know this about their pets; accurate translation would avoid this misunderstanding. Man's uniqueness is creation in the *imago Dei*, not in having a soul.

Yahweh placed Adam over the plant and animal kingdoms. When the Serpent spoke to the woman in the presence of Adam, neither seemed surprised that the Serpent could communicate with them. This suggests that Adam and his wife had direct communication with the animals before they sinned. Why did the LORD create this arrangement between the animal kingdom and man? The Bible teaches that there are many creatures with animal characteristics in heaven that are far superior to humans (Isa. 6:1-4, Ezek. 1:1-28, Rev. 4:5-11). A careful review of these references indicates that these beings have major functions to perform in heaven. In the future, they will have prominent roles at the time of the Apocalypse (Rev. 6:1-8).

These heavenly creatures have characteristics of man, birds, and animals; they worship in close proximity to God. In the book of Isaiah, there is a description of six-winged creatures called seraphim (Isa. 6: 2). In the book of Ezekiel, there is a description of creatures who have four faces each: man, lion, bull, and eagle. Each one possesses four wings. They are called cherubim (Ezek. 1:10, 10:1-22). There is a description of an individual cherub with the face of a bull (Ezek. 10:14).

In the book of Revelation, four awesome creatures have elements of both the seraphim and cherubim. These four creatures have six wings each like the seraphim. They each have one of the faces of the cherubim. One has the characteristics of a lion, one a calf, one a man, and one a flying eagle. These descriptions differ from the description of the cherubim in Ezekiel where each one has all four faces (Rev. 4:7-8). They all delight to be in perpetual worship of the LORD near His throne.

When the LORD returns to the earth, He and His armies will ride white horses (Rev. 19:11-14). Therefore, there must be horses in heaven.

It is possible that the reason Adam was given responsibility for supervision of the animal kingdom in the Garden of Eden is that man will one day have some responsibility in heaven in association with these awesome creatures who are close to the throne of God (Heb. 2:5-8). Our Creator has purpose for the animals that He created; they have *nephesh*. Since these awesome creatures already exist in heaven, it should not be surprising to see some of the earthly animal kingdom in heaven after this life:

"Your righteousness is like the mountains of God; Your judgments are like a great deep. O LORD, You preserve man and beast" (Psa. 36:6).

In this verse, the Hebrew word translated as "preserve" should be "save" (*yaŝha'*, ישע) (Psa. 36:6). A reasonable translation would be, "You save man and beast." This is the same Hebrew root that is related to its corresponding noun, "salvation" (*yeshuʾaĥ`*, ישועה):

"Oh, that the salvation of Israel would come out of Zion! When the LORD restores His captive people, Jacob will rejoice, Israel will be glad" (Psa. 14:7).

If man fails in his present responsibility to the animal kingdom and turns them into evil creatures, it is possible that some of the animal kingdom will suffer just as man will, if he rejects the salvation offered to him. Since Adam had responsibility over the animal kingdom, mankind must take this same responsibility seriously and not demean what the Bible clearly teaches about these creatures.

THE FALL AND ITS CONSEQUENCES

Adam was created first and was the intended leader in marriage (1 Tim. 2:12-13). Leadership did not mean inequality between the leader and the one led. The distortion in this relationship can best be understood by examining the Fall.

The Lie That Murdered

Genesis 3:1-24

Gen. 3:1: The serpent, a beast of the field, was a wild animal. Since Satan was wild, he chose to inhabit the serpent; the serpent acquiesced (Gen. 3:14). *Yahweh Elohim* judged the Serpent (*naĉhaŝh,* נחש) to be crafty. The Hebrew word, "crafty" (*'aȓuȋm,* ערום), is from the same Hebrew root as the word, "naked" (*'aȓuȋm,* ערום). This suggests that the Serpent had become spiritually disrobed and was capable of naked evil.

Since he did not acknowledge *Yahweh* as LORD, Satan spoke only of *Elohim* (1 Cor. 12:3). Satan may have accepted *Elohim* as the Creator of the man and woman, but not his Creator (Gen. 1:6-8; 2:1, 20-23; Isa. 14:13-14). Note that the woman followed the Serpent's lead and referred to God as *Elohim*, instead of *Yahweh Elohim*, the name used by God when He gave the command about the fruit of the trees to Adam, not to the woman.

The Fall of Satan

Lucifer, created on the second day fell soon thereafter (Ezek. 28:12-17): "He was a murderer from the beginning" (John 8:44a). He led one-third of the angels to a spiritual death and then proceeded to murder Adam and his wife (Rev. 12:4).

The 28th chapter of Ezekiel speaks of the Garden of Eden; the text tells of the holy mountain of *Elohim* in heaven. The context indicates that Satan, in the guise of the "king" (*melek,* מלך) of Tyre, rebelled in the heavenly Eden and became violent. Because of Satan's violence and pride, God cast him from the heavenly Eden. It may have been at this time that he entered the serpent in the earthly Eden to tempt the woman (Ezek. 28:12-19).

He was to be the guardian of the Garden (Ezek. 28:14, 16). In the ephod, the jewels represented the 12 tribes of Israel. Satan was bejeweled in his being with jewels of the same type as those on the ephod worn by the high priest, but not in the same order and number. Specifically, the third row of three jewels is missing; the reason for this is not clear (Ezek. 28:13, Exod. 28:15-30). The numbers of jewels vary between nine in the Hebrew text and 14 in the Septuagint. The text is suggestive, but not conclusive, that the covering jewels of Lucifer represented jewels from the ephod. Before his rebellion, *Helel*, "the shining one," "the morning star," may have been charged to be the shining jewel and spiritual leader of mankind (Isa. 14:12 NASB margin).

Thus, if the jewels here represented the ephod, it suggests that the responsibility given to Lucifer in Eden was to be the High Priest of man. He was to provide spiritual guidance and protection for man as his guardian. Apparently, Lucifer deemed it below his dignity to supervise man who he believed had lesser spiritual and animal characteristics. Lucifer, who became Satan, wanted to ascend to compete with *Yahweh* (Isa. 14:12-14).

As previously discussed, beings with animal and human characteristics exist in heaven around the throne of God. Since Satan was a cherub (Ezek. 28:14), he may have viewed animals as the greater creation and the supervision of animals by man as demeaning (Isa. 14:12-14, Ezek. 28:4-21). It may have been on this premise that he suggested to Darwin, and others who had rejected God as Creator, the theory of man evolving from animals. If Darwin did not serve God, he served Satan (John 3:19-21).

Furthermore, Satan's observation of man being placed over animals in the Garden of Eden may have suggested to him that man would eventually be over angelic beings like himself. That thought would have created jealousy and anger in such a proud creature (Psa. 8:3-8, Heb. 2:5-8).

Satan did not like the fact that he was a created being and less than God. The basic tenet of evolutionary theory is to continue to evolve, to ascend to be one's own god. Satan's distorted mind may have suggested to him that he was not created but had evolved and would **"ascend** (*'al̂ah,* עלה)...and **make himself to be like** (*dam̂ah,* דמה) the Most High, *Elyon* (*'elyon̂,* עליון)." Satan, the fallen angel, *Helel*, wanted to be over the other angels and compete with God:

"But you said in your heart, 'I will ascend to heaven; I will raise my throne above the stars of God, and I will sit on the mount of assembly in the recesses of the north. 'I will ascend above the heights of the clouds; I will make myself like the Most High'" (Isa. 14:13-14).

Gen. 3:2-3: Satan, in the guise of the Serpent, spoke only to the woman, but Adam was present with his wife (Gen. 3:6, 17). In Hebrew, the pronominal suffixes for "you" and "your" are common plural, and their corresponding verbs are plural; they refer to both Adam and his wife in this passage.

Instead of addressing Adam, the Serpent revealed his craftiness by addressing the woman. The creation of the woman followed the creation of Adam. Satan suggested to her, by innuendo, that God had discriminated against her. By ignoring Adam, the Serpent was indicating to the woman that she needed to exercise authority over Adam and assume leadership. Adam did not speak during the interchange between the Serpent and his wife. He failed in his leadership assignment as the woman's leader and guardian.

When *Yahweh Elohim* gave the command to Adam about the tree of the knowledge of good and evil, the woman did not exist (Gen. 2:16-17). Therefore, she did not personally know what

Yahweh Elohim had said; she had to have learned it from Adam. Satan's transmission of pride to the woman had its desired result. By not asking her husband to refute the Serpent, she took his leadership role.

Satan suggested, by innuendo, that God had done something wrong. He impugned *Elohim* (*Yahweh Elohim*) by raising a question about His word: "Indeed, has God said, 'You shall not eat from every tree of the garden?'" (Gen. 3:1b).

The woman received her information from Adam. He would not have misled her before the Fall. Therefore, her statements were exaggerations. Adam did not intervene and correct her. There were three inaccuracies in the woman's reply:

1. God did not say that they could not touch the tree of knowledge of good and evil (Gen. 2:16-17). It is always dangerous to add to God's word (Deut. 4:2, Rev. 22:18-19).

2. There were two trees, not one, in the middle of the garden. The construction of the sentence in the Hebrew text indicates the tree of life and the tree of knowledge of good and evil were in the middle of the garden (ועץ החיים בתוך הגן ועץ הדעת טוב ורע) (Gen. 2:9). She failed to mention the tree of life in the middle of the garden; she focused on "the tree of the knowledge of good and evil" (Gen. 2:17a). It is dangerous to subtract from God's Word (Deut. 4:2, Rev. 22:18-19). Satan hoped they would eat from both trees and share sin and eternal damnation with him.

3. Since she knew that Adam had heard the command, and she had not, and Adam was her leader, the woman should have asked him to speak for her.

Gen. 3:4-5: The reply from the Serpent was referred to by the LORD Jesus Christ. While speaking to the religious leaders of His day, the LORD confronted them with the following:

"Jesus said to them, 'If God were your Father, you would love Me, for I proceeded forth and have come from God, for I have not even come on My own initiative, but He sent Me. Why do you not understand My way of speaking? Because you cannot hear My word. You are of your father the devil, and you want to do the desires of your father. He was a murderer from the beginning, and does not stand in the truth because there is no truth in him. Whenever he speaks the lie, he speaks from his own, for he is a liar and the father of it'" (John 8:42-44 NASB margin).

What is **the** lie that murdered? It was previously noted that the judgment, "dying you will die," means spiritual death, spiritual separation from *Yahweh Elohim* immediately after the commission of sin followed by physical death at a future time. Therefore, when the Serpent said that this would not happen to them, he uttered **the** lie that murdered Adam and Eve spiritually and physically. "There is no truth in him" (John 8:44b).

The next part of **the** lie was impugning the character of *Elohim* (*Yahweh Elohim*). Satan mocked God's authority by refusing to acknowledge him as LORD, *Yahweh*:

"Therefore I make known to you that no one speaking by the Spirit of God says, 'Jesus is accursed'; and no one can say, 'Jesus is Lord,' except by the Holy Spirit" (1 Cor. 12:3).

The innuendo that knowing good and evil allowed one to be like *Elohim* (*Yahweh Elohim*) implied that God had experienced evil. Evil is the opposite of the character of *Yahweh Elohim*; His attributes include absolute good and holiness.

Finally, **the** lie presented to every individual by Satan is the belief that he can consider himself to be "like God" with eyes opened to receive special knowledge. That is, each person wishes to be his own god, believing he knows better how to run his life than his Creator and LORD. Implicit in this lie of the Serpent to Adam and his wife was the suggestion that they could determine their own future. Since they were not able to control all the variables of life, this was a patent absurdity. Since Satan deals in this lie and others, all followers of the LORD must ever be truthful in all matters lest they fall heir to Satan's devices.

Gen. 3:6: Because of its implication for all the daughters of the woman, it is important to understand this verse. The spiritual inheritance from the Fall for all women is detailed in this verse. The woman decided to eat of the fruit of the tree of knowledge of good and evil for three reasons:

1. It was good for food, the temptation to satisfy the body.

2. It looked enticing, the temptation to satisfy the mind and emotions.

3. It could give "wisdom," the temptation to satisfy the spirit of the mind.

Adam was with the woman. She ate of the fruit before giving it to Adam. While she was eating, she must have experienced the pleasure and/or guilt of sin. After this sensation, instead of telling Adam not to eat, she desired that Adam experience the same thing, even though this act was under the sentence of death, "dying, you will die." She wanted Adam to participate in her folly. Adam remained silent and followed the leading of the woman and through her the leading of the Serpent.

Perhaps the greatest irony is the fact that authority over the animal kingdom was given to Adam and his wife (Gen. 1:28). Instead of exercising authority over the inhabited serpent, they allowed Satan to exercise authority over them. They had the authority to kill the fallen serpent and disembody Satan.

Gen. 3:7: Their spiritual eyes were opened, and they believed their nudity was something bad. Even though *Yahweh Elohim* had blessed their physical union and nudity, they experienced shame about it. Before they sinned, they had no shame. Why did eating the fruit produce shame about their sexuality and nudity? There is no recorded evidence that they were involved in sexual activity at the time of Satan's intervention, but that is a possibility.

The Serpent succeeded in transferring to them a sense of shame about their nudity that demeaned their "animalistic" sexual relationship. They became spiritually naked, clothed with sin, instead of the righteousness of *Yahweh Elohim*. Instead of being like *Yahweh Elohim*, the opening of their spiritual eyes made them like Satan. The only way to be like *Yahweh Elohim* is to obey Him. He desires and designs the best for each person.

Adam kept silent and became the follower, not speaking out against the Serpent and the woman's desire to follow the Serpent, instead of *Yahweh Elohim*. The Serpent succeeded in getting them to believe they were no longer complementary to each other as equals; they perceived themselves as unequal and competitive with each other.

Adam knew what *Yahweh Elohim* said. He did not object to referring to God just as *Elohim*. He did not correct the Serpent's innuendo. He did not object to the Serpent addressing the woman instead of him. Neither of them called upon *Yahweh Elohim* for help against this wily tempter.

Because of the induced shame of their sexuality and nudity, they made girdles for themselves. It is not clear whether the girdles covered only their genitals or included their breasts. Since they were ashamed of the very differences that previously were their glory, they may have covered both. They made the girdles of fig leaves sewn together. Their covering was a futile attempt to absolve their sin (Gen. 3:21).

Communion with God in the Garden

Gen. 3:8: The translation of the Hebrew word, *ruach* (*rûach,* רוח), can be "spirit" or "wind." The Spirit of God is *Ruach* (Gen. 1:2). The sound of *Yahweh Elohim* walking in the garden, heard like the wind, *ruach*, is a *double entendre*. God was present in Spirit; it was the wind of the day (NASB margin). God may have visited them to review the end of their day at eventide, when the gentle breezes blew. The new day started after sundown.

This may have been the basis for the LORD Jesus' comment to Nicodemus. He told him that being born of the Spirit was like the wind, and he should know that as **the** (definite article in Greek) teacher in Israel (John 3:8-10). Nicodemus should have understood this verse from the book of Genesis. He was **the** teacher of the *Tanakh*, the Old Testament.

Before the sin of Adam and the woman, *Yahweh Elohim* must have regularly visited His creation in the Garden of Eden. His sound and presence were known by Adam and his wife. They were able to commune spirit to Spirit. Consider how much they lost, when that relationship was broken!

Now they hid themselves from the presence of *Yahweh Elohim*. They were dead spiritually and dying physically. Furthermore, they hid near where they sinned, "The tree of life also in the midst of the garden, and the tree of the knowledge of good and evil" (Gen. 2:9b, 3:8). Thus, they were near both the tree of the knowledge of good and evil and the tree of life. If they had eaten fruit from the tree of life, they would have suffered the fate of the fallen angels. Their fear kept them from this—until *Yahweh Elohim* came and provided a way for redemption predicated on their confession of sin, repentance, and acceptance of the provision of the sacrifice to come.

THE PENALTIES FOR SIN

Gen. 3:9: Since *Yahweh* knew where Adam was in his physical and spiritual state, His question, "Where are you?" was for Adam's benefit. Since he was now unfit to stand in the presence of the Absolute Holy, Adam needed to understand his spiritual condition. Note that *Yahweh* called for Adam, not the woman. Since Adam was responsible for the woman, He expected her to be with him.

One of the fathomless wonders is that God wants our worship and fellowship. Before Adam and the woman sinned, they had fellowship with God; now *Yahweh* sought them out in order to renew that fellowship. Their sin would have to be covered, atoned for, before they could worship Him again in Spirit and truth (John 4:23-24).

Gen. 3:10-11: Sin produced not only shame of sexuality and nudity but also its corollary, fear of *Yahweh Elohim*. They tried to hide from Him. Adam spoke only of hiding himself while trying to shield his wife. After he had failed to protect his wife from the Serpent, he tried to protect her from *Yahweh Elohim*. Adam was attempting to keep his wife from her Judge and Savior. God's judgment can lead to salvation.

Note that *Yahweh* dealt with sin by asking questions of the sinner. This gave the potential for recognition of personal sin and repentance. Does not the LORD still use this method when dealing with each person and his sins? When we sin, questions arise in our minds. Passive sin is the failure to do what we know is right; active sin is a willful act that we know is wrong. If we are not hardened, our consciences prick us for both types of sin.

"Where are you?" Adam answered this question correctly by stating that he was afraid to be in the presence of the holy God. He affirmed that he sensed his nudity. He was nude before he sinned and unashamed; now he was ashamed.

"And He said, 'Who told you that you were naked? Have you eaten from the tree of which I commanded you not to eat?'" (Gen. 3:11)

Adam's statement about nudity assumed the answer to these two questions. Because of his disobedience, he felt his nudity.

Gen. 3:12-13: Adam's sequences of answers resulted in a lateral to his wife in an effort to blame her for his sin. Since God had given the woman to Adam, he inferred that God was partially responsible for the sin that occurred. This means that he accepted Satan's argument that God could be in error. Thus, men have ever sought to blame God and their wives for their personal sin.

Yahweh Elohim asked the woman only one question, "What is this you have done?" She confessed her sin but blamed the Serpent for her action. *Yahweh Elohim* accepted the fact that the Serpent had practiced deceit, lying, and murder and turned to him last. He would subsequently return to the woman and Adam, in that order, and deal with each one.

This sequence is informative in understanding how God deals with multiple parties responsible for sin. Judgment occurred in the correct order and with the correct punishment. The guiltiest party, Satan, was dealt with first, then the woman, and finally, Adam.

Redemption is always nigh, but there is an inherent price to pay for any sin. It does not help to point to the environment, Satan, and/or others; each person is responsible for his own sin. Conversion requires repentance and acknowledgment of God as LORD and Savior (Rom. 10:9-10). Those who can hear the words of the LORD, and apply them by faith and obedience, receive His forgiveness and redemption.

Gen. 3:14: The Serpent is the deceiver. When deceit is present, Satan is behind it. He deceived the woman. *Yahweh* accepted her confession, but not her effort to blame Satan for her action.

When the LORD addressed the Serpent, He spoke as *Yahweh Elohim*, not *Elohim*. Whether Satan accepted it or not, God is both LORD and Creator. Since there was no possibility for confession and repentance, *Yahweh Elohim* did not question him. Satan was beyond redemption.

Satan was already condemned for his rebellion in heaven against *El Elyon*, God Most High (Isa. 14:14, Ezek. 28:14-19). He was now condemned while inhabiting the serpent in the earthly Garden of Eden. *El Elyon* rules all of His creation in the heavens and the earth.

The sentence of the serpent, who allowed Satan to enter its body, was to crawl in the dust as the lowest of the wild beasts. This implies that serpents could walk, and/or fly, before the Fall:

"The oracle concerning the beasts of the Negev. Through a land of distress and anguish, from where come lioness and lion, viper and flying serpent, they carry their riches on the backs of young donkeys and their treasures on camels' humps, to a people who cannot profit them" (Isa. 30:6).

Dust is also a symbol; it indicates that Satan has an unnatural appetite for the bodies of men made from the dust of the ground, the place where the serpent now grovels. *Yahweh Elohim* commands; Satan must obey. Those who believe in *Yahweh Elohim* need not fear Satan or any of his followers.

Gen. 3:15: There would be enmity between the seed of the woman and the Serpent. In Hebrew, "seed" (*zeh'-rah,* זרעה) is singular with a feminine ending. Redemption would come through the seed of the Virgin Mary and the Seed implanted by the Holy Spirit. The God-Man, the LORD Jesus Christ would provide redemption for sin (Luke 1:26-35, Gal. 3:16, 19).

Thus, this enmity was ultimately between the LORD-Jesus-Christ/*YHWH-Yeshua-Mashiach*, the "seed" (*zeh'-rah,* זרעה) of the woman, and Satan whom He defeated (Luke 10:18). It would also be between all the seed of Satan, fallen angels and humans who choose to follow him, and all the "seed" (*zera',* זרע) of the LORD Jesus Christ, heavenly beings who never sinned and humans who accept the redemption offered to them (John 3:16-21).

This is the first of many prophecies that the LORD Jesus Christ would suffer before He triumphed over Satan:

"And I will put enmity between you and the woman, and between your seed and her seed; He shall bruise you on the head, and you shall bruise him on the heel" (Gen. 3:15).

"But the LORD was pleased to crush Him, putting Him to grief; if He would render Himself as a guilt offering, He will see His offspring, He will prolong His days, and the good pleasure of the LORD will prosper in His hand" (Isa. 53:10).

In this latter verse, "seed" (*zera',* זרע) (Isa. 53:10) does not have a feminine ending (*zeh'-rah*, זרעה) (Gen. 3:15). It refers to the multiplied seed of believers who accept the sacrifice of the LORD-Jesus-Christ/*YHWH-Yeshua-Mashiach*.

Gen. 3:16: The condemnation to the woman contained three elements: multiplied "conception and pregnancy" (one Hebrew word, *herôn,* הרן), "sorrow and pain" (one Hebrew word, *'itstsâbôn,* עצבון) in delivering babies, and "desire" (*teshûqah,* תשוקה) for her husband and his rule over her:

"To the woman He said, 'I will greatly multiply your pain and your conception and pregnancy in pain you will bring forth children; yet your desire will be for your husband, and he will rule over you'" (Gen. 3:16 NASB margin).

The Menses

The Bible speaks of the menses in the negative; some writers refer to this as a menstrual taboo (Lev. 12:5, 15:26).

In the law, sexual intercourse during the menses was harshly condemned and resulted in excommunication from Israel:

"If there is a man who lies with a menstruous woman and uncovers her nakedness, he has laid bare her flow, and she has exposed the flow of her blood; thus both of them shall be cut off from among their people" (Lev. 20:18).

After childbirth, the days of impurity were extended twice as long for a female as a male. The purification applied to the mother, but both were isolated. Therefore, the female child endured the isolation period with her mother (Lev. 12:1-8).

Since the menses are merely the slough of the endometrium (lining of the womb) that completes the menstrual cycle, how can menstruation be "rejected as impure" (*niddah,* נדה) and "be foul," (*tamê',* טמא)? Although menstrual periods are messy, there is no known medical reason to call the menses, the dead cells, physical impurity. Therefore, the explanation is unlikely to be physiologic but related to the condemnation of the woman after the Fall.

If the menstrual cycle was not present before the Fall, the addition of a monthly cycle could have been the method to "greatly multiply conception and pregnancy" (*h'rab̂aĥ 'arbaĥ her̂on̂,* הרנ הרבה ארבה). If it became the sign of the first woman's Fall, one can understand how its addition would have become a sign of spiritual impurity. This would explain the negative aspects of the mention of the menses in the Scriptures. The righteous deeds of men, proclaims the prophet, are like "bloody menstrual rags":

"For all of us have become like one who is unclean, and all our righteous deeds are like a filthy garment; and all of us wither like a leaf, and our iniquities, like the wind, take us away" (Isa. 64:6).

Thus, the prophet compares man's righteous works to "a filthy garment," i.e., "like bloody menstrual rags" (**כטמא** כלנו וכבגד **עדים**). In this gruesome example, the best man can do, his righteousness, hearkens back to the curse given to the woman. All the sons and daughters of the first woman suffer from her initial sin. Israel was similarly "rejected as impure" (*niddaĥ,* הנדה) and was "unclean" ("foul," *tam̂e',* טמא):

"Then the word of the LORD came to me saying, Son of man, when the house of Israel was living in their own land, they defiled it by their ways and their deeds; their way before Me was like the uncleanness of a woman in her impurity" (Ezek. 36:16-17).

It appears that the original plan for the woman was to have less frequent pregnancies without pain over an unending lifespan. Death was not in the plan. If the menstrual cycle was absent before the Fall, one can only speculate about God's design for procreation. Certainly the couple had the pleasure of two becoming one and all that that entailed. Perhaps conception and pregnancy would have occurred via a very different hormonal system. Perhaps the couple could have voluntarily triggered the necessary physiologic changes by their mutual desire to have children.

If the menstrual cycle was intact before the Fall, another explanation for the increase in conception and pregnancy is men and women increased the frequency of sexual intercourse after the

Fall. Sexual intercourse was designed as a means to know the spouse more completely, to give pleasure to a married couple, and for procreation. At mid-cycle, when the ovum is released from the ovary, the change in the woman's hormones increases receptivity. Women have less response to pressure pain and are more appreciative of visual and oral stimuli. This increases the possibility of sexual intercourse and conception. Because of quantitative distortion of its original purposes, it is likely that sexual intercourse became more frequent after the Fall. However, increased frequency of sexual intercourse does not explain the negative Scriptures that associate spiritual uncleanness and impurity with the menses.

Whatever the pre-Fall condition, the establishment of the menstrual cycle after the Fall seems the likely explanation for the method of multiplying conception and pregnancy. If so, the menstrual cycle became the sign of the woman's sin in the Fall and the reason for the spiritual negativity in the Bible about the menses (Gen. 3:16). Indeed, it may well be the sign of the curse for the female. Because of discomfort and/or inconvenience, many young women refer to it as "a curse," not realizing the implication of their dissatisfaction.

Redemption for the Wife and Mother

Modern medicine has done much to alleviate pain in childbearing. However, the Hebrew word translated pain can also mean "sorrow and grief" (*'itstsab̂ôn̂,* עצבון). This is a prophetic word that tells much about what mothers experience as their babies develop into adults. The only remedy for such sorrow and grief is to turn to the LORD for His salvation for themselves and their children and for His help in raising them.

Whereas the woman wanted to lead her husband, now her "desire" (*teshûq̂aĥ,* תשׁוקה), her longing, would be for her husband, and he would rule over her. Contained within this judgment is the root of feminism that revolts against this command. The distorted relationship from pre-Fall equality has resulted in an imbalance for all marriages. The resolution of conflict between husbands and wives can only approach the pre-Fall condition through the Biblical rules now governing the post-Fall marriage relationship.

Redemption brings about reversal to the pre-Fall state in some arenas, but not all. While it is true that redemption provides salvation from the effects of the Fall for wives who accept the LORD's salvation and rule in their lives, there are specific restrictions (Eph. 5:22-33). The advice of the Apostle Paul to Timothy specifies one aspect of redemption for this matter to a saved woman along with the restrictions imposed upon her:

"Likewise, I want women to adorn themselves with proper clothing, modestly and discreetly, not with braided hair and gold or pearls or costly garments, but rather by means of good works as is proper for women making a claim to godliness. A woman must quietly receive instruction with entire submissiveness. But I do not allow a woman to teach or exercise authority over a man, but to remain quiet. For it was Adam who was first formed, then Eve. And it was not Adam who was deceived, but the woman being deceived, has come into transgression. But women will be saved through the bearing of children if they continue in faith and love and sanctity with self-restraint" (1 Tim. 2:9-15).

A godly lifestyle, modest dress, submission of the wife to the authority of her husband, and effectively utilizing her role as wife and mother can revitalize her from the effects of the Fall. If she manifests the qualities described in this passage, she becomes a redemptive force for her husband and children.

There are other redemptive roles for women described in the Scriptures. Believing women assumed the prophetic office after their redemption (Exod. 15:20, Jdg. 4:4, 2 Kin. 22:14, 2 Chr. 34:22, Neh. 6:14, Isa. 8:3, Luke 2:36, Acts 21:8-9). Women as well as men receive spiritual gifts from the Holy Spirit that are to be utilized for the good of the body of Christ, the church (1 Cor. 12:4-11).

The LORD Jesus Christ, by word and example, elevated the position of women in their families and in society. Note the following.

1. The woman with chronic vaginal bleeding who touched the hem of His garment received health, salvation, and restoration within society (Matt. 9:20-22).

2. The daughter of the Gentile mother at Sidon was delivered from demon possession (Matt. 15:22-28).

3. He forgave the sins of a prostitute and granted her salvation (Luke 7:37-48).

4. He responded to Mary's desire to learn. He approved of education for women in a society that disdained the same (Luke 10:39-42).

5. At his mother's request, He turned water into wine at a wedding feast (John 2:3-10).

6. He brought salvation to the Samaritan woman who was a social and religious outcast (John 4:1-43).

7. He showed compassion to the woman who was set up and caught during the act of illicit sexual intercourse; the male partner was not brought before Him. The religious leaders wanted to condemn her; He judged them and forgave her (John 8:3-11).

Gen. 3:17-19: Adam's sentence was brief and to the point. When he should have been leading and defending his wife by taking authority over the Serpent, and/or calling on *Yahweh Elohim* for His help, he listened to his wife and followed her leading. He directly disobeyed the LORD's command about eating from the tree of the knowledge of good and evil.

The curse on the ground changed the role of work for Adam. The whole creation started its decline and still awaits it redemption (Rom. 8:19-22). Work changed from being a joy to becoming a toilsome activity. Farming was less fruitful; the ground would produce thorns and thistles.

The Hebrew word translated as "toil" is the same word that is translated as "pain and sorrow" (*'itstsaḇôn,* עצבון). This is the word that described the woman's "pain and sorrow" (*'itstsaḇôn,* עצבון) in childbirth and motherhood (Gen. 3:16). Men and women suffer the same condemnation but in different realms. Pain and sorrow for men are symptoms that come from their work. For men work is often nonproductive, burdensome, and occupies a great amount of time to the detriment of relationships within their families and the family of God.

The Spiritual Application of the Curse on the Ground

The lack of productivity in the soil is symbolic of a lack of productivity in one's spiritual life. An illustration of this occurs in the book of Hebrews (Heb. 10:26-31):

"For in the case of those who have once been enlightened and have tasted of the heavenly gift and have been made partakers of the Holy Spirit, and have tasted the good word of God and the powers of the age to come, and have fallen away, it is impossible to renew them again to repentance, while they again crucify to themselves the Son of God and put Him to open shame. For ground that drinks the rain which often comes on it and brings forth vegetation useful to those for whose sake it is also tilled, receives a blessing from God; but if it yields thorns and thistles it is worthless and close to being a curse, and it ends up being burned" (Heb. 6:4-8).

The similarity of the words in Hebrews to the words in these verses in Genesis suggests the writer of Hebrews may have been thinking of them. The LORD said that seed that fell on thorny ground resulted in an unfruitful life (Luke 8:7, 14). The writer of Hebrews gives an illustration of a life of spiritual thorns and thistles that dishonors the LORD. This passage describes a lifestyle that brings disrepute to the name of the LORD. If such behavior continues, one can reach a point where repentance is no longer possible; it is "close to being a curse" (Heb. 6:4-8). If such a condition materializes, the kindness of the LORD puts the believer to sleep, i.e., removes him/her from this life. Thus, just like soil that loses its productivity, poor spiritual soil can suffer with poor productivity and dire results. Individuals may lose their body but still gain their spirit:

"I have decided to deliver such a one to Satan for the destruction of his flesh, so that his spirit may be saved in the day of the Lord Jesus" (1 Cor. 5:5).

The Condemnation to the Rest of the Creation

It is possible that the decreased food supply contributed to some animals turning from the vegetarian diet originally prescribed to become omnivores or carnivores (Gen. 1:29-30, Isa. 65:25). In addition, the violence of some fallen men toward animals may have altered the behavior between men and animals to become an adversarial one (Gen. 6:11-12). A time will come when the original plan for animals will undergo redemption:

"And the wolf will dwell with the lamb, and the leopard will lie down with the young goat, and the calf and the young lion and the fatling together; and a little boy will lead them. Also the cow and the bear will graze, their young will lie down together, and the lion will eat straw like the ox. The nursing child will play by the hole of the cobra, and the weaned child will put his hand on the viper's den. They will not hurt or destroy in all My holy mountain, for the earth will be full of the knowledge of the LORD as the waters cover the sea" (Isa. 11:6-9).

"The wolf and the lamb will graze together, and the lion will eat straw like the ox; and dust will be the serpent's food. They will do no evil or harm in all My holy mountain, says the LORD" (Isa. 65:25).

"Natural disasters," e.g., tsunamis, tornadoes, hurricanes, and earthquakes trace their origin to the Fall. Many natural disasters are unnatural "acts of Satan," not "acts of God" as the insurance companies and legal profession use the phrase. Satan is limited in what he can do with these disasters and must seek permission before he can act (Job 1:12-19).

When evil is so all consuming that it overcomes an individual, a community, or the world, God may intervene and render such judgment. Examples include: individuals (pages 85-86) (1 Cor. 5:5, Heb. 6:4-8); Sodom, Gomorrah, and the cities of the valley (Genesis 19); the flood (Genesis 7); and the prophecy of future destruction during the days of God's wrath (Rev. 6:12-17, 10:7).

The Ramifications of Death

Adam's body suffered from the blight of sin; it had to be returned to the dust of the ground. There can be no resurrection without physical death and redemption. Since the LORD Jesus Christ conquered the devil and death, those who believe in Him can be free of the fear of death. All people subject to such fear must turn to the LORD to receive His peace:

"Therefore, since the children share in flesh and blood, He Himself likewise also partook of the same, that through death He might render powerless him who had the power of death, that is, the devil, and might free those who through fear of death were subject to slavery all their lives" (Heb. 2:14-15).

Redemption results in a spiritual new birth, and eventually, a new body (1 Cor. 15:42-44). For the Christian, death becomes a birth into a new life:

"'Truly, truly, I say to you, if anyone keeps My word he will never see death.' The Jews said to Him, 'Now we know that You have a demon. Abraham died, and the prophets also, and You say, 'If anyone keeps My word, he will never taste of death'" (John 8:51-52).

The LORD Jesus Christ herein defines a believer as one who keeps His word. The two Greek verbs describing death have similar shades of meaning. Not "to see" (*theōreō*, θεωρέω) death indicates that believers will go to their family reunion with the saints without the visual sense of death. Not "to taste" (*geuomai*, γεύομαι) of death means that believers will not experience death. Death is an immediate transition into a new and blessed life.

After the flood, the genealogies in chapters five and 11 of Genesis depict a shortening of the life span (Table 10, page 397). This may have occurred as man switched from a vegetarian diet to one that included animal meat that resulted in a change in metabolism (Gen. 1:29-30, 6:3, 9:3-4; Psa. 90:10). That change increased the incidence of hardening of the arteries in the cardiovascular system and its related morbidity and mortality.

Gen. 3:20: Prior to this time, the woman had not received a name. Adam understood and accepted *Yahweh Elohim*'s redemptive plan. By choosing to name his wife, Eve ("life," *chavvaĥ,* חוה), Adam had faith that life would spring from death through the seed that came from Eve. This action meant that they had forgiven each other.

Redemption is spiritual, physical, mental, emotional, familial, and social. *Yahweh Elohim's* sacrifice of animals to clothe them foretold of a sacrifice to come that would be the means of their redemption. His questions to them, and His teaching, addressed the need to renew their minds, so they could understand what had happened to them and understand the way of redemption. God sequentially dealt with all of Adam and Eve's needs. Since they would no longer be in the Garden of Eden, He "covered" them in order to reduce their embarrassment over their nudity and protect them from the elements. Subsequently, He would provide "cover" ("atonement," *kaphar,* כפר) for their sin.

In like manner, when Elijah fled from Jezebel, God fed him and met his physical need. He then let him ventilate and met his psychological need. Finally, He dealt with his spiritual need (1 Kin. 19:1-18). Those who counsel others should be sensitive to God's care for the entire person, even when the primary need is spiritual.

It is unwise to judge spiritual sins in others without knowing all the facts; only God has the capability to know all the **subjective** issues. In the future, God would give authority to man to judge **objective** sins by the criteria described in His law.

Husbands and Wives

Husbands are to love their wives the same way that Christ loved His church, His bride, and gave Himself for it. He is to love his wife the same way that he loves his own body.

Part of the mystery of the apostle's comparison of the husband-wife relationship to the church is that the husband is deficient in his experience as a member of the bride of Christ. He must learn from his wife's obedient example of submission to him how he should subject himself to the LORD (Eph. 5:23-32). The husband as a leader is in a masculine role; the husband as part of the bride of Christ is in a feminine role. By studying his wife's godly relationship to him, he can improve in his obedience to his LORD. He must love his wife as he does his own body. The Bible does not sanction a domineering, self-gratifying husband. He is dependent on his wife's example for part of his spiritual development.

The subsequent deterioration of the sexual relationship in marriage is illustrated by the situation of former slaves in Corinth (1 Cor. 7:1-40). The owners of slaves bred them. They may have had multiple sexual partners. While in such relationships, many came to salvation. In that abnormal situation, the Apostle Paul gave his advice about how to manage sexual relations within marriage. He further advised that the unmarried should not seek marriage in the difficult times faced by Christians in the Corinthian environment, except for inability to control their sexual appetite (1 Cor. 7:6-9, 25-38).

The content of this chapter is good advice for all marriages in the trying times in which we live where many have had several sexual partners before marriage. When there is a desire for sexual relations, the basic rule of thumb is that one partner should submit to the other partner (1 Cor. 7:2-4). The only exception is when both, by common agreement, devote themselves to prayer; prolonged separation can result in sexual temptation (1 Cor. 7:5). Authority over the wife's body belongs to her husband, and authority over the husband's body belongs to his wife—shared, coequal authority in sexual matters (1 Cor. 7:4).

When married to an unbelieving spouse, the believer is to accept this arrangement for the sake of the sanctification of their children and the possibility that the unbelieving spouse might come to know the LORD. If the unbelieving spouse leaves, the believing spouse is not to interfere with his or her departure (1 Cor. 7:10-16). Remarriage after the death of a spouse is permissible, but not advisable, unless the surviving spouse is still young (1 Cor. 7:39-40, 1 Tim. 5:9-16). When a woman is married to a husband who is disobedient to God's word, the Apostle Peter emphasized the following behavior for the wife: submission, chaste behavior, modest attire, respect, a gentle and quiet spirit, and a person with inner strength and character (1 Pet. 3:1-6). A verbal witness will be of little value without such demeanor.

The unique submission required of the wife to the husband does not apply to other men. Wives are to respect their husbands and obey them as part of their service to the LORD (Eph. 5:22-24, 33). It is good advice for a young woman never to date a man that she does not respect. If the relationship blossoms, she should ask herself if she would be willing to obey this man.

Sarah, who accepted Abraham's direction to call herself his sister on two occasions that resulted in being placed in harems, is a prime example of such obedience (Gen. 12:10-20, 20:1-18). The second time this occurred could have interfered with the birth of the promised son (Gen. 17:21). In both situations, Abram-Abraham was wrong, but God protected Sarah; she had obeyed her husband (Gen. 12:11-20, 18:12, 20:1-17).

A vital prayer life is dependent upon the husband honoring his wife as a fellow heir of "the grace of life" (1 Pet. 3:7). Married couples must consider the effect of their relationship on their prayers. They were joined to show forth the *imago Dei* (page 62).

THE FUTURE SACRIFICE FOR SIN

Gen. 3:21: The exclamation point on this redemptive plan was now given by *Yahweh Elohim* who made garments from animal skins for Adam and Eve, instead of the sewn fig girdles they had made for themselves. Note that He did this after Adam gave his wife the redemptive name, Eve ("life," *chavvaĥ*, חוה). Adam needed to express faith in Eve, and *Yahweh Elohim*'s promise of her redemptive seed, before He provided the animal sacrifice for them.

Their "works" approach to redemption, trying to cover their sinful state without the sacrifice of innocent blood, was not acceptable. Animal sacrifice to clothe the sinner foretold the sacrificial system—the shedding of blood that was symbolic of the shed blood of the Savior on Calvary's cross. His sacrifice provides the means for redemption to all who trust Him (Heb. 9:10-14). By faith, Adam and Eve repented and accepted God's redemption in the sacrifice to come (Gen. 3:20-21).

Redemption for Adam and Eve

Gen. 3:22: If they had eaten from the tree of life, eternal damnation awaited Adam and Eve. *Yahweh Elohim*, in His mercy, did not allow that to happen.

He stated that man now knew good and evil "like **One** (כאחד) of Us." Once again, the emphasis was on the coming of the LORD Jesus Christ, the **One** person in the Trinity who would come to know evil. He would experience evil as the innocent sacrifice who bore the sin of the world on the cross.

Gen. 3:23: Adam was not only banished from the Garden of Eden but now had to obtain his food by working the ground outside the lush garden. Work is under the condemnation of sin; redemption in work is through faith in *Yahweh*. To experience true redemption from the negative aspects of work, one must enter into God's rest (Heb. 4:1-11).

Gen. 3:24: *Yahweh Elohim* drove the man out of the garden. Subsequently, the Bible and other historical documents testify to the fact that man went from the garden to the east. "Civilized" men dwelt on the Babylonian side of the Fertile Crescent. The Garden of Eden must have been somewhere near the top of the Fertile Crescent. The cherubim and the revolving, flaming sword guarded the entrance to the Garden of Eden until the time of the flood.

ENERGY TO MATTER
EVOLUTION WITHIN THE SPECIES

The fourth chapter commences the discussion of children within the family.

Energy from God resulted in the creation of matter (Gen. 1:1-2). God utilizes energy placed within man in the creation of a baby by a myriad of energy requiring processes; every step in the creation of another human involves energy. The complexity is much greater than can be described here; a few examples will suffice. The energy of a couple during sexual intercourse results in the release of germ cells. The union of a spermatozoon and egg in the female tubes also forms from energy within the body. The implantation of the fertilized ovum into the endometrium of the uterus (lining of the womb) occurs with the release of energy. The subsequent evolution to embryo, fetus, and a complete human baby requires energy in multiple processes. Energy for the body comes from the intake of food and water as the child evolves to be an adult. The adult marries another and the cycle of life is repeated.

This is an example of creative forces within the husband and wife. Energy becomes matter, which in a small way, allows humans to participate in the creation of another person, even as God's energy manifested itself in the creation. Adam and Eve participated in this miracle of the creation of another human being (Gen. 2:7, Acts 17:24-28). This is Biblical evolution, energy to matter in the formation of a child within the confines of marriage. This evolution from energy to life only occurs within species, never between species (Gen. 1:12, 21, 24-25)!

THE UNRIGHTEOUS LINE

Cain, the First Murderer, not the Redeemer

Genesis 4:1-26

Gen. 4:1-2: The Hebrew verb used here for Adam's sexual intercourse with Eve is "to know" (*yadâ',* ידע) her. As previously discussed, this verb implies more than physical knowledge; it includes mental, emotional, and spiritual knowledge. God's intent for sexual intercourse is to develop an intimate physical, mental, emotional, and spiritual union. As a couple continues to unite in sexual intercourse over the course of their marriage, there is the potential for greater knowledge about each other, an evolving union of two souls with their bodies, minds, and spirits.

This should give us insight into the LORD Jesus' use of the Greek equivalent of this verb to define eternal life. The relationship between a believer and God is "to know" (*ginōskō,* γινώσκω) the only true God and Jesus Christ whom He sent (John 17:3). The union between God and the believer is to be a total one with submission of body, mind, and spirit (Rom. 12:1-2).

This fourth chapter starts with the first **single** use of the Tetragrammaton, *YHWH* (יהוה), in Genesis (page 50). The sign of the DDO appears before *YHWH* (**את**־יהוה) (Gen. 4:1). As previously stated, when it is the DDO, this two letter Hebrew word is not translated in English. Here it retains its original meaning; *YHWH* is the essence of being (page 18).

Eve may have believed that she had "gotten" *YHWH*, the Redeemer. Cain means "gotten one" (*qayin,* קין). It is probable that Eve thought Cain was the Promised Seed who would be the Redeemer. It is unlikely that Eve perceived the need for the virgin birth at this stage of her understanding, even though she had been told that redemption would come through her seed (Gen. 3:15). She did not understand that "her seed" meant that conception would take place in a virgin. She probably thought the promise would simply come through her child and looked for it in her firstborn son.

Eve statement, “I have gotten a man, the LORD,” is commonly translated, “**with** *the help of* the LORD” (Gen. 4:1 NASB margin). However, *“the help of”* is in italics in the NASB; this indicates that these words are not present in the original Hebrew. Those who choose to translate את as the preposition, “with,” believe that Eve was simply acknowledging God’s direct involvement in conception and birth and choose to interpolate “*the help of.*”

Eve experienced pain and sorrow in childbirth. She did not complain of her pain (Isa. 51:2). Sorrow would eventuate in the murder of Abel by Cain (Gen. 3:16, 4:8). In a greater sense, the seed that became the nation of Israel would bring forth “pain and sorrow” (*'itstsaḃoṅ,* עצבון) through their disobedience to *Yahweh Elohim*, their LORD and Creator.

In Hebrew, the normal word pattern to describe the birth of another son is to repeat the words, “and she conceived” (*v’tar̂ah̆,* ותהר) and bore another son or daughter (Genesis 29:32-30:24). Those words are absent for Abel’s birth; conception is mentioned once, not twice. Instead, the Hebrew states, “and she added” (*v’taŝaph,* ותסף) and bore Cain’s brother. This is suggestive that Abel was Cain’s twin brother. Some have suggested Abel’s name means “vapor” or “breath” (*hebel,* הבל) (James 4:14).

Adam and Eve had daughters, but there is no detailed information about them (Gen. 5:4). During the early years of creation, the bloodline was pure without inheritable diseases, so the brothers married their sisters. As the number of families increased, there was a prohibition on marriage between siblings in order to minimize genetic diseases, psychosexual disorders, and to maintain the sanctity of each individual in the family.

Adam had responsibility for both the plant and animal kingdoms. This responsibility descended upon his two sons. Cain supervised the plant kingdom, and Abel supervised the animal kingdom.

The Effect of Sin on Families and Society

It is pertinent to note that both sons raised in the same household and environment had the same advantages. Nowhere in the text does God condemn Adam and Eve for sin that Cain committed or for the aberrancy in Cain that led to his sin. The current teaching of psychology and sociology, when children go wrong their environment or their parents are at fault, destroys individual responsibility. Personal responsibility is necessary for a safe society:

"Fathers shall not be put to death for their sons, nor shall sons be put to death for their fathers; everyone shall be put to death for his own sin" (Deut. 24:16).

Cain was personally responsible for his brother's murder. He deserved death, but *Yahweh* was merciful to him.

The Bible acknowledges that sinful behavior in parents and societies can result in carryover of sin to the third and fourth generation of parents that **hate God** (Exod. 20:5):

"You shall not worship them or serve them; for I, the LORD your God, am a jealous God, visiting the iniquity of the fathers on the children, on the third and the fourth generations of those who hate Me" (Exod. 20:5).

Such carryover may be physical, and/or psychological, and/or spiritual, and/or social. Sexually transmitted disease in the father can infect the mother who can infect the fetus in the womb. Aberrant mental problems in parents can affect the psyche of their children. Spiritual sin is rebellion against God. Social sin is the composite of physical, psychological, and spiritual sins from multiple individuals living together in a community.

After the Fall, the Biblical evidence indicates that Adam and Eve were redeemed, loved God, and kept his commandments. Those who **love God and keep His commandments** can experience His redemption in the family and lovingkindness carried over to the thousandth generation, because of His faithfulness and grace:

"Know therefore that the LORD your God, He is God, the faithful God, who keeps His covenant and His lovingkindness to a thousandth generation with those who love Him and keep His commandments" (Deut. 7:9).

There is redemption for these three types of sin. If we turn from our sin to the LORD, He will change us with a positive carryover to the thousandth generation for those members of our families who choose to obey Him. If many in the society turn to the LORD and honor Him in their lives, the effects of personal salvation can bring about a healthy community (Exod. 15:26) or prevent destruction of one; it would only have taken ten righteous people to prevent the demise of Sodom (Gen. 18:32). People who practice righteousness become the salt that preserves, and the light that enlightens, their families and their society (Matt. 5:13-16).

Commandments involving the family are pivotal for a healthy society. The prescription for children in the nuclear family is obedience and honor to both father and mother. Such obedience and honor can preserve an individual's longevity and contribute to the longevity of the community. This is the first commandment with a promise, but not the only one. Following all of God's commandments will result in a society where longevity is the rule (Exod. 20:12; Deut. 5:16, 33, 6:2, 11:8, 9; Eph. 6:1-3). Fathers must not provoke their children to anger but bring them up in the discipline and instruction of the LORD (Eph. 6:4). This will lessen the carryover of sin from parents to their children.

Gen. 4:3-4: Both Cain and Abel would have known about the sacrifice of animals used to clothe the bodies of their parents, and thus, the need for the shedding of blood to atone for sin (Gen. 3:20-21).

After the initial sacrifice "to cover" Adam and Eve, it is not clear whether regular sacrifice of animals continued. Animal skins would have become the standard apparel for the fallen race. Thus, animals would have been killed, so their skins could be used for clothing. Alternatively, the slaughter of an animal could be done to commemorate the LORD's promised sacrifice. Before the flood, the righteous line who obeyed *Elohim* were vegetarians; animals were not to be killed for food (Gen. 1:30, 9:3-4).

Since the incident here occurred at the time of the ingathering of crops, it must have been harvest time. In Hebrew, "in the course of time" is literally, "the end of days" (*qeṩ yom̂im,* קץ ימים). This suggests the time of the fall harvest.

"The end of days" (*qeṩ yom̂im,* קץ ימים) may also have been prophetic concerning the end times. From the time of Cain and Abel until the end of time, mankind would divide into two categories based on their choices. Men could believe God and bring their best to Him in faith in the Promised Seed who would be the sacrifice for all sin, or not believe Him and seek to control their own lives. The latter always leads to further sin and degradation.

The Bible subsequently unveiled two representative symbols of the Messiah, the sacrificial Lamb and the Bread of Life (Lev. 2:1-16; John 1:29, 6:31-35). In the Levitical law, if a poor person could not afford an animal or bird sacrifice, he was allowed to use flour (from grain) without oil or incense for a sin offering, (Lev. 5:11-13).

"According to the Law, one may almost say, all things are cleansed with blood, and without shedding of blood there is no forgiveness" (Heb. 9:22).

Therefore, these offerings by Cain and Abel, which antedated the Law, represented the two symbols of the Messiah that came from agricultural and animal life, the Bread and the Lamb. Since the offerings looked forward to the sacrifice on the cross of Calvary, there had to be a blood sacrifice for forgiveness of sin.

Subsequently, grain offerings were offered with animal offerings to illustrate the offering up of the Messiah's body as the Bread of Life and His shed blood as the sacrifice for sin (Lev.

23:5-13). In order to receive *Yahweh*'s acceptance, the offerings had to be the first and best of the grain and the first and best of the flock given together (Lev. 1:3, Num. 18:29-30, Mal. 1:12-14).

Cain knew about the blood sacrifice of animals for his parents' sins. Cain, as the elder brother, should have suggested to Abel the need to combine **the first and best of their respective offerings, the grain and the blood**. He did not do this. Neither did Cain bring the first and best of his grain (fruit of the ground) offering from the crops (Gen. 4:3). Abel did bring the first and best portions of the animal blood sacrifice to *Yahweh* (Gen. 4:4). Therefore, *Yahweh* accepted Abel's offering, but not Cain's.

Gen. 4:5-8: Cain never asked *Yahweh* for the reason for the rejection of his offering. Instead, Cain frowned when his offering was not accepted. *Yahweh*'s rebuke for Cain's frown and red face that "burned" (*charâh,* חרה) with anger suggests that this was a new experience. *Yahweh* spoke to Cain and indicated that the frown and anger were harbingers of sin that was "crouching" (*rabats,* רבץ) at the door. The Hebrew word used for crouching, *rabats*, suggests a serpent ready to spring and strike. *Yahweh* further indicated that sin, personalized in the Serpent, Satan, desired Cain. He had to master his propensity to sin; personal response was required. If he wished to lose his anger with its resultant frown and smile again, he must rule over it (Gen. 4:6-7). God ever convicts of sin, righteousness, and judgment (John 16:8-11).

Cain must have known of the Promised Seed of the woman. His mother may have thought that Cain was the Promised Seed (pages 93-94). She must have discussed this matter with him (Gen. 3:15, 4:1). He knew of the animals sacrificed to clothe Adam and Eve (Gen. 3:21). If he was to overcome his great anger that would lead to hatred and murder, he had to trust in the future sacrifice of the One who had just visited him.

Cain discussed the matter with Abel, possibly to lure him out to the field. There he rose up and murdered him. His subsequent behavior confirms that this was not a spontaneous crime of passion. Cain was in close personal contact with Abel, when he murdered him; his rising up suggests the use of some object to hit him. Abel's blood shouted from the ground; it testified of his traumatic death (Gen. 4:10-11).

Gen. 4:9-10: *Yahweh* once again led the sinner to recognize his sin by asking a question, just as He had done in trying to keep Cain from sinning in the first place: "Where is Abel your brother?" He was the elder brother and responsible for Abel. A correct answer could have resulted in confession, repentance, forgiveness, and restoration through the promise of the coming Redeemer. Instead, Cain responded with a lie and sarcasm.

Since Cain responded with further sin, *Yahweh*'s next question produced judgment: "What have you done?" *Yahweh* who knew what had happened stated that Abel's blood "shrieks" (*tsaʔaqim,* צעקים) to Him from the ground; this Hebrew verb is plural (*tsaʔ**aqim,*** **צעקים**). Abel's departed spirit repeatedly cried out for the injustice of his life prematurely taken.

The blood of aborted embryos and fetuses, babies, and other murdered humans cries out to God today. The pain experienced by embryos, fetuses, and babies who are aborted has been adequately demonstrated by medical studies on the same. Their innocent blood shrieks to God for vengeance; that vengeance will descend to the earth in the days of the wrath of God (Isa. 63:1-6, Rev. 10:7).

Gen. 4:11-12: The ground that had received Abel's blood was cursed. The banishment from the garden to till the ground by sweaty toil had already been administered (Gen. 3:19, 23-24). Now the ground received **an additional curse**; it would not yield its strength. Cain became a vagrant and wanderer on the earth. Sinful man cannot dwell in the presence of the Holy God without redemption and purification.

Gen. 4:13-15: Cain, still unrepentant, sought a lesser punishment, not accepting the fact that his sin isolated him from God and resulted in further condemnation to the soil. Even in his rebellion, Cain desired the presence of God. Fallen man yearns for his Creator and LORD and is restless until he makes peace with Him. There is no peace without confession, repentance, and redemption. Instead of repenting and making peace with God, Cain blamed Him for driving him from His presence. He also blamed him for the punishment of more work to produce less food from the soil (Gen. 4:2, 11). Man ever seeks to blame God for the results of his personal sin!

He had murdered; now he was afraid that someone would murder him. At the time he killed Abel, Cain must have had other adult brothers, or his fear would have had no basis in fact. Cain and Abel were adults. He believed his other brothers would seek vengeance on him for killing Abel. *Yahweh* answered Cain's plea by proclaiming a sevenfold vengeance on anyone who murdered Cain. He made him a "marked man" (Gen. 4:15). This latter judgment was gracefully given in an attempt to halt further murder, but alas, murder continued in the land (Gen. 4:23). The nature of the sign given to Cain, possibly a mark, is problematic.

Gen. 4:16: Cain had already settled east of Eden, but now he dwelt further to the east in the land of "wandering and vagrancy" (*nod̂,* נוד) (Gen. 3:24). Cain became a vagrant and wandered away from *Yahweh.* It is probable that this was the east side of the Fertile Crescent in the land that became Assyria and Babylon.

The Genealogy of the Unrighteous Line

Gen. 4:17-24: Since he accepted his promised redemption, Adam was the progenitor of the righteous line. Cain rejected *Yahweh*'s redemption and became the progenitor of the unrighteous line.

Cain forsook his agricultural assignment. He tried to avoid *Yahweh*'s judgment on the soil and the environment. He became a city dweller and built a city named after his son. This was further rebellion against the judgment given to him for his sin.

The first seven generations in the unrighteous line set the tone for repetitive sin throughout that line until the end of the present age (Gen. 2:2-3). The list includes nine men and three women.

TABLE 2: THE MEANING OF THE NAMES OF THE FIRST SEVEN GENERATIONS OF THE UNRIGHTEOUS LINE	
NAME	**MEANING**
1. Cain	"Gotten One" (*qayin,* קין)
2. Enoch	"Dedicated" (*chaňok̂,* חנוך)
3. Irad	"Fugitive" (*'iyrad̂,* עירד)
4. Mehujael	"Smitten of El" (*mechiŷya'el̂,* מחייאל)
5. Methushael	"Man of El" (*methuŝha'el̂,* מתושאל)
6. Lamech	"Powerful" (*lemek,* למך)
6a. Adah	"Ornament" (*'ad̂aĥ,* עדה)
6b. Zillah	"Shade" (*tsillaĥ,* צלה)
7a. Jabal	"A Stream from Bel" (*yab̂al̂,* יבל)
7b. Jubal	"Conducted from Bel" (*yub̂al̂,* יובל)
7c. Tubal-Cain	"Begotten of Bel" (*tub̂al qayin,* תובל קין)
7d. Naamah	"Delightful, pleasant, lovely" (*naamah,* נעמה)

There is no record of the ages of the unrighteous line, only their names. God records time by His righteous line who will continue with Him throughout eternity. Only the wives of Lamech are recorded. This may be due to the probability that this was the first practice of polygamy:

"Lamech took to himself two wives: the name of the one was Adah, and the name of the other, Zillah" (Gen. 4:19).

These are names of antiquity; their exact meaning is problematic (Table 2, this page). Their names suggest service to a false god.

Two of the names, Enoch and Lamech, also occur in the righteous line. The names may have different applications based on the individual character of the person. Enoch, from the righteous line, was a **dedicated** prophet (Gen. 5:21-24, Jude 1:14-15). The meaning of Enoch, in the unrighteous line, may have referred to the pride of Cain in **dedicating** a city and naming it after his son (Gen. 4:17).

Lamech, from the unrighteous line, was **powerful** and slaughtered a man and a boy. Lamech, from the righteous line, died at an earlier age than most of his line; the cause of his death is not given (Table 10, page 397). His **power** was in fatherhood and the prophecy that his son, Noah, would bring rest to mankind with some relief from the curse on the ground. The righteous line took over the toil of the agricultural work that had been the assignment of Cain and his progeny (Gen. 5:28-31).

Lamech was the sixth man in the unrighteous line. He typified the evil of the unrighteous line. Six is the Biblical number that signifies rebellion against God (Rev. 13:18). Lamech wounded and slaughtered a man and a boy. He then committed sacrilege against *Yahweh* by suggesting that he be protected seventy-sevenfold, since Cain received sevenfold protection, not understanding the significance of the number seven, i.e., unending (Matt. 18:21-22).

The words, "Lamech took to himself," and his subsequent actions, suggest a self-centered man who took what he wanted. There is no indication of knowing and loving his wives.

He married Adah whose name means "an ornament." She was an ornament for Lamech's use. His second wife was Zillah whose name means "shade." This may have been a reference to her skin complexion and/or involvement in the occult (page 123). Lamech sought physical attributes, and possibly, involvement in the occult, in his wives.

There is a record of one daughter, Naamah. Naamah may mean "to be delightful, pleasant, and lovely." This may have been a reference to her physical and psychological attributes. Naamah completed the initial record of the unrighteous line as the twelfth recorded person in the seventh generation.

It is likely that the feminine attributes exhibited by these three women in the unrighteous line, considering the nature of their husband/father and sons/brothers, were actually feminine wiles. Perhaps these three women in the list are there to indicate their contributions to unrighteousness by the misuse of natural beauty and charm:

"Charm is deceitful and beauty is vain, but a woman who fears the LORD, she shall be praised" (Prov. 31:30).

As previously stated, the names of the sons are problematic and depend on how one interprets the syllables in the Hebrew words. All three of Lamech's sons end in "bal." Since Cain settled in the area that became Babylon, this may be a reference to Bel, the primitive Babylonian god, probably the equivalent of Baal in Canaan (Isa. 46:1; Jer. 50:2, 51:44). If that interpretation is correct, Cain's line had become instruments of Bel, the god of the "gotten one," Cain.

Tubal-Cain, "begotten of Bel," made bronze and iron implements, possibly weapons of war (Ezek. 27:13). It is possible that Lamech used the latter to slay the man and the boy.

The first syllable of Jabal is in the active voice in Hebrew. Jubal's first syllable is in the passive voice. Jabal's work may have been an active agent of Bel, and Jubal's work a passive one. Jabal completed Cain's rebellion from an agrarian life style and took over the livestock and herdsman role originally given to Abel.

Jubal's passive rebellion was through music with musical instruments that honored a false god. In Cainite worship, Jubal made instruments to praise Bel with his music. Passive service to Satan is more subtle in its negative effect on righteousness, but not less effective.

THE ORIGIN OF MUSIC

The first music of the creation of the earth occurred at its initiation with the singing of the morning stars and the angels:

"Where were you when I laid the foundation of the earth? Tell Me, if you have understanding, Who set its measurements? Since you know. Or who stretched the line on it? On what were its bases sunk? Or who laid its cornerstone, when the morning stars sang together and all the sons of God shouted for joy?" (Job 38:4-7).

In 1619, Johannes Kepler, the famous astronomer, placed musical notes in the position of each of the then known heavenly bodies in his work, *Harmonice Mundi* (The Harmonies of the World).[31] In that treatise, Kepler tells of the satisfaction of God in His work as revealed in the music of His creation. Indeed, the "morning stars" (*kok̂ab̂i boq̂er,* כוכבי בקר) sang at the creation by the emanations of their tones.

"All the sons of God" (כל־בני אלהים) refer to the angels that, "shouted with ear-splitting gusto" (*ruâ',* רוע) during the earth's creation. An alternate translation is, "All the sons of God shouted for joy" (Job 38:7 NASB). The creatures around the throne break forth in worship and song in God's presence (Rev. 5:9, 14:2). The voice of God reverberates; it is musical in tone. Music is part of His nature. The descriptions of His voice include being like—a trumpet, thunder, and many waters (Rev. 1:10, 4:1, 14:2). He is the great Musician that conducted His orchestra during the creation.

When he saw the woman God had created, Adam's poetic stanza may have been in the form of a song. Thus, he may have sung at the creation of his soul mate (Gen. 2:22-23).

The Music of Ancient Middle Eastern Religious Rites

Music was part of the religious services of the various gods of the ancient Middle East. The musical rhythm derived from the Cainites stirred emotions through words and rhythms that utilized fertility rites (sexual orgies) to praise their gods.

This commentary has already discussed the beauty of the sexual relationship within the confines of marriage that *Yahweh Elohim* ordained in the Garden of Eden (pages 65-66). The emphasis here is on the perversion of that beautiful relationship used in the development of man-made religions that purported to worship God, but in reality, worshiped Satan. Ancient Middle Eastern religions practiced fertility rites, male and female prostitution, and child sacrifice. Such perverted worship was commonplace in these religions, except for that prescribed in the worship of *Yahweh*. However, the Hebrews departed from *Yahweh* and joined in these religious rites, which contributed to their exile:

"But they mingled with the nations and learned their practices, and served their idols, which became a snare to them. They even sacrificed their sons and their daughters to the demons, and shed innocent blood, the blood of their sons and their daughters, whom they sacrificed to the idols of Canaan; and the land was polluted with the blood. Thus they became unclean in their practices, and played the harlot in their deeds" (Psa. 106:35-39).

In ancient Ur [map site 1] of the Chaldees, the discovery of a plaque that depicts various animals playing the instruments of the time in an orchestra is suggestive of a singular truth—the music's appeal was to the primitive, sensual, negative, animalistic qualities of people.[32] The Bible and ancient literature refer to the worship of false gods. In these orgiastic "worship services," idols that represented female and male sexuality, e.g., the Asherim and the Baalim, respectively, were the center of worship.

Original Meaning of "Jazz" and "Rock and Roll"

Although few people are aware of it today, the phrase, "rock and roll," was made popular in modern society by a disc jockey in the early 1950s.[33] The term referred to sexual intercourse depicted in the music of "rhythm and blues" that was recast as "rock and roll." At that time, "rock and roll" was believed to be a socially acceptable term; "rhythm and blues" was not. The term, "jazz," originally, "jass," also had a similar derivation as an euphemism for sexual intercourse. Jazz music became popular in the first half of the 20th century.[34] Early in their history, both of these forms of music were commonly played in brothels. Thus, this music has a similar history to the music of worship in ancient Middle Eastern cultures as detailed above. The basic appeal of rock and roll and jazz is rhythm that depicts sexual activity.

Evangelism

The argument goes that many accept the LORD with the use of this music in evangelism, so the method is appropriate. This is another version of "the ends justify the means argument," i.e., the idea that any action is okay as long as there is a "good outcome." The use of this music as a method for evangelistic outreach should give Christians pause for concern. This is a dissenting note to many Christians who like these musical styles:

"To avoid personal involvement with the cross we have become adept at finding or creating religious projects to soothe our conscience and make things look good. Among these are evangelism and foreign missions. These are good, Scriptural activities, incumbent upon all Christians, but all presuppose that they who engage in them should be holy, Spirit-filled and totally committed to God...For a worldly, weak, decadent church to make converts is but to bring forth after her own kind and extend her weakness and decadence a bit further out."[35]

Dr. A. W. Tozer of the Christian Missionary Alliance made these insightful comments about this problem nearly a half-century ago. Dr. Tozer has been with the LORD for a little over four decades, but his prophetic truth continues. The church has continued to decline in its spiritual quality while it boasts of an increasing number of adherents, often in mega-churches.

One must ask whether many of those who respond in current evangelistic campaigns are genuinely converted. It also belies the question as to whether those who do convert by such methods will progress to a path of holy living or will merely reflect the mores of the culture around them—further weakening the church.

The seed is the Word of God; those who sow the seed must not adulterate it by the use of these deplorable methods (Luke 8:11).

What happened to the LORD's teaching about the four types of response to the sowing of the seed of the Word of God (Matt. 13:1-23)? Might the "harvest" of today be mostly from the first three types of responders to the seed: those where Satan obliterates the seed immediately, those who fall during temptation, and those in whom the cares of this life choke the seed, so that no fruit is produced (Luke 8:5-15)? The present condition of the church suggests that this is true. Furthermore, the LORD stated we could only identify true Christians by the fourth response, those who bear fruit (Matt. 7:15-20; Luke 8:15, 43-46).

Lastly, it belies the question of the Biblical emphasis on evangelism that demands quality in believers rather than quantity. The LORD Jesus Christ was concerned about those that joined the crowd without understanding the cost of commitment to Him. It is standard today to avoid His hard sayings:

"Now large crowds were going along with Him; and He turned and said to them, if anyone comes to Me, and does not hate his own father and mother and wife and children and brothers and sisters, yes, and even his own life, he cannot be My disciple. Whoever does not carry his own cross and come after Me cannot be My disciple…So then, none of you can be My disciple who does not give up all his own possessions" (Luke 14:25-27, 33).

Individuals that consider their family members and their own lives to be their possessions must hate the same if they would follow the LORD Jesus. Only when we learn to love the LORD more than self, any other person, and any possession are we fit to love ourselves and our family members with pure love. The LORD taught that to be worthy of Him, His followers must be willing to take up a cross and follow Him. A true believer wants to know Him, be a true disciple and learn of Him, a student that applies His teaching (John 17:3). The LORD did not soften His message for the sake of obtaining more disciples. He did not want pseudo converts!

The message of the gospel, the Good News, is so much greater than anything the world has to offer. The church belittles the message when it joins in the methodology of the world to seek lost people. Any effort to merge the pagan with the Biblically prescribed worship of God is syncretism. Such worship cannot be pleasing to a Holy God. He repeatedly judged Israel for such attempts (2 Kin. 17:9-23).

There is a need for believers to review the LORD's comments about what He expects the condition of the church to be like when He returns:

"Now, will not God bring about justice for His elect who cry to Him day and night, and will He delay long over them? I tell you that He will bring about justice for them quickly. However, when the Son of Man comes, will He find the faith on the earth?" (Luke 18:7-8).

In Greek, the definite article is present before "faith." The LORD expressed concern about finding **"the faith"** (την πιστιν) on the earth at His return. His brother Jude (Judah) expressed the need for believers to contend for **"the faith"** (τοις αγιοις πιστει):

"Beloved, while I was making every effort to write you about our common salvation, I felt the necessity to write to you appealing that you contend earnestly for the faith which was once for all handed down to the saints" (Jude 1:3).

Has the church deluded itself into thinking that large numbers of superficial adherents to the gospel are genuine converts? In church history, greater numbers of superficial adherents have always come during times of prosperity. Contrariwise, times of tribulation have produced fewer believers, but ones who understood and accepted the unadulterated faith taught by the LORD and His apostles.

The LORD stated that the preaching of the gospel to the whole world would occur during a time of tribulation, just before the "end" (*telos*, τέλος) of the present age. He will return after the worldwide evangelization that will occur during that tribulation. Pseudo believers will fall away at that time:

"Then they will deliver you to tribulation, and will kill you, and you will be hated by all nations because of My name. At that time many will fall away and will betray one another and hate one another. Many false prophets will arise and will mislead many. Because lawlessness is increased, most people's love will grow cold. But the one who endures to the end, he will be saved. This gospel of the kingdom shall be preached in the whole world as a testimony to all the nations, and then the end will come" (Matt. 24:9-14).

It is unlikely that the prosperity evangelism of today is the "gospel of the kingdom" that will be preached to the world during the tribulation that occurs just before the end of this age. However, there are places in the world today where believers experience tribulation. In those places, growth is through the use of sound Scriptural methods with converts who produce fruit in their lives.

Worship

Many feel that musical rhythm of any type (rock and roll, jazz, and love ballads) with praiseworthy lyrics (instead of cultural lyrics that glorify sex, drugs, and rebellion) sanctify the rhythm. The validity of such an argument depends on the premise that the rhythm need not be synergistic with the words. The suggestion is that God will be pleased with such worship. The argument that the rhythm need not be synergistic with the words is an erroneous one. Musical rhythm **and** the words are meant to stir the emotions of the worshiper to glorify the LORD of all creation (Eph. 5:19, Col. 3:14-17).

We must not ignore the Scriptural admonitions about music in worship of the LORD. The Bible repeatedly refers to men and angels praising the LORD through music. The book of Psalms gives many examples of words and musical instruments that honor the one true God (Psa. 150:1-6). The music of the temple exuded such worship and is a model for churches today.[36]

One wise servant of God likens the rock musician to an individual shipwrecked on an isolated island. He finds the proverbial bottle in the ocean that drifts upon the beach with a message in it. Upon reading the message, he finds that the message is from himself. Could it be that the rhythms adopted by the church from rock and roll, jazz, and love ballads are depicting the ravished emotions of the "worshipers"? King David and other writers of the Psalms carefully designed instruments, words, and services to glorify God, not the worshiper (1 Chr. 25:1-31).

If we make melody in our hearts to the LORD, it must not be with a rhythm whose history glorified sex, illicit drugs, and rebellion. Music with rhythm that originated from Satan with a primitive beat or a sensual sway, introduced into the church, will bring along with it the very sin that it represents.

The church today suffers from sexual immorality, perhaps as at no previous time in history. Divorce rates are at historic highs. Many Christians who have suffered a divorce often continue sexual liaisons outside the marriage union without seeing harm in the same. Teenagers in public and "Christian" schools, having observed the disintegration of the marital relationships in their homes, fall heir to premarital sexual involvement.

The outcome of a permissive attitude to sexual practices and relationships increases the incidence of sexually transmitted diseases. These can spread to the embryo, fetus, or baby and maim or kill. Other types of child abuse can result from these practices: abortions, unwanted babies, physical and sexual abuse—all forms of child sacrifice. Whenever the church mingles in these societal practices, it differs little from apostate Israel (Psa. 106:35-39).

Note Dr. Tozer's prophetic statements about worship:

"Evangelical Christianity is now tragically below the New Testament standard. We have lost the art of worship. We are not producing saints. Our models are successful businessmen, celebrated athletes and theatrical personalities. We carry on our religious activities after the methods of the modern advertiser. Our homes have been turned into theaters. **Our literature is shallow and our hymnody borders on sacrilege...scarcely anyone appears to care. We must have a better kind of Christian soon, or within another half century, we may have no true Christianity at all. Increased numbers of demi-Christians is not enough. We must have reformation.”**[37]

The half century is upon us. Does the church seek quality of Christians today or simply large numbers of adherents by using societal methods to evangelize and have the “converts” join in our “worship” services? Dr. Tozer warned of the weak condition of the church during his time of ministry and the fact that it would weaken further if there were not a return to true worship and obedience to the faith. Careful observation supports his thesis—the church is much weaker today than it was in the middle of the last century.

The music of the church should speak to the LORD, high and lifted up—a music that lifts the inner person in spirit and truth. The Father seeks such people to be His worshipers (Isa. 6:1, John 4:24). One can often measure the spiritual caliber of a local church by noting whether its music primarily concentrates on the personhood of God with lofty words and rhythm or on its people and their damaged emotions or for their own entertainment:

“Many of our popular songs and choruses in praise of Christ are hollow and unconvincing. Some are even shocking in their amorous endearments, and strike a reverent soul as being a kind of flattery offered to One with whom neither composer nor singer is acquainted. **The whole thing is in the mood of the love ditty, the only difference being the substitution of the name of Christ for that of the earthly love...Our meetings are characterized by cordiality, humor, affability, zeal and high animal spirits...correct doctrine, fast tunes, pleasing personalities and religious amusements**.”[38]

Should not we be listening to anointed leaders like Dr. Tozer and heed their insights and warnings? Let the church return to careful Biblical study to ascertain what methods are suitable for evangelism and worship.

Many of the psalms with their uplifting words, associated with the music instruments described at the beginning of many of them, became the basis for worship in the temple and synagogue, and subsequently, in Christian churches. Such lofty words, with the aid of the older and newer musical instruments, has benefited believers from all cultures throughout the world. Let us emulate these Biblical examples, not the examples from the music of the world. It behooves all who have joined the righteous line to examine carefully the Scriptural basis for worship in the church. The Bible admonishes us to return to the bedrock of our faith, to **the** faith once delivered to the saints (Luke 18:8, Jude 1:3).

The Righteous Line

Genealogy of the Righteous Line

Gen. 4:25-26: Adam and Eve accepted their redemption and started the righteous line. Seth means "to make" or "to appoint" (*shet̂h,* שׁת); his name indicates his appointment to replace Abel. The hope that Cain would be the righteous seed was crushed when he killed Abel. Seth's son, Enosh (*'ĕnôsh,* אנוֹשׁ), was so named, "when men began to call upon the name of *Yahweh*" (Table 3, page 117).

In the first ten generations of the righteous line, **mankind** deteriorated spiritually to the degree that *Yahweh* sent a worldwide flood during the time of Noah, the tenth from Adam. In the next ten generations from Shem to Abram, **the righteous line** had a decline in their spiritual status:

"Now, therefore, fear the LORD and serve Him in sincerity and truth; and put away the gods which your fathers served beyond the River and in Egypt, and serve the LORD" (Josh. 24:14).

The righteous line had drifted into polytheism and the worship of the moon god in Babylon. When *Yahweh* appeared to Abram in

Ur of the Chaldees, and took him on a spiritual journey through the earthly Promised Land to his final destination in the heavenly Promised Land, the righteousness of the line was revitalized.

Transmission of the History of the Creation and the Genealogy from Adam to Moses

Methuselah was born in 687 AA (After Adam's creation). Adam died in 930. They could have known each other for 243 years. Shem was born in 1558 AA; Methuselah died in 1656 AA, the year of the flood. They could have known each other for 98 years. Isaac was born in 2108 AA; Shem died in 2158 AA. They could have known each other for 50 years. When he was between 17 and 20 years of age, Levi returned to the family homestead at Hebron [map site 13] (Gen. 29:34, 30:24-25, 37:2). Isaac was between 164 and 167 years of age. They could have known each other for 13 to 16 years before Isaac died at 180 years of age (Table 10, page 397). These observations suggest that the early history of creation was transmitted orally (Bar Graph, page 115). Part of it may have been transmitted in written form. Jochebed, Moses' mother, or someone who antedated Jochebed, or Moses himself may have penned the **book** of Adam's generation (Gen. 5:1).

Jochebed, "*Yahweh* is glory" (*yok̂ebed,* יוכבד), was Levi's daughter. The youngest age for Jochebed at Moses' birth was 234 Biblical years (2626 AA [Moses' birth] - 2392 AA [Levi's death] = 234 years) (Exod. 6:20, Num. 26:59). She was probably older than that because the assumption of Levi fathering her in his last year of life is not likely. She must have been old enough to obtain historical information from Levi before he died. As Moses' mother, wet-nurse, and nanny, Jochebed was the one chosen to transmit to Moses the history of the creation of the heavens and earth and the genealogy from Adam to Moses. She was a unique woman chosen by God to live longer then her contemporaries for this special purpose.

Based on the analysis of the ages of individuals described in this section, and their crossover with one another, the following

Bar Graph (page 115) depicts the crossover of seven individuals from Adam to Moses who could have transmitted much of the information that Moses wrote down in the book of Genesis.

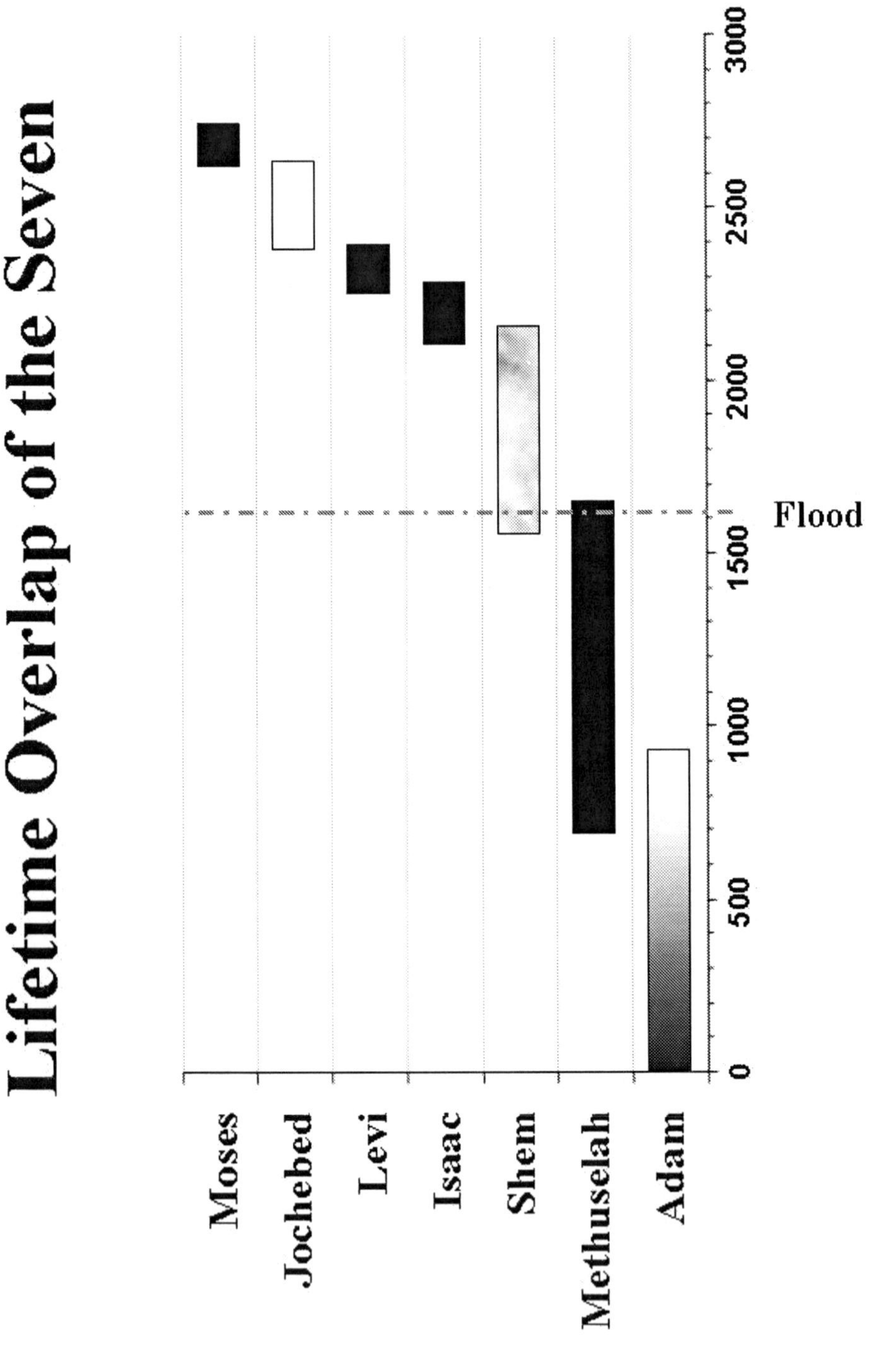
Lifetime Overlap of the Seven
Moses
Jochebed
Levi
Isaac
Shem
Methuselah
Adam
0
500
1000
1500
2000
2500
3000
Flood

CHAPTER 2

THE GENERATIONS OF ADAM

Genesis 5:1-32

Chapter five starts the book of the generations of Adam; this is the second of the generations in the book of Genesis. The first was the generations of the heavens and the earth (Gen. 2:4). The generations of Adam describe the righteous line up until the time of Noah and the flood, 1656 Biblical years AA (After Adam's creation) (Table 3, page 117; Table 10, page 397).

The description of Seth was in the likeness and image of Adam. Adam was in the likeness and image of God. The choice of subsequent individuals in the first ten generations of the righteous line occurred because they were appropriate representatives of the character of God. Since Seth was the third born, others in the righteous line may not have been the firstborn, but the selected righteous son (pages 140-141, 156).

Enoch, as a prophet, anticipated the time of the flood; Methuselah died the year that the flood came as judgment to the earth. Enoch named his son, Methuselah, "man of the dart"; Methuselah's name may have been prophetic of the piercing of the LORD Jesus Christ on the cross. Enoch was translated because he "walked with God." He was a prophet who condemned the antediluvian world. The judgment of the worldwide flood foreshadowed the future judgment to the world by fire (Zep. 3:8). Enoch also prophesied of this future judgment to the world that will occur upon the return of the LORD Jesus Christ:

"It was also about these men that Enoch, in the seventh generation from Adam, prophesied, saying, 'Behold, the Lord came with many thousands of His holy ones, to execute judgment upon all, and to convict all the ungodly of all their ungodly deeds which they have done in an ungodly way, and of all the harsh things which ungodly sinners have spoken against Him'" (Jude 1:14-15).

Lamech died five years before the flood. Noah means "rest" (Table 2, 101). Lamech prophesied that Noah would relieve them from the "toil" ("sorrow and pain," *'itstsâbôn,* עצבון, the same word used in each judgment of Adam and Eve, pages 80-82) of working the soil (Gen. 3:16-17, 5:29). The cleansing of evil from the earth by the worldwide flood resulted in a new beginning for all life and enrichment and rest to the soil. The unrighteous line had abdicated their responsibility for their agrarian assignment. A new beginning came from Noah's family who had the same charge as Adam for caring for the animals that disembarked from the ark and for tilling the soil.

Noah had three sons after his 500th year: Japheth was the eldest, Ham the youngest, and Shem the middle son (Gen. 9:24, 10:21).

TABLE 3: THE MEANING OF THE NAMES OF THE FIRST TEN GENERATIONS OF THE RIGHTEOUS LINE	
NAME	MEANING OF THE NAME
1. Adam	"Man" (*adâm,* אדם) from *adamah*
2. Seth	"Appointed" (*shêth,* שׁת)
3. Enosh	"Man" (*'enôsh,* אנוש) calling on *Yahweh*
4. Kenan	"Possession" (*qêynân,* קין)
5. Mahalalel	"Praise of God" (*mahălal'êl,* מהללאל)
6. Jared	"Descent" (*yered,* ירד)
7. Enoch	"Dedicated" (*chănôk,* חנוך)
8. Methuselah	"Man of the Dart" (*methûshelach,* מתוּשלח)
9. Lamech	"Powerful" (*lemek,* למך)
10. Noah	"Rest" (*nôach,* נח)

EVIL THAT DEMANDED CLEANSING

Genesis 6:1-22

Gen. 6:1-2: In the second verse, the basic question is whether "the sons of God" (*benî Elohim,* בני־האלהים) refer to fallen angels, demons, who directly impregnated women and/or to fallen men. The same phrase (*beni Elohim,* בני־האלהים) is used in the book of Job to refer to angels, not men (Job 1:6, 2:1, 38:7). Elsewhere a slightly different phrase refers to angels, "sons of the mighty" (*beni Elim,* בני אלים) (Psa. 29:1, 89:6). *Elohim* and "sons of the Most High" (*beni 'elyon,* בני עליון) can refer to men (Psa. 82:6, Luke 6:35, John 10:34-35).

All mankind had rebelled against God, except Noah and his family. Some of the men whose thoughts were continually evil came under the control of the fallen angels after voluntarily submitting to them. The fallen angels may have created an abnormal seed by using the agency of fallen men. If that was the situation, "sons of God" may have referred to the fallen angels inhabiting the fallen men that they demonized.

However, the linguistic argument would suggest fallen angels only. They may have been able to impregnate women without the intervention of a body of a fallen man: "The sons of God came into the daughters of men" (*y'b'o beni h'elohim banot h'adam,* יבאו בני האלהים אל־בנות האדם) (Gen. 6:4). The LORD said the angels of heaven do not marry; He did not say that fallen angels did not have the ability to impregnate a woman (Matt. 22:30).

In either case, the purpose of Satan was clear; his primary aim was to try to prevent the promised Seed who would crush him from being born (Gen. 3:15).

The word, "came," indicates sexual intercourse with the sole purpose of using a woman to achieve a selfish end. Perhaps the derivation of its slang usage today evolved from the same depreciative approach to sex. In this situation, the fallen angels were attempting to achieve Satan's goal of an abnormal, demonized race, so that a pure birth could not take place, and they could dominate mankind.

These fallen angels underwent confinement at the time of the flood:

"God did not spare angels when they sinned, but cast them into hell and committed them to pits of darkness, reserved for judgment" (2 Pet. 2:4).

In the New Testament, the usual Greek word for Hell is Gehenna (*geenna,* γέεννα), the place of confinement after the final judgment. This verse states that the fallen angels are awaiting judgment in "Hell" (*tartaroo,̄* ταρταρόω) and "pits of darkness" (*seirais zophos*, σειραις ζοφου). Hell must be an incorrect translation of *tartaroo*. The probable meaning is "the recesses of Hades" (*tartaroo,̄* ταρταρόω), not Gehenna. The Old Testament also speaks of this region as being "in the remotest parts of the pit" (*berek̂aṫi-bor,* בירכתי־בור):

"Assyria is there and all her company; her graves are round about her. All of them are slain, fallen by the sword, whose graves are set in the remotest parts of the pit and her company is round about her grave. All of them are slain, fallen by the sword, who spread terror in the land of the living" (Ezek. 32:22-23).

Strictly speaking, Hell is not yet occupied. Individuals are sent to Hell after the Great White Throne judgment (Rev. 20:11-15). The known exceptions will be the False Prophet and the Antichrist who will be sentenced to the lake of fire at the end of the present age (Rev. 19:20). Pending the Great White Throne judgment, fallen men and fallen angels await that judgment in Hades, "the pit," "the abyss," i.e., not in Hell (Luke 8:31, 2 Pet. 2:4, Jude 1:6).

Gen. 6:3: In the depravity of that time, *Yahweh* stated that His Spirit would not continue to strive with man. Each man had a restraint against doing evil by the Spirit of *Yahweh*.

There are two possible interpretations of the 120 years. It could mean that there would be 120 years until the flood. However, the text indicates that men grew progressively more evil as they aged. The verse states, "nevertheless **his** days shall be 120 years"; the pronoun suggests a shortening of the life span of individuals. Thus, its primary meaning is a shortening of the life span that became necessary to decrease the amount of accumulated evil in the world.

Indeed, after the flood, there was a progressive shortening of the life span over several centuries. Noah lived 950 years, Shem-600 years, Eber-464 years, Peleg-239 years, and Moses-120 years (Table 10, page 397). Moses' only known psalm (in the Book of Psalms) tells of the further shortening of the life span to an average of 70 years, or 80 years if a person possesses physical and/or spiritual strength (Psa. 90:10, Isa. 40:29-31). It is also possible that both interpretations were correct. The lifespan was shortened, and it was 120 years until the flood.

Gen. 6:4: The Nephilim were the giants that came from these abnormal unions (Num. 13:33). Their name comes from the Hebrew infinitive that means "to fall" (*naphal,* נפל). The Nephilim were "the fallen giants/tyrants" (*nephilim,* נפלים). They were an abnormal race developed from the seed of demons and humans who ruled the earth at the time of Noah.

The LORD went into the abyss to preach to those from the generation of the flood who had been dominated by the Nephilim (Luke 8:30-31, Eph. 4:8-10, 1 Pet. 4:6, 2 Pet. 2:4-10, Jude 1:6-7):

"For Christ also died for sins once for all, the just for the unjust, so that He might bring us to God, having been put to death in the flesh, but made alive in the spirit; in which also He went and made proclamation to the spirits now in prison, who once were disobedient, when the patience of God kept waiting in the days of Noah during the construction of the ark, in which a few, that is, eight persons, were brought safely through the water" (1 Pet. 3:18-20).

"For the gospel has for this purpose been preached even to those who are dead, that though they are judged in the flesh as men, they may live in the spirit according to the will of God" (1 Pet. 4:6).

Perhaps He preached to the people from the time of the flood, who were "guarded" (*phulakē,* φυλακή) in Hades, because of the gross abnormality of the situation described in these few verses in Genesis where the seed of demons and women, the Nephilim, ruled over all of society, except for Noah and his family. They had no power over Noah and his family because they were protected by the LORD. The Nephilim reign created an atmosphere where men had only evil thoughts in their hearts all day long (וכל־יצר מחשבת לבו רק רע כל־היום).

The LORD Jesus stated there would be a recurrence of a time like this before His return (Matt. 24:37-39, Luke 17:26-30).

As stated above, the LORD visited the generation of people from the time of the flood in Hades. Some of these may have responded to His message; He led them out of the captivity of Hades:

"You have ascended on high, You have led captive *your* captives; You have received gifts *among* men, even among the rebellious also, that the LORD God may dwell *there*" (Psa. 68:18 NASB margin: *your, among,* and *there* are absent in the Hebrew text). Therefore, the literal translation is, "You have ascended on high, You have led captive captives; You have received gifts, men, even the rebellious also, to dwell with *Yah Elohim*": (עלית למרום שבית שבי לקחת מתנות באדם ואף סוררים לשכן יה אלהים).

The Apostle Paul gave his interpretation of this verse (Psa. 68:18). He clearly indicated that the captives in questions were those from "the lower parts of the earth":

"Therefore it says, 'WHEN HE ASCENDED ON HIGH, HE LED CAPTIVE A HOST OF CAPTIVES, AND HE GAVE GIFTS TO MEN' (Now this expression, 'He ascended,' what does it mean except that He also had descended into the lower parts of the earth? He who descended is Himself also He who ascended far above all the heavens, so that He might fill all things)" (Eph. 4:8-10).

Some suggest the captives (Psa. 68:18) were the saints who came out of the graves that were opened following the earthquake at the time of the crucifixion; they appeared to many in Jerusalem on resurrection day (Matt. 27:52-53). If that interpretation is correct, it assumes that those who re-inhabited their bodies had not previously ascended to Paradise. That is contrary to the LORD's teaching about Paradise. The believing thief went to Paradise the day of the crucifixion, not on resurrection Sunday (Luke 23:43). It seems more likely that these saints left Paradise to re-inhabit their former bodies and come forth from their graves as a testimony to other believers of the power of the resurrection.

A review of the aforementioned Scriptures should lead one to conclude that captives from the time of the flood were the ones that ascended with the LORD after responding to His preaching in Hades. It is likely that these were the people subjugated by the Nephilim. There is no indication as to how many believed and responded to the LORD. It is unlikely that the Nephilim would have responded because of the demonic part of their nature.

It is possible that the Nephilim will reappear for a brief period at the end of the present age (Rev. 9:1-10). Those that will come forth are waiting in **the opening (***phrear,* φρεατος**) of the shaft of the abyss** (Rev. 9:1), **not the remotest parts of the pit** (*tartaroo̅,* ταρταρόω) where the demons "who did not keep their own domain" are awaiting judgment (1 Pet. 2:4, Jude 1:6).

The creatures described in the Revelation demonstrate horrible characteristics of fallen angels and humans. It is possible that these are the Nephilim in their **unmasked** (more demonic) forms. The attributes of these beings, that Satan will be permitted to send forth near the end of the present age, suggest an abnormal hybridization (Rev. 9:7-10). Instead of the normal characteristics of humans and the awesome holy angels, seraphim, and cherubim described in the Scriptures, these beings have deteriorated into horrendous creatures with distorted animal, insect, human, and mineral attributes (Isa. 6:1-4, 14:9-12; Ezek. 28:12-19; Rev. 4:7-9, 9:7-10).

The fact that the seed of the Nephilim continued to exist after the flood suggests a similar demonization of some fallen men. The Bible indicates that all these were tyrants, giants in human form. The long-necked Anakim (*'anaq̂îm,* כענקים) were descended from the Nephilim (Num. 13:32-33). Goliath was 9.75 feet tall; his armor weighed 157 pounds, and the head of his spear weighed 17 to 18 pounds (1 Sam. 17:4-7). In addition, the Rephaim, a name that means "shades" (*h'râphaîm,* **הרפאים**), were abnormal giants (page 102). Og, king of Bashan, whose iron bedstead measured 13.5 feet by 6 feet, was one of the Rephaim (Deut. 3:11). Satan tries to dominate by size. These Biblical accounts, subsequent to the flood, indicate that only a few such beings were alive, and they were restricted to small geographical areas.

One must not conclude that all giants are evil; there are genetic differences in the height of people and hormonal abnormalities of the pituitary gland that can produce gigantism unrelated to sin in an individual. There is fossil evidence for giants based on large footprints found with the structure of human feet. In the Paluxy River bed in Texas, there are human footprints 18 inches long associated with footprints of dinosaurs. A person with this size foot could have been eight to nine feet tall. In addition, there is a report of a skeleton 11.5 feet tall from an Italian coal mine.[39] These may have been normal giants, but that is problematic.

Gen. 6:5-7, 11-13: *Yahweh*'s judgment on mankind for their continuous evil thoughts, their corruption, and their violence was a worldwide flood to destroy all human, animal, bird, and insect life, except the occupants of the ark. Since the Nephilim dominated mankind at the time of the flood, the flood was a blessing sent by *Yahweh* to cleanse the earth and remove those led astray by the Nephilim (pages 121-122). Hence, God was merciful in cleansing the earth and allowing Noah and his family a second opportunity. The situation will be the same at the end of the present age just before the LORD's return:

"And just as it happened in the days of Noah, so it will be also in the days of the Son of Man: they were eating, they were drinking, they were marrying, they were being given in marriage, until the day that Noah entered the ark, and the flood came and destroyed them all. It was the same as happened in the days of Lot: they were eating, they were drinking, they were buying, they were selling, they were planting, they were building; but on the day that Lot went out from Sodom it rained fire and brimstone from heaven and destroyed them all. It will be just the same on the day that the Son of Man is revealed" (Luke 17:26-30).

Multiplication of evil would have eventually resulted in mutual destruction during the antediluvian days and the days of Lot. The world faces the same dilemma today as it awaits the return of the LORD Jesus Christ.[40] If mankind continues in their Hell-bent ways, self-destruction of the human race will occur unless the LORD intervenes. Before that happens, He has promised to return to judge the evil and deliver those who trust in Him and anticipate His coming (Zep. 2:3, John 14:1-3).

CHAPTER 3

THE GENERATIONS OF NOAH

The generations of Noah are the third of the generations in the book of Genesis. This was the time where the fallen condition of mankind resulted in the need to cleanse the earth of its evil by a worldwide flood. A new start came to Noah, his family, and all creation after the flood.

Gen. 6:8-10: In such a time, Noah, a preacher of righteousness, found favor in the eyes of *Yahweh* (2 Pet. 2:5). Noah had complete integrity and righteousness comparable to that of Daniel and Job. It could, and did, deliver him from social destruction (Ezek. 14:12-20). In addition, his wife, his three sons, and their wives went into the ark with him and were delivered from certain destruction.

The words, "Noah walked with God" (*'elohîym tehalak noâch,* את־האלהים התהלך־נח), are similar to the ones that described Enoch (*tehalak chanok 'elohîym,* ויתהלך חנוך את־האלהים) who was translated to be with God (Gen. 5:24). There is a spiritual essence in the names of Enoch ("dedicated," *h'chanok,* חנוך) and Noah ("rest," *noâch,* נח). Each had his calling to fulfill. One dedicated servant went to the LORD by translation. The other one stayed to preserve mankind, animals, birds, insects, and some marine life and to provide some rest from the curse to the soil.

Gen. 6:14-16: The ark's dimensions were 450 by 75 by 45 feet. Dividing the dimensions by 75 reduces this to 6 by 1 by 0.6, the dimensions of a man; the ark's structure was a symbol of salvation for man.

The ark had three decks with an opening about 18 inches from the top of the wall just beneath the "roof," i.e., "covering" (*mikseh,* מכסה) (Gen. 8:13). The ark had an estimated living area of nearly 95,700 square feet and could support approximately 13,900 tons.[41]

The Hebrew root used for "cover" (כפר) and "pitch" (כפר) in the 14th verse is the same as the root for "atonement" (*kaphar,* כפר)

(Lev. 9:7). It was "covered" with "pitch" inside and outside. The atonement applies to the inner man and to the physical body. Therefore, the ark's covering and pitch were symbols of atonement for man.

Whereas adult dinosaurs would not be able to come into the ark, their young were small enough to do so. The newborn Ultrasaurus, with its 120 feet long parent, measured about six feet in length.[42] Adult dinosaurs died at the time of the flood. Young dinosaurs may not have developed after the flood, or they may have survived and become extinct later (Job 40:15-24).

Gen. 6:17: The flood covered the earth and destroyed everything that had breath under heaven that was not in the ark. This included humans, animals, insects, and birds, and some of the sea creatures. Some of the latter were the only creatures preserved outside the ark during the flood.

The ark was the sanctuary from the world in a time when evil ruled. The church of the LORD Jesus Christ should be that ark in the times in which we live. Alas, the present condition of the church is such that many members swim with the world doomed to destruction, instead of floating above the world by entering the sanctuary of God's provision:

"For whatever is born of God overcomes the world; and this is the victory that has overcome the world—our faith. Who is the one who overcomes the world, but he who believes that Jesus is the Son of God?" (1 John 5:4-5).

Gen. 6:18-20: A new covenant was given to Noah, his family, and the occupants of the ark. Since the text states that the animals "will come to you," *Elohim* brought the creatures to Noah. Two of each sex of animals, insects, and birds came into the ark without Noah's searching for the same.

Gen. 6:21: The edible food for all the souls in the ark was plant life (Gen. 1:29-30, 9:3). These chosen animals had not yet resorted to violence against each other as omnivores or carnivores, even though mankind was filling the earth with violence. It is possible that some of the beasts outside the ark may have become violent and become omnivores or carnivores. The unrighteous line may have become omnivores before the flood.

Gen. 6:22: Noah did all that God commanded him. Undoubtedly, he suffered much ridicule directed towards him and his family. He continued to preach during the time that the ark was built (2 Pet. 2:5, Ezek. 14:12-20). Noah is a beautiful illustration of one faithful to *Yahweh* in a completely evil generation. He obeyed the commands given to him with no questions asked or any attempt to try to dissuade *Yahweh* from His judgment on the world.

THE WORLDWIDE FLOOD

Genesis 7:1-24

Gen. 7:1: *Yahweh* saw Noah as righteous before Him in his generation, a time of maximum unrighteousness that demanded a cleansing of the earth by the worldwide flood. Multiple ancient cultures describe a massive flood.

The Hebrew text indicates that *Yahweh* invited Noah to "come" (*boʾ*, בא), not "enter" into the ark with his family. This would indicate that *Yahweh* was speaking to him from the ark and would be present with them in the ark. The ark represents salvation through the atonement of the LORD Jesus Christ who never leaves those who believe in Him (Matt. 28:18-20). His call was to Noah, his family, the animals, the birds, and the insects to come into the ark. He was the One who invited them to come through the door, the One who sealed the ark, the One who went with them during the flood, and the One who opened the ark's door when they disembarked.

The LORD Jesus Christ is the door, the One who atoned for our sins, the One who saves us from sin, and the One who sanctifies us as we go through life. He invites us to dine with Him in His kingdom (Luke 22:15-16, John 10:1-18). Those outside the ark perished; those who do not accept the LORD-Jesus-Christ/*YHWH-Yeshua-Mashiach* will suffer in Hell (John 3:16-21).

Gen. 7:2: Seven couples of clean animals were taken compared to one couple of unclean animals. The Hebrew word for these couples is the same as that used for Adam and his wife in their relationship as "husband" (*'îŷsh,* אִישׁ) and "his wife" (*ishshto,* אשׁתו); *Ishshto* is the possessive of "wife" (*'ishshaĥ,* אִשָּׁה) (Gen. 2:23). At that time in history, these animals paired for life.

After the flood, mankind received permission to eat animal meat (Gen. 9:3). Thus, there would have been a need to have available more clean than unclean animals for food.

Gen. 7:3: The Hebrew word denoting the relationship between birds refers only to their gender, "male and female" (*zak̂ar̂ neqeb̂aĥ,* זכר ונקבה), not their relationship.

Gen. 7:4: Noah received seven days advance warning of the 40 days and nights of rain that came with the flood. Forty would become the symbol of judgment to unbelievers and trial to believers. Noah did not know about other cataclysmic events, the opening of the windows of the heavens (plural) and the fountains of the deep (Gen. 7:11). That information was not necessary for his obedience. God does not tell us everything He will do, only what is necessary for our obedience.

Some have speculated that the earth did not experience rain before this time. Rain was necessary for the growth of plants after Adam started tilling the Garden of Eden; it is unlikely that this was the first rain that fell (page 55). Since Noah did not ask for a description of rain, the supposition is that he had experienced rain many times.

Gen. 7:5-6: Noah did all that *Yahweh* commanded him. In spite of the circumstances, he gave unquestioning obedience to *Yahweh*. Noah was 600 years old.

Gen. 7:7-10: Noah, his family, and all selected animal, insect, and bird life came into the ark during the seven days. This gave him time to prepare the animals and his family for life aboard the ark. On the eighth day, Noah and his family came into the ark to join all the animals, insects, and birds that had boarded during the previous week (Gen. 7:1-4).

Gen. 7:11-16: The flood started in Noah's 600th year of life, 1,656 Biblical years AA (After Adam's creation) (Table 10, page 397). It started on the 17th day of the second month. God chose a 30-day month and a 360-day year for the Biblical method for recording time (Gen. 7:11, 8:3-4). Biblical history must be calculated in Biblical years, not Julian years (Appendix II, page 394) (Dan. 12:7; Rev. 11:2-3; 12:6, 14; 13:5).

The production of the water for the flood came from three separate sources during 40 days and nights: rain, the fountains of the deep burst (volcanic eruptions from the area of tectonic plates), and the windows of the heavens opened (Gen. 7:11 NASB margin).

Several phenomena occurred during the eruption of Mount St. Helens on May 18, 1980, in the state of Washington. Almost 1300 feet of rock was blown off the side of the mountain with volcanic ash ascending about 60,000 feet. The ash circled the earth three times before dissipating. Glaciers atop Mount St. Helens turned to steam during its eruption. This mixed with silica to produce a hot liquid. As these particles rapidly cooled, they came back to the earth as a dark rain containing sharp particles. The molten lava stream, pyroclastic flow, and the sharp particles contributed to the death of animals and humans.[43]

In 1883, an eruption in Krakatoa, Indonesia, shot about a hundred thousand feet in the air and modified the sunset for three years.[44] Most of the deaths were due to massive tsunamis. Others died from the combination of the tephra and expanding volcanic gases produced by pyroclastic airfall and flows. Many suffered hearing loss from the noise of the major eruption. Two-thirds of the island collapsed in upon itself. The Krakatoa eruption was ten times greater than the one at Mount St. Helens. Over 36,000 people died during the Krakatoa eruption. The sequence of events recorded in the Bible was qualitatively similar to these eruptions, but quantitatively so much greater.

During the flood, separation of the original landmass, Pangaea, must have occurred at the time of the disruption of the tectonic plates and resulted in the continents that exist today. One need only examine a world map and look at their coastlines to see the similarity in the borders of the separated continents (Gen. 1:9-10).

Thus, the fountains of the deep opened the fissures at the edges of the tectonic plates and came forth in a volcanic eruption associated with salt water from the oceans. This massive worldwide eruption from the tectonic plates contributed to the deadly rain that lasted for 40 days and 40 nights (Gen. 7:11-12, 8:1-2). The physical and chemical particles secondary to the volcanic eruption may have caused immediate death to many of the inhabitants of the earth. Some would have succumbed to the tsunamis, some to the tephra, and some to the pyroclastic airfall and flow.

Everything that had breath perished, except some of the sea creatures and those in the ark. The effort of the animals to escape the rise and force of the waters accounts for the currently described distribution of a plethora of animal skeletons found on continents where they were not expected.[45] Only Noah, those with him in the ark, and some of the sea creatures survived.

The Cambrian Explosion was the time of the sudden appearance of a variety of complex animal fossils in one geological stratum. No transitional forms from early ancestors were present. The theory of evolution cannot adequately explain the Cambrian Explosion. This finding is supportive of sudden destruction of all life forms exposed to the worldwide flood (pages 37-38).[46]

The windows of "the heavens" (*shamayim*, השמים)—"sky" is an incorrect translation—opened at the same time as the fountains of the deep. Rain was a separate entity, not part of the windows of the heavens. At the end of the release of these three sources of water, the windows of the heavens "closed" (*sakar,* סכר) (Gen. 8:2).

The Hebrew word translated as "windows" (*'ărubbaĥ,* ארבה) does not have a clear meaning. Some translate it as "lattice" of the heavens (like the lattice plate over a chimney) or "floodgates" of the heavens. The waters from the windows of the heavens (Gen. 7:11) contributed to the cataclysm. The word, "heavens," is plural. The water from the windows of the heavens may have come from third heaven where God's keeps His "chambers" (Psa. 104:3, 13).

Since the windows of the heavens closed, they may open again. The same Hebrew word for this phenomenon foretells a future opening of these "windows" (*'ărubbaĥ,* ארבה) at the time of a future destruction to the earth:

"Then it will be that he who flees the report of disaster will fall into the pit, and he who climbs out of the pit will be caught in the snare; for the windows above are opened, and the foundations of the earth shake. The earth is broken asunder, the earth is split through, the earth is shaken violently. The earth reels to and fro like a drunkard and it totters like a shack, for its transgression is heavy upon it, and it will fall, never to rise again" (Isa. 24:18-20).

The recurrence of the windows of the heavens will happen at the time of destruction on the earth during the period of the wrath of God at the end of the present age (Isa. 24:1-23). Since this destruction will occur by fire, the release of waters from the windows of the heavens may be the means of putting the fire out (Gen. 8:21-22, 2 Pet. 3:7-12). Final destruction of the first earth and first heaven will not occur until the end of the millennium, a thousand years later (Rev. 21:1):

"Then I saw a great white throne and Him who sat upon it, from whose presence earth and heaven fled away, and no place was found for them" (Rev. 20:11).

Gen. 7:17-24: The flood covered the whole earth. In Hebrew, the text clearly confirms the accuracy of the English translation: "All the high mountains which were under all the heavens were covered." The waters rose about 22.5 feet, approximately one-half the height of the ark, above "all the highest mountains" (*kol̂ h'harim,* כל־ההר) under "all the heavens" (*kol̂ h'sham̂ayim,* כל־השמים).[47] The water prevailed upon the earth for 150 days.

Purification and Redemption

Genesis 8:1-22

Gen. 8:1: God remembered Noah—God took action. The Hebrew word used here for "wind" (*ruâch,* רוח) is the same as the word for the Holy Spirit (*ruâch,* רוח). The Spirit of God brought a wind and physically dried and spiritually cleansed the earth from the evil that had dominated it. The earth was now ready for a new beginning. The wind may have caused a rapid cooling of the atmosphere that resulted in an ice age in the polar regions of the earth.[48]

Gen. 8:2-4: The fountains of the deep and the windows of the heavens were closed and the rain was restrained. The fact that different verbs describe rain and the windows of the heavens verifies that these were two different sources of water (page 129).

Since the waters started to recede at 150 days on the 17th day of the seventh month and the flood started on the 17th day of the second month, it follows that a Biblical month consists of 30 days.

The ark rested on the mountain range of Ararat (Gen. 8:4).

Gen. 8:5: The tops of the mountains were visible on the first day of the tenth month (Table 4, page 133).

Gen. 8:6-7: Noah could have viewed the recession of the waters from the opening at the top of the ark but would not have been able to see much of the land below the mountains. The waters producing the flood occurred over a period of 40 days. After the recession of the waters, Noah waited until the tenth day of the 11th month before he sent out a raven. The raven did not return; it may have become an omnivore and may have survived by eating dead flesh.

Gen. 8:8-12: When the raven did not return, Noah sent a dove out at seven-day intervals. The first time the dove did not find a place to rest. The second time she returned with a freshly picked olive leaf in her beak. The third time the dove did not return; she now had adequate plant life for food.

Since that time, the dove and the olive leaf have become symbols of peace. In addition, the dove became a symbol of the Holy Spirit who gives inner peace for one who believes in the LORD Jesus Christ (Mark 1:10, Rom. 10:9-10).

TABLE 4: TIME IN THE ARK

THE TIME OF THE FLOOD BY CHAPTER AND VERSE	DAYS OF THE MONTHS DURING THE FLOOD
7:10: Intake into the ark	Pre-flood—2/10
7:12: Waters released	2/17-3/27
7:11, 24; 8:3-4: Ark on Ararat	7/17
8:5: Mountain peaks visible	10/1
8:6: Raven sent out	11/10
8:7-12: Dove sent out three times	12/9-12/30?
8:13-14: Noah's 601st year	1/1
8:14-19: Debarkation from the ark	2/27—370 days from the start of the flood, 377 days in the ark

Gen. 8:13: On the first day of the new year, Noah removed the covering from the ark and saw that the land was dry. He continued to wait for God to open the door and give him permission to disembark. The date of the new year was relative to the 601st year of Noah's life. God's dating in Scripture relates to events in the lives of those who believe and obey Him (Table 10, page 397).

Gen. 8:14-19: On the 27th day of the second month, God told Noah to come out of the ark with all his family, the animals, the insects, and the birds. It is likely that the door to the ark was near ground level, so large animals could easily enter and leave the ark. *Yahweh* had sealed and shut the door of the ark. Now He removed the seal and opened the door of the ark. As previously stated, this is a picture of His complete atonement in closing the door of the ark, sustaining it during the time of the flood, and opening the door afterwards to a new life.

Gen. 8:20-22: After the flood, Noah built an altar and offered to God of every clean animal and every clean bird. He started the era of the new, cleansed earth by offerings that represented the sacrifice to come, the LORD-Jesus-Christ/*YHWH-Yeshua-Mashiach*. This was an offering of a sweet aroma resulting in a blessing from *Yahweh* who stated that He would never again destroy every living thing on the earth. Thus, during the coming days of the wrath of God, not everyone will be destroyed (Isa. 24:14-16, Zech. 14:16).

In *Yahweh*'s blessing, there was recognition of the evil within man from his youth throughout his adult life. God now rules the earth with that as an acknowledged fact. A psychology that teaches that man is inherently good, and young people will do what is right if left to their desires, is not concordant with *Yahweh*'s evaluation. The truth uttered by *Yahweh* is correct and borne out by mankind's behavior throughout the history of the human race. Children are the seed sown by their parents; they may lead good, productive lives or contribute to the evil of the world.

The soil again yielded its produce; the ground was not cursed (Gen. 8:21). Lamech's prophecy about Noah was fulfilled (Gen. 5:29).

Seed

We lose the spiritual impact of seed by translating it as offspring or descendants. The Hebrew word for all types of "seed" (*zera'*, זרע) is found 229 times in 204 verses in the Old Testament.

The Greek word for "human seed" (*sperma,* σπέρμα) is found 43 times in 40 verses in the New Testament. Seed is a spiritual word with spiritual significance. Each human soul is a special "seed" (*zera',* זרע) that is sown by the Creator. Each person was designed to become a righteous seed that would honor the Savior who became a guilt offering for the purpose of transforming the spoiled seed into one that is fruitful (Isa. 53:10).

Before the Fall, it applied to the reproduction of all life forms (Genesis 1). After the Fall, the word was first used to promise the seed of the woman that would contribute to the Savior's birth; He would triumph over Satan and his progeny (Gen. 3:15).

Human seed denotes taking something microscopic, female egg and male spermatozoon, joining them after sexual intercourse, nourishing the seed during pregnancy, and delivering a beautiful baby. These individuals become adults who start families who evolve nations. The children that are sown into the world are to produce fruit that glorifies God. Until they attain physical **and** spiritual maturity, parents are obligated to nurture their children.

The word, seed, is descriptive of all life forms, including human progeny and the One who saves us. The LORD Jesus repeatedly related plant and human seed to His kingdom, e.g., the seed of the Word of God (Matt. 13:18-30, 37-42), the mustard seed and the kingdom of heaven (Matt. 13:31-32), the sower and the kingdom of God (Mark 4:26-29), and faith like a mustard seed (Luke 17:6).

In poetic stanza, *Yahweh* stated that seedtime and harvest, summer and winter, cold and heat, and day and night would continue as long as the earth remains. Within this latter promise dwells the truth of spiritual seedtime and harvest until the end of the age (John 4:35-38, Gal. 6:8).[49] Godly seed will grow and produce a spiritual harvest. There will be a season for reaping healthy seed that is sown in good soil, even in times of famine.

One example of seedtime and harvest, based on personal faith in *Yahweh*, is Elijah's interaction with the widow of Zarephath when both of them were in the throes of a famine:

"Then the word of the LORD came to him, saying, 'Arise, go to Zarephath, which belongs to Sidon, and stay there; behold, I have commanded a widow there to provide for you.' So he arose and went to Zarephath, and when he came to the gate of the city, behold, a widow was there gathering sticks; and he called to her and said, 'Please get me a little water in a jar that I may drink.' As she was going to get it, he called to her and said, 'Please bring me a piece of bread in your hand.' But she said, 'As the LORD your God lives, I have no bread, only a handful of flour in the bowl and a little oil in the jar; and behold, I am gathering a few sticks that I may go in and prepare for me and my son, that we may eat it and die.' Then Elijah said to her, 'Do not fear; go, do as you have said, but make me a little bread cake from it first and bring it out to me, and afterward you may make one for yourself and for your son. For thus says the LORD God of Israel, 'The bowl of flour shall not be exhausted, nor shall the jar of oil be empty, until the day that the LORD sends rain on the face of the earth.' So she went and did according to the word of Elijah, and she and he and her household ate for many days" (1 Kin. 17:8-15).

Yahweh had given a command to the widow of Zarephath to provide for Elijah. She knew *Yahweh Elohim*; therefore, she was a believer. As the representative of *Yahweh*, Elijah asked her to provide for him first. This required a faith response to believe *Yahweh's* previous command to her and to give to another in need before meeting the legitimate needs of herself and her son. Because of her obedience, they all had ample supply during the remainder of the three and one-half years of famine.

The LORD Jesus declared to the people of his hometown, Nazareth, that no widow in Israel had this type of faith during the time of Elijah. Therefore, *Yahweh* sent Elijah to a foreign widow. Because of this observation, the self-righteous Jews in Nazareth tried to throw Him off a cliff (Luke 4:25-26).

Another example is the widow who went to Elisha in her time of need:

"Now a certain woman of the wives of the sons of the prophets cried out to Elisha, 'Your servant my husband is dead, and you know that your servant feared the LORD; and the creditor has come to take my two children to be his slaves.' Elisha said to her, 'What shall I do for you? Tell me, what do you have in the house?' And she said, 'Your maidservant has nothing in the house except a jar of oil.' 'Then he said, 'Go, borrow vessels at large for yourself from all your neighbors, even empty vessels; do not get a few. And you shall go in and shut the door behind you and your sons, and pour out into all these vessels, and you shall set aside what is full.' So she went from him and shut the door behind her and her sons; they were bringing the vessels to her and she poured. When the vessels were full, she said to her son, 'Bring me another vessel.' And he said to her, 'There is not one vessel more.' And the oil stopped. Then she came and told the man of God. And he said, 'Go, sell the oil and pay your debt, and you and your sons can live on the rest'" (2 Kin. 4:1-7).

Elisha did not give the widow something; he asked her to act and believe for the miraculous harvest that she needed. He instructed her to "sow" what she had left, a jar of oil. By faith, she acted and received a harvest of oil that allowed her to pay her debt and have enough left over for her and her sons to live on.

There are practical ramifications to the concept of seedtime and harvest as revealed in these two examples. People in need, like the two widows, have to plant their seed of faith before they can realize their harvest.[50] This is an important principle for missionary endeavors in needy countries. We may do a disservice to people in need when we give them money instead of teaching them how to sow and reap by faith in the LORD who is their Source! Seed can be time, talent, evangelism, possessions, children, worship—anything that can be sown to produce a needed harvest within the kingdom of God. We are to sow in faith, believing God to bring in the harvest that He wishes to give us in His time and His way.

CHAPTER 4

THE GENERATIONS AFTER THE FLOOD

The covenant made with the generations after the flood, the fourth of the generations in the book of Genesis, is inclusive of all subsequent generations. The Adamic covenant, renewed through the Noahic covenant with modifications, applies to all mankind as an everlasting covenant (Gen. 9:16).

THE NOAHIC COVENANT; MAN'S RESPONSE

Genesis 9:1-29

Gen. 9:1-2: The command first given by *Elohim* to Adam was now given by *Elohim* to Noah for his sons to multiply and fill the earth (Gen. 1:28). However, there was a major difference in the relationship of man with the beasts and birds. Instead of having a cooperative, loving supervisor, the terror of man was on every beast and bird.

Gen. 9:3-6: A major change occurred; man was given permission to eat animal flesh, not just plant life (Gen. 1:29-30). The status of the eating habits of those who perished in the flood is not stated. It is likely that the introduction of animal flesh into the diet was related to the progressive shortening of the lifespan (Table 10, page 397) (Gen. 6:3).

A command was given not to eat animal blood; it had a two-fold meaning. One was not to eat the blood (rare meat) of an animal; this would hasten the development of atherosclerosis and the heart and blood vessel diseases related thereto. The other was not to eat the flesh while the animal still showed signs of life, because its life ("soul," *nephesh*, נפשׁ) was in the blood (אך־בשׂר בנפשו דמו לא תאכלו). For such cruelty *Elohim* required the life of any person so doing by the animals themselves (Gen. 9:4-5).

Yahweh would require the life of any person who murdered another person. Murder makes mockery of the fact that each person is created in the *imago Dei*. The command of capital punishment for murder originated from the Creator. Capital punishment is not an option for governments that wish to obey the LORD. Subsequently, the law would define the penalty for accidental death (Deut. 19:1-13).

Gen. 9:7: They were to multiply and "swarm in the earth" (Gen. 9:7 NASB margin). Verses one and seven are the same; they encapsulate the topic of life after the flood.

Gen. 9:8-11: A new covenant was ratified by *Elohim* to Noah, his sons, their seed, and every living creature. "All souls" (*kol nephesh,* ואת כל־נפש) will never again be destroyed by water that came from the three sources that caused the flood, and never again will there be a generalized flood to destroy the earth (Gen. 7:11). The word, "covenant," occurs seven times in these verses. The duration of the covenant is "to everlasting generations" (*dorôt 'olâm,* לדרת עולם) (Gen. 9:12 NASB margin).

Relevant to this is the fact that there will be no sea in the new earth (Rev. 21:1). Its absence may be related to the destructive forces of the flood and Satan's abode in the abyss of the sea (Rev. 11:7).

Gen. 9:12-17: The association of the clouds with rain suggests that rain was a known and recurrent event. The sign of the covenant would be the rainbow with its full spectrum of colors. With every rainbow *Elohim* would remember His covenant. The rainbow is for man's benefit to remember that God remembers and honors His covenant.

Gen. 9:18-19: Attention turns to the three sons of Noah: Shem, Ham, and Japheth. The three sons of Noah were to replenish the earth through their progeny, their seed.

Gen. 9:20-27: Noah became drunk after planting a vineyard and drinking from its produce. It is not clear whether this was deliberate, or he simply did not know the alcoholic content of what he brewed. The soil was enriched in the aftermath of the flood. It may have resulted in a grape with greater alcoholic content than Noah was accustomed to before the flood.

The central point of the story is that Noah was naked in his tent, and Ham "saw" his nakedness (Gen. 9:22). In Hebrew, the infinitive, "to see" (*raʾaĥ,* ראה), can mean "to act." In the command to Abraham at Mount Moriah to offer up Isaac, the Hebrew infinitive, "to see" (*raʾaĥ,* ראה), is translated into English as "to provide." God saw and provided what was needed (Gen. 22:8, 14).

Ham's action is confirmed by the Hebrew text that states he "did" (*'aŝaĥ,* עשה) something to Noah:

"When Noah awoke from his wine, he knew what his youngest son had done to him" (Gen. 9:24).

In Hebrew, Ham means "hot" (*cham̂,* חם). Canaan means "merchant" (*kena'an,* כנען) (Hos. 12:7). The name may symbolize the land of unscrupulous businessmen (page 304) (Zech. 14:21). Greed in dehumanizing business practices is often accompanied by immoral behavior. Note that part of Canaan's seed populated Sodom and Gomorrah (Gen. 10:19).

Why did Canaan, one of four of Ham's sons, receive condemnation for Ham's act (Gen. 9:25, 10:6)? In the righteous line, the most righteous son is listed first, not the firstborn; in the unrighteous line the firstborn is listed first (Gen. 5:3, 11:26). Ham was the youngest son of Noah who departed from the righteous line (Gen. 9:24, 10:6). Noah was prophesying that the progeny of Ham's youngest son, Canaan, would reap the harvest of Ham's homosexual act (Gen. 10:6). Sodom, Gomorrah, and the villages of the Jordan valley would be destroyed for similar behavior (Genesis 19). These cities were part of the land of Canaan.

Noah had his first son, when he was 500 years old (Gen. 5:32). Shem had his firstborn son two years after the flood when he was 100 years old (Gen. 7:11, 11:10). Therefore, there had to be a son who was two years older than Shem. Shem was the middle son; Japheth was the eldest:

"Also to Shem, the father of all the children of Eber, the brother of Japheth the elder, children were born" (Gen. 10:21 NASB margin).

Shem and Japheth received a blessing for covering their father's nakedness without seeing the same. The seed of Shem was the righteous line from which Abraham was born. Japheth was the father of the Gentile nations that inhabit the coastlands of the world (Gen. 10:2-5). The primary blessing to Shem suggests he may have initiated the kind act of covering their father:

"May God enlarge Japheth, and let him dwell in the tents of Shem; and let Canaan be his servant" (Gen. 9:27).

In Hebrew, Japheth means "to enlarge." The enlargement of the seed of Japheth resulted in the large population that would occupy most of the landmass of the earth, "the coastlands," i.e., Europe, Asia, the Americas, and several islands (Gen. 10:2-5).

Yahweh blessed Shem as the forebear of the future Hebrew nation. The Hebrew infinitive, "to dwell" (*shak̂an,* שׁכן), can also mean "to abide." It is problematic whether this refers to Japheth "abiding" in the tents of Shem, i.e., being blessed from Shem, or alternatively, He (*Elohim*) shall "abide" in the tents of Shem. (יפת אלהים ליפת וישכן באהלי־שם) Since both meanings can be justified linguistically, and in reality, it is probable that this is a *double entendre*. The gospel came from the descendants of Shem through Abraham and his seed to bless the nations of the world. God created the nation of Israel, His chosen people, through the seed of Shem, and He abides with them. In the future, this blessing will merge with the formation of the Israel of God.

Ham was not included in the blessing; judgment came to his youngest son. Noah's curse to Canaan was to be the lowest of servants to both brothers. This judgment has been variable in its application throughout history. Therefore, it must have a future fulfillment when Canaanites will be absent from the house of *Yahweh Tza'vot*:

"Every cooking pot in Jerusalem and in Judah will be holy to the LORD of hosts; and all who sacrifice will come and take of them and boil in them. And there will no longer be a Canaanite in the house of the LORD of hosts in that day" (Zech. 14:21).

Representatives of the three sons would eventually be welcomed into the family of God. In Old Testament times, salvation came to men through faith in *Yahweh-Yeshua-Mashiach*. Examples include: Japheth—Job's faith in *Yahweh*, Shem—Abraham's faith in *Yahweh*, and Ham—Hagar's faith and Ishmael's faith in *Yahweh* (Gen. 12:1, 16:9-10, 25:17; Job 1:8).

Representatives of the three sons entered the family of God, during New Testament times, through faith in the LORD Jesus Christ. Examples include: Japheth—the conversion of Cornelius and his household, Shem—the conversion of Saul to become the Apostle Paul, and Ham—the Ethiopian eunuch's conversion (Acts 8:25-40, 9:1-19, 10:1-48).

Gen. 9:28-29: Noah could have known all of the righteous line from Enosh (except Enoch) down through Terah, the father of Abram (Table 10, page 397). Noah lived more than a third of his life after the flood. He saw the earth divided in the days of Peleg when *Elohim* confused the languages at the Tower of Babel (Gen. 10:25-29; 11:1-9, 18-28). He died two years before Abram was born (Table 10, page 397).

CHAPTER 5

THE GENERATIONS OF SHEM, HAM, AND JAPHETH

The record of the fifth of the generations in Genesis, the sons of Noah, is recorded in the tenth chapter. The derivation of all of the peoples of the earth can be traced back to these three: Shem, Ham, and Japheth.

THE TABLE OF NATIONS

Genesis 10:1-32

Gen. 10:1: Philologists can trace the 6,000 or more languages of the earth, with myriads of dialects, back to three basic root languages emanating from the three sons of Noah and their progeny.

Gen. 10:2-5: The oldest son, Japheth, is first on the list. There are 14 individual descendants of Japheth: seven sons (Gomer, Magog, Madai, Javan, Tubal, Meshech, and Tiras) and seven grandsons (Ashkenaz, Riphath, Togarmah, Elishah, Tarshish, Kittim, and Dodanim).

Although many scholars give several variations in the interpretation of the territory of each of the sons and grandsons, there is agreement that Japheth's progeny started the Indo-European nations that became the coastlands of the world and make up most of the landmass and population of the earth. This resulted in the fulfillment of part of the prophecy given by Noah to enlarge Japheth (Gen. 9:27). Therefore, when the prophets speak of the coastlands in the Bible, without further specification, they are referring to the progeny of Japheth with their lands, languages, families, and nations.

Gen. 10:6-20: Next on the list are 30 descendants of Ham: four sons (Cush, Mizraim, Put, and Canaan), eight grandsons (Seba, Havilah, Sabtah, Raamah, Sabteca, Nimrod, Sidon, and Heth), two great-grandsons (Sheba and Dedan), seven people-groups (Ludim,

Anamim, Lehabim, Naphtuhim, Pathrusim, Casluhim, and Caphtorim), and nine separate tribes (Jebusite, Amorite, Girgashite, Hivite, Arkite, Sinite, Arvadite, Zemarite, and Hamathite). The list includes the person and tribe of Canaan. This emphasis may relate to the prophecy given by Noah and the subsequent history of Canaan relative to Israel (Gen. 9:25-27). Several tribes came from individuals, e.g. the Philistines came from the Casluhim, one of seven tribes of the progeny of Mizraim.

Nimrod is introduced as a mighty one on the earth: "He was a mighty hunter before the LORD." He dominated the people of the earth. His kingdom started with Babel; he was the leader of the revolt against *Yahweh* at the Tower of Babel (Gen. 11:1-9). Thus, he was "in the face" (*l'pañeh*, לפני) of *Yahweh*, the literal Hebrew translation of "before" *Yahweh* (Gen. 10:9). In the revolt at Babel, led by Nimrod, the latter phrase more aptly describes his attitude toward *Yahweh*.

He built three cities in Shinar (Babylon): Erech, Accad, and Calneh and then went forth to Assyria and built four more cities: Nineveh, Rehoboth-Ir, Calah, and Resen. The Hebrew word construction allows for the possibility that the four latter "cities" were part of a great city complex known as Nineveh, a city first located in Assyria that later became part of Babylon:

מן־הארץ ההוא יצא אשור ויבן את־נינוה ואת־רחבת עיר ואת־כלח: ואת־רסן בין נינוה ובין כלח הוא העיר הגדלה:

Later in Scripture, Nineveh is called "the great city." This suggests that it is correct to view Nineveh as a complex of these four cities (Jon. 3:2). "The great city" is also the phrase used to describe two cities that will undergo destruction during the wrath of God. Jerusalem will be split into three parts (Rev. 11:8, 16:19). Nineveh will be completely destroyed (Zep. 2:13-15).

Nimrod was the leader that attempted to unify the world in rebellion against God. He is a symbol of the Antichrist who will appear at the end of the age and try to do the same thing. The latter event will occur during the final half-week (three and one-half years) of Daniel's prophecy of 70 weeks of years (490 Biblical years) (Dan. 9:24-27).

Mizraim's progeny occupied many of the countries that border the Mediterranean. Mizraim ("two straits," *mitsrayim*, מצרים) is the name for Upper and Lower Egypt. The Philistines settled in the Promised Land. They came from the sea and were descended from the Casluhim from the progeny of Mizraim.

The progeny of Canaan occupied the Promised Land until the time of Joshua; they were subjugated, because of their disobedience to *Elohim* (Gen. 15:16). The prophecy of Noah that the progeny of Canaan would become slaves to the progeny of Shem had partial fulfillment at that time.

The effect of Ham's homosexual act upon his father would eventuate in judgment during the destruction of Sodom, Gomorrah, and the cities of the valley. The inhabitants of those cities came from Canaan's seed (Gen. 19:1-29). The progeny of Ham is primarily located in the lands, families, languages, and nations of the Middle East and Africa, but several descendants have been scattered throughout the earth, some as slaves.

Gen. 10:21-31: The last mentioned son of Noah is Shem, the second born (Gen. 5:32, 11:10). He was the father of the children of Eber. In Hebrew, Eber means "a region beyond" (*'eb̂er,* עבר). The word may mean that the spiritual progeny of Eber is destined for "a region beyond," a promise given to the true seed of Abraham. "Hebrew" (*'ibriŷ,* עברי) is a name derived from Eber (*'eb̂er,* עבר) (Gen. 14:13, Rom. 2:28-29, Gal. 3:29).

The list of 26 descendants of Shem follows: five sons (Elam, Asshur, Arpachshad, Lud, and Aram), five grandsons (Uz, Hul, Gether, Mash, and Shelah), one great-grandson (Eber), two great-great-grandsons (Peleg and Joktan), and 13 great-great-great-grandsons (Almodad, Sheleph, Hazarmaveth, Jeran, Hadoram, Uzal, Diklah, Obal, Abimael, Sheba, Ophir, Havilah, and Jobab).

Shem's first listed grandson, Uz, may have been the person who founded the land of Uz. Job was from the land of Uz. Satan persecuted Job, a name that means "persecuted" (*'iŷoḃ,* איוב). Some believe the book of Job to be the oldest book in the Bible. He lived to a great age; he may have been as old as the early patriarchs (Table 10, page 397) (Job 1:1, 42:16-17).

Peleg was born about a century after the flood (Table 10, page 397). Hence, he would have been a contemporary of Nimrod. Peleg's name means "to divide" (*peleg,* פלג). In Peleg's time, the earth was "divided" (*pelegah,* פלגה). *Pelegah* is a word that is derived from the same Hebrew root as Peleg. This division is highly suggestive that this was the time of the revolt at Babel that resulted in the divisions of mankind into different people-groups with different languages (Gen. 11:9).

Joktan (*yoqtaŋ̂,* יקטן) means "little." Joktan and his sons branched off from the righteous line at the time of Babel. Joktan's progeny remained in the Middle East. The righteous line descended through Eber and Peleg down to Abram who settled in the Promised Land.

The Shemites were the third language group; they became part of the lands, families, and nations in the Middle East. The line from Shem to Eber is included in the Shemite line in the genealogy table (Genesis 11) (Table 10, page 397).

Gen. 10:32: Thus, there is a record of 70 generations from the three sons of Noah: Shem (26), Ham (30), and Japheth (14). The progeny of these three "were separated on the earth after the flood." Out of these three men came the families, nations, and people-groups of the earth.

Babel

Genesis 11:1-32

Gen. 11:1-9: Peleg was born around a century after the flood and died 340 years after the flood at the age of 239 (Table 10, page

397). Note that a significant shortening of the life span occurred at the time of Peleg. Noah was the tenth in the righteous line, each of whom lived nearly a millennium (except Enoch who was translated). Shem lived 600 years. From Arpachshad to Eber men lived to 400 years plus; from Peleg to Serug there was a drop in age to 200 years plus; from Nahor to Abram the age span dropped to between 100 and 200 years.

There are at least three variables involved in the shortening of the lifespan after Noah.

1. The first variable can be attributed to the changes at the time of Babel that resulted in the need for men to adjust to different climatological conditions and diets based on their varied environments as they scattered on the earth.

2. The second variable was the effect on metabolism in changing from an herbivore to becoming an omnivore after the flood.

3. The third variable was the violent lifestyle and further destruction of the environment by Nimrod and his followers with their move to urban centers.

They departed from an agrarian lifestyle and rebelled against the command to "swarm in the earth" (Gen. 9:1 NASB margin).

Nimrod, Ham's grandson, formed the kingdoms of Babel (Babylon) and Assyria. Nimrod was a contemporary of the righteous line from at least Shem through Peleg; thus, it is likely that he lived more than 400 years as did his contemporaries. Therefore, Nimrod was the leader of the unrighteous line at the time of the formation of the Tower of Babel; he built Babel (Gen. 10:10).

Babel is a name associated with the confusion of languages (Gen. 10:8-12, 11:9). Babel (*bab̂el,* בבל) comes from the Hebrew word, *"balal"* (*bal̂al,* בלל), that means "confused." The English word, "babble," has a similar meaning. Babylon is the land of spiritual confusion.

The building of the tower occurred on the plain of Shinar. This is concordant with the previous discussion about the unrighteous line of Cain settling on the east side of the Fertile Crescent. After the flood, the unrighteous line gravitated back to the same geographical area.

The command to Noah and his sons was to multiply and swarm in the earth (Gen. 9:1, 7 NASB margin). Filling the earth required scattering abroad upon it (Gen. 9:19). Instead of obeying this command, Nimrod and his followers decided to concentrate in one geographical area and build a tower whose top would "reach into heaven" (Gen. 11:4). They wanted to dominate earth and heaven. The latter suggests demonic participation in their effort.

The Babylonian name for such a tower was a *ziggurat*. The Hebrew word for tower is *"migdal"* (*migdal̂,* מגדל) (Gen. 11:5). The *ziggurat* was made of burnt brick with some type of mortar.[51] The common language, purpose, and help from the fallen angels in rebellion against *Yahweh* contributed to the ingenuity necessary to build the tower (Gen. 11:1, 6).

Their motives included the following:

1. They wanted to confront heaven by building a tower that would "reach into heaven" (Isa. 14:13-14).

2. They wished to avoid dispersal throughout the earth by uniting to build one city and continue to disobey the agrarian assignment given to Cain (Gen. 4:3).

3. They wanted to honor their own name instead of the name of God.

4. They may have wanted an elevated structure to try to avoid destruction from another flood. The content of the bricks included

tar in the mortar. This was an attempt to make the structure resistant to the waters of a flood.

5. Their main motive was the worship of the heavenly bodies—the stars, sun, and moon—in defiance of *Elohim*. Fallen angels could have provoked this form of idolatry as a means of diverting men from the worship of the One Triune God to the worship of demons (Psa. 106:37, 1 Cor. 10:20).

Stars represent angels in the Bible. This planetary worship represented union with Satan, fallen Lucifer, the shining one—*Helel*, and his demons; Satan helps people who worship him (Isa. 14:12, Luke 4:5-8 NASB margin). The origin of planetary worship was from the proud, fallen one, Satan. All religions influenced by him appeal to man's pride, either pseudo exaltation or pseudo humiliation.

One *ziggurat* had progressive levels relative to the size of the planets that started from the largest on the bottom to the smallest one on top. The latter was the moon. This is concordant with the worship of the moon god that was prevalent in ancient Babylon.[52] There is historical evidence that the worship of the moon god was eventually transmitted to the monotheism that Muhammad evolved. The crescent moon is still part of the symbol of Islam. The name, Allah, may have been derived from the name of one of the ancient Babylonian gods, *Il*.[53]

Rulers usually account for a small percentage of the general population. The rest of the population either follows or submits. *Yahweh* came down at Babel as protector of believers from those unbelievers who wished to rule the earth and subjugate or destroy them. If *Yahweh* had not come down and confused the languages, these evil rulers would have succeeded in subjugating the earth and its peoples, just as the Nephilim did before the flood:

"Come, let Us go down and there confuse their language, so that they will not understand one another's speech" (Gen. 11:7).

Yahweh used the same words, "go down" (*yaradah,* ארדה), when he spoke to Abraham of the upcoming destruction of Sodom and Gomorrah (page 203):

"I will go down now, and see if they have done entirely according to its outcry, which has come to Me; and if not, I will know" (Gen. 18:21).

The LORD was the only member of the Trinity that went "down" (*aradah,* ארדה) at the time of Abraham. It is likely that all three members of the Trinity descended into Babel; let **Us** "go down" (*naradah,* נרדה). Since the Trinity descended to the earth, it speaks of the spiritual significance of man trying to unite against God and God's response (Gen. 1:26, 11:7). The command to confuse their speech so they could "not hear" (*lo shama',* לא ישמעו) each other's language came from *Yahweh*, the pre-incarnate LORD Jesus Christ.

Yahweh sent two angels to Sodom to meet with Lot and his family and bring about deliverance for Lot and his two daughters. At Babel, *Yahweh* may have spoken to the righteous before they were scattered on the earth. This would be concordant with His commission to the two angels who spoke to righteous Lot and delivered him from Sodom (Genesis 19).

The missionary movement of the last couple of centuries has attested to finding an unusual understanding of God in many tribal areas. In several folk cultures, there is definitive evidence of an understanding of the Most High God, *El Elyon*, passed down from generation to generation.[54] Several people-groups have oral traditions of someone coming with a book that would explain the way of God to them. That book was the Bible. Other people-groups have ceremonies depicting a sacrifice that would produce peace within their tribes.[55] The sacrifice of peace ceremonies were symbolic of the need for Christ's sacrifice for all who would come to Him and find peace. The commonality of these truths in many tribal cultures suggests a uniform revelation to them in the distant past (page 42).

If there was a Christophany at Babel, the LORD Himself may have preached to the people of the earth concerning these truths. They would have carried this information with them after He confused their languages and scattered them abroad. Hence, the continued stories and customs that were handed down over the centuries. Such a supposition does not rule out subsequent revelation to righteous individuals in different people-groups in different ages, e.g., Abram and Job.

Yahweh would eventually descend to the earth in the incarnation and be born from the power of *El Elyon*. Why did God use the name *El Elyon* at the time of the birth of the Son of God? Surely, it was to indicate that His Son was "the Anointed One" (*Maschiach*-Christ) to be the Savior (*Moshee'a`*) for all who believe in Him.

The power of *El Elyon* would overshadow the Virgin Mary:

"The angel answered and said to her, 'The Holy Spirit will come upon you, and the power of the Most High will overshadow you; and for that reason the holy Child shall be called the Son of God'" (Luke 1:35).

Overshadowing carries with it the idea of God's presence enveloping the Virgin Mary. As explained in this same text by Dr. Luke, the Holy Spirit would implant the Seed of the Son of God within her womb, not her female tubes where fertilization would normally take place (Luke 1:31).

The same infinitives are used for sexual intercourse in marriage in the two Biblical languages: in Hebrew, "to know" (*yâda', ידע*), and in Greek, "to know" (*ginōsko̅,* γινώσκω) (Gen. 4:1, Matt. 1:25).

"To overshadow" (*episkiazo̅,* ἐπισκιάζω) bears no relationship to the Greek infinitive for sexual intercourse, "to know" (*ginōsko̅,* γινώσκω). The negative of *ginosko*, not "kept," is used to describe the virginal state of Mary. Joseph "did not know her" (*ouk ginōskoen,* ουκ εγινωσκεν) until after the birth of the LORD:

"And Joseph awoke from his sleep and did as the angel of the Lord commanded him, and took Mary as his wife, but kept her a virgin until she gave birth to a Son; and he called His name Jesus" (Matt. 1:24-25).

In Greek, "Most High" (*Hupsistos,* ὕψιστος) is the equivalent of the Hebrew, *El Elyon*. The LORD Jesus Christ was a priest after the order of Melchizedek, priest of *El Elyon* (Gen. 14:18, Heb. 5:6):

"The LORD has sworn and will not change His mind, 'You are a priest forever According to the order of Melchizedek'" (Psa. 110:4).

The Messiah came as the Savior for all peoples who respond to Him in any culture; this includes those who know Him only as *El Elyon*.

The people who left Babel to scatter throughout the earth may have known three things that testified to them about God.

1. They had the light of the creation:

"For since the creation of the world His invisible attributes, His eternal power and divine nature, have been clearly seen, being understood through what has been made, so that they are without excuse" (Rom. 1:20).

Is there evidence that people respond through the light of creation? Pachacuti, ruler of the South American Incas from 1438-1471, observed the limitations of worship of the sun as god. The sun was unable to give light to all, could be covered with a cloud, and was confined to the same daily journey across the heavens. Therefore, he reasoned that the sun could not be god. Pachacuti and his leaders turned to the worship of Viracocha, their name for the Creator, and developed hymns and godly traditions for that worship.[56] Unfortunately, they did not teach that truth to their people. Nevertheless, this example verifies that the creation can point people to the worship of the one true God who created them.

2. They knew of a generalized flood that wiped out all of mankind, except for the few that survived in the ark."[57]

3. They knew about the Most High God, *El Elyon*. He came down to Babel. He may have preached to them before their scattering throughout the earth. God will respond to anyone, anywhere, who seeks Him with all his/her heart (Deut. 4:29, Jer. 29:13):

"Opening his mouth, Peter said: 'I most certainly understand now that God is not one to show partiality, but in every nation the man who fears Him and does what is right is welcome to Him'" (Acts 10:34-35).

Some had to await the specific knowledge from the book, the Bible, and its story of the interaction between God and His creation that culminated in the sacrifice of His Son for the salvation of all who would respond to Him (John 3:16-21). Just as the Apostle Peter was sent to Cornelius, anyone who has responded to the LORD Jesus Christ is obligated to propagate the complete message to all the peoples of the earth. There are still other people-groups awaiting this message of the Bible (Matt. 28:18-20).

THE ANTITHESIS OF BABEL

Pentecost was the spiritual reversal of Babel. At Pentecost, believers in the one true God experienced the reunification of the understanding of languages through the agency of the Holy Spirit (Acts 2:1-11).

"And when this sound occurred, the crowd came together and was bewildered, because each one of them was hearing them speak in his own language" (Acts 2:6).

Pentecost (*pentekoste,* πεντηκοστή) means "fiftieth" in Greek; the Jews celebrated this day as the 50th day of the Feast of *Shavuot* (*shabuîot,* שׁבתות), the festival of seven weeks, derived from the Hebrew word, "seven" (*sheba',* שׁבע). The closing Feast of Shavuot occurred on the 50th day after the offering of the firstfruits of the spring harvest (Lev. 23:5-21). Shavuot, Pentecost, celebrated the ingathering of the spring harvest.

The gift of the Holy Spirit to the apostles was given on Resurrection Sunday when the LORD breathed on them (John 20:19-23). The Holy Spirit in the "born from above" believer is the evidence of salvation (John 3:3 NASB margin). The purpose of Pentecost was for the power of the Holy Spirit to spread the gospel to all nations. This came at the Feast of *Shavuot* (*shabuôt,* שׁבתות), the Feast of Pentecost (*pentēkostē,* πεντηκοστή). The spring harvest, i.e., the early harvest of believers followed.

The special manifestation of the Holy Spirit coming as a mighty wind and as tongues of fire had a twofold meaning. The 120 or so persons on whom the tongues of fire were distributed **spoke** in other languages by the power of the Holy Spirit. "Devout men from every nation under heaven" **heard** them speak in their own languages and dialects; 16 are listed. The words spoken were of praise to the LORD (Acts 2:11).

At Pentecost, the miracle of speaking this many languages and dialects would have been sheer confusion to the hearers in the crowd, unless each one was able to hear above the crowd and noise in his own language and dialect; they were accused of drunkenness (Acts 2:11-13). Note the reversal of the difficulty with hearing ("not hear," *lo shâma',* לא ישמעו) languages that had produced the confusion at Babel (Gen. 11:7, Acts 2:6).

Pentecost was both a speaking and a hearing miracle. Subsequent to Pentecost, the miracle of speaking in other languages occurred when the gospel was preached to other people-groups, and they received the Holy Spirit. The language continued to be one that praised God.

According to the command of the LORD, the gospel was to go to Jerusalem, Judea, Samaria, and the remotest part of earth (Acts 1:8). The miracle of Pentecost occurred first with Hebrews and proselytes, then Samaritans, and finally, Gentiles.

The conversion of the Hebrews and proselytes in Jerusalem occurred at Pentecost. Subsequently, the Apostle Peter and the Apostle John laid hands on believers in Samaria. The Apostle Peter was sent to Cornelius and his household. Each group exhibited the same manifestation as at Pentecost (Acts 8:5, 14-17; 10:1-48).

The disciples at Ephesus had received a baptism of repentance as taught by John the Baptist, but not one of faith in the LORD Jesus Christ. They manifested the same miracle when they were baptized in the name of the LORD Jesus Christ: "And when Paul had laid his hands upon them, the Holy Spirit came on them, and they began speaking with tongues and prophesying" (Acts 19:6). Repentance without faith in the LORD Jesus Christ is not adequate for salvation (Rom. 10:9-10).

The task of the church is to take the gospel to every people, tribe, and nation in their languages and dialects by the empowerment of the Holy Spirit. To accomplish this witnesses must be purged by the fire of the Holy Spirit, i.e., made pure and holy. The result will be a remnant, the Israel of God (Gal. 6:15-16). The redeemed will unite with the LORD in His kingdom and serve and praise Him. They will not continue their rebellion against Him.

The rebellion against God fizzled at Babel when mankind was scattered over the earth. Thus, God's original command was fulfilled. Nimrod, as the ancient world leader who developed the kingdoms of Babylon and Assyria and attempted to unite the world against God, failed. He was a prototype of the Antichrist who will come and try to do the same thing at the end of the present age by uniting with Satan and his demons; he will fail.

It is likely that the Antichrist to come will try to unify the world through one spoken language. Either one language will become worldwide (English?) or the use of computers will allow simultaneous translation of all languages. Another possibility is the development of one worldwide computer language.

CHAPTER 6

THE GENERATIONS OF SHEM

Gen. 11:10-25: The stated order of Noah's three sons is Shem (middle brother), Ham (youngest brother), and Japheth (eldest brother). The two sons whose progeny would inhabit the Middle East are listed first. Ham would dominate the territory of the Middle East. Shem would continue with the smaller, righteous progeny in the Promised Land. Japheth, the eldest son, is listed last; his progeny would spread abroad over the earth and be blessed by the message that would come from the seed of Shem.

The sequence of names given for the righteous line does not list the eldest sons first but the selected righteous son (page 116).

The generations of Shem are the sixth recorded in the book of Genesis. The meaning of Shem is "name" (*shem̂,* שֵׁם).

Some of the progeny of Shem continued the righteous line, but others departed to form part of the unrighteous line (Gen. 11:10-26, 14:1-2). As can be seen throughout the book of Genesis, splits from the righteous line in the Middle East resulted in progeny that subsequently became enemies of Israel.

Shem bridges the time of the righteous line from the flood to the time of Abram. After Babel, the Biblical history of mankind is sparse until the time of Abram.

If Shem initially lived on the east side of the Fertile Crescent, he may have borne witness to Abram. There is no Biblical history of the same, but their ages suggest that possibility. When Abram was 50 years old, Shem would have been 500 with a hundred more years to live. Shem would die in Abraham's 150th year and Isaac's 50th year (Table 10, page 397). The different trials of Abram-Abraham, and the first five decades of Isaac's life, would have occurred during Shem's lifetime. It is possible that Abram had contact with Shem on the east side of the Fertile Crescent. In addition, it is possible that Shem migrated to the west side of the Fertile Crescent.

Probably due to the age crossover between Shem and Abraham, some rabbis believed that Melchizedek was Shem.[58] Melchizedek did not have a genealogy; Shem did (Heb. 7:3). However, if the writer to Hebrews was merely indicating that a genealogy was not recorded for Melchizedek by the use of his titles, it is still possible that Shem was Melchizedek. The word, Melchizedek, actually denotes his titles, not his personal name (pages 169-171) (Gen. 14:18-24).

Since Shem means "name," it may be an allusion to bearing the "Name" as a representative of *El Elyon*. The length of Shem's life after the flood suggests that he had a special service to perform for the LORD. There is a significant drop in the ages of men after Shem died (Table 10, page 397). If Shem was the one of the seven who transmitted to Isaac the history of the creation, and the genealogy starting with Adam, he may have lived in the land and communicated with Abraham and Isaac. Therefore, it is possible that Shem was Melchizedek (Bar Graph, page 115).

CHAPTER 7

THE GENERATIONS OF TERAH

The generations of Terah are the seventh recorded in the book of Genesis. His generations included the polytheists from Babylon and Abram in the righteous line. Representatives from Terah's generations, other than Abram, split from the righteous line.

ABRAM'S LIFE

Gen. 11:26-32: According to Joshua, "the fathers" served other gods in Babylon (Josh. 24:2). The documentation of idol worship by Laban, the great-great-grandson of Nahor (Terah's father), and Lot's propensity to materialism are evidence of such worship, and its sinful effect on those involved (Gen. 13:10-11, 22:20-24, 31:19).

Spiritually speaking, Terah was the father of Abram, not Abraham. Abram would become Abraham after Terah's death. The fulfillment of the promises would occur after Abram became Abraham who initiated the eighth of the generations in Genesis. Israel's history as a nation begins with its progenitor, Abraham.

The God of glory appeared to Abram prompting him to leave Ur of the Chaldees to go to a land he would after receive for an inheritance (Gen. 11:26-32, 12:1-4, 15:7; Acts 7:2). Terah, Abram's father, left Ur of the Chaldees with Abram and Lot a significant time before his death. Haran, the father of Lot and Milcah, died in Ur of the Chaldees (Gen. 11:32, 12:4). Abram's goal was the land of Canaan; there is no recorded explanation as to why they settled in Haran [map site 2] (Gen. 11:31).

Terah and Abram lived in Haran in Paddam-Aram at the top of the Fertile Crescent. Since the city was named after Terah's son, Haran, it must have been developed by Abram and Terah.

Terah was father to both Abram and Sarai, but they had different mothers (Gen. 20:12). Terah may have had sequential wives, or he may have been a polygamist. The intermarriage within the family suggests little opportunity for suitable wives in the surrounding culture and/or the acceptance of marriage between half-sisters and half-brothers (Josh. 24:2).

Terah started his "generations" at the age of 70 (Gen. 11:26). Since Abram was 75 years old when Terah died at the age of 205 years, he had to have been the youngest son (Gen. 11:32, 12:4). Since Haran's daughter, Milcah, was the wife of Nahor, the probable middle son, it seems likely that Haran was the eldest. Thus Lot, Milcah's brother and the son of Haran, may have been younger, the same age, or older than Abram (pages, 165, 204). Milcah's age may have been similar to Lot's age, but that is problematic.

Ur was the center of worship of the moon-god in Babylon.[59] After the LORD appeared to Abram, Terah and Lot joined him in leaving Ur of the Chaldees. However, settlement at Haran resulted in a delay in answering the call until Abram's father died.

Property rights went to the sons before grandsons. Lot was the son of Haran; he was the grandson of Terah. After Terah died, Nahor, Lot's uncle and Abram's older brother, had the legal right to the settlement at Haran. Subsequent to Abram and Lot's departure, Nahor, the middle son of Terah, settled Haran. Nahor's pride is illustrated by the fact that he changed the name of the city from Haran to Nahor (Gen. 24:10). Nahor's leaving Ur for economic gain is compatible with the character of Laban, his grandson, and Laban's efforts to "divine" financial gain from Jacob (Gen. 22:20-24, 30:27).

Because of *Yahweh's* call to go on to the land of Canaan after Terah's death, Abram did not contest the material rights to the city of Haran. Those rights passed to Nahor. Abram still had many possessions when he left Haran (Gen. 13:2, 14:14). Since material gain was not Abram's goal, *Yahweh* could bless him with possessions. Abram's primary goal was to know God, to experience Him. Lot chose to go with Abram who was a worshiper of *Yahweh*. He did not wish to stay with his sister and her husband.

Map of Patriarchs' Travels

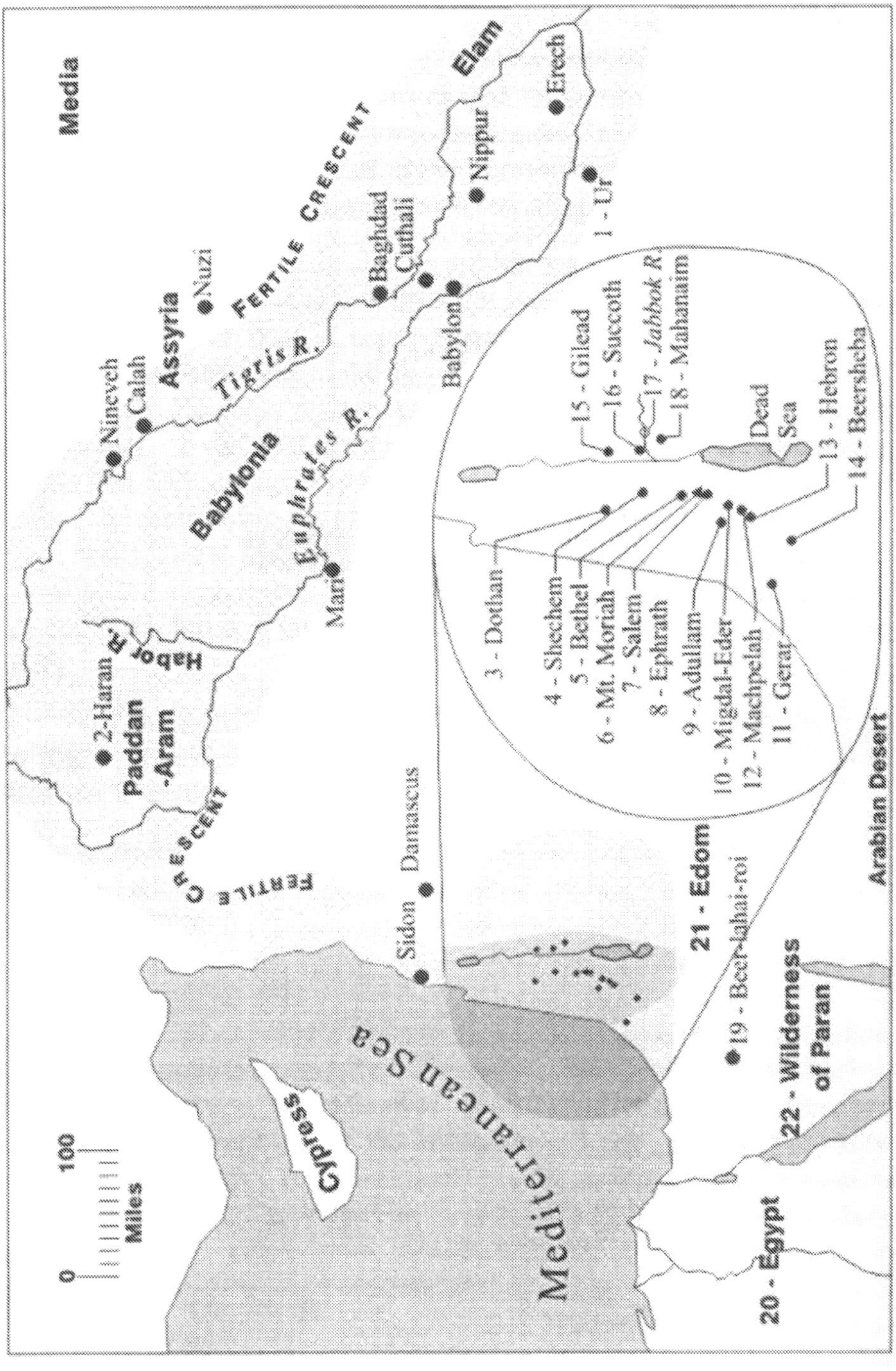

Renewal of the Call to Abram and His Obedient Response
Haran; Abram, Age 75

Genesis 12:1-20

Gen. 12:1-5: Stephen, in his sermon before the Sanhedrin, stated the following:

"The God of glory appeared to our father Abraham when he was in Mesopotamia, before he lived in Haran, and said to him, 'LEAVE YOUR COUNTRY AND YOUR RELATIVES, AND COME INTO THE LAND THAT I WILL SHOW YOU.' Then he left the land of the Chaldeans and settled in Haran. From there, after his father died, God had him move to this country in which you are now living" (Acts 7:2-4).

Therefore, a **Christophany** occurred in Ur (the **first** direct communication between God and Abram). Abram must have testified to Terah and Lot of the LORD's appearance to him. As discussed, Abram's call to leave their home may have influenced them to accompany him out of Ur of the Chaldees. Therefore, Abram must have felt a responsibility to his father; he took care of him until his death. Nahor stayed in Ur until he inherited the city of Haran. Nahor's response created a situation where it would be difficult for Abram to stay in Haran. After Terah's death, *Yahweh* reissued the call to Abram and **spoke** to him (the **second** direct communication) to leave his country (now Haran), relatives, and his father's house to go to the land of his original call (Gen. 12:1).

God Is No Respecter of Persons

God, who is no respecter of persons, responds to any individual who turns to Him and seeks Him with all his heart (Deut. 4:29, Jer. 29:13):

"I most certainly understand that God is not one to show partiality, but in every nation the man who fears Him and does what is right is welcome to Him" (Acts 10:34-35).

As previously discussed, the LORD responds to people in all times and cultures who search for Him with all their heart, not trusting in their own righteousness.[60] Sometimes the LORD communicates directly to Gentiles as He did with Abram and with Job. Sometimes He sends someone to reveal to them the message of salvation through the LORD Jesus Christ as He did when he sent the Apostle Peter to Cornelius (Acts 10:1-48). Salvation comes through no other name under heaven given to men. Personal revelation in special circumstances in no way lessens the responsibility of believers to carry out the Great Commission (Matt. 28:19-20, Acts 4:12).

First Altar at Shechem; Abram, Age 75

Gen. 12:6-7: *Yahweh* **appeared** to Abram and promised to give the land to his seed (**third** direct communication). Abram's seed would include his genetic seed, the nation of Israel, and his (Abraham's) spiritual seed, the Israel of God. The latter are reborn through faith in the LORD-Jesus-Christ/*YHWH-Yeshua-Mashiach*.

Abram responded by building his first altar in the Promised Land at the oak (*terebinth*) of Moreh at Shechem [map site 4]. This would become an important site in the life of Jacob (Gen. 33:18-20, 35:1-4). In Hebrew, *moreh* means "teacher" (*mor̂eh,* מורה). It is likely that the *terebinth* of Moreh was a religious worship site where religious teaching took place. The Canaanites and their false religions were in the land at the time. Abram introduced the worship of *Yahweh* at this site, possibly by teaching there. In addition, he offered sacrifices on the altar he built there.

Second Altar at Bethel; Abram, Age 75

Gen. 12:8-9: By faith, Abram continued his occupation of the land by building his second altar to Yahweh on a mountain east of Bethel [map site 5] and west of Ai. He called upon the name (character) of *Yahweh* as he worshiped at that altar. This place was to become an important site in the life of Jacob (Gen. 28:10-22, 35:1-15).

The fact that Bethel and Ai are mentioned long before Bethel (Luz) received its name is supportive evidence that Moses was the writer of this record and used names that were known at the time in which he lived (Gen. 28:19). His mother, Jochebed, transmitted to Moses the story of Bethel and Jacob's visits there (Bar Graph, page 115). Abram continued his journey to the south country, the Negev.

Sarai's Obedience—Abram's Deceit; Egypt; Abram, Age 75 to 85

Gen. 12:10-20: Abram had 318 warriors in his household (Gen. 14:14). His entire household may have numbered a thousand or more; he was responsible for them during the famine. However, he did not seek God's direction for his move to Egypt. Isaac would learn that God could bless him during a famine without going to Egypt (Gen. 26:1-3, 12-14). Since Abram did not inquire of God, he may have missed a great blessing. "Abram went down to Egypt," according to the topography of the land, but he also made a decision that led downward in his spiritual journey (Gen. 12:10).

When Sarai was between 65 and 75 years old, her beauty resulted in her selection for Pharaoh's harem. Women did not have equal rights in the culture. Abram allowed Sarai to go into Pharaoh's harem; he received sheep, oxen, donkeys, and male and female servants for her. Hagar may have been one of the female servants that he received (Gen. 16:1).

Abram's allowing Sarai to enter the harem was not worthy of his calling. He placed the value of his own life over the value of his relationship with Sarai. Since Sarai was unable to become pregnant by Abram, it is possible that he risked Sarai's impregnation by the Pharaoh in an effort to obtain a royal scion.

Sarai's obedience on this occasion was truly remarkable. Note that *Yahweh* struck Pharaoh and his house with great plagues on behalf of Sarai, not for Abram's sake. He was protecting Sarai in her obedience to Abram as unto the LORD (Eph. 5:22).

When Sarai was in Pharaoh's harem, Abram must have sought *Yahweh* on her behalf and may have repented for his sin of not seeking *Yahweh* before the move. During his sojourn in Egypt, *Yahweh* kept His promise to Abram. He blessed those that blessed him (Gen. 12:3).

Pharaoh discovered that Sarai was Abram's wife. Presumably, she may have revealed this to avoid sexual intercourse with him. The revelation that Sarai was Abram's wife gave an explanation for the plagues to Pharaoh. After Sarai's return to Abram, they received a special escort out of the land.

Abram's Wealth Grew in Egypt
Back to Bethel; Abram, Age 75 To 85

Genesis 13:1-18

Gen. 13:1-4: Abram journeyed from Egypt to the Negev and back to the altar between Bethel and Ai where he had been prior to his journey to Egypt. Before further spiritual progress could occur, Abram had to repent and return to the place where he had deviated from *Yahweh's* call. He renewed his relationship with *Yahweh* and called upon His name (Gen. 12:8, 13:3-4).

Sin interrupts spiritual progress. Before embarking further on one's spiritual journey, repentance may require returning to the place of one's departure from the LORD.

Abram's Deference to Lot and His Materialism

Gen. 13:5-13: Lot had journeyed with Abram to Egypt. He saw the riches of Egypt; he saw Abram's wealth. The strife between the herdsmen of Lot and Abram suggests Lot was competing to obtain more wealth than Abram had.

During the strife between Abram's shepherds and Lot's shepherds, there is emphasis on the fact that the Perizzites and Canaanites were in the land. Unbelievers are always watching believers; they notice when believers fight among themselves and exhibit a poor witness for the LORD. Rather than discredit the name of *Yahweh* before unbelievers, Abram decided to resolve the conflict by deferring to Lot.

Thus, Abram gave the choice to Lot as to which part of the land to occupy. If Lot was older than Abram, he should have been the one to offer the choice of the land to Abram (page 159). "Lot chose for himself." He made a selfish choice; he was motivated by materialism. He chose the land that would give him wealth, even though it was spiritually bankrupt (Gen. 13:11-13). Lot's choice foretold a downward spiritual spiral in Sodom:

"For the love of money is a root of all the evils, and some by longing for it have wandered away from the faith and pierced themselves with many griefs" (1 Tim. 6:10 NASB margin).

God's Blessing after Abram's Deference to Lot

Gen. 13:14-17: After Abram deferred to Lot, a decision reflecting spiritual progress, *Yahweh* blessed Abram further. It was then that *Yahweh* **spoke (fourth** direct communication) to him and renewed the promised blessing. He promised that all the land he could see would be his and his seed forever. Abram's seed would be as numerous as the dust of the earth. Abram was to walk through the length and breadth of the land and possess it by faith.

Abram's Third Altar
Hebron; Abram, Age 75 to 83

Gen. 13:18: The *terebinths* of Mamre may have been another religious site around ancient, large trees. Abram moved to Hebron (Mamre) and built his third altar to *Yahweh*. Hebron became the primary homestead for Abraham, Isaac, and Jacob. Mamre is the name of an Amorite who lived in the land. Hebron means "an alliance" (*chebrôn,* חברון). Abram developed an alliance with Mamre and his brothers, Eschol and Aner (Gen. 14:13).

The Battle of the Four Kings against Five

Genesis 14:1-24

Gen. 14:1-12: The four eastern kings ruled over the five kings of the Amorite nations. Amraphel, king of Shinar, was from Babylon; Shinar is another term for Babylon. Since Arioch, king of Ellasar, is a Babylonian name, he also was from Babylon. Chedorlaomer, king of Elam, was from the Shemite line; Elam was the eldest son of Shem (Gen. 10:22). Since Tidal, king of *Goyim*, is a Canaanite name, he may have been an ally from the Canaanite nations. The name used throughout the Old Testament for non-Hebrews is the *Goyim*, i.e., the Gentiles.

These names suggest a Shemite-Babylonian-Canaanite alliance with significant military power. It is noteworthy that the main king, Chedorlaomer, was a descendant of Shem, the son of Noah from the righteous line. Chedorlaomer had departed from the righteous line and opted for wealth and military might. The five Canaanite kings had served Chedorlaomer for 12 years; they rebelled in the 13th year and went to war in the 14th year.

The Meaning of the Hebrew Names and Places

The translation of Hebrew names is informative about the places and peoples involved in this war.

Bera means "son of evil" (*bera',* ברע). Sodom comes from a Hebrew root that means "burnt" (*sedôm,* סדם). It was the chief city in the circle of cities around the valley of the Jordan (Gen. 13:10).

Birsha means "wickedness" (*birsha',* ברשע). Gomorrah means "a heap" (*'ămôrâh,* עמרה). Together the names mean "a heap of wickedness."

The wickedness of Sodom and Gomorrah had prophetically been denounced (Gen. 9:22-25, 10:19, 13:13).

Shinab means "a father has turned" (*shin'ab̂,* שׁנאב). Admah means "red earth" (*'admaĥ,* אדמה).

Shemeber is a combination of Shem and Eber. Shem means "name" (*shem̂,* שׁם); Eber is the root (*'eb̂er,* עבר) from which the word, Hebrew, is derived. Shemeber was a sacrilegious name, a king whose character did not honor his name.

Zeboim means "gazelles" (*tsebo'iŷm,* צביים).

Bela means "destruction" (*bela',* בלע). Zoar means "small, insignificant" (*tso'ar,* צער).

Before the battle with the five southern kings, the four kings with Chedorlaomer leading them defeated several of the giants who were north of them.

The Rephaim (*rap̂haîm,* רפאים) were evil giants; the name means "shades." The Ashteroth (pl., *ashtar̄oth̄,* עשׁתרות) were idols that represented female sexuality. Asherah (sg.) may have been the original "moon-goddess" of Babylon. Israel was guilty of the apostate worship of the "Queen of Heaven" in later times (Jer. 7:18). Karnaim means "double-horned" (*qarnayim,* קרנים). In the Old Testament, horns often refer to military might.

Zuzim comes from a Hebrew root that means "roving creatures" (*zuẑiŷm,* זוזים) and may refer to beastly behavior. Ham means "hot" (*cham̂,* חם). This suggests behavior that was like beasts, possibly homosexual/bisexual behavior.

Emim means "terrors" (*emim,* אימים). Shaveh-kiriathaim can be translated as "plain of the 'double' city" (*shav̂eh̄ qiryath̄atim,* שׁוה קריתים). These were the evil ones, noted for their terrorism, who lived on the "plain of the 'double' city."

The Horites were a people that came from the mountains; *har* is the Hebrew word for "mountain" (*har,* הר). Here it may refer to, "cave dwellers" (*chor̂iŷ,* חרי). Seir means "hairy" (*se'iŷr,* שׂעיר).

"Hairy mountaineer" is a possible translation (Gen. 27:11, 32:3). El-paran means "a tree near a place of caverns" (*'eyl paʼrân̂m,* איל פארן). The prefix, *eyl*, refers to "a tree"; it may be a reference to a worship site. It may have been near the location where Ishmael would eventually live on the eastern side of the wilderness (Gen. 21:21).

En-mishpat means "spring of judgment" (*'eyn mishpaṭ̂,* עין משפט). Kadesh means "holy" (*qad̂esĥ*, קדש).

Amalekites comes from a Hebrew root that means "valley dwellers" (*'amal̂eq̂*, עמלקי).

Amorites comes from a Hebrew root that means "mountain dwellers" (*'emor̂iŷ,* אמרי). Hazazon-Tamar may mean "a row of palm trees" (*chatstson̂ tam̂ar̂,* חצצן תמר). This may have been another religious site around palm trees (Jdg. 20:33).

Siddim means "fields" (*siddiŷm,* שדים); they were located near the area that became the Dead Sea.

The translation of these names suggests that God, from His holy throne, represented by the holy place, Kadesh, pronounced His judgment on these evil tribes and nations at the spring of judgment, En-mishpat. The LORD rules over the affairs of mankind; sometimes He uses evil people to render His righteous judgment on other evil people and places (Gen. 18:25).

Abram Delivers Lot and Others

Gen. 14:13-16: The battle between the four evil, eastern kings and the five evil, local kings resulted in Lot's capture. Abram and his allies were protected by God and were not involved in the conflict. An escapee, the fugitive, reported Lot's capture to Abram. The definite article (ה) occurs before "fugitive" (*pal̂iŷṭ,* הפליט) and suggests the fugitive was the only one who escaped. God delivered this individual, so he could inform Abram of Lot's capture. Perhaps Lot sent him to inform Abram about the battle.

Abram was the seventh generation from Eber (*'eber,* עבר) (Table 10, page 397). In Hebrew, Eber means "a region beyond" (*'eber,* עבר). Abram was the first Hebrew (*'ebriŷ,* עברי); this is the first use of this word in Genesis. Abram would become Abraham, the father of the Hebrews. People who believe as Abraham believed are heaven bound. Hence, a true Hebrew is one who believes in the one true God and accepts His provision for salvation that leads to "the region beyond" (Rom. 2:28-29).

Abram went with his three Amorite allies and the 318 men born in his own household and recovered the people and the spoils of war. The number of men in the allies' armies is not stated. The literal translation for allies is "masters of the covenant" (*ba'ali beriŷth,* בעלי ברית). This could have been a routine alliance, or it could have been a spiritual alliance also. It is possible that Abram had witnessed to one or more of the men who had accepted *Yahweh* as his LORD. Because of their covenant with Abram, and Abram's relationship with his LORD, the allies were protected from the eastern kings.

Since Dan had not been born yet, the northern location of Dan is a detail that was added later. Indeed, the name of Dan for this location did not occur until after Moses' death (Josh. 19:47). Samuel, Nathan, Gad, or one of the later prophets may have been the compiler who added this information (1 Sam. 10:25, 1 Chr. 29:29). Some geographical names in the book of Genesis come from later times and reflect details added after the described event.

Melchizedek, Priest of *El Elyon*
Salem; Abram, Age 75 to 85

Gen. 14:17-24: Since Melchizedek's genealogy is not recorded, he became an example of the LORD Jesus Christ who is a priest forever (Psa. 110:4; Heb. 5:5-10, 7:1-28). Melchizedek means "King of Righteousness" (*malkiŷ'tsedeq,* מלכי־צדק). Salem (*shalêm,* שׁלם) [map site 7] is an ancient name (Psa. 76:2). Salem is related to the word, "shalom." Both words mean peace. Hence, he was "King of Peace." These are titles; Melchizedek is not a personal name (pages 156-157).

They met in *Shaveh*, "the valley of the king" (עמק המלך). The valley belonged to Melchizedek who represented the King, the LORD Jesus Christ. The valley did not belong to the heathen kings meeting there; they had no authority.

Melchizedek was priest of God Most High, *El Elyon* (*el 'elyôn*, אל עליון). He blessed Abram in the name of *El Elyon*, "Possessor" (*qânâh*, קנה) of the "heavens" (*shâmayim*, שמים) and the "earth" (*'erets*, ארץ).

This is the first occurrence of these two names for God in the book of Genesis, *El Elyon* and the *Qanah* of the heavens and earth (page 50). The Hebrew word for Creator comes from the root, *bara* (*bârâ'*, ברא). Here the emphasis is on God who possesses the earth, not his capacity as Creator. The goods of war were of little significance to the God who owns the earth. Melchizedek testified this truth to the materialistic kings.

When speaking to the new king of Sodom of his oath, Abram used these names of God—*El Yahweh*, *El Elyon* (אל יהוה אל עליון), Possessor of heaven and earth. (The translators choose to translate the first אל as "to" *Yahweh*, not *El Yahweh*.) When Abram spoke of his oath, why did he add that *El* (God) was *Yahweh*? The use of *El* with *Yahweh* was a means of testifying to the heathen kings that *Yahweh* was God.

Often *Yahweh* is used as the name of the pre-incarnate LORD: "Abram said to the king of Sodom, 'I have sworn to the LORD God Most High, Possessor of heaven and earth'" (Gen. 14:22). If Melchizedek was *El Elyon*, he would have been *Yahweh*, the pre-incarnate LORD Jesus Christ, and Abram should have addressed Melchizedek with obeisance (page 199). Note that Abram affirmed Melchizedek's declaration that *El Elyon* is the "Possesser" (*qânâh*, קנה) of the heavens and earth. Consider the following verse:

"Without father, without mother, without genealogy, having neither beginning of days nor end of life, but made like the Son of God, he remains a priest perpetually" (Heb. 7:3).

Melchizedek was "**made like** the Son of God" (Heb. 7:3). If Melchizedek was the LORD Jesus Christ, the writer to Hebrews should have stated the same (pages 156-157).

In addition, the LORD Jesus Christ came "**according to the likeness** of Melchizedek": "And this is clearer still, if another priest arises according to the likeness of Melchizedek, who has become such not on the basis of a law of physical requirement, but according to the power of an indestructible life. For it is attested of Him, 'YOU ARE A PRIEST FOREVER ACCORDING TO THE ORDER OF MELCHIZEDEK'" (Heb. 7:15-17).

These statements indicate that Melchizedek's appearance was not a Christophany. Instead, the Son of God came **according to the likeness and order** of Melchizedek who was **made like** Him in his combined role of King of Righteousness and King of Peace in ancient Salem.

Why did the LORD come as a priest according to the order of Melchizedek? *Yahweh*'s intent was for His message of salvation to spread to the entire world. Many cultures have a history of believing in the one true God, *El Elyon*, God Most High. Some anthropologists refer to this in folk religions as belief in a "Sky" God (pages 150-151).[61]

Jesus came as the Anointed One, the Messiah, not just for the Jewish people, but for all who would accept Him as such. Abram gave allegiance to *El Elyon* and related that name to *Yahweh*. Missionaries who uncover the belief in a Most High God in a culture, and/or unusual customs of a sacrifice for peace, and relate the same to the LORD Jesus Christ as *El Elyon*, have often seen mass conversions.[62] The wicked kings from the valley of the Jordan would have known about *El Elyon* through the ministry of Melchizedek. Someday every person will bow to the LORD, the Most High God (Isa. 45:23, Rom. 14:11).

The spokesman for the cities of the valley was the king of Sodom. This indicates that Sodom was the chief city in the valley of the Jordan. Abram's vow to take nothing from the new king of

Sodom contrasted with Lot's materialism (Gen. 14:10). Lot observed Abram's words and actions; he did not learn from them. He may have had a competitive spirit, even though Abram did not compete with him. Lot had the opportunity to depart from Sodom at this time, but chose not to do so. This would have dire results for him and his family.

Why did Abram decide to give a tenth to Melchizedek? Abram may have equally divided the spoil between the ten "leaders" involved: the five local kings, his three allies, Lot, and himself. Abram did not take a share but gave his entire portion to Melchizedek, the priest of *El Elyon*.

The tithe became the symbol of the whole. Everything any person has belongs to God; the giving of the tithe is symbolic of that truth. All possessions belong to the One who is the "Possessor of the heavens and earth." We are stewards of His beneficence.

This is the first tithe recorded in the Bible and given before the law. Giving should be based on devotion to God, not legal requirement. Exposition on the significance of the giving of the tenth before the Levitical covenant occurs in the letter to the Hebrews (Heb. 7:4-10). Believers are minimally responsible for the tithe; it represents their entire stewardship.

The Promise of the Heir
Hebron; Abram, Age 75 to 85

Genesis 15:1-21

Gen. 15:1-5: *Yahweh* **appeared** (**fifth** direct communication) to Abram in a vision. This occurred after their military victory and Abram's testimony before Melchizedek, the local kings, the allies, Lot, and the rest of the people. *Yahweh* responded positively to Abram's actions and testimony in this incident. He told Abram not to fear. Abram may have been afraid of reprisal following his military victory; *Yahweh* promised to be a shield to him. As a minority believer in an evil, violent land, Abram needed God's protection. This promise must have been reassuring to him. He had given the "tithe of all"; it was his seed of faith (Gen. 14:20). In return for the seed sown and the testimony given, God gave him a new hope, the promised son. His works demonstrated his faith (James 2:19-24).

Abram was between 75 and 85 years of age, probably closer to 85. He was concerned about Sarai's ability to bear a child; she was near the time of her menopause (Gen. 16:1-2). He received the promise that the righteous seed would come from his body (Gen. 15:4).

There is a change in the simile. Instead of seed as numerous as the dust of the earth, the promise is seed as numerous as the stars of the heaven. Dust and stars both give the idea that his seed would be beyond enumeration. Perhaps the addition of stars is intended to indicate that Abram's true seed, believers, will graduate from the dust of the earth to the stars of heaven (Gen. 1:1, Deut. 10:14, 1 Kin. 8:27, Neh. 9:6).

Righteousness Based on Faith

Gen. 15:6: Abram believed God. The exposition of the theme of righteousness by faith followed by obedient works occurs in the New Testament. Justification occurs by faith, but works are the evidence of faith. The Apostle Paul expounds on the doctrine of righteousness by faith based on this verse (Gen. 15:6; Rom. 4:3, 9, 22). There is less emphasis today on the corresponding exposition about works in the epistle of James. Salvation does not come by doctrine that does not result in a changed life; salvation comes to the one whose faith results in righteous living:

"Even so faith, if it has no works, is dead, being by itself. But someone may well say, 'You have faith and I have works; show me your faith without the works, and I will show you my faith by my works'" (James 2:17-18).

The recognition of true believers and true prophets is by their "fruit," the produce of their lives. The test the LORD gave to the religious leaders was whether they did the works of Abraham:

"They answered and said to Him, 'Abraham is our father.' Jesus said to them, 'If you are Abraham's children, do the deeds of Abraham'" (John 8:39).

If the fruit is not present, it cannot be know that individuals are true believers according to the LORD Jesus Christ:

"Beware of the false prophets, who come to you in sheep's clothing, but inwardly are ravenous wolves. You will know them by their fruits. Grapes are not gathered from thorn bushes nor figs from thistles, are they? So every good tree bears good fruit, but the bad tree bears bad fruit. A good tree cannot produce bad fruit, nor can a bad tree produce good fruit. Every tree that does not bear good fruit is cut down and thrown into the fire. So then, you will know them by their fruits. Not everyone who says to Me, 'Lord, Lord,' will enter the kingdom of heaven, but he who does the will of My Father who is in heaven will enter. Many will say to Me on that day, 'Lord, Lord, did we not prophesy in Your name, and in Your name cast out demons, and in Your name perform many miracles?' And then I will declare to them, 'I never knew you; depart from me, you who practice lawlessness'" (Matt. 7:15-23).

The Covenant

Gen. 15:7-21: *Yahweh* reminded Abram that He called him out of Ur of the Chaldeans. Ur means "luminary" (*'ur,* אוּר); it was the center for moon worship in southern Babylon. The Chaldeans were the dominant aristocratic tribe of astrologers and wise men in southern Babylon (Dan. 2:4-11). The call to Abram was to leave the land of moon worship and this priestly caste of the same. Babylon was the land of spiritual confusion. *Yahweh* reminded Abram of the great deliverance he had received from that evil country. Because of his obedience, he would inherit the Promised Land.

Abram addressed God as *Adonai Yahweh*, the first use of this compound name of God in Genesis (page 50).

Under the Levitical code, the enumerated animal sacrifices had several applications (Lev. 1:14, 3:1, 4:28, 6:6). The sacrifices could have represented peace (heifer), sin (female goat), guilt (ram), and burnt (turtledove and young pigeon) offerings, respectively. The fact that the animals were three years old may have been a reference to the time of the LORD Jesus Christ's subsequent ministry upon the earth for three years. However, the total consumption of the animals and birds was typical of burnt offerings; the animals represented the life of one totally consumed in service to God (Lev. 1:4, 9).

The ratifying of a covenant required both parties to pass between the sacrificial animals (Jer. 34:18-19). However, this covenant was dependent on *Yahweh's* word; Abram participated by faith (Heb. 6:13-18). Satan's attempt to prevent the covenant was through the birds of prey that tried to destroy the sacrificial animals. Only after Abram had obeyed, by bringing the sacrifices and defending them from the birds of prey, did *Yahweh* **speak** (the **sixth** direct communication) to Abram. In the terror of the great darkness of this world, *Yahweh*'s covenant to the man of faith shone through with His flaming torch and smoking oven that passed between the sacrificial animals. The flame consumed and the oven smoked, thereby indicating *Yahweh*'s acceptance of the sacrifice.

God informed Abram that it would take four hundred years of oppression in a foreign land before his seed would possess the Promised Land. The reason given was that God, as the Judge of the nations, had determined in His foreknowledge that the "iniquity" ("moral perversity," *'âvôn,* עון) of the Amorite nations would not be full until that time. The Exodus from Egypt occurred 1,050 years after the flood and more than six hundred years after this covenant was made with Abram (Table 10, page 397) (Gen. 15:16).

An enumeration of ten Gentile nations follows; in this context, ten is a complete number, a symbol for all nations. The nations of the world are under continual judgment by God. They will undergo a final judgment at the end of the present age (Isa. 40:15-17).

The progeny of Abraham would spend 430 years in Egypt. The nation of Israel would be "enslaved and oppressed" for 400 of those years (Exod. 12:40-41). The Hebrew word translated as "oppressed" (*'ănāh,* ענה) is the same Hebrew word translated as "affliction" during the early years that Joseph was in Egypt (Gen. 41:52). Affliction and oppression can be mental harassment as well as poverty and physical torture. The Israelites were "an abomination" (*toʿēbah,* תועבה) to the Egyptians during the time of Joseph; slavery followed later (Gen. 43:32, Exod. 1:8-22).

If Abram was 84 years of age at the time of this covenant, it would be 184 Biblical years before Joseph would enter Egypt to initiate the 430 Biblical years of sojourn there (Table 10, page 397) (Gen. 37:2, 39:1):

"Now the time that the sons of Israel lived in Egypt was **four hundred and thirty years. And at the end of four hundred and thirty years, to the very day**, all the hosts of the LORD went out from the land of Egypt" (Exod. 12:40-41).

"What I am saying is this: the Law, which came **four hundred and thirty years later**, does not invalidate a covenant previously ratified by God, so as to nullify the promise" (Gal. 3:17).

Some have interpreted the Apostle Paul's statement as meaning that the 430 years started at the time of the covenant with Abram. If one allows for the crossover of the ages of the four patriarchs: Abraham, Isaac, Jacob, and Joseph, such an interpretation would be impossible (Tables 8 and 9, page 390) (Gen. 15:16, Exod. 12:40-41). The nation of Israel was in Egypt long after the death of Joseph. Therefore, it is likely that the statement, "The Law, which came 430 years later," refers to the time of the law at Mount Sinai, after the sojourn of 430 years by **Abraham's progeny** in Egypt (Gal. 3:16-17).

The four generations of the family of Levi: Levi, Kohath, Amram, and Moses account for the time in Egypt (Gen. 15:16, Exod. 6:16-20). An analysis of the ages of these four Levites is compatible with the stated 430 years in Egypt (Appendix III, pages

398-399). Their ages are the only way by which one can calculate the genealogy of the righteous line during that time. God records Biblical time by his righteous people.

Abram Trusts in the Flesh
Hebron; Abram, Age 85

Genesis 16:1-16

Gen. 16:1-6: The text indicates that Sarai had gone through menopause by the age of 75, so she saw no biological way of bearing a son to Abram (Gen. 18:11-12, 31:35; Rom. 4:19). Sarai gave Hagar to Abram in an effort to obtain a male heir, a practice that was acceptable for concubines in the culture of that time (Gen. 22:24, 25:1-6; 1 Chr. 1:32). It is likely that Abram obtained Hagar as a gift from Pharaoh during his misadventure in Egypt (Gen. 12:16). Sarai's request was for Abram "to come" (*bo,* בוא) into Hagar, not "to know" (*yada,* ידע) her. The first word simply meant for Abram to have sexual intercourse with Hagar for the purpose of impregnation; the second word indicated intimate knowledge of the sexual partner as a wife (Gen. 4:1). Sarai did not want Hagar to disrupt her relationship with Abram.

Abram's acceptance of the advice of Sarai was similar to Adam's acceptance of the advice of his wife when each should have been exercising the leadership role God gave to them (Gen. 3:17). *Yahweh* said the heir would come from his body; Abram rationalized that the heir would not come from Sarai's body (Gen. 15:4). Abram did not inquire of *Yahweh* as to whether Sarai was right in giving Hagar to him.

Since he asked *Adonai Yahweh* for an heir before Sarai went through the menopause, Abram's disappointment in Sarai's failure to conceive before her menopause may have clouded his thinking. He accepted the social mores of the day as being in accord with the will of God. He tried to fulfill God's promise by means of his flesh, rather than by faith. This is a lesson for all who accept cultural norms without examining them according to the precepts of God that are enunciated in His Word.

After becoming pregnant, Hagar reacted to Sarai with disdain. Sarai then gained permission from Abram to deal severely with Hagar. Sarai's appeal to Abram indicated that she believed Hagar wronged her. Her inability to get pregnant resulted in frustration that she took out on Hagar.

However, Sarai was the one who initiated the union between Hagar and Abram. Sarai appealed to *Yahweh* for judgment between her and Abram. Since she asked for judgment between herself and her husband, not between herself and Hagar, she felt that Abram now preferred Hagar as a wife. Sarai was post-menopausal, and Hagar was a young woman who succeeded where Sarai had failed. Sarai was jealous. Sarai went into a harem for the sake of her husband, but she could not endure another woman taking her place as wife.

Abram understood and discerned the jealous response of Sarai. The two women could not coexist peacefully without God's intervention. Abram stated that Hagar was Sarai's maid, her property, he allowed her to determine the outcome. Later, God would hold Abram responsible for Hagar as his maid; she was not Sarai's responsibility (page 219).

Sarai's jealousy turned on Hagar; Sarai treated her "harshly" (*'ănaĥ,* ענה). The latter word indicates she afflicted and humbled her, even though she was pregnant with the assumed heir of the promised son.

ISHMAEL'S LIFE-I

Ishmael, the Son of the Flesh
Beer-Lahai-Roi; Abram, Age 85 to 86

Gen. 16:7-16: Sarai's harsh treatment resulted in Hagar fleeing her mistress. She probably attempted to return to Egypt through the wilderness of Shur (Gen. 16:7). *Yahweh*'s subsequent judgment was in favor of Hagar. The word, "angel," means "messenger." Since the text reveals multiple titles: the Angel of *Yahweh*, *Elohim*, *Elroi,* and *Yahweh*, and Hagar called Him, *Yahweh*, this was an appearance of the pre-incarnate LORD Jesus Christ, a Christophany (Gen. 16:13). The Angel of *Yahweh* appeared in person to Hagar, a female servant, at a spring (Gen. 16:7). This is the first use of this name of God in Genesis (page 50). God is no respecter of persons; He was just as faithful to Hagar as He was to the Abram and Sarai (Acts 10:34-35). His love and justice does not discriminate. He is fair to all and loves all, the Hebrew and the Egyptian, the rich and the poor.

Hagar answered the question of where she had come from, not the question of where she was going. She was a young woman, pregnant, alone, afraid, and unsure of where she was going. She had lost her way.

Yahweh's command was difficult; Hagar was to return to Sarai and submit to her authority. *Yahweh* had heard about her affliction; her son was to be named Ishmael, "God hears" (*yishmaʾeʾl*, ישמעאל) (pages 220-221). He would dwell "in the face of all his brothers"; the usual translation is "before all his brothers" or "to the east of all his brothers." One can speculate that the literal Hebrew, "in the face of," may have given rise to the English idiom, "in your face," which denotes an angry response. In this context, the latter may be the preferable translation.

Although Hagar bore Ishmael, he was not the promised son. The promise was that Hagar's seed would be numerous. Still there is a sense in which her seed was part of the blessing to all nations that would come through Abraham. Some of the progeny of Ishmael have become believers in the LORD-Jesus-Christ/*YHWH-Yeshua-Mashiach*.

Hagar would be unable to understand that Ishmael would not be Abram's heir until 14 years later when Sarah became pregnant. Muslims believe that Ishmael is the promised son. Hagar and/or Ishmael may have felt that he should have been the promised son and passed that belief on to Ishmael's progeny.[63] Only after Isaac was born could Hagar understand the conflict that would occur between Ishmael's progeny and Isaac's progeny.

God appeared to Hagar as *Elroi*, "God who sees me" (*'êl ro'îy,* אל ראי), another new name for God in the book of Genesis (page 50). Hagar named the well, *Beer-Lahai-Roi*, "the well of the Living One who sees me" [map site 19] (Gen. 16:14, NASB margin). *Yahweh* met her at a spring (Gen. 16:7). The literal translation of spring water is "living water" (Gen. 26:19). God grants living water to those who believe Him (John 4:13-15, 37-28). The spring was located between Kadesh, "holy" (*qâdêsh,* קדשׁ), and Bered, "hail" (*beh'-red,* ברד). Hagar saw *Yahweh* between the sites of the sacred and holy and the hail that represented the adverse storms of this life. She made the right choice and obeyed *Yahweh*.

Hagar told the story of this incident to Abram and Sarai. At that time Hagar, Abram, and Sarai interpreted *Yahweh's* encounter with Hagar as evidence that Ishmael would be the promised son (Gen. 17:18).

After Sarai heard of *Yahweh*'s appearance and message to Hagar, it is likely that she dealt with Hagar in a more reasonable manner. At least, she tolerated her. Hagar was pregnant with "their" son. In order to minimize feelings of jealousy on the part of Sarai, one suspects that Abram was judicious in his treatment of Hagar. Thus, it is likely that he did not have further sexual relations with Hagar (page 196). Ishmael was born in Abram's 86th year.

CHAPTER 8

THE GENERATIONS OF ABRAHAM

The generations of Abraham are the eighth in the book of Genesis. Ishmael's progeny would eventually become enemies of Israel. In addition, the six sons of Abraham and Keturah would result in additional Middle Eastern tribes who would join with the progeny of Ishmael in enmity against the nation of Israel. Abraham would become the father of a multitude of nations from which a remnant would turn to the one true God.

Abraham's son was Isaac. Isaac's son was Jacob. Jacob engendered the family that became the nation of Israel. Thus, the progeny of these three patriarchs would contribute to the birth of the Messiah (Matt. 1:1-17). The Messiah would come from the seed of the woman through the virgin birth (Gen. 3:15, Isa. 7:14, Gal. 3:16-19, Matt. 1:18-25).

ABRAHAM'S LIFE-I

Abram Becomes Abraham
Hebron; Abraham, Age 99

Genesis 17:1-27

Gen. 17:1-8: God waited until Ishmael was 13 years old before fulfilling the promise Abram had tried to fulfill through his own potency. It is likely that He waited so that Abram and Sarai knew they would not be able to produce a child. They would have to believe Him before the promised son could be born and disavow Ishmael who they believed to be the promised son. When Abram was 99 years old, *Yahweh* **appeared** to him as *El Shaddai* (the **seventh** direct communication) with the promise of a son to be born through Sarai. Abraham's seed came through the provision of *El Shaddai*, the All-Bountiful One. This is the first occurrence of this name of God in Genesis (page 51).

Abram's name, "exalted father," was changed to Abraham, "father of a multitude," denoting the many peoples, kings, and nations that would come from his seed. The change from Abram to Abraham, a change in name and character, was necessary in order to understand the design of God for the nation of Israel. Jacob would become Israel as he went through a similar transformation.

In Hebrew, the word describing the friendship between God and Abraham is "love" (*'ahab,* אהב). In Greek, the word is *philos* (*philos,* φίλος). Both of these words indicate that Abraham was the friend, the "love" (*ahab/philos*) of God:

"Did You not, O our God, drive out the inhabitants of this land before Your people Israel and give it to the descendants of Abraham Your friend forever?" (2 Chr. 20:7).

"You see that faith was working with his works, and as a result of the works, faith was perfected; and the Scripture was fulfilled which says, 'And Abraham believed God, and it was reckoned to him as righteousness,' and he was called the friend of God" (James 2:22-23).

The Abramic-Abrahamic Covenant

There was a three-part progression to the Abramic Covenant (Gen. 12:1-3, 13:14-17, 15:4-6). It would conclude with the final part, the Abrahamic Covenant (Gen. 17:1-10). *Yahweh* revealed significant details in each of the four stages of the covenant.

Part I—Abramic Covenant, Chapter 12

1. "Now the LORD said to Abram, 'Go forth from your country, and from your relatives and from your father's house, to the land which I will show you'" (Gen. 12:1).

Abram received the initial Abramic Covenant as one of the generations of Terah. Abram gave up his country, his relatives, and his father's house. He went to the new land that *Yahweh* would show to him. The land of Canaan, the land of merchants, would become the land of Israel. He received a commendation for this in the annals of the faithful ones who obeyed the LORD:

"By faith Abraham, when he was called, obeyed by going out to a place which he was to receive for an inheritance; and he went out, not knowing where he was going" (Heb. 11:8).

2. "And I will make you a great nation" (Gen. 12:2).

Yahweh would make Abram, "a great nation" (*l'goŷim gad̂ol̂*, לגוי גדול). The use of *Goyim* may indicate the nation of all Jewish and Gentile believers who would become part of the Israel of God.

3. "And I will bless you, and make your name great; and so you shall be a blessing" (Gen. 12:2).

Yahweh's promise was to make Abram's name great, so he could become a blessing to others. *Yahweh* was not saying that he would make the name of Abram great in the way that it is common to think of in Western culture. *Yahweh* was promising to change the character of Abram into one that would be great. Abram would become Abraham as he continued in obedience to *Yahweh*. As that change occurred, Abraham would become a blessing to others.

From this new life, this new character, all the families of the earth would receive a blessing. The families from which the nations sprung (Genesis 10) have benefited, and will continue to benefit, from the Promised Seed, the Messiah (Gen. 3:15; Gal. 3:16, 28-29).

4. "And I will bless those who bless you, and the one who curses you I will curse" (Gen. 12:3).

Those who blessed Abram would receive a blessing, and the one that cursed Abram would receive a curse. The blessing was plural, to the many; the curse was singular, to an individual. *Yahweh* is just and gracious to all.

5. "And in you all the families of the earth will be blessed" (Gen. 12:3).

The blessing extends to "all the families of the earth" (*kol̂ mishpaĉhaî 'ad̃am̂ah̆,* כל משפחת האדמה). *Adamah* is the Hebrew word that refers to the ground of the earth, so this is a generalized blessing that goes beyond the blessing to the nation of Israel. *Yahweh* sees peoples as families; the family is the basic unit that represents His corporate relationship to His people. Preservation of the nuclear family is vital to any nation.

Part II—Abramic Covenant, Chapter 13

"The LORD said to Abram, after Lot had separated from him, 'Now lift up your eyes and look from the place where you are, northward and southward and eastward and westward; for all the land which you see, I will give it to you and to your descendants forever. I will make your descendants as the dust of the earth, so that if anyone can number the dust of the earth, then your descendants can also be numbered. Arise, walk about the land through its length and breadth; for I will give it to you'" (Gen. 13:14-17).

Abram was promised the land of Israel forever with numberless seed, even as the dust of the earth. He could now grasp the extent of the land.

Part III—Abramic Covenant, Chapter 15

1. "And Abram said, 'Since You have given no offspring to me, one born in my house is my heir. Then behold, the word of the LORD came to him, saying, 'This man will not be your heir; but one who will come forth from your own body, he shall be your heir.' And He took him outside and said, 'Now look toward the heavens, and count the stars, if you are able to count them.' And He said to him, 'So shall your descendants be'" (Gen. 15:3-5).

Abram requested a single "seed" (*zera',* זרע) as his "heir" (*yar̂ash,* ירש). *Yahweh* extended the covenant to include the birth of a baby boy from Abram's own body who would be his "seed" (*zera',* זרע). That single seed would multiply and become numberless.

2. "On that day the LORD made a covenant with Abram, saying, 'To your descendants I have given this land, from the river of Egypt as far as the great river, the river Euphrates'" (Gen. 15:18).

The boundaries of the land of Israel were further delineated.

The Abrahamic Covenant, Chapter 17

Finally, the capstone of the covenant was the change from Abram to Abraham (Gen. 17:1-9). The covenant was dependent on Abraham's faith in the Word of God, not trusting in his own flesh, his own potency. *Yahweh* was the One who gave, ratified, and fulfilled the covenant with its added provisions.

1. "I will establish My covenant between Me and you, and I will multiply you exceedingly" (Gen. 17:2).

Abraham would be "greatly multiplied" (*b'me'od̂ me'od̂,* במאד מאד).

2. "As for Me, behold, My covenant is with you, and you will be the father of a multitude of nations" (Gen. 17:4).

The promise was to be a father of a multitude of "Gentile nations" (*goŷim,* גוים), not just the nation of Israel.

3. "No longer shall your name be called Abram, But your name shall be Abraham; for I have made you the father of a multitude of nations" (Gen. 17:5).

Abram means "exalted father" (*'abram̂,* אברם); Abraham means "father of a multitude" (*'abraĥam̂,* אברהם). The name change, character change, was necessary to become a father of many nations. The change was already made (past tense) by *Yahweh*; He is omniscient and sees the end from the beginning.

4. "I will make you exceedingly fruitful, and I will make nations of you, and kings will come forth from you" (Gen. 17:6).

The promise is dependent on *Yahweh's* word.

5. "I will establish My covenant between Me and you and your descendants after you throughout their generations for an everlasting covenant, to be God to you and to your descendants after you" (Gen. 17:7).

The covenant is everlasting for Abraham's progeny ("your seed," *zeraq',* זרעך), those who believe in the LORD-Jesus-Christ/*YHWH-Yeshua-Mashiach*. The covenant extends beyond this world; it is "everlasting" (*'oîâm,* עולם):

"By faith he lived as an alien in the land of promise, as in a foreign land dwelling in tents with Isaac and Jacob, fellow heirs of the same promise; for he was looking for the city which has foundations, whose architect and builder is God" (Heb. 11:9-10).

Abraham's seed, the seed of faith, would eventuate in the Messiah: "Now the promises were spoken to Abraham and to his seed. He does not say, 'and to seeds,' as referring to many, but rather to one, 'and to your seed,' that is, Christ" (Gal. 3:16). Christ was born through "the seed" (και τω σπερματι αυτου) of the woman, not "the seeds" (και τοις σπερμασιν). This was the prophecy of the virgin birth (Gen. 3:15, 22:17-18). *Yahweh* would accomplish what seemed to be impossible to Abraham. Sarah would bear the promised son, Isaac. In the fullness of time, the Holy Spirit would birth the Messiah for all peoples through the Virgin Mary.

6. "I will give to you and to your descendants after you, the land of your sojournings, all the land of Canaan, for an everlasting possession; and I will be their God" (Gen. 17:8).

Abraham's progeny is promised the land as an everlasting possession. Israel, after the flesh, would become Israel, after the Spirit, the Israel of God, an everlasting kingdom (Gal. 6:15-16).

7. "God said further to Abraham, 'Now as for you, you shall keep My covenant, you and your descendants after you throughout their generations'" (Gen. 17:9).

In order to benefit from the covenant, the generations to come would need to demonstrate faith and obedience like Abraham's.

8. "This is My covenant, which you shall keep, between Me and you and your descendants after you: every male among you shall be circumcised" (Gen. 17:10).

Abram had tried to fulfill *Yahweh*'s promise by impregnating Hagar. He was given the covenant of circumcision, cutting away the foreskin of the penis, to signify that he was no longer to attempt to fulfill the promises of *Yahweh* by his own potency. His seed must also trust *Yahweh*, not their own potency.

The Israel of God

The Fulfillment of the Promises Made to Abram-Abraham

During their sojourn in Egypt, the family of Abraham would become the nation of Israel. *Yahweh*'s first promise and blessing was to make Abram into a great nation. The initial fulfillment of this was at Mount Sinai: "Now then, if you will indeed obey My voice and keep My covenant, then you shall be My own possession among all the peoples, for all the earth is Mine; and you shall be to Me a kingdom of priests and a holy nation. These are the words that you shall speak to the sons of Israel" (Exod. 19:5-6).

However, Israel failed to live up to their calling culminating in their rejection as a nation by the LORD Jesus Christ, but that rejection did not include the remnant of the people within the nation that accepted their Messiah: "THE STONE WHICH THE BUILDERS REJECTED, THIS BECAME THE CHIEF CORNER

STONE: THIS CAME ABOUT FROM THE LORD, AND IT IS MARVELOUS IN OUR EYES. Therefore I say to you, the kingdom of God will be taken away from you and given to a nation, producing the fruit of it" (Matt. 21:42-43 NASB margin).

The Apostle Peter, probably in remembrance of this statement that the LORD made during Passion Week, quoted the same verse from the Psalms that the LORD did and stated that the church has become the nation that displaced Israel according to genes: "The stone which the builders rejected has become the chief corner stone. This is the LORD'S doing; It is marvelous in our eyes" (Psa. 118:22-23).

"This precious value, then, is for you who believe; but for those who disbelieve, THE STONE WHICH THE BUILDERS REJECTED, THIS BECAME THE CORNER STONE, and, 'A STONE OF STUMBLING AND A ROCK OF OFFENSE'; for they stumble because they are disobedient to the word, and to this doom they were also appointed. But you are A CHOSEN RACE, A ROYAL PRIESTHOOD, A HOLY NATION, A PEOPLE FOR GOD'S OWN POSSESSION that you may proclaim the excellencies of Him who has called you out of darkness into His marvelous light; for you once were NOT A PEOPLE, but now you are THE PEOPLE OF GOD; you had NOT RECEIVED MERCY, but now you have RECEIVED MERCY" (1 Pet. 2:7-10).

The Apostle Peter defines the holy nation as "a people for God's own possession" (Exod. 19:5-6, Matt. 21:42-43, 1 Pet. 2:9-10). That people cannot include the apostate within Israel according to the flesh, the apostate from the genetic seed, the sons of Jacob. The church of the LORD Jesus Christ, composed of Jews and Gentiles, became the nation, the people, the kingdom of priests that inherited the promises originally given to the nation of Israel, the sons of Jacob (Rom. 2:25-29). The Apostle Peter cannot be referring to Jewish Christians only; otherwise he would be making a nonsense statement, i.e., the Jewish nation lost the spiritual inheritance, and Jewish Christians received it. He is speaking of the church of God whose Gentile members are grafted into the spiritual nation of Israel.

Some have argued that the Apostle Peter was writing only to Jewish Christians based on the fact that the book is addressed to "aliens" in the areas of dispersion:

"Peter, an apostle of Jesus Christ, To those who reside as aliens, scattered throughout Pontus, Galatia, Cappadocia, Asia, and Bithynia, who are chosen according to the foreknowledge of God the Father, by the sanctifying work of the Spirit, to obey Jesus Christ and be sprinkled with His blood: May grace and peace be yours in the fullest measure" (1 Pet. 1:1-2).

Note the Greek word for "aliens" (*parepidēmos,* παρεπίδημος) in the first verse (1 Pet. 1:1) is the same Greek word that is translated as "strangers" (*parepidēmos,* παρεπίδημος) in the second chapter (1 Pet. 2:11). Furthermore, in the latter verse, "aliens" is translated by a different Greek word (*paroikos,* πάροικος) (1 Pet. 2:11). This same Greek root is translated as "stay" (*paroikia,* παροικία), "a foreign residence," in the first chapter (1 Pet. 1:17). A study of the Greek words, variously translated into English in these verses, indicates that the Apostle Peter is writing to Christians (Jewish and Gentile believers) who are aliens and strangers (pilgrims) on the earth. He is not writing to just Jewish believers dispersed in Gentile lands!

A careful reading of the book would verify this. He even indicates that he is writing to Christians (*Christianos,* Χριστιανός) later in the book:

"But if anyone suffers as a Christian, he is not to be ashamed, but is to glorify God in this name" (1 Pet. 4:16).

The Apostle Paul confirmed the same teaching by also quoting from the Old Testament (Hos. 1:10, 2:23):

"Even us, whom He also called, not from among Jews only, but also from among Gentiles. As He says also in Hosea, 'I WILL CALL THOSE WHO WERE NOT MY PEOPLE, MY PEOPLE, AND HER WHO WAS NOT BELOVED, BELOVED, AND IT SHALL BE THAT IN THE PLACE WHERE IT WAS SAID TO

THEM, YOU ARE NOT MY PEOPLE, THERE THEY SHALL BE CALLED SONS OF THE LIVING GOD'" (Rom. 9:24-26).

Isaiah stated the same truth: "Also the foreigners who join themselves to the LORD, to minister to Him, and to love the name of the LORD, to be His servants, every one who keeps from profaning the sabbath and holds fast My covenant; even those I will bring to My holy mountain and make them joyful in My house of prayer. Their burnt offerings and their sacrifices will be acceptable on My altar; for My house will be called a house of prayer for all the peoples" (Isa. 56:6-7).

After the fullness of the Gentiles is grafted in, the nation of Israel will accept their Messiah:

"For I do not want you, brethren, to be uninformed of this mystery—so that you will not be wise in your own estimation—that a partial hardening has happened to Israel until the fullness of the Gentiles has come in; and so all Israel will be saved; just as it is written, 'THE DELIVERER WILL COME FROM ZION, HE WILL REMOVE UNGODLINESS FROM JACOB. THIS IS MY COVENANT WITH THEM, WHEN I TAKE AWAY THEIR SINS'" (Rom. 11:25-27).

The Apostle Paul further states that the church, made up of the circumcision (Jews) and uncircumcision (Gentiles), becomes the Israel of God:

"For neither is circumcision anything, nor uncircumcision, but a new creation. And those who will walk by this rule, peace and mercy be upon them, and upon the Israel of God" (Gal. 6:15-16).

The LORD Jesus referred to the church two different times in the gospel of Matthew (Matt. 16:15-19, 18:17-18). Relevant to this discussion is His first statement:

"He said to them, 'But who do you say that I am?' Simon Peter answered, 'You are the Christ, the Son of the living God.' And Jesus said to him, 'Blessed are you, Simon Barjona, because flesh and blood did not reveal this to you, but My Father who is in heaven. I also say to you that you are Peter, and upon this rock I will build My church; and the gates of Hades will not overpower it'" (Matt. 16:15-18).

Christ (*Christos* in Greek) and Messiah (*Mashiach* in Hebrew) both mean "the Anointed One." The LORD stated that he would build His church upon the rock of the Apostle Peter's confession that the LORD Jesus was the Messiah (*Christos/Mashiach*). Therefore, the Messiah is the Messiah of the church composed of Jewish and Gentile believers. Thus, based on the LORD's statement and the quoted verses above, the church, composed of Jews and Gentiles who accept their Messiah, is the entity upon which the LORD will build His kingdom (Matt. 21:42-43).

The Apostle John described the church, Jewish and Gentile believers, as a "kingdom of priests." He utilized these words three different times in Revelation (Rev. 1:6, 5:10, 20:6). In the new heaven, the names of the tribes of Israel will be inscribed on the gates of the holy city, and the names of the apostles will be inscribed on the foundation stones (Rev. 21:12-14).

Church History and the Israel of God

Therefore, based on the writing of these apostles and the statements of the LORD, the church becomes the new Israel, the Israel of God, made up of Jewish and Gentile believers. The Israel of God is the nation (people) that inherits the spiritual promises given in the Old Testament to the nation of Israel and in the New Testament to the church. The Israel of God will continue forever!

Through personal study of the Scriptures, it is the author's conclusion that the Israel of God is composed of Jewish and Gentile believers who trust in the LORD-Jesus-Christ/*YHWH-Yeshua-Mashiach* (Gal. 5:15-16). After coming to this conclusion and discussing it with several pastors and scholars of evangelical persuasion, it became clear that this was not the dictum of many of the evangelical Bible schools and seminaries in the U.S., and thus, not the teaching from the pulpit of many evangelical churches.

This triggered additional research on the matter. It appears the current position is that only the sons of Jacob, i.e., Israel according to genes, will inherit the promises given to Israel in the Old Testament. This is a relative new theological position in church history that started in the 1800s. In the 18 centuries before that time, Christians accepted that the church's Gentile believers were grafted into Israel, as the Apostle Paul declared, to join with Jewish believers to become the new creation, the Israel of God (Rom. 9:25-26, 11:16-27; Gal. 6:15-16).

That thinking changed in this country when John Nelson Darby, a Plymouth Brethren theologian from England, gave a series of lectures in the United States in the 1860s that has influenced evangelical scholars since that time. Darby believed that references to Israel in the Old Testament belonged only to the progeny of Jacob, "the sons of Jacob," not to the church.

Benjamin Wills Newton, a contemporary Plymouth Brethren theologian of Darby, took exception to Darby's teachings. Newton believed the Old Testament saints were part of the church, i.e., spiritual Israel. Newton was opposed to Darby's view of Israel and several other doctrinal issues. Newton's scholarship is either not known, or not accepted, by many evangelicals in the United States and has had little sway in this country.[64] Darby had a charismatic personality and a persuasive political presence; Newton did not, but he was known for his scholarship.

Current evangelical scholarship in the United States argues against the Israel of God being the church, in spite of the fact that the Apostle Paul stated that the new creation goes beyond the "uncircumcision" (the Gentiles) and the "circumcision" (the Jews) (Gal. 6:15).[65]

Alfred Edersheim was a converted Jew who also was a contemporary of Darby and Newton. Edersheim may well be the foremost Jewish authority on the interpretation of the Scriptures as it pertains to Israel. Most people who are interested in the Jewish understanding of the Scriptures have read his best-known work, *The Life and Times of Jesus the Messiah.*

In the Barburton lectures, Edersheim stated that the church, since its inception and throughout its history, has believed that it becomes the fulfillment of Old Testament teaching and prophecy. Edersheim declared that the church is the true Israel of God. For those who have carefully read his writings on this subject, Edersheim's scholarship is difficult to challenge. After reviewing the books enumerated in the References, and others, and further searching the Scriptures, the author agrees with Edersheim's conclusion that the church becomes the Israel of God composed of believing Jews and Gentiles. The church will receive the spiritual promises from both the Old and New Testaments.[66]

ABRAHAM'S LIFE-II

Abraham's responsibility in the covenant was to walk before *Yahweh* and be "complete, perfect, having integrity" (*tam̂iŷm,* תמים) (Gen. 17:1 NASB margin). Again, a better translation of "before" is "in the face of" (*paneh,* פנה). Abraham was to have a righteous walk under the watchful care of *Yahweh*, not "in your face" as a negative idiom. The context and the character of the person involved determine the interpretation. Linguistic variables must be subject to context!

The goal was to be perfect as the Father is perfect (Matt. 5:48). Abraham could have perfect integrity with *Yahweh* and become a complete man with evolving perfection (sanctification) in this life. The name change was illustrative of the change in the character of Abram that was necessary to become the new man, Abraham.

Second works of grace come at different times for different believers (Isa. 6:1-7). The condition for such a work is the response of the individual to the LORD's prompting to further trust in Him and demonstrate the same through obedience to Him.

In order to receive the promises made to Abraham, his seed would be obligated to show faith like his and do the works of Abraham (John 8:37-39). The covenant was an everlasting one for the true seed of Abraham, believers in the LORD-Jesus-Christ/*YHWH-Yeshua-Mashiach* (Rom. 2:28-29, 4:11-13). The land would belong to the physical seed of Abraham, the land of Israel. The expansion of Israel will include the spiritual seed of Abraham, Jews and Gentiles who are believers in the LORD Jesus Christ, their Messiah. The latter are grafted into Israel, the Israel of God that will occupy the land during the future millennial reign of the LORD (Ezek. 47:21-23, Rom. 11:16-27, Gal. 6:15-16).

Circumcision, the Sign of the Covenant

Gen. 17:9-14: The covenant of circumcision was a lifelong sign to Abraham to denote in his flesh that he was not to attain God's promise by his own potency but by the promise of *El Shaddai* (Gen. 17:13). Ishmael was the son obtained by Abram's own potency, not by his faith.

Circumcision, the sign of the covenant, benefited the servants and slaves of Abraham. It is supportive of the fact that he was to bless the peoples of the world (Gen. 12:2-3). As emphasized above, Gentile believers are grafted into Israel (Rom. 9:6, 11:16-24; Gal. 6:15-16).

There is no definitive medical evidence to suggest that the uncircumcised state decreases the ability to impregnate a woman. When he was uncircumcised, Abraham had impregnated Hagar 14 years previously. The purpose of circumcision was to illustrate that individual potency did not achieve the will of God. Circumcision of the heart was required (Deut. 30:6).

Sarai Becomes Sarah

Gen. 17:15-16: *Elohim* honored Sarai's spiritual character, exemplified by her obedience to Abram in the incident with the Pharaoh, and her deference to Abraham as her lord, by changing her name to Sarah. She received her spiritual recognition from the LORD by obeying her husband (Gen. 3:16b).

In Hebrew, "sar" (*śar,* שׂר) means "a ruler." The "ai" is a suffix denoting possession. Therefore, Sarai (*sarai,* שׂרי) may mean "my princess," Abram's princess. Dropping this suffix was symbolic of her independent spiritual attainment. Adding an "h" at the end of her name (*saraĥ,* שׂרה) produced the feminine singular ending in Hebrew. Sarah was honored as a mother of the son of promise, and therefore, queen mother of kings and nations.

Yahweh saw Sarah's motherhood as a type of royalty. Thus, she received equal honor with Abraham for her unique role as mother and wife as symbolized by her name change, her new spiritual character. Abraham was the kingly father and Sarah was the queenly mother of the righteous:

"Listen to me, you who pursue righteousness, who seek the LORD: Look to the rock from which you were hewn and to the quarry from which you were dug. Look to Abraham your father and to Sarah who gave birth to you in pain; when he was but one I called him, then I blessed him and multiplied him" (Isa. 51:1-2).

Today there is a need for believers to restore the LORD's benediction on the holy calling of fatherhood and motherhood.

Abraham's Laughter

Gen. 17:17: Upon hearing of the promised son, Abraham fell on his face and laughed. This was an act of both unbelief and submission to *Elohim*, the Creator, for his creative act of the promised son, Isaac ("he laughs," *yitschaq̂,* יצחק). The laughter depicted his joy at the possibility of a son through Sarah. The question in his heart, which *Elohim* heard, depicted human logic and unbelief. Many of us, like Abraham, are ambivalent when it comes to believing God for a miracle that He reveals to us. However, note that Abraham immediately prostrated himself and accepted the name change for Sarai. He called her Sarah in the subsequent conversation with *Elohim* and followed through with the circumcision of his entire household (Gen. 17:17, 23-27). During this spiritual struggle, his works verified his faith.

Since his father was 130 years old when Abram was born, it is a little difficult to understand why Abraham found it unlikely that a man of the age of 100 could father a child (Gen. 11:32, 12:4). It is likely that Terah, Abram's father, had a younger wife that became Abram's mother. However, Sarah would be 90 years old at the time of the birth of Isaac.

Sarah had undergone menopausal changes in her female organs that would have made it difficult to have had sexual intercourse during the previous ten to 15 years. Exogenous estrogen was not available as it is today for local or systemic use to maintain the vagina for sexual function.

There is no Biblical evidence for Abraham having sexual relations with any other woman than Sarah, the temporary alliance with Hagar, and the relationship with Keturah after Sarah's death. Abram had depended on his potency to impregnate Hagar at the age of 85 (Gen. 16:1-4). His last sexual intercourse may have been with Hagar 14 years previously (page 180) (Gen. 16:2).

If Abraham had not had sexual intercourse for several years, and had become impotent, he may have doubted the possibility of regaining his potency. Sarah was 14 years post-menopausal (Gen. 16:2). Abraham may have been declaring that they both were too old to have sexual intercourse (Rom. 4:19). Confirmation of Abraham's impotence appears in the New Testament:

"Therefore there was born even of one man, and him as good as dead at that, as many descendants AS THE STARS OF HEAVEN IN NUMBER, AND INNUMERABLE AS THE SAND WHICH IS BY THE SEASHORE" (Heb. 11:12).

There is no evidence that Abraham was near death at 100 years of age; he would live another 75 years. The Hebrew writer knew that. He was writing about Abraham's impotency, dead in the sense that he could not achieve erections and reproduce, "an impotent old man" (και ταυτα νενεκρωμενου).

At the time of *Elohim*'s (the Creator's) promise, Abraham recognized that he could not father the son of promise through Sarah except by faith in *Elohim*'s word. Subsequently, after he was 140 years old, the renewal of his potency would allow Abraham to father six more sons by Keturah. Keturah would have been a younger pre-menopausal woman (Gen. 25:1-2).

Both Sarah and Abraham would have to believe God in order to receive the necessary physiologic changes in their bodies that would allow them to produce the promised son. Abraham would need to believe for changes in Sarah that would allow the possibility of sexual intercourse with her and for his own potency—now given as a gift of God, not a personal achievement. Sarah would need to believe for a reversal of the post-menopausal changes in her body and a renewal of her interest in having sexual intercourse with Abraham. It is pertinent to note the emphasis in the New Testament statement about Sarah's struggle:

"By faith even Sarah herself received ability to conceive, even beyond the proper time of life" (Heb. 11:11a).

Thus, the Holy Spirit indicated that the major issue in conception for Sarah was her faith that God would do what He said. The time of the event was to be the same season the following year. Since Sarah had gone through menopause, it would be necessary to reverse the aging process by secreting hormones necessary to prepare her body for sexual relations and conception before she could become pregnant. These changes would occur over the following three months, during which their faith would be tested. Abraham was 99 years old, Sarah was 89 years old, and Ishmael was 13 years old.

I-Isaac, Son of Promise
Ishmael, Son of Flesh

Gen. 17:18-22: God accepted Abraham's prayer for Ishmael. This mixed blessing resulted in the development of 12 princes that would become a nation that would be hostile to the progeny of Isaac, the nation of Israel (Gen. 25:13-25, Gal. 4:28-29). Ishmael was not the son of promise. Since the Bible records that he was "gathered to his people," he must have been a believer in *Yahweh*. "His people" would have included Abram, his father (Gen. 25:17).

Thus, he would have gone to Abraham's bosom after passing the portals of death (Luke 16:22).

The Year of the Birth of the Promised Son

Yahweh Elohim told Abraham twice that the promise's fulfillment would be at the "appointed time" (*moʾeḏ,* מוֹעֵד) in the following year (Gen. 17:21, 18:14). There was specificity in the year selected by God.

The 100th year of Abraham's life was 2,108 Biblical years AA (After Adam's creation). The birth of Isaac in 2108 AA was halfway between the creation of Adam and the birth of Christ around 4 BC (2108 X 2 = 4216) (Appendix III, page 396). Therefore, the birth of the promised son, Isaac, was equidistant between the creation of Adam and the birth of the promised Son of God, the Messiah (Table 10, page 397). Since there is no Biblical evidence for the specific month and day of the birth of the Messiah, one can only speculate as to whether the birth of Isaac occurred on the same month and day as the LORD's birthday: "The secret things belong to the LORD our God" (Deut. 29:29a).

Immediate Obedience to the Sign of the Covenant

Gen. 17:23-27: Circumcision was a sign of Abram's sin of trying to do the will of God by his own potency and a continual reminder of the same. Immediate obedience to the command of God that same day illustrated the beauty of Abraham's faith and spiritual character. Three times in this passage, it states that Abraham's servants and slaves were to be circumcised. God's plan was for Abraham to bless the peoples of the earth. That blessing included the foreign servants and slaves within his household (Gen. 17:2-13, 23, 27).

Abraham had 318 warriors in his household. Those men and their male relatives were unlikely to submit to circumcision without knowing the reason for it. Therefore, it is probable that Abraham witnessed to them about the Christophany, the previously mentioned seventh communication between him and *Yahweh* (Gen.

17:22). Abraham must have continually taught his household about *Yahweh*. If the men were to accept circumcision for themselves and their sons, there had to be an underlying mutual trust. Abraham was the object lesson. He must have told them that he learned that he could not achieve the will of God by his own potency, neither could they. He must have testified to them about the promised son.

Abraham's Spiritual Sensitivity and Hospitality

Genesis 18:1-33

Gen. 18:1-8: Abraham allowed Sarah to go into the harem of Abimelech for about three months (page 216). Therefore, the events of the 18th and 19th chapters follow soon after the events of the 17th chapter.

Abraham's tent was near the religious site of the *terebinths* of Mamre. Abraham had built an altar at that site several years before (Gen. 13:18). A **Christophany** (the **eighth** direct communication) occurred in the heat of the day. When Abraham looked up, he saw three men opposite him. Abraham recognized that *Yahweh* was visiting him with two of His angels. Since these three looked like other men, only one who walked with *Yahweh* would be spiritually sensitive to the identification of the visitors. Abraham was able to distinguish the person of *Yahweh*; He had appeared to Abraham before (Gen. 12:7, 17:1).

They came to Abraham "in the heat of the day." Major events often happen in the heat of the day when there is no time to prepare for them. Actions taken at that time are dependent upon one's previous walk with the LORD.

Abraham's response was to run to them in the heat of the day and worship by bowing to the ground, an act of obeisance and worship not given to mortal men. He addressed Him as "my Lord" (*'ădônîy*, אדני), the first use of *Adonai* (Lord, i.e., Sovereign) as a single name of God in the book of Genesis (page 50). If Abraham found favor in His sight, he did not want the Lord to pass by him.

Would that all men would fall in obedience to the Lord when He reveals Himself to them and pray that He not pass by them.

Abraham then became host to his Lord and served him a tender calf from the herd that he personally selected; the servant and Sarah prepared the meal. It would have taken time to slay and barbecue the calf and prepare the meal. These heavenly visitors patiently waited for Abraham to perform his act of service for them. The LORD is never in a hurry; He waited to enjoy the fellowship of His faithful servant over a meal.

Sarah's Silent Laughter

Gen. 18:9-15: The following dialogue confirmed that Abraham knew who his guests were. After finishing the meal, they asked where Sarah, not Sarai, was. Sarah needed her faith stirred up, so she would be able to birth the promised son and function with her new name, her new spiritual nature.

The angels spoke as one with their Lord, "They said." At the announcement to Zacharias of the birth of John the Baptist, Gabriel replied immediately to Zacharias' unbelief, "I am Gabriel who stands in the presence of God" (Luke 1:19a). It is glorious to note the angels' unity with the Lord and immediate response in both these scenes.

After his previous encounter with *Yahweh*, the circumcision of all the males within the household implies that there had been discussion between Abraham and Sarah about the reason for that action. In addition, Abraham must have communicated to her *Yahweh's* change of her name to Sarah and his name to Abraham. Furthermore, he would have told her of *El Shaddai's* promise that she would bear a son the following year.

Sarah must not have believed Abraham as revealed by her inward statement of unbelief and laughter upon overhearing the reaffirmation of the promise to Abraham. *Yahweh* now dealt with her unbelief and communicated the name change of Sarah and the birth of the promised son through Abraham within earshot of

Sarah. It must have been after this that Sarah's faith was stirred to believe the promise of God that enabled her to conceive (Heb. 11:11). The rebuke of the Lord (*Adonai*) resulted in the development of Sarah's life-giving faith. Honest rebuke can be an effective teaching method that inspires a faith response.

Yahweh previously stated the "appointed time" (*moʾêd*, מועד) to be "at this season next year" (Gen. 17:21). Sarah would bear a son, "at the appointed time" and "when the time revives" (Gen. 18:14 NASB margin). The latter phrase is an elaboration of the former one; the Lord was reminding Sarah of the fulfillment of the original time promised to Abraham.

This was dependent on the return of *Yahweh* at that time who would supervise the birth of the promised son. This action foreshadowed the Father who would supervise the birth of the promised Son, the Messiah. *Yahweh's* supervision would protect the birth of Isaac from harm, just as the Father would protect the Messiah at the time of His birth (Matt. 2:13-15).

Sarah was past the time of bearing children, "the manner of women"; her menses had ceased (Gen. 16:2, 18:11, 31:35 NASB margin). Thus, at the ages of 99 for Abraham and 89 for Sarah, *Yahweh* reiterated His promise to both.

It was at this time that the Biblical record records that Sarah called Abraham her lord; this was her habit. In this age of feminism, it is well to reflect on the admirable traits of Sarah, and God's commendation of her in her name change. The Apostle Peter discussed this submission by Sarah to her lord:

"In the same way, you wives, be submissive to your own husbands so that even if any of them are disobedient to the word, they may be won without a word by the behavior of their wives as they observe your chaste and respectful behavior. Your adornment must not be merely external—braiding the hair, and wearing gold jewelry, or putting on dresses; but let it be the hidden person of the heart, with the imperishable quality of a gentle and quiet spirit, which is precious in the sight of God. For in this way in former times the holy women also, who hoped in God, used to adorn themselves, being submissive to their own husbands; just as Sarah obeyed Abraham, calling him lord, and you have become her children if you do what is right without being frightened by any fear" (1 Pet. 3:1-6).

Sarah's "pleasure" was to undergo a renewal of sexual function, conception, pregnancy, birth of Isaac, and the opportunity to nurse him.

Nevertheless, Sarah's silent laughter while listening at the tent door and her harsh dealing with Hagar are illustrative of her spiritual deficiencies. "All who have this treasure in earthen vessels" suffer the same malady (2 Cor. 4:7). One wag has suggested that the translation should be, "All have this treasure in cracked pots."

Yahweh heard her and reproached her when she silently laughed at His promise. Abraham's laughter had been audible (Gen. 17:17). Sarah's question was whether sexual function could be restored in her "worn out" (*balah,* בלה) body and her lord's "old" (*zaqen,* זקן) body (Gen. 18:12, Heb. 11:12).

Yahweh did not speak of difficulty; instead, the text states, "Is anything too wonderful for the LORD?" (Gen. 18:14a NASB margin). God was going to do something that was "wonderful" (*pala',* פלא), marvelous, extraordinary, surpassing their fondest dreams. Difficulty does not exist in the vocabulary of the omnipotent God.

God Honors Abraham

Gen. 18:16-19: Abraham was a good host; he walked with his guests to send them off. The angels, in the guise of men, looked toward Sodom. *Yahweh*'s singular honor was to relate to Abraham the judgment on Sodom, Gomorrah, and the villages of the valley before it happened. He had selected Abraham as the one to be a father to a multitude of nations.

The promise of God was conditional. Abraham's responsibility was to be just and righteous and command his children and household to be just and righteous (Gen. 18:19). If they wish to see the possibility of the same outcome, all believing parents have the same responsibility. Children, for their part, must believe and obey their parents (Eph. 6:1-3). Obedience to parents teaches obedience to the LORD.

Abraham's Intercession—*Yahweh*'s Righteousness

Gen. 18:20-33: *Yahweh* introduced the great sin of Sodom and Gomorrah into the conversation. He is omniscient and omnipresent. He was with the two angels in spirit and with Abraham in person (page 344) (Gen. 19:12-14). The idea that He must "go down" was compatible with the topography of the land. "Go down" were the same words used when the Triune God went down to judge the tower of Babel and confuse the languages (page 150) (Gen. 11:1-9). The angels went toward Sodom, the chief village of the valley, the town where Lot and his family lived.

When he began his intercession, Abraham did not specify Sodom. *Yahweh* used the name of Sodom, thereby indicating that He understood that the intent of Abraham's intercession was the preservation of Lot and his family, and thus, He understood the cry of Abraham's heart. The loss of Lot's family, home, and possessions would occur upon the destruction of the city. This may have been the reason that Abraham prayed for the city of Sodom. He did not consider praying to remove Lot and his family from Sodom. Loss of possessions was necessary for Lot's spiritual progress. One must discern when to pray for the person, but not for their possessions. The latter may hinder their walk with the Lord.

The Lord did not rebuke Abraham for not interceding for the other cities of the valley; they were already under condemnation. Abraham accepted that judgment; he must have known about the sin in those cities. Abraham's initial request was to appeal to the nature of God not to kill the righteous with the wicked. He must have believed there were other righteous people in Sodom, or that Lot's extended family made up ten or more persons.

Yahweh, the righteous Judge of all the earth, will do what is just. *Yahweh* graciously accepted Abraham's sequential six appeals without rebuke. Abraham finished his prayer without making a seventh appeal. Perhaps there should have been a seventh appeal for the members of Lot's family who were, or who would become, believers. Prayer, at best, is learning God's thoughts and expressing them back to Him; we must learn to align our thoughts with the LORD's (Exod. 32:9-14). *Yahweh* was teaching Abraham how to intercede and persist in prayer until the correct request was made. This is an example for all of us (1 Cor. 10:11).

Abraham learned that *Yahweh*'s mercy was greater than his. *Yahweh*'s righteousness was greater in that He delivered Lot and his two daughters, even though their righteousness was in decline (Gen. 19:29). In addition, God delivered Lot from the materialism that had ensnared him. *Yahweh* is the righteous Judge who read Abraham's heart, not just his words. How comforting it is to know that the Lord responds to the intent of our prayers, even when our thoughts and words are not clear.

The Two Angels at Sodom

Genesis 19:1-38

Gen. 19:1-3: Lot could have been younger, older, or about the same age as Abraham. Lot's father, Haran, was born 70 years before Abram (page 159). He died before Abram's move from Ur of the Chaldees (Gen. 11:26-12:4). Lot could have been over 100 years old at the time of this event. When he originally separated from Abram, Lot had chosen to go to the valley of the Jordan. He also chose to return there after being rescued by Abram following the battle of the four kings against five (Gen. 13:10, 14:16, 19:1).

There is no evidence that Lot was a polygamist. Since he was married to a woman that had two daughters of marriageable age, probably in their teens, it is probable that Lot's first wife had died (page 211). His present wife would have been younger and would have come from Sodom or the surrounding area.

The two angels arrived at Sodom in the evening; the Bible often associates sin with darkness (Prov. 4:19). Lot sat at the gate, the meeting place of the elders of the city where court was held (Ruth 4:1-2). The absence of anyone else at the gate suggests a lack of effective leadership in Sodom. Lot was alone; he may have wanted to protect strangers coming into the town by offering them hospitality. He recognized the two angels as heavenly visitors and prostrated himself before them (Gen. 18:1-2, 19:1).

"And if He rescued righteous Lot, oppressed by the sensual conduct of unprincipled men (for by what he saw and heard that righteous man, while living among them, felt his righteous soul tormented day after day by their lawless deeds)" (2 Pet. 2:7-8).

These verses tell of the torment of Lot's soul by what he heard and saw, but he did not attempt to leave. He would have to have abandoned some of his family, wealth, and position. He may have had the lingering hope that he could influence change in his family and this sinful city through his witness. Believers whose family members have strayed, and who are blessed with wealth and social status, find it difficult to leave all at the command of the LORD.

Lot knew the type of activity that went on in Sodom at night. He called the angels his lords; he may have recognized that they were servants of the LORD. He pleaded with them to stay the night with him. At first, they declined.

Angels are not omnipresent; they act by command from their LORD and learn by obeying that command. They came to see how evil the city was and could do this better by observing activity in the city square at night.

After they accepted the invitation, Lot prepared a feast for his guests and baked unleavened bread for them. In the Bible, leaven often speaks of the burgeoning effect of sin that is symbolized by the effect of yeast on dough. Since they were sinless, the two angels accepted the meal. They feasted with Abraham at midday; they shared a meal with Lot in the evening (Gen. 19:3).

Nighttime in Sodom

Gen. 19:4-11: Lot had recognized the heavenly stature of the two angels. The men of Sodom responded to their appearance with wicked desire; Satan hates the pure of body and spirit. During the night, the young and old men from all parts of the city sought the two angels to rape them.

In addition, the text states "all the people" (*kol̂ h'am,* כל־העם) came to Lot's house, even from as far away as the borders of the town. This means that people from all parts of the town, men and women, viewed homosexual rape as a public, spectator sport. The women of the town were as perverse as the men were. One suspects that sexual abuse of children was rampant in the cities (Mark 9:42). The behavior of the people of Sodom suggests that each person did what was right in his own eyes (Jdg. 17:6, 21:25). It is easy to understand why God obliterated this community and others like it. Woe to the cities of our day that sanction such behavior. When judgment comes, they will go the way of Sodom and Gomorrah. The Judge of all the earth will do right!

The term for sexual intercourse, "to know" (*yad̂a',* ידע), is used here (Gen. 4:1). As is true for homosexuals and bisexuals today, these men distorted this God given term for heterosexual intercourse within the boundaries of marriage in an effort to defend their aberrant sexuality as normal.

Male homosexuality and bisexuality were rampant. Studies have shown bisexuals to be more promiscuous than homosexual males. Such sexual behavior was one of the sins that produced the outcry to heaven with pending judgment in the wings. As revealed in this episode, male bisexuals and homosexuals can be violent in their sexual activity. Anorectal intercourse is damaging to the anal sphincter. Its design was for the control and elimination of fecal waste, not sex.

Scientific efforts to prove a biologic basis for homosexuality are inconclusive. The available data has never shown what is chicken versus what is egg. Biological and mental changes in homosexuals may be secondary to their practices, not genetic traits. The Bible denounces such behavior. Since the Creator did not design men and women for such practices, one can conclude that any biological and mental changes that occur in homosexuals are secondary to the practices themselves, not due to genes that predispose to such behavior (Rom. 1:18-32).

Lot negotiated by offering his virgin daughters for sexual abuse instead of the two angels. This revealed how far Lot had succumbed to the mores of the city. It is remarkable that the daughters were virgins. Their environment was not conducive to sexual conservatism. Lot must have set a righteous standard for them in an unrighteous society. However, their subsequent behavior depicted a decline in their attitude about normal sexuality.

The men of the city became angry with Lot. They criticized him for offering his daughters. They believed that heterosexual intercourse with virginal females was less desirous than homosexual intercourse with males. In response to his offer, “They pressed against him,” an action that suggests an attempt at homosexual rape. Lot had recognized the spiritual quality of the angels, but not their power. They saved Lot by pulling him inside and striking the men with blindness; they could not find the door. Blindness was symbolic of their perverse attitudes about human sexuality and violence.

Gen. 19:12-14: The angels indicated that Lot had daughters, sons, and a son-in-law. The plural for sons suggests that Lot had one or more sons that had married and left home. If his present marriage was to a second wife, that would have been likely. Sons from his previous marriage would have been much older at this time with their own families. They may have succumbed to the mores of Sodom. They may even have been in the crowd that was present. Lot did not attempt to contact anyone other than those in the home. Therefore, Lot saw no hope for his sons responding to his plea.

Lot spoke to the “two” sons-in-law, those legally pledged to marry his two virgin daughters. They thought he was joking. The discrepancy between the angel's assessment of only one son-in-law, instead of two, may have been due to God's appraisal that one intended to seduce one of the daughters without commitment.

The angels commanded Lot to bring out his wife and daughters. Because of the outcry that had come up to Him, *Yahweh* had already condemned the cities of the valley (Gen. 19:13).

Gen. 19:15-22: Why did the angels tell them not to look back after leaving Sodom? Those who deserve the same judgment, and receive deliverance instead, are not to view the LORD's judgment on those who do not escape. The LORD and His angels knew about the future, final judgment that will be in the presence of the holy angels and the LORD, not in the presence of saved sinners:

"He also will drink of the wine of the wrath of God, which is mixed in full strength in the cup of His anger; and he will be tormented with fire and brimstone in the presence of the holy angels and in the presence of the Lamb" (Rev. 14:10).

Lot procrastinated all night until dawn. Because of *Yahweh*'s compassion, the angels seized Lot, his wife, and his two daughters and brought them out of the city. These were the only ones in all the cities of the valley that received *Yahweh*'s deliverance, except for the village of Zoar.

Lot, still clinging to the hope that disaster could be avoided, begged to go to the small village of Zoar, instead of fleeing to the mountains as commanded. It was at this time that the village was named Zoar, "small, insignificant" (*tsoʾar,* צער), based on Lot's faulty plea (Gen. 19:20). The angels told Lot they could not destroy the cities until Lot was safe; the intent of Abraham's prayer had been answered (Gen. 19:22).

Why did God grant Lot's request to preserve Zoar? Zoar was located at the southern tip of the Dead Sea; the destruction of the other cities would not have affected the preservation of Zoar. It was under the original sentence of destruction, just like the other cities of the valley. Perhaps some of the residents of Zoar had potential for repentance after they saw the destruction that occurred. On the other hand, answers to the wrong prayer request can result in multiplied evil in the world and in one's life:

"So He gave them their request, But sent **leanness into their souls**" (*shal̂ach raẑon̂ b'nepheshim,* וישלח רזון בנפשם) (Psa. 106:15 NASB margin).

Subsequent to the destruction of the area, Lot's fear caused him to flee to the mountains. The evidence indicates that Lot did not completely believe the angels concerning the destruction that was coming. Thus, he made the request to go to Zoar. After he observed the destruction of the cities, he was afraid not to obey. Many who do not accept God's forewarning of judgment react the same way after judgment has been rendered.

Judgment on Evil Communities

Gen. 19:23-26: *Yahweh* used two angels to destroy the cities of the valley (Gen. 19:13, 22, 24). Angels have powers given to them about which humans know very little; they operate through the power of their Lord.

The destruction of the cities of the valley, their inhabitants, and the countryside was complete, except for Zoar. *Yahweh* rained brimstone and fire out of heaven on them (Gen. 19:24). A volcanic eruption that sent molten, sulfurous crystals into the air and rained back on the inhabitants of the cities could account for this outcome. They would have died quickly from the fiery missiles produced or from asphyxiation caused by the gasses. The air pollution, "like the smoke of a furnace," that Abraham would see the next day lends support to this probability (Gen. 19:28).

Sodom and Gomorrah lived "down" to their names; Sodom means "burnt" (*sedom̂,* סדם) and Gomorrah means "a heap" (*'am̆or̂aĥ,* עמרה). God burned the cities of the valley and turned them into a heap of ruins. Destruction is the highest good for a city consumed with evil; otherwise, its sin continues to multiply and harm the innocent. Only the LORD knew the extent of the sexual abuse of men, women and children that occurred in the cities of the valley.

The previously described well-watered valley of the Jordan in this area no longer exists (Gen. 13:10). The lush environment suffered. No longer could evil men seek to exploit the area for economic gain (Gen. 19:25). The valley became the area of the Dead Sea, appropriately named, approximately 1300 feet below sea level, the lowest point on earth. The perversity in these cities and their rebellion against God was also the lowest on earth. The Dead Sea contains high levels of salt. Salt replaced the people of the valley who failed to be salt in their communities:

"For everyone will be salted with fire. Salt is good; but if the salt becomes unsalty, with what will you make it salty again? Have salt in yourselves, and be at peace with one another" (Mark. 9:49-50).

Lot's wife, who lingered in the rear, looked back in spite of the command not to do so. Lot would not have known that she had perished until afterwards. Her act indicated a lack of faith in what the angels said. If she was originally from Sodom or the vicinity, she may never have come to the faith that her husband had in *Yahweh*. She became "a pillar of salt" during the volcanic eruption when tephra, filled with the high salt content in the Dead Sea area, rained down on her. She lagged behind, just one step ahead of the devastation; she must have felt the heat. One turn to look back was enough to seal her fate.

A similar moral decline in the majority of mankind will occur as the end of the age approaches. Abnormal sexual activity will be the accepted standard. When the LORD is revealed upon His return to the earth, He said it would be like the days of Noah and the days of Sodom (Luke 17:22-37).

At the end of the millennium, fire will come down from heaven to judge Satan and the last set of rebels who war against *Yahweh Tza'vot*. These cities of the valley of the Jordan are a harbinger of the final judgment that will come to the world (Rev. 20:9-10).

After the LORD's coming return to the earth, the reorganization of the earth's topography will result in geographical changes in this area. There will be a river flowing out from the temple in Jerusalem with fresh waters that flow to the eastern sea. If the Pishon and Gihon rivers went under the surface of the earth during the flood, they may reappear. One river may flow through Israel; the other may take this new course. The area surrounding the fresh waters will still contain salt marshes; they will be a reminder not to forget the lesson of Sodom, Gomorrah, and the cities of the valley (Ezek. 47:1-12).

The Judge of All the Earth Does Right

Gen. 19:27-29: God's judgment and mercy are never in conflict. Abraham observed the destruction from the place where he had met with *Yahweh*. Abraham interceded for ten in the city of Sodom; *Yahweh* delivered Lot and his two daughters. Lot's wife chose her own judgment through unbelief.

Yahweh's righteousness was greater than Abraham's righteousness. To repeat, God hears the cry of our heart, even though our words may not match our inner thoughts.

The Carryover Effect of Incest

Gen. 19:30-38: During these ancient times, most young women were married in their teenage years. Since they were engaged to be married, it is likely that Lot's daughters were teenagers (page 204). The deterioration in righteousness, depicted by the behavior of Lot's daughters, was typical of the effect of an evil environment on teenagers. In spite of the fact that their father must have been of great age at the time, and may have been near the end of his life, they despaired of finding suitable husbands in their present circumstances.

Since the daughters had anticipated having sexual intercourse with the men of their betrothal, the primary motivation in their actions might have been sexual, not preservation of the family. The elder daughter suggested to the younger that they get their father drunk and have sexual intercourse with him. Their sexual drive overruled common sense and patience. They showed no signs of faith in *Yahweh* who cared for them.

They knew of the sexual deviancy of the inhabitants of Sodom: bisexuality, homosexuality, incest, drunkenness, and probable child abuse. Their actions suggest that they thought incest to be a form of acceptable sexual behavior. Thus, they employed alcohol to accomplish their incestuous actions. They got their father drunk on two consecutive nights; each one, in turn, had sexual intercourse with him. Both became pregnant.

Lot did not know that he had impregnated his two daughters. Note the repetition of the words after each of the two nights:

"He did not know when she lay down or when she arose" (Gen. 19:33b, 35b).

It is unlikely that the daughters would have told their father that he had had sexual intercourse with them. In Biblical times, engagement was a legal commitment without consummation until after the marriage ceremony, which may have been months after the betrothal (Gen. 19:12, 14; Matt. 1:18-19). Given the condition of the sexual mores in Sodom, Lot probably thought his daughters became pregnant by the two "sons-in-law" before they left Sodom. Therefore, Lot may have died without realizing the truth.

Just as happened with Abraham's impregnation of Hagar, their sin resulted in the development of two more nations in perpetual enmity with Israel. Moab means "from the mother's father" (*moʾab̂,* מואב). Ben-ammi means "inbred son of the mother" (*benʿammiŷ,* בן־עמי). Ben-Ammon can be translated as "sons by tribal inbreeding."

These names raise the question of whether sexual immorality persisted in the tribes of Moab and Ammon and affected Israel (1 Kin. 14:21; 15:2, 10; 2 Chr. 11:21-22, 15:16). In the future, their perpetual conflict with Israel would be illustrated by the sexually transmitted disease epidemic that would occur after Balaam's advice to the leaders of Moab, Ammon, and Midian to initiate a religious "fertility rite" at Baal-Peor. Sexual intercourse in a bordello tent near the tabernacle would occur in an effort to merge a pagan religion with the worship of *Yahweh* (syncretism) (pages 374-378). Thus, that attempt at syncretism would produce evidence that endemic sexually transmitted diseases would develop in some of the tribes of Moab, Ammon, and Midian.

Abraham's Second Deceit with Sarah
Gerar in the Negev; Abraham, Age 99

Genesis 20:1-18

Gen. 20:1-13: Since Lot had gone to the mountains, it is probable that Abraham did not know what had happened to him. He may have thought that he perished in the destruction of Sodom. This may have been the reason for Abraham's departure from Hebron. If he believed that God had not spared Lot, he may have been disgruntled. It is possible to receive a positive answer to prayer and not find this out for some time afterwards. He did not ask God what had happened to Lot; he did not seek God's direction for the move. He had committed this same sin earlier in life, when he went down to Egypt during a time of famine (Gen. 12:10).

"Be anxious for nothing, but in everything by prayer and supplication with thanksgiving let your requests be made known to God. And the peace of God, which surpasses all comprehension, will guard your hearts and your minds in Christ Jesus" (Phil. 4:6-7).

He progressively moved from the Negev to a place between Kadesh and Shur and then to Gerar [map site 11] in the land of the Philistines. When believers are depressed or dissatisfied, they may wander about without specific direction and become susceptible to sin. The failure to seek God's direction for his move led to a repeat of the same sin that he committed in Egypt a quarter of a century earlier. During his 99th year, Abraham represented his wife as his sister. This time it was to a Philistine chieftain, Abimelech, a title that means "my father the king" (*'aḇiŷ melek,* אבימלך).

Abraham risked the impregnation of Sarah by Abimelech during the year that *Yahweh* said she would conceive and bear Isaac. He had not learned the lesson from his previous deceit in Egypt (Gen. 12:10-20). His faith had wavered. He may have expected God to protect Sarah just as He had done in Egypt. God did protect Sarah for the sake of His word concerning the promised son and Sarah's faithful obedience to her husband. If his potency had not been restored yet, Abraham may have chosen to risk having Sarah impregnated by the Philistine chieftain. He may have reasoned that it was no worse than his use of Hagar.

Why would Abimelech want an 89-year-old woman as a wife? The likelihood is that he viewed this as a way to form an alliance with Abraham, a wealthy chieftain. Abraham had wealth, a trained army of 318 men, servants, etc. (Gen. 13:6, 14:14). Another possibility is that the hormonal changes in Sarah's body necessary to become pregnant may have reversed some of the changes that occurred during her menopause; her pre-menopausal beauty may have blossomed (Gen. 12:11, 14; 16:1-2; 18:11).

God appeared to Abimelech in a dream as *Elohim*, the Creator. Abimelech may have initially interpreted this name to mean that God was one of many gods; he may have been a polytheist.

Elohim is the name of God used in the first chapter of Genesis to describe the creation. God may have used this name to denote that the critical question was whether Abimelech would interfere with His creative act in Sarah to conceive the promised son. If he did not let Sarah go, He threatened Abimelech with death.

Since Abimelech had not touched Sarah, he stated that he had acted in the "integrity of my heart and **the innocence of my hands**." He pled for himself and his people (Gen. 20:4-5). Furthermore, he pointed out that Abraham was the one who had lied. After the threat of his demise, he acknowledged God as Sovereign and Lord (*'ădōnāŷ,* אדני). He rapidly developed a higher opinion of the One dealing with him.

God answered him in the dream and affirmed that he did act in the integrity of his heart. However, He did not authenticate that Abimelech acted in the innocence of his hands (page 253). God kept him from touching Sarah: "Then God said to him in the dream, 'Yes, I know that in the integrity of your heart you have done this, and I also kept you from sinning against Me; therefore I did not let you touch her'" (Gen. 20:6).

God accepted Abimelech's plea for himself and his people. Abimelech's relationship with God was not as Sovereign and Lord. God's response to Abimelech was still as *Elohim*, not as *Adonai*. Not everyone who calls God Lord is accepted by Him (Matt. 7:21). If he did not repent and submit to God as his personal Lord, Abimelech's eternal destiny would have been unchanged.

If Abimelech did not restore Sarah to Abraham, God proceeded to repeat the penalty of death, not only to Abimelech but to all that belonged to him in his tribe. The threatened penalty was necessary to ensure that Abimelech did not have sexual intercourse with Sarah and interfere with the miracle birth of the promised son. This would have allowed Satan to trumpet that the conception of Isaac was due to sexual intercourse with an unbeliever.

God told Abimelech that Abraham was a prophet. If he wanted to live, he had to ask Abraham to pray for him. Abimelech was unable to sleep after the dream. He was frightened and recounted the message in the dream from *Elohim* to his servants early the next morning. His men and servants also reacted with great fear.

He then reproached Abraham for bringing this sin upon him and his kingdom. Since God told him that Abraham was a prophet, Abimelech's interaction with Abraham suggests that he believed Abraham had the ability to bring a curse on him (Gen. 12:3, 20:7).

Abraham knew that polytheists interpreted *Elohim* as many gods, not the One Triune God. Abraham believed there was no fear of *Elohim*, the One Triune God, in that place. Nevertheless, his prior experience indicated that God was able to protect His servant from murder in any environment; he failed to trust Him.

Different mothers bore Abram and Sarai, but they had the same father. Abraham gave the weak excuse, the modified truth, that Sarah was his half-sister. However, by so doing, he confessed that Sarah was his wife. He then repeated to Abimelech the faithless charge that he had given to Sarah. She was to declare that she was his sister in order to protect him (Gen. 12:13).

Abraham's persistence in this charade, in spite of all that God had done before in Egypt, was remarkable. However, it points out the fact that many have at least one persistent problem for which faith is weak. God kept His covenant with Abraham, but Abraham failed. Isaac became heir to this same deceitful action several years later (Gen. 26:1-11). Sometimes the same sin, which is secondary to lack of trust in the LORD, is handed down in families.

Abimelech's Sarcasm; Gifts to Abraham

Gen. 20:14-18: Abimelech enriched Abraham with a gift of animals and servants and sarcastically stated to Sarah that he gave "her brother" a thousand pieces of silver. The literal translation is "for you a covering of the eyes," not "your vindication" (Gen. 20:16 NASB margin). This could have been an idiom, but it seems that a literal meaning is justified—Abimelech was apologizing to Sarah for having gazed at her with sexual desire. He offered Abraham to settle anywhere in the land. Abraham settled in Beersheba [map site 14] about 30 miles from Gerar. Beersheba did not belong to Abimelech (Gen. 15:18, 21:14, 31).

Based on the prior promise of *Yahweh*, this would be just before the time of Sarah's conception (Gen. 17:21). Since sexual intercourse with Sarah would have interfered with the conception of the promised son, *Elohim* had produced infertility in the Philistine women as a symbol of the protection given to Sarah who had been infertile in the past. It is likely that Abimelech and the men of his tribe were polygamists. Since many women would have been involved, infertility would have been obvious within three months. Because of the infertility in the other women, Abimelech may have been considering trying to impregnate Sarah. God intervened. Sarah's remarkable obedience demonstrated her faith; *Yahweh* protected her this time also (Gen. 12:10-20).

Abimelech's obedience to the command of *Elohim* resulted in the prayer from Abraham to restore fertility to his household.

Abraham and his seed were to be the means of spreading the good news about *Yahweh* to all mankind. God, through Abimelech, gave to Abraham additional male and female servants, *goyim*. This was one of the ways that Abraham could bless those of other tribes and nations by instructing them in saving faith and obedience to *Yahweh* (Gen. 12:16, 20:14). Many of the rabbis failed to recognize this obvious way God used Abraham to bless individuals from other nations. It was better to be a slave in Abraham's house, and a believer in *Yahweh*, than to dwell in the tents of the wicked (Psa. 84:10).

Laughter—Son of Promise
Beersheba; Abraham, Age 100 to 103

Genesis 21:1-34

Gen. 21:1-7: After the episode with Abimelech, Abraham believed *Yahweh* for the restoration of his potency and the ability to impregnate Sarah. During the previous three months, the restoration of Sarah's pre-menopausal beauty may have been an encouragement to him. Hormonal changes would occur in Sarah's hair, skin, breasts, and reproductive organs. Necessary hormonal changes would also occur in Abraham. During this season of maturity, they both would have rejoiced at a return to earlier, intimate times.

Yahweh fulfilled the promise to both of them. Abraham received his potency and Sarah conceived. The promised son of Abraham and Sarah was born to one who was nearly 15 years past her menopause (Gen. 16:1-2, 18:11; Rom. 4:19; Heb. 11:11). This occurred "at the appointed time" promised by *Yahweh*. However, Sarah was heir to the curse on all women who bear children, to have pain and sorrow in childbirth; she did not complain (Gen. 3:16):

"Look to Abraham your father and to Sarah who gave birth to you in pain; when he was but one I called him, then I blessed him and multiplied him" (Isa. 51:2).

Thus, Isaac ("he laughs," *yitschaq̂,* יצחק) was born at the half-way mark between the creation of Adam and the birth of the Son of Promise, the LORD Jesus Christ, whose miraculous birth came through the Virgin Mary (Appendix III, page 396). The son of promise and the Son of Promise were miraculously born through a post-menopausal woman and a teenage virgin, respectively.

At the age of 100, Abraham's promised son was born. Abraham's and Sarah's laughter were shared with all who heard of the birth and celebrated the name of Isaac given by *Yahweh* to their son. Childbearing is a mark of the blessing of God. Sarah was 90; she rejoiced that her breasts were productive in her old age, and she was able to nurse her son. The circumcision of Isaac was done on the eighth day according to the command of God (Gen. 17:12).

There is a propensity to bleeding in the newborn between the second and fifth days after birth due to low levels of vitamin K. Vitamin K is necessary for the synthesis of prothrombin, a major factor necessary for blood clotting. In the newborn, its concentration is at a peak on the eighth day. This bit of scientific knowledge became available in the 20th century, nearly four millennia after the time of Abraham. Subsequently, the eighth day was also the time selected for dedication of firstborn males who were consecrated to *Yahweh* and for animals offered in sacrifice to God (Exod. 22:29-30; Lev. 12:2-3; 22:19, 27). God, in His compassion, does not want babies of humans and animals to suffer.

II-Isaac, Son of Promise
Ishmael, Son of Flesh

Gen. 21:8-13: Weaning usually occurred when the child was three years old. A feast occurred at the time of weaning. Ishmael would have been 17 years old, Abraham 103, and Sarah 93. The taunting by Ishmael, and Sarah's dismay, resulted in Abraham obeying Sarah's wish to send him away, but only after *Elohim* **spoke** to him (the **ninth** direct communication), even though it distressed him greatly. *Elohim* intervened directly without Abraham's intercession; God is sovereign (Gen. 21:12).

The son of flesh persecuted the son of promise. This gave rise to the Apostle Paul's great discourse on this theme (Gal. 4:22-31). Since his message had to do with the creation of two different nations, God spoke as *Elohim*. Hagar was Abraham's maid, not Sarah's maid; he was responsible for her (page 178):

"But God said to Abraham, 'Do not be distressed because of the lad and your maid; Whatever Sarah tells you, listen to her, for through Isaac your seed will be called'" (Gen. 21:12 NASB margin).

ISHMAEL'S LIFE-II

God's Protection and Blessing of Hagar and Ishmael

Gen. 21:14-21: Because he was Abraham's seed, the promise that Ishmael would become a great nation would come to fulfillment. Abraham gave Hagar and Ishmael a supply of bread and a skin of water; they departed. Presumably, there was enough bread and water to get Hagar and Ishmael back to Egypt. Abraham must have given her instructions about springs, roads, etc. However, Hagar lost her way.

Hagar was stronger than her teenage son, but she was not accustomed to life in the wilderness. They wandered about in the wilderness of Beersheba. They were out of water. They were near, or in, the wilderness that Hagar had been in at the time she ran away from Sarah when she was pregnant with Ishmael (Gen. 16:6-14). She would have recalled the promise given 17 years previously by *Yahweh* about Ishmael (Gen. 16:10-12). Now she needed further clarification as to how the blessing could come to

Ishmael. Clearly, he was not the promised son, or they would not be in their present predicament.

The pathos of the weeping of Hagar and Ishmael's crying resulted in *Elohim* speaking to her from heaven. He had visited her in person on that previous occasion and promised her that Ishmael would become a great nation. This time He came using His name, *Elohim*, renewing His creative promise to her. He had compassion on Ishmael's crying, but He spoke to Hagar; she was the one who needed to understand what the promise really meant. He told her not to fear; He had heard the agonizing cry of Ishmael.

In her previous excursion into the wilderness, Hagar had called the place *Beer-Lahai-Roi*, "the well of the Living One who sees me" (Gen. 16:14 NASB margin). However, the present well was not one with "living water," i.e., a spring. She was unable to see the well due to her anguish and weeping; *Elohim* directed her attention to the well. It is likely that it was a hole in the ground, so it would have been difficult to see.

Many times in life, we are unable to see the LORD's provision for us due to similar distress. The LORD has to open our eyes, so we can see that His solution is already present. It is necessary to see the solution with the eyes of faith before observing with our physical eyes.

We often find ourselves in places of the past with no apparent progress. Hagar had gone from the height of believing that Ishmael would be the promised son of Abraham to the depth of seeing another claim that right and the rejection of both of them. She needed to hear from the One who gave the promise, possibly near the place of His original revelation to her (pages 179-180).

It was an experience of faith for Ishmael. Ishmael ("God hears," *yishma'e'l*, ישמעאל) did not see God who was just a bowshot away, but he undoubtedly **heard** the voice of *Elohim* who saved him. Thus, it is clear why *Elohim* spoke from heaven instead of appearing in person as He did the first time (Gen. 16:7). Hearing the voice of God must have brought Ishmael to personal faith in

Him. Since Ishmael means "God hears," the prophecy of his name was fulfilled for him, not just for his mother. Since he was "gathered to his people" (*y'aŝaph 'el̂ 'amiv,* ויאסף אל־עמיו) at the end of his life, he was saved. "Gathered to his people" denotes a believer in *Yahweh* going to a family reunion (Gen. 25:17).

Hagar and Ishmael were protected by *Elohim* and sent forth to dwell in the Wilderness of Paran [map site 22]. Their rejection caused both to desire to live away from other people. They were in the wilderness; they would conquer the wilderness. Ishmael became an archer. His mother, an Egyptian, obtained an Egyptian wife for him.

Abraham's Life—III

The Covenant with Abimelech

Gen. 21:22-34: The Philistine chieftain, Abimelech, brought the commander of his army, Phicol, with him to make a covenant with Abraham, even though they were separated by about 30 miles. Their last meeting had been three years earlier (Gen. 20:1-18). It is probable that that incident, the history of the victory of Abraham and his allies over the five kings, Abraham's personal army, and the observation that *Elohim* was with Abraham, a prophet, prompted the visit (Gen. 21:22). Abimelech feared for himself and his progeny. He may have expected an attack from Abraham, perhaps as revenge for the episode with Sarah. Since he came after the time of Isaac's weaning, he may have been afraid that the newborn son would continue a vendetta against his progeny in coming generations (Gen. 21:23). The leaders of this world project on godly leaders their own motives and actions.

Abraham covenanted with Abimelech but reproved him for the loss of a well (page 255). Abimelech pleaded ignorance; that was unlikely. Abraham gave to Abimelech sheep and oxen, even though there was no reciprocity on Abimelech's part. This may have been due to Abimelech's generosity with sheep, oxen, servants, and a thousand pieces of silver following the previous episode with Sarah (Gen. 20:14-16).

Abraham set apart seven ewe lambs to symbolize the covenant. Seven is the perfect number in Scripture (Gen. 2:2-3). Ewe lambs would be productive. Beersheba literally means "the well of the seven." After this event, its additional name was "the well of the oath" (Gen. 21:31). Abraham acted in the Spirit of his LORD and Savior.

Abimelech returned "to the land of the Philistines." This statement verifies that Abimelech's bravado in claiming that Abraham was living on his land was false (Gen. 21:23, 32). Abimelech did not own Beersheba (Gen. 15:18; 21:14, 31). Therefore, it is likely that the last verse of this chapter is a summary verse of the experience of Abraham "in the land of the Philistines."

Tamarisk trees are **evergreen**. Therefore, Abraham planted a tamarisk tree and called on "*Yahweh*, the **Everlasting** *El* (God)." *Yahweh* was the one who made the perfect covenant with Abraham.

Abraham's promised son foreshadowed the promised Son of God. The covenant included blessing for those who blessed Abraham and cursing to the one who cursed him. In this incident, the Philistines received a covenant of peace with Abraham, the servant of *Yahweh* (Gen. 12:3, 20:17). The LORD ever takes sin and turns it about for good for repentant and obedient believers; Abraham had ceased his wandering (Gen. 50:20).

The Offering of the Son of Promise
Mount Moriah; Abraham, Age 117?

Genesis 22:1-24

Gen. 22:1-14: "After these things," i.e., the events of the 21st chapter are connected to the events of this chapter. The birth of Isaac fulfilled *Yahweh's* promise to Abraham about his promised son. Abraham had already sent Hagar and Ishmael into the wilderness, so Ishmael would not be an heir with Isaac (Gen. 21:14, 21). Since this is the next major event, there must be a correlation with the story of Hagar and Ishmael in the previous chapter. Abraham sent Ishmael away at the age of 17 when he was a "lad" (*na'ar,* נער). Since Isaac is described by the same Hebrew word, "lad" (*na'ar,* נער), it may suggest that he was similar in age to Ishmael when he was sent away (Gen. 22:5). If so, the timing of the command would have been particularly stressful to Abraham. Since the weaning of Isaac and the departure of Hagar and Ishmael, it is possible that 14 years had elapsed.

Elohim tested Abraham and **spoke** to him (the **tenth** direct communication). Abraham went on a three-day journey from Beersheba to Mount Moriah [map site 6] followed by a three-day journey back to Beersheba, "the well of the sevenfold oath." The covenant and oath that *Yahweh* had made to Abraham about the promised son was the major consideration (Gen. 15:1-6). Moriah means "chosen by *Yah*" (*moȓiŷaȟ,* מריה) (Gen. 22:14).

Since Abraham rose early in the morning to carry out the command, this tenth communication must have occurred during the nighttime hours. *Elohim* seemed to require the sacrifice of the son of promise at a specific location, one of the peaks of Mount Moriah.

Abraham had to decide if *Elohim* was one of many gods of the surrounding nations who demanded child sacrifice. He knew *Elohim* as the Creator, the One Triune God. Abraham had to reconcile the demand for child sacrifice with the character of *Yahweh* and His promise concerning Isaac. Abraham's familiarity with God's voice, and His messages through the previous nine direct communications with him, convinced him that this was *Elohim*, the One Triune God.

Although Abraham took two young men with him, he split the wood for the sacrifice. This was a sign of total obedience; he did the menial job of preparing the wood for the sacrifice.

Abraham expressed his faith and understanding of *Elohim* as the One Triune God, and *Yahweh* as the One who had covenanted with him, by telling the young men that he and Isaac would go to the mountain **to worship and return** to them. He believed that obedience and sacrificial giving to God were acts of worship. Furthermore, if the sacrifice were carried to completion, his understanding of the character of *Yahweh Elohim* demanded that He raise Isaac from the dead (Gen. 22:5, Heb. 11:17-19). Abraham, the father, and Isaac, the promised son, foreshadowed the offering of a life totally consumed for the Father by the Son of God on the cross of Calvary followed by His resurrection. The burnt offering was the offering totally consumed; it illustrated the life totally consumed for *Yahweh* (Lev. 1:9). The LORD Jesus Christ's goal was to obey the Father, to be consumed doing the Father's will (John 17:1-8).

The young men were to stay with the donkey. They had walked all the way from Beersheba to Mount Moriah (Gen. 22:5-6). The donkey carried the wood. They transferred the wood from the donkey onto Isaac's back. Since Isaac was able to carry all the wood for the sacrifice, he was at least a teenager. If Isaac were 17, Abraham would have been 117 years old. Abraham was still in prime physical condition. Abraham prepared the wood; Isaac carried it. In the future, the Father would prepare the cross for his Son to die for the sins of the world; the Son would bear the wood of that cross (Isa. 53:1-12; John 3:14-21, 19:17).

The place was one of "the mountains" (*h'harim,* ההרים) of Moriah (Gen. 22:2). Abraham "saw the place **from a distance.**" He may have been instructed to look for the highest peak on Mount Moriah, 777 meters. Sacrifice usually was carried out at the highest level. The temple built by Solomon on Mount Moriah is believed to have been at a lower level, 741 meters; the present temple site is at this height (2 Sam. 24:1-25, 1 Chr. 21:1-30, 2 Chr. 3:1).[67]

Some historical and archeological findings support the highest peak on Mount Moriah, 777 meters, as the place of the crucifixion. If so, God saw the place of the offering of Abraham's son as the place where the Father would see His Son become the sacrifice for the sins of the world.[68]

Abraham answered Isaac's question about the provision of the lamb for the sacrifice by telling him that *Elohim Yireh* would be the sacrifice. The literal translation is, "*Elohim* sees Himself the Lamb for the burnt offering my son" (אלהים יראה־לו השׂה לעלה בני) (Gen. 22:8a). Isaac's acceptance of his father's explanation for the absence of the lamb for a sacrifice indicated that Isaac had had previous conversations with his father about the subject of the promised Seed who would come, the Lamb of God.

Abraham foresaw the day when the Lamb of God would live a sinless life and die as a burnt offering, a life totally consumed by obedience to His Father:

"Your father Abraham rejoiced to see My day, and he saw it and was glad.' So the Jews said to Him, 'You are not yet fifty years old, and have You seen Abraham?' Jesus said to them, 'Truly, truly, I say to you, before Abraham was born, I am'" (John 8:56-58).

Abraham had been told previously that it was in his "seed" (sg. noun, *zera'*, זרע) that all the nations of the earth would be blessed (Gen. 15:5, 17:7, 26:4; Gal. 3:15-16, 29). By faith, Abraham had received the promised son. He would have observed that Isaac was not perfect. Abraham must have understood that there would be a perfect Seed that would provide redemption and resurrection for him, for Isaac, and those in the world that would believe in Him (John 3:16-21). Isaac was willing to trust his father and his father's God, even as his father obeyed and trusted Him. Abraham modeled faith to his son.

Isaac must have voluntarily allowed Abraham to bind him. It is likely that Isaac could have successfully wrestled with his father and run. However, he submitted and demonstrated his trust in his father and his father's God. Abraham built the altar, took the wood from Isaac, arranged the wood on the altar, and bound Isaac. Then Abraham laid him on top of the wood; he was still a strong man (Gen. 22:9). The day would come when the promised Son would voluntarily be nailed to a cross that the Father placed Him on and become the sacrifice for the sins of the world; He too, trusted His

Father (John 3:14-16). The Son of the Father also would become a guilt offering to produce a righteous "seed" (zeraʿ, זרע):

"But the LORD was pleased to crush Him, putting Him to grief; if He would render Himself as a guilt offering, He will see His offspring, He will prolong His days, and the good pleasure of the LORD will prosper in His hand" (Isa. 53:10).

Upon seeing Abraham with Isaac bound and the upraised hand with the knife in it, *Yahweh* stopped Abraham. In this circumstance faith had to be carried nearly to "execution" before it could be honored by *Yahweh* (James 2:20-24). God commanded as *Elohim* and intervened as *Yahweh*. Abraham was correct; ***Elohim Yireh*** was ***Yahweh Yireh*** (Gen. 22:8, 14).

"*Yireh*" (*yiraʾaĥ,* יראה) means "He sees"; when the LORD sees, He acts.

"The LORD will provide," literally means, "*Yahweh* sees" (יהוה יראה). (Gen. 22:14a).

Both statements are true: "*Yahweh* sees" and "*Elohim* sees." Therefore, this statement must be connected to the prior one, "*Elohim* sees Himself the Lamb for the burnt offering my son" (אלהים יראה־לו השׂה לעלה בני) (Gen. 22:8a).

In the great mystery of the sacrifice on Calvary's cross, the One Triune God, *Elohim*, would participate as Father, Son, and Holy Spirit, but the Angel of *Yahweh,* the Son, the one "chosen by *Yah*" (*moȓiŷaĥ,* מריה) would be the One on the cross.

This experience for Isaac of being bound on the altar, seeing his father's upraised hand with a knife in it, and the halting of the sacrifice by **the voice** from heaven (the **11th** direct communication) of the Angel of *Yahweh*, the LORD Jesus Christ, explains Isaac's personal name for God, "the Fear of Isaac." This was the name that Isaac used early in his spiritual development (Gen. 31:42, 53). Fear can be a motivating factor in the initiation and continuation of gaining personal knowledge of the LORD, but it should eventually lead to a greater understanding of God's character and His love (Prov. 1:7, Matt. 11:28-30).

The revelation of three more names of God occurs in this chapter: *Elohim Yireh*, "*Elohim* sees" (*'eľoȟiŷm raʿaȟ,* אלהים יראה), *Yahweh Yireh,* "*Yahweh* sees" (*YHWH raʿaȟ,* יהוה יראה), and the Fear of Isaac (page 51) (Gen. 31:53).

The LORD Jesus Christ's sacrifice would take place in the future on Calvary's cross on Mount Moriah, the site "chosen by *Yah*" (*moȓiŷaȟ,* מריה). *Elohim* did "see Himself the sacrifice." The provision of a ram was symbolic of the guilt offering. That sacrifice would be offered by a young male in the prime of life, the One speaking to Abraham (Lev. 5:14-6:7). Abraham received Isaac back, as it were, from the dead. God the Father would receive His Son back from the dead at the time of His resurrection!

Abraham's Sacrificial Offering

Gen. 22:15-19: After the substitutionary sacrifice of the ram for Isaac, the Angel of *Yahweh* **spoke** again (the **12th** direct communication). This implies that *Yahweh* would not have spoken again unless Abraham had sacrificed the ram. There was no command for Abraham to do so; he acted on his own volition and faith. Abraham understood the need for a substitutionary sacrifice for his son.

Since God spoke of Isaac as Abraham's "only son" three different times in this chapter, God disavowed Ishmael as the promised son (Gen. 22:2, 12, 16).

In verse 17, "seed" is singular with a singular pronoun. A better translation would be, "Your seed (*zeraq,* זרעך) shall possess the gate of **his** enemies (*ayabiv,* איביו)," instead of "their enemies" (Gen. 22:17 NASB margin). Certainly, this was the prophecy of the One who would be sacrificed on Mount Moriah, the One who would come, die, and rise from the dead and rule over **His** enemies. The LORD defeated His enemies, Satan and those who yield allegiance to him.

The covenant was renewed, but this time the simile changes from dust of the earth to the stars of the heavens and the sand of the seashore. Believers are creatures made from the dust of the earth. The action of the sea on the dust of the earth is to form sand. This action illustrates the continual cleansing, sometimes abrasive scrubbing, of believers by the Spirit of God until they become sand, crystals without adherent dirt. That process allows them to triumph over their enemies through this cleansing action by the Holy Spirit. Believers will graduate to become the stars of heaven. After the test at Mount Moriah, the confirmation of the promises of *Yahweh* was given to Abraham. Through his seed, the blessing would go to the nations of the earth (Gen. 13:16, 22:17).

Abraham then returned with Isaac and the two young men to Beersheba, the Well of the Sevenfold Oath. Thus, Abraham received further confirmation of *Yahweh*'s promise and oath.

Relatives of Abraham

Gen. 22:20-24: A list follows with the names of the eight sons of Nahor and Milcah, Abraham's brother and niece, respectively, and the four sons of Nahor's concubine, Reumah. The 12 sons mirror the eventual 12 sons of Jacob, the son of Isaac. Specific mention is made of Bethuel, the father of Rebekah who would become Isaac's bride. The son of Kemuel ("raised of God," *qemu'el,* קמואל), Aram, was the only grandson mentioned. This suggests that he was the one after whom Paddan-Aram ("the plateau of Aram," *paddan 'aram,* פדן ארם) was named.

Progeny from five different sources would form part of the Middle Eastern nations other than Israel: Nahor, Ishmael, and Esau; two additional peoples came through Lot and his daughters, Moab and Ammon; and at a later time, the six sons of Keturah and Abraham were added (Gen. 19:30-38; 25:1-4, 16; 36:40-43).

Today, the progeny of these men are devotees of Muhammad who espouse the Islamic religion that proclaims Ishmael as the promised son. They have all become enemies of Israel, the nation that accepts Isaac as the promised son. Unfortunately, Israel has rejected its promised Son, the Messiah (*maŝhiŷach,* מָשִׁיחַ).

Why does this genealogy come right after the incident at Mount Moriah? Abraham's role was to produce one son, the promised son who engendered the nation of Israel through his grandson. Jacob, Abraham's grandson, would be the one to produce 12 sons whose families evolved to become the nation of Israel. That seed would engender the Messiah through the seed of a Jewish virgin (Isa. 7:13-14, Luke 1:26-37). The LORD Jesus Christ came to bless all nations. He would fulfill the promise He gave to Abraham and Sarah to be the father and mother of a multitude of nations.

Sarah's Homegoing, Age 127
Machpelah; Abraham, Age 137

Genesis 23:1-20

If Abraham were 117 years old during the episode in the 22nd chapter, he would have been 20 years older, or 137, at the time of Sarah's death at the age of 127. Sarah's Biblical epitaph includes a record of her age, a unique honor among the women of the Bible. Sarah died at Kiriath-arba, "the city of the four" (*qiryath 'arba',* קרית ארבע), also known as Hebron, "an association or an alliance" (*chebrôn,* חברון).

This was the place where Abraham made a covenant with Mamre, Eshcol, and Aner, and thus, was formerly known as "the oaks of Mamre" (Gen. 14:13). The names suggest a gradual transfer from dominant individuals like Mamre and his brothers to the four giants driven out by Caleb at the time of the conquest: Anak, Sheshai, Ahiman, and Talmi. After the conquest, it became the city of Hebron (Josh. 15:13-14). Thus, the names of Kiriath-arba and Hebron occurred subsequent to the time of Abraham.

Abraham would live to be 175 years of age (Gen. 25:7). Most of the events recorded in Abraham's life occurred between 75 and 140 years of age, just 65 of those years. Believers may live many years before they are ready to carry out special assignments given by the LORD. The early years are training years that prepare for such assignments. All believers have one major task to perform in their old age, to pass their experience and knowledge of the LORD to the following generations, their children and grandchildren. Abraham became a mentor to his twin grandsons for 15 years before his death (Tables 8 and 9, page 390).

Believers are to live in peace with all men whenever possible (Rom. 12:18). Abraham had a positive witness in this city. The fact that Sarah died at Hebron indicates that they had moved from Beersheba back to Hebron (Gen. 14:13, 22:19, 23:2). Abraham and Sarah wished to die at their old family homestead.

Upon her death, Abraham purchased the only ground he would possess during his lifetime in the Promised Land. This was the field and cave at Machpelah [map site 12], which became the family burial site for Abraham and Sarah, Isaac and Rebekah, and Jacob and Leah. Since those buried there would all have faith in *Yahweh*, this was a commemorative site for the transition from earth to Paradise. For Old Testament saints, "Abraham's bosom" would become another name for Paradise (Luke 16:22, 23:43).

Abraham introduced himself to the sons of Heth, "sons of terror," as "a stranger and a sojourner among you." All believers are strangers and sojourners in this world. They await the Promised Land of Israel during the millennium; their final destination will be the new heaven and earth.

That evil clan knew that Abraham was "a prince of God" and recognized that God, *Elohim*, had blessed and protected him (Gen. 23:6 NASB margin). They were polytheists and would have interpreted *Elohim* as many gods, but they may have acknowledged the One Triune God, *Elohim*, through Abraham's witness. Abraham appealed to their "soul" (*nephesh,* נפש), not their "wish." Sarah's soul had departed; it was a solemn and spiritual occasion (Gen. 23:8). The Scriptural record continues with an ancient Middle Eastern negotiation of a contract. Each party was polite and "gave," not bought or sold the property.

"Abraham bowed before the people of the land" (Gen. 23:12). Even though he had a reputation as "a mighty prince," he negotiated according to custom and in a peaceful manner with the ungodly (Gen. 23:6). His spiritual heirs have the same obligation in dealing with unbelievers.

Machpelah comes from a Hebrew root that means "a double portion" (*makpel̂ah̑,* מכפלה). Machpelah's name occurs at the beginning of the negotiation; its name anticipated the event, possibly due to the presence of the field and cave (Gen. 23:9). Abraham asked to buy the cave only. Ephron the Hittite offered him the field and cave for 400 shekels of silver. Abraham paid the price without argument. He departed from the usual method of negotiation. One suspects that the name of the place, Machpelah, reflected the necessity of buying both the field and the cave. In addition, it might have cost double the going rate. Special note is given that the deed included the field with all its trees as well as the cave (Gen. 23:17).

The seller, Ephron the Hittite, probably believed that Abraham was naïve in accepting a high price without negotiation. However, there are times that a believer's witness is more important than the loss of money; Abraham judged this time of mourning to be such an occasion. He did not haggle over the purchase of his wife's gravesite and wished to honor her at the stated price without argument. He may have selected a beautiful site to commemorate Sarah's physical and spiritual beauty.

Believers will undergo many different kinds of burials: in caves, in soil, in water, by fire, or simple decay above ground. They should give each other wide latitude in the method used for disposal of their earthly bodies. Regardless of the method, because of the promise of the one who conquered death, they will rise again (Heb. 2:9-15).

Abraham's Faithful Servant
Hebron; Abraham, Age 140

Genesis 24:1-67

Gen. 24:1-61: Three years after the death of Sarah, when Abraham was 140 years old, he sent his servant to his relatives in Nahor, previously Haran, to obtain a wife for Isaac (Gen. 25:20). When Nahor came from Ur of the Chaldees to claim his inheritance after his father died, he renamed the city after himself; he was a proud man (Gen. 11:31; 24:10).

Yahweh had blessed Abraham in every way: physically, mentally, and spiritually. Even though he was old, he would marry again and produce six more sons (Gen. 25:1-6). By faith, the restoration of his potency in his 99th year continued for a half-century or more.

The story of singular obedience and faith of the oldest servant of Abraham, possibly Eliezer of Damascus, is thrilling and instructive (Gen. 15:2). If this was Eliezer of Damascus, he is another example of Abraham's carrying the good news of *Yahweh* to individuals from other lands. Let us review the remarkable characteristics of this trusted servant who is an example for all in obedience to the LORD.

1. His master trusted his oldest servant; this speaks of a long period of faithful service to his lord. He was in charge of all that Abraham owned. Considering the wealth and number of servants that Abraham possessed, he judged him a remarkably competent and trustworthy steward.

2. Abraham invited him to swear through placement of his hand under Abraham's thigh, a picture of an intimate method for sealing an oath and a symbol of the importance of Abraham's seed (Gen. 24:2, 9).

3. Abraham asked him to swear in the name of *Yahweh*, Creator of heaven and earth. The servant was a believer. Abraham

had faithfully taught him about God and His names. One suspects that he had heard the testimony of the 12 interactions between Abraham and *Yahweh* many times.

4. The servant was careful to clarify the boundaries of his charge to obtain a wife for Isaac from Abraham's country and relatives with absolutely no option for obtaining a wife from Canaan.

5. He received the promise from Abraham that *Yahweh* would send His angel before him to guide him. He believed this, and the subsequent story substantiated his belief.

6. Only if the chosen woman refused to accompany him could he be relieved of his commission. After being sure of his charge, he agreed to swear to the oath.

7. He was an overseer of Abraham's possessions and did not ask what he could or could not take with him. Abraham trusted him and delegated authority to him over his entire household; Abraham was not a micro-manager. The servant chose ten camels, their baggage, and selected servants to take with him. The gifts that he would give to Rebekah, Laban, and Milcah verified his careful selection.

8. He looked for a woman at a water fountain at eventide when the flocks were watered. If there were many wells in the district, the well fed by a spring would be the choice one (Gen. 24:13, 20, 42). His possible selection of a shepherdess meant he was looking for a young girl of marriageable age, trustworthy, and used to hard work. The servant used the common sense that God had given to him.

9. He prayed for God's wisdom and direction. His prayer was to *Yahweh*, the *Elohim* of his master. The prayer was silent and specific (Gen. 24:12-15). His prayer indicated his belief that God arranges marriages for His children who trust Him. He wanted *Yahweh* to show him the one He had "appointed for Your servant

Isaac." He wanted a, young lady who was polite to strangers and industrious enough to volunteer to draw water for ten camels.

Such a young girl might be curious about a wealthy stranger coming to their village and might be motivated by that alone. However, the servant knew that *Yahweh* could change young people who had less than forthright motives (page 238).

10. The answer came as he was completing his silent prayer. It verified that *Yahweh* had indeed sanctioned Abraham's word to go before him and had honored the servant's faithfulness. Rebekah was a virgin and very beautiful, positive characteristics provided by the LORD. In addition, she had "not known" (*lo yâdah*ʻ, לא ידעה) any man, testimony of no sexual interaction of any type with the opposite sex.

After he had observed her going to and from the spring, sensing the answer to his prayer, he ran to meet Rebekah. She addressed him with respect as "my lord." Many young people who choose to disrespect their elders and foreigners may lose God's special blessings in their lives (Gen. 24:17-18).

11. She answered according to the specific requirements of his prayer. He was not content to have her volunteer to water the camels; he waited for her to complete the task. Since camels drink a lot of water after a journey, this took some time. Since she started at eventide, it must have been dark before she finished. (Oh for a restoration of the time when young women are safe in the presence of strangers after dark!) Before inquiring about her family, he rewarded her with gifts; this elicited her cooperation. She received a nose ring and bracelets (pl. noun, *tsâmîŷd,* צמידים) that were for "one hand" (*yâdiĥ,* על־ידיה).

The placement of more than one bracelet on one hand means the wrist was considered part of the hand. An amplification occurs in Ezekiel where the wrists are described as "the joints of the hand" (*kol̂ 'atstsiŷl yâdi,̂* כל־אצילי ידי) (Ezek. 13:18). This Biblical understanding that the hand includes the wrist area is informative in understanding the placement of the spikes, not simple nails, in the wrists, not hands, of the LORD at His crucifixion. The medical and historical evidence indicates the spikes went through the indentation between the carpal bones of the lower wrist area, not the middle of the palm. If they had penetrated the LORD's palms, the spikes would have ripped through between his fingers, since there would have been no way to immobilize them.

When the servant enquired about her family, she volunteered to have him lodge with them. The servant had not revealed his identity yet. Her family was wealthy; they had lodging for a caravan with ten camels. Her answers verified that she had position in the family; she had authority to provide lodging for a stranger. Her offer also suggests the aggressive character of this young woman. Her curiosity was piqued. She knew her brother Laban's materialistic outlook on life; he would be interested in a stranger who gave gifts and had ten camels of merchandise.

12. After the confirmation of his silent prayer, he immediately bowed low in worship and thanksgiving to *Yahweh*, a testimony to all that were present. The content of this public prayer that mentioned Abraham and *Yahweh*, the *Elohim* of his master, caused Rebekah to run and relate the entire incident to her mother's household.

It is a beautiful love story written by God for two of His special children. It is likely that Rebekah would repeat this story to Jacob, just before he would leave home, nearly a century in the future (page 271) (Gen. 29:2-3).

13. After Laban saw the ring and bracelets and listened to Rebekah's story, he ran to meet the servant of Abraham. The servant identified himself to Laban as Abraham's servant; he never revealed his name in the whole story. He was a humble man, not seeking his own honor. He sought his master's honor and interests.

Laban invoked the name of *Yahweh* as though he were a believer. Laban was not a worshiper of *Yahweh*; he still worshiped the Babylonian pantheon of gods (Gen. 31:19). He probably knew of Abraham and the fact that he worshiped *Yahweh*. Abram had left Ur of the Chaldees, and subsequently, Haran, because of *Yahweh's* call. Otherwise *Yahweh* was just the name of another god to Laban. His use of this holy name merely indicated that Rebekah had accurately related the account of the servant's prayer to Laban.

Laban unloaded the camels and provided fodder for them, not allowing the servants brought from Abraham's household or his own servants to do this. He wanted to be alone as he took inventory of the merchandise in the loads carried by the camels.

14. Abraham's servant accepted the hospitality of feet washing after the journey. He broke custom by refusing to eat until he had stated his mission. Accepting a meal would have allowed his host to try to influence him; he would be under obligation to him for his hospitality. He received permission to speak. Thus, he continued to hold the stronger hand in the negotiations that followed.

15. He credited *Yahweh*'s blessing to Abraham for his wealth and the miraculous birth of an heir through Sarah. Since Nahor's progeny amounted to 12 sons, comparatively speaking, Abraham's fathering one child was a minor event (Gen. 22:20-24). On the other hand, all of Abraham's inheritance would go to Isaac.

16. He recounted the specifics of his journey, his prayer, and the answer given as testimony to *Yahweh*'s faithfulness. He bore witness that the task given to him came from *Yahweh* through his master.

He reversed the order of his inquiry to Rebekah and the time that he gave her the gifts. He stated that he asked about the family prior to giving gifts to Rebekah. He wanted them to understand that they must give their answer before he gave them any gifts.

He indicated that he would be free of his oath to Abraham, regardless of what they decided concerning Rebekah. He did not pressure or manipulate. He indicated that *Yahweh* had appointed Rebekah for his master's son. If they did not release her to go with him, he was inferring that they would be disobeying *Yahweh*. If they refused, he believed that God had another to take her place. He invited a righteous response:

"So now if you are going to show lovingkindness and truth to my master, tell me; and if not, let me know, that I may turn to the right hand or to the left" (Gen. 24:49 NASB margin)

17. His testimony to Bethuel and Laban, father and son, respectively, was accepted. Since Laban seemed to be in charge, it is likely that Bethuel was old, perhaps in poor health.

"The matter comes from *Yahweh*; we cannot speak to you bad or good" (Gen. 24:50b). Laban would repeat this answer to Jacob 117 years later. On that future occasion, he would use the name, *Elohim*, not *Yahweh* (page 285). They understood the message of Abraham's servant; as polytheists they were unwilling to offend any of the gods. They gave permission, without qualification, for Rebekah to go with them. It would be a good match with the potential for a possible increase in the family's wealth. Abraham's servant again bore testimony by bowing to the ground to *Yahweh*.

18. Until they accepted his request to take Rebekah to Isaac, Abraham's servant did not give gifts to the family. He correctly analyzed their materialism (Gen. 24:30, 31:38-42). His insight about the character of Laban would be substantiated by his future interactions with Jacob. The text suggests that Rebekah received more gifts than her mother and Laban. This may have served as an inducement to Rebekah to accompany him back to Isaac. Abraham's servant was careful in the use of his master's possessions; most of these gifts returned home with Rebekah.

19. He did not allow the family members to change their minds and use a delaying tactic the next day. Laban's wish to negotiate further gain probably came from his knowledge of the produce on the ten camels; he wanted more. They transferred the decision to Rebekah who immediately agreed to go with Abraham's servant.

20. The servant had understood Rebekah's curiosity about a stranger that had ten camels and servants. She may have been

attracted to the wealth that Isaac would inherit; after all, her upbringing was in a materialistic home. He knew that the LORD overcomes such traits in young people (page 234). The LORD calls young people and changes their aspirations and their character to become obedient believers.

21. The servant did not pressure Rebekah to go with him. Once the family allowed Rebekah to make her own decision, he simply waited to hear her response. It would not do to bring home a reluctant bride. His insight into Rebekah's character was correct. The family could not "lose face," so they sent Rebekah with her maids and her nurse. Deborah, her nurse, must have been older than Rebekah and her maids (page 307). Deborah would eventually become the nurse of Jacob and his children (Gen. 35:8).

The family gave Rebekah a prophetic blessing:

"And may your descendants possess the gate of those who hate them" (Gen. 24:60b).

Laban subsequently acted hatefully to Jacob, Rebekah's seed; the blessing Laban pronounced would come back in judgment to him (page 288).

Summary Comments on the Faithful Servant

Abraham's servant bypassed Hebron and completed his mission by bringing Rebekah to Isaac. Abraham did not ask to inspect Rebekah before giving her to Isaac. The servant knew that the bride needed to meet her husband first, not her father-in-law.

The servant took no credit for his role in the undertaking; this story is his Biblical epitaph. He successfully served *Yahweh* by serving his master. God often places people in positions of trust and servanthood to develop their character and relationship with Him. If this servant was Eliezer of Damascus, which seems likely, when Isaac was born, he lost the inheritance (Gen. 15:2). He showed no evidence of discontent about this. However, he did receive a spiritual inheritance from Abraham as revealed by this chapter in the Bible. He delighted to serve his lord, always placing the name of his lord above his own. He is a model to all in service to the LORD of heaven and earth. He trusted *Yahweh* and served Him by serving Abraham. He completed his mission when he delivered Rebekah to Isaac:

"The servant told Isaac all the things that he had done" (Gen. 24:66).

Gen. 24:62-67, 25:11: Isaac's awe of Abraham may have played a role in his leaving home. It is possible that Abraham had already married Keturah, but the recorded sequence suggests that that occurred after Isaac's marriage (Gen. 25:1). The servant knew that Isaac was not living at home. Sometime after his mother's death, he left Hebron and dwelt in the Negev, the south country, in his mother's tent. He wanted to be around his old homestead and the things that reminded him of his mother. In addition, he wanted his mother's tent to be the home of his wife.

He had just visited *Beer-Lahai-Roi*, the place where Hagar met with *Yahweh* when she was pregnant with Ishmael and cast out by Sarah. The fact that Isaac was dwelling in the Negev near *Beer-Lahai-Roi* suggests that he was on good terms with Ishmael who lived with his mother in the Wilderness of Paran, south of *Beer-Lahai-Roi* (Gen. 21:21, 25:18).

Isaac was in the field at eventide. He may have been meditating or looking for the arrival of his bride. He may have heard the sound of the camels and looked up.

A possible translation of the name of Rebekah is "to ensnare with beauty" (*ribqaĥ*, רבקה). Sarah never had the opportunity to see her daughter-in-law. It is likely that she designed bridal clothes, jewelry, and other gifts for her. In anticipation of her meeting with Isaac, the servant must have given the jewelry and bridal garments to Rebekah to wear; Isaac would have recognized them. Both Isaac and Rebekah "lifted up his/her eyes" and saw each other (Gen. 24:63-64). Surely this is poetic authentication of *Yahweh*'s benediction on a marriage arranged in heaven.

Rebekah modestly covered her face with her veil. Isaac received her as a chaste virgin who was clothed and bejeweled in items familiar to him. She is a picture of the bride of the LORD (Song 4:1-16, Rev. 14:3-5). At the age of 40, Isaac took Rebekah, as his wife into his mother's tent. It is probable that Rebekah was still a teenager. Isaac loved her and was comforted three years after his mother's death.

The beauty and simplicity of this union goes far beyond the description of an ornate wedding feast that is absent from the record. The size and festivity of the wedding ceremony does not determine the love of a couple designed for each other by the living LORD.

THE SIX SONS OF ABRAHAM AND KETURAH

Abraham's Only Wife Was Sarah—Their Heir Was Isaac

Genesis 25:1-34

Gen. 25:1-6: Sometime after Sarah's death, and probably after Rebekah came to comfort Isaac as his wife, Abraham, around 140 years of age, married Keturah ("incense or perfume," *qẹṭûrāĥ,* קְטוּרָה) who bore him six more sons. Abraham retained his potency as a gift from *Yahweh* in whom he trusted. Since she bore six sons, Keturah had to have been a young woman.

When they were adults, Abraham gave gifts to their sons and sent them to the land of the east, so there would be no interference with the inheritance of Isaac (Gen. 25:6, 37:25-28). This may have been a short time before Abraham's death at 175 years of age. Sixteen names are recorded in their progeny.

Abraham became the father of a multitude of nations (Gen. 17:5-6). The progeny of Abraham and Keturah are part of the Arabic nations that would be scattered throughout the Arabian Peninsula. The list includes six sons, seven grandsons, and three people-groups. Some of their names suggest future interactions that would take place between Israel and these Arabic tribes. For example, a princess from Midian ("strife," *midyañ*, מדין) was involved in the sexually transmitted disease outbreak at Baal-Peor (Num. 25:15); in the future, the Queen of Sheba would visit King Solomon (1 Kin. 10:1), etc.

1. Zimran ("musician," *zimrañ*, זמרן)

2. Jokshan ("ensnarer," *yoqshañ*, יקשן)

3. Medan ("contention," *medañ*, מדן)

4. Midian ("strife," *midyañ*, מדין)—Moses' wife came from Midian (Exod. 2:15-21)

5. Ishbak ("leave alone," *shebaq*, שבק)

6. Shuah ("wealth," *shu'a'*, שועא)

7. Sheba ("seven," *sheba'*, שבא); perhaps he was the ancestor of the Queen of Sheba. He may have settled in southern Arabia (1 Kin. 10:1)

8. Dedan ("low country," *dedañ*, דדן)

9. Asshurim ("Assyrians," *ashshurim*, אשורם)

10. Letushim ("hammered," *letushim*, לטושם)

11. Leummim ("communities," *le'ummiym*, לאמי)

12. Ephah ("gloomy," *'eyphah*, עיפה)

13. Epher ("gazelle," *'epher*, עפר)

14. Hannoch ("dedicated," *chañok*, חנוך)

15. Abida ("father of knowledge," *'abiyda'*, אבידע)

16. Eldaah ("god of knowledge," *'elda'ah,* אלדעה)

The plural noun, "concubines," suggests that Ishmael, the son of Hagar, was included as a concubine's son. There are careful Biblical records of all of Abraham's progeny. Sarah was the only wife, and Hagar and Keturah were concubines. In circumstances unrelated to the laws of inheritance, but related to their role in reproduction, the record indicates that Keturah and Hagar were wives of Abraham. Here the text notes the legal distinction between wives and concubines as governed by the laws of inheritance of that period (Gen. 16:3; 25:1, 6; 1 Chr. 1:32).

Subsequently, the Ishmaelites, Medanites, and Midianites formed a trading alliance with a caravan that carried goods and slaves between the East and Egypt. This business enterprise would produce a caravan that would take Joseph to Egypt as a slave (pages 321 and 329) (Gen. 37:25-36).

Family Reunion

Isaac and Ishmael at Abraham's Homegoing Machpelah; Abraham, Age 175

Gen. 25:7-11: Abraham "was satisfied" at the time, "he was gathered to his people." The words, "*with life*," are not in the Hebrew text as indicated by the use of italics in the NASB (Gen. 25:8). Such satisfaction may have referred to this life as well as his transition. He was satisfied with death, i.e., his birth to a new life. He was going to his LORD and a reunion with the righteous line.

God directly communicated with Abraham on 12 different occasions during his life: seven times by speaking to him and five times in appearance by vision or in person. The first was an appearance, a Christophany, in Ur of the Chaldees before he was 75 years old. It is probable that the next 11 times occurred between the ages of 75 and 117, a period of 42 years. The "silent years" were as important in the development of Abraham's character, and the development of his seed, as the ones where there is a Biblical record. God is ever shaping His children in His image.

The epitaph of Abraham is in the New Testament:

"By faith Abraham, when he was called, obeyed to go out to a place which he was to receive for an inheritance; and he went out, not knowing where he was going. By faith he lived as an alien in the land of promise, as in a foreign land, dwelling in tents with Isaac and Jacob, fellow heirs of the same promise; for he was looking for the city which has foundations whose architect and builder is God...Therefore there was born even of one man, and him as good as dead at that, as many descendants AS THE STARS OF HEAVEN IN NUMBER, AND INNUMERABLE AS THE SAND WHICH IS BY THE SEASHORE" (Heb. 11:8-10, 12).

Abraham died at the age of 175. After Abraham had answered the LORD's call to leave Haran, the LORD gave him a full century of life in the Promised Land (Gen 12:1-4). Both his sons, Isaac and Ishmael, buried him at Machpelah. This suggests that relations between Isaac and Ishmael were satisfactory. They may have had frequent communication with each other.

In this day of conflict between Muslims and Christians and Jews, we do well to remember that Abraham is the father of a multitude of nations. The LORD loves all who embrace Him by faith in all people-groups.

The phrase, "gathered to his people," indicates that Abraham was going to a family reunion with believers in the one true God. The believing patriarchs did not see or taste of death (John 8:51-59). Abraham's people had to be all those of the righteous line that had gone before him. Subsequently, there is a similar statement made about Isaac, Ishmael, and Jacob at their homegoings, but not Esau (Gen. 25:8, 25:17; 35:29).

CHART 1: ABRAM-ABRAHAM'S LIFE	
AGE	**EVENT**
Born	Abram was born in Ur of the Chaldees (Babylon).
Adult	He left Ur for Haran and stayed there until his father died.
75-85	He left Haran and went to Shechem, then to Bethel, then to Egypt, and back to Bethel. Sarai went into Pharaoh's harem in Egypt; God protected her. He gave the valley of the Jordan to Lot. After the fight of the kings, he recovered Lot and the other captives. He gave the tithe to Melchizedek. He returned home to Hebron.
85-86	Hagar was impregnated by Abram with the subsequent birth of Ishmael.
99-100	Abram was given the covenant of circumcision and renamed Abraham; Sarai was renamed Sarah. They were given the promise of Isaac. The Lord appeared to Abraham at Hebron. The cities of the valley, except Zoar, were destroyed; Lot and his daughters escaped. Abraham moved to Gerar and represented Sarah as his sister for the second time. Sarah was again protected by God. Isaac, the promised son, was born at Beersheba.
103?	The family homestead was at Beersheba. Ishmael and Hagar were sent away.
117?	Isaac was offered on Mount Moriah and received back.
137	They had moved back to Hebron. Sarah died at the age of 127. Machpelah was purchased as a burial site.
140	Rebekah was brought to Isaac by the servant of Abraham (Eliezer?). Abraham married Keturah. Years later, Abraham gave gifts to the concubines' sons and sent them to the east. Isaac became the sole heir.
160	The twin grandsons, Jacob and Esau, were born.
175	Abraham died and was gathered to his people. Ishmael and Isaac buried Abraham at Machpelah.

CHAPTER 9

THE GENERATIONS OF ISHMAEL

The generations of Ishmael are the ninth recorded in the book of Genesis. As promised by *Yahweh* to Hagar, a great nation would come from her seed and Abraham's (Gen. 21:18). Ishmael produced 12 sons, 12 tribes (Gen. 17:20). *Yahweh* would fulfill his promise to Abraham; he would be the father of a multitude of nations.

Gen. 25:12-18: Even though Ishmael went with the progeny of Keturah to the sons of the east and developed a caravan transporting goods from the east, he settled in the Wilderness of Paran in the northern Sinai Peninsula. "East of Egypt as one goes toward Assyria" probably refers to the caravan trade route that Ishmael and two of the sons of Keturah developed (Gen. 21:21; 25:1-6, 18; 37:27-28, 36; 39:1).

After the weaning of Isaac, Hagar ("flight," *hâgâr̂,* הגר) took her flight for the second time with Ishmael. Ishmael ("God hears," *yishmaʿeľ,* ישמעאל) engendered 12 sons as promised by *Yahweh Elohim* (Gen. 16:10, 17:20, 21:18).

1. Nebaioth ("heights," *nebaŷôth,* נבית)
2. Kedar ("dark Bedouins," *qêdâr̂,* קדר)
3. Adbeel ("disciplined of God," *'adbe'eľ,* אדבאל)
4. Mibsam ("fragrant," *mibśâm̂,* מבשׂם)
5. Mishma ("a hearing," *mishmaʿ,* משמע)
6. Dumah ("silence," *dûmâĥ,* דומה)
7. Massa ("burden," *maśśaʿ,* משׂא)

8. Hadad ("mighty," *chad̆ad,* חדד)

9. Tema ("desert," *têma',* תֵּימא)

10. Jetur ("enclosed," *yeṭûr,* יטור)

11. Naphish ("refreshment," *nâphîysh,* נפיש)

12. Kedemah ("precedence," *qêdemâh,* קדמה)

Nebaioth may have been the ancestor of the Nabataeans who built Petra. Kedar's and Tema's names suggest that some of the sons of Ishmael may have been Bedouins. This is buttressed by the Hebrew word for "tribes" (*'ûmmah,* אמה) (Gen. 25:16). Since they lived in a circumscribed area east of Egypt and south of Israel, this supports the suggestion that they were Bedouins.

They settled from Havilah ("circle," *chăvîylâh,* חוילה) to Shur ("wall," *shûr,* שׁור). The Pishon ("increase," *pîyshôn,* פישׁון) River was a branch from the river that watered the Garden of Eden. Since the Pishon river flowed around Havilah, it must have flowed through Israel (page 60). This suggests that the land of Israel was originally planned as a land rich in minerals (Gen. 2:10-11).

The different translations of the phrase, "in the face," include: "in defiance of," "before," "in front of," and "to the east of." The settlement was east of Egypt (Gen. 25:18). Because of the subsequent relationship between Ishmael's and Isaac's seed, it may be prudent to interpret it with its literal meaning "in the face of" or, "in defiance of" his brothers (page 179). The meaning is compatible with the English idiom, "in your face" (Gen. 25:18).

The Bible indicates that Ishmael was a believer at his death in that he was "gathered to his people" (Gen. 25:17). "His people" must have referred to Abraham and believers that antedated him. Remember that Ishmael heard the voice of God from heaven, when he was a teenager. That incident may have resulted in his spiritual salvation as well as his physical deliverance.

Salvation can come to an individual, but his seed can carry on a perceived injustice done to them. The progeny of the Arabic nations became enemies of the nation of Israel by adopting Ishmael as the promised son in the Muslim religion (page 179). Mohammed sought to unify the world by having everyone submit to the monotheistic religion of Islam, instead of the worship of the Babylonian pantheon of Gods. Islam literally means "submission." Radical Islam wishes to dominate the world. They are still "in the face" of their brothers.[69]

The Family of Isaac

Conflict in the Family
Negev Near *Beer-Lahai-Roi*; Isaac, Age 40

Gen. 25:19-26: After 20 years of marriage, Isaac interceded with *Yahweh* on behalf of Rebekah who was barren. Isaac may have been worried that Rebekah would be infertile like his mother had been until God miraculously intervened. Why did Isaac wait 20 years before making such intercession? It seems likely that Isaac needed this time with Rebekah to develop their relationship. During the 20 years, Rebekah had to learn to trust in *Yahweh* and give up the Babylonian gods of her family. They both needed time to develop spiritually prior to becoming parents. God provided that possibility through initial infertility.

Yahweh answered Isaac's prayer; Rebekah conceived and became pregnant with twins. It is likely that she was 20-25 years younger than Isaac and would have been 35 to 40 years old at the time of her pregnancy and the birth of the twins.

After becoming pregnant, increased fetal activity, described by *Yahweh* as an intrauterine struggle, resulted in Rebekah inquiring of *Yahweh* as to why this was happening. *Yahweh* spoke to her and revealed that two nations and peoples were in her womb; the elder would serve the younger. Only God knows the beginning and end of our lives before we live them. It is inconceivable that Rebekah would not have related this direct communication from *Yahweh* to Isaac.

This is definitive Biblical evidence that a fetus is a human being in the eyes of God. An additional example is John the Baptist expressing joy from his mother's womb (Luke 1:44).

When Isaac was 60, they became the parents of Esau and Jacob. The character of Jacob ("heel catcher/supplanter," *ya'ăq̆ob̂,* יעקב) is foretold in the grasping of Esau's heel to attempt to supplant him from being the firstborn. Jacob was the "grabber," one who obtained things by his own aggressiveness.

Esau means "rough" and/or "hairy" (*'eśav̂,* עשׂו). Esau received his name because of his abundant hair present at birth that was like a hairy garment (Gen. 25:25). Edom comes from a Hebrew root that means "red" (אדום). Adam (אדם) comes from the same root; Adam may have had red hair. "Ruddy" (*'admon̂iŷ,* אדמוני) King David may have had red hair also (1 Sam. 16:12). The LORD enjoys a variety of color in His creation.

Parental Favoritism

Gen. 25:27-28: Esau became a skillful hunter, "a man of the field"; Jacob became "a complete man who lived in tents" (Gen. 25:27 NASB margin). These descriptions contrast the hunting versus domestic interests of Esau and Jacob, respectively. It also suggests that Esau was narrow in his interests. Jacob had broad interests and did his work well. Isaac loved Esau and Rebekah loved Jacob.

The Hebrew word for "complete" is the singular form (*tam̂,* תם) of the plural noun used to describe Abraham in his covenant with *Yahweh*, "to be complete, perfect, having integrity" (*tam̂im,* תמים) (Gen. 17:1 NASB margin). Even though characterized as a "grabber," Jacob was a complete man and did seek the rights of the firstborn. He wanted the blessing handed down from Abraham to Isaac by *Yahweh*. God develops those who want the right things. Jacob would need to learn that the gift of God does not come by personal manipulation, "by grabbing." He needed to develop personal integrity.

Isaac was the one that interceded on behalf of Rebekah for her conception; *Yahweh* responded with a positive answer (Gen. 25:21). Isaac may have felt that *Yahweh* should have spoken to him, instead of Rebekah, about Jacob receiving the inheritance of the elder son. He never sought *Yahweh* for confirmation of the revelation that was given to Rebekah.

Esau's Loss of the Birthright

Gen. 25:29-34: Isaac was 60 years old when the twins were born; he was 75 years old when Abraham died at the age of 175. The twins would have known Abraham during the first 15 years of their lives, the last 15 years of Abraham's life (Tables 8 and 9, page 390). They would have heard the remarkable stories of the promises of *Yahweh* to Abraham and his seed. Indeed, Abraham did dwell in tents with Isaac and Jacob:

"By faith he lived as an alien in the land of promise, as in a foreign land, dwelling in tents with Isaac and Jacob, fellow heirs of the same promise" (Heb. 11:9).

Rebekah's favoritism to Jacob suggests that she had told him about *Yahweh*'s direct communication to her when she was pregnant. Jacob would have known that his parents disagreed about this matter. Because of her experience, Rebekah taught Jacob to believe that he was the one chosen to receive the spiritual blessing originally given to Abraham. Jacob wanted that blessing; Esau showed no interest in it. If Esau knew of the prophetic word to his mother, he minimized its importance. Isaac, by his behavior as recorded in the text, discounted the prophecy given to Rebekah.

After the record of their intrauterine struggle, the significant incident of the exchange of the meal of bread and red, lentil stew for Esau's birthright is the next one recorded between Esau and Jacob.

Abraham's death may have renewed Jacob's interest in the birthright and blessing. Since Esau showed no inclination for the birthright, one suspects that Abraham was a direct stimulus to

Jacob's quest. It is likely that the exchange of the birthright happened near the time of Abraham's death when the twins were 15 years old (Tables 8 and 9, page 390). After Abraham's death, the 26th chapter continues with Isaac's life at age 75 (Gen. 25:7-8). The twins would have been 15 years old then.

Since Edom sounds like the Hebrew word for "red" and comes from the same Hebrew root, there is emphasis on the symbolism of the color of the stew. Esau was more concerned about his stomach than *Yahweh's* promises. Esau was willing to exchange his birthright for a bowl of red, lentil stew; he despised his birthright:

"See to it that no one comes short of the grace of God; that no root of bitterness springing up causes trouble, and by it many be defiled; that there be no immoral or godless person like Esau, who sold his own birthright for a single meal. For you know that even afterwards, when he desired to inherit the blessing, he was rejected, for he found no place for repentance, though he sought for it with tears" (Heb. 12:15-17).

The Abrahamic Covenant Transmitted to Isaac
Gerar in the Negev; Isaac, Age 75

Genesis 26:1-35

Gen. 26:1-5: Another famine occurred during the time of Isaac. Isaac did not inquire of *Yahweh* about his move to Gerar in the land of the Philistines. This move was closer to Egypt. It is possible that Isaac was considering going down to Egypt, following in the footsteps of his father, even though he knew the adverse consequences of the same.

It was at this time that *Yahweh* transmitted to Isaac the blessing originally given to Abraham. Since there is no further discussion about Abraham, it would indicate that Abraham had gone to his heavenly home at 175 years of age (Gen. 25:7). The command not to go down to Egypt would have reminded Isaac of the previous famine when Abram was 75 years old. Isaac would now be the same age as Abram when he failed to inquire of God about this same move (Gen. 12:4, 10).

Since Abram did not inquire of *Yahweh* and went down to Egypt during the previous famine, his misdirected journey resulted in Sarai's placement in Pharaoh's harem, the probable acquisition of Hagar, and a need to return to Bethel to renew his walk with *Yahweh* (Gen. 12:4, 10-20; 13:1-4).

On that occasion, *Yahweh* did not stop Abram; He let Abram learn from his disobedience. However, Isaac who was in awe of his father had not developed to the spiritual level of Abram. *Yahweh* **appeared** to Isaac and commanded him not to go down to Egypt as his father had done in the previous famine. He was not tested beyond his ability (1 Cor. 10:13).

Yahweh said, "Stay in the land of which I shall tell you" (שׁכן בארץ אשׁר אמר אליך) (Gen. 26:2b). The use of the imperfect ("future") tense indicates that the land of Gerar was not the place where He wanted Isaac to reside. Isaac did not ask whether his present sojourn in the land of Abimelech was "the land of which I shall tell you." Isaac interpreted that land as the place where he was currently living. The LORD's commands are specific in every detail.

The reason given by *Yahweh* of the transfer of the blessing to Isaac was Abraham's keeping *Yahweh*'s covenant with him (Gen. 17:1, 26:5). Isaac needed to trust *Yahweh* and obey the terms of the covenant, even as Abraham had done.

Abraham listened to *Yahweh* and his "charges, commandments, statutes, and laws" (*mishmereth,* משׁמרת; *mitsvot,* מצות; *chuq̂qot,* חקות; and *tor̂ot,* תורת) (Gen. 26:5).

Charges—Abraham guarded, watched, and preserved them.

Commandments—He obeyed them.

Statutes—He understood and implemented any ordinance, prescription, and custom given by *Yahweh*.

Laws—He understood God's design for good in all His laws. He kept them, i.e., obeyed them.

Yahweh commended Abraham for obeying Him and hearkening to his voice in these four different areas. Isaac was to do the same. Abraham's seed, believers in the LORD, need to obey in these four areas just as Abraham did.

Isaac Repeats His Father's Deceit

Gen. 26:6-11: At Gerar, Isaac, because of fear for his life, as his father before him had done, represented his wife as his sister. The fact that she was his cousin, and not his half-sister as Sarah had been to Abraham, did not enter into the decision. Isaac repeated the same folly his father had committed on two separate occasions (Gen. 12:10-20, 20:1-18).

The discovery of the relationship occurred when Abimelech observed Isaac's intimate caress of Rebekah. The Hebrew word used to describe this action means "laughter" (*tsaĉhaq,* צחק); it comes from the same root as the name of Isaac, "he laughs" (*yitschaq̂,* יצחק) (pages 330-331). This suggests they were having a hilarious time in sexual play that left no doubt that Rebekah was Isaac's wife. Isaac's charade had deprived them of the privacy of the God given right of sexual relations in marriage.

This demonstrates the beauty of shared intimacy between a husband and wife. God designed sex for fun and enjoyment as well as procreation. It also illustrates that such intimacy is not for public consumption.

Probably at the same age that his father had done the same thing, Isaac sinned by passing his wife off as his sister.

Abimelech, warned by God through this public display of affection, instead of a dream as his ancestor had been, gave command for no one to touch Rebekah. The use of the word, touch, suggests exact detail of the episode of his forebear's interaction with the living Lord (page 215). That history, passed down to this Abimelech, told of potential death to his forebears. He did not want to receive the same condemnation (Gen. 26:10). His concern that one of his men might easily have had sexual intercourse with Rebekah indicates that this was a permissive, male dominated culture (Gen. 26:10).

Yahweh protected Rebekah and Isaac, even as He had Sarah and Abraham. However, *Yahweh* did this in a way that rebuked Isaac for his deceit and allowed both of them to suffer embarrassment for their public display.

Isaac's Obedience and Blessing

Gen. 26:12-16: *Yahweh* provided additional riches following Isaac's obedience in not going down to Egypt; he reaped a hundredfold during the famine. Reaping during a famine is impossible without the LORD's intervention.

It is possible that Abram could have experienced a similar blessing, but his disobedience precluded that possibility (Gen. 12:10). When one departs from the LORD's chosen way, the blessing for obedience is lost.

It is unlikely that the Philistines increased their wealth during the famine. Therefore, they were envious of Isaac. However, they were afraid of Isaac's God who increased his wealth and "the army" in his household. Isaac had become more powerful than they were. They requested him to leave. Isaac did not return to Beersheba but stayed nearby in the valley of Gerar.

Isaac Repeats His Father's Labors

Gen. 26:17-22: The Philistines had filled the wells with dirt that Abraham had dug. When Isaac started digging the wells again, they claimed the first well because it had "living water," a spring. Because of the contention between the two tribes, it was named

Esek ("contention," *'eŝeq,* עשק). Similarly, the Philistines laid claim to the second well, Sitnah ("strife," *śiṭnaĥ,* שׂטנה). The third well was named Rehoboth ("broad places," *rechoɓoṫ,* רחבות), because *Yahweh* made room for them in the land. The aim of the Philistines was to get Isaac out of "their territory."

There is a lesson in Isaac digging again the wells that his father had dug. Each generation of believers must trust the LORD for every need in their lives. They cannot live off the accomplishments of their forebears.

The "living water" that the LORD Jesus described to the woman at the well was interpreted by her as water from a spring, which is the literal translation of the water from the well at Esek ("living water," *mah'-yim chayim,* מים חיים). The LORD Jesus taught the woman at the well that He was the source of the true "living water" (*hudor̄ zao,̄* υδωρ ζων) (John 4:10-14). All believers must experience this living water by having the dirt and mud of their lives cleansed by the LORD. It is only then that the free Source of "living water" can well up unto eternal life. Isaac was learning from these experiences that he needed this living water to cleanse him and make him whole.

The men of Gerar took economic advantage of Isaac. *Yahweh* had provided for him in spite of the thievery of the Philistines. He did not fight with them. He let them have the wells until he dug the well, Rehoboth ("broad places," *rechoɓoṫh,* רחבות); there was now provision for him and the Philistines:

"Never pay back evil for evil to anyone. Respect what is right in the sight of all men. If possible, so far as it depends on you, be at peace with all men. Never take your own revenge, beloved, but leave room for the wrath of God for it is written, 'VENGEANCE IS MINE, I WILL REPAY,' says the Lord. 'BUT IF YOUR ENEMY IS HUNGRY, FEED HIM, AND IF HE IS THIRSTY, GIVE HIM A DRINK; FOR IN SO DOING YOU WILL HEAP BURNING COALS ON HIS HEAD.' DO NOT BE OVERCOME BY EVIL, BUT OVERCOME EVIL WITH GOOD" (Rom. 12:17-21).

The Well of the Sevenfold Oath
Beersheba; Isaac, Age 100

Gen. 26:23-33: After Abram wandered about following the destruction of Sodom and the assumed death of Lot, he passed Sarah off as his sister to the Abimelech of that time. After making peace with Abimelech, he dug these same wells and experienced seizure of at least one of them (page 221).

It may have appeared to Isaac that the injustice of the Philistines was not for his benefit. Since Isaac had not looked for the land that *Yahweh* had told him about, *Yahweh* used the Philistines unfair tactics to move Isaac to that place, just as He had moved his father before him (Gen. 20:1-18, 21:22-34).

Nevertheless, the one whose God is the LORD cannot be defeated by the aggression of unbelievers. When the believer obeys the LORD, the aggression of the unbeliever can be turned into a blessing.

Beersheba was "the land of which I shall tell you," the land that God promised to him (Gen. 26:2). *Yahweh* **appeared** to Isaac the night of his arrival in Beersheba, "the well of the sevenfold oath" (*be'er̂ sheba',* באר שׁבע), by incident and translation (Gen. 21:30-31). He was not to fear; previously, Isaac had known *Yahweh* as his Fear (Gen. 31:53). Isaac received a renewal of the blessing from *Yahweh* "for the sake of my servant Abraham" (Gen. 26:24). Isaac still needed to improve in his spiritual state in order to receive the blessing for his own sake.

Isaac built an altar to *Yahweh* at Beersheba and called on Him by that name. This suggests a lessening of his fear of *Yahweh* with his experience of Him over the previous quarter of a century. He had experienced many blessings: answer to his prayer for Rebekah's conception, *Yahweh*'s appearance to him warning him not to go down to Egypt, His blessing during the famine, His protection from the Philistines, and now, *Yahweh's* appearance at Beersheba.

Abraham had not built an altar at Beersheba but had planted a Tamarisk **(evergreen)** tree. *Yahweh,* the **Everlasting** *El* (God), was continuing to provide for and spiritually develop Abraham's son, Isaac (Gen. 21:33). The tree was about a century old now. It would have been a reminder to Isaac of his father's faith and *Yahweh*'s faithfulness.

Just as Isaac needed to dig the wells again in order to experience "living water," it was necessary for him to build an altar to *Yahweh* to thank and praise Him as "the Living Water."

After observing that God was with him in all that he did, the following three dignitaries met with Isaac: Abimelech, the chieftain ("my father the king," *'abiŷ melek,* אבימלך), Ahuzzah, his manager ("possession," *'achuẑzath,* אחזת), and Phicol, his army commander ("strong," *piŷkol̂,* פיכל).

They came to make a covenant at Beersheba because they feared Isaac. Isaac was aware of a similar meeting between the former Abimelech and Phicol with his father (pages 221-222). Abraham would have been over 103 years old at that time. If this was the time of Esau's marriages, as the record suggests, Isaac was 100 years old (Gen. 26:34).

Isaac's response was similar to Abraham's response. Isaac first talked of the Philistines' hatred and rejection of him. When the Philistine leaders used God's name, *Yahweh*, Isaac did not argue further. Isaac had borne witness to them of *Yahweh's* blessing in his life and wanted to continue that witness; he then hosted a feast for them.

The Philistines lied about doing Isaac no harm. Nevertheless, whenever possible, the people of God must live peaceably with all men (Rom. 12:18).

While the conversation was taking place with the Philistines, and the covenant with the swearing of oaths, Isaac's servants were in the process of digging a well. It was christened based on "an oath" (*shib'aĥ,* שבעה) on the very day of the completion of the covenant (Gen. 26:25, 32-33). Abraham had christened the well, Beersheba after his experience with the Philistines. Isaac had a similar experience and gave the same name to the well. He was learning to appreciate his spiritual heritage as he learned the same lessons his father had learned (Gen. 21:22-32).

Esau's Polygamy

Gen. 26:34-35: When Isaac was 100 years old, Esau married at age 40, the same age that his father had married. This suggests continued favoritism by Isaac to Esau, and Esau's adulation, or manipulation, of his father. However, he married two Hittite women who were "a bitterness of spirit" to Isaac and Rebekah, probably because they came from an immoral culture with the trappings of the same (Gen. 26:35 NASB margin). By this decision, Esau gave testimony to a lack of concern about spiritual matters and accepted polygamy as a way of life. Esau was godless, had despised his birthright, and now embarked on an immoral life style (Heb. 12:16).

Isaac's Rumination on Death

Genesis 27:1-46

Gen. 27:1-4: Isaac was 137 years old. His age of 137 and Jacob's age of 77 are determined as follows. Jacob was 130 years old when he went down to Egypt (Gen. 47:9). Joseph was 39 years old at that time (Gen. 40:29-30, 41:46, 45:6). Joseph was born when Jacob was 91 (130 – 39 = 91). Joseph was born after Jacob had served Laban 14 years (Gen. 29:18, 30; 30:25; 31:41). Therefore, Jacob was 77 years old when he left home (91 - 14 = 77). Since Jacob left home at the age of 77, and Isaac was 60 years old when the twins were born, Isaac was 137 (60 + 77 = 137) (Gen. 25:26).

Thus, when Isaac was 137 years old, possibly on his birthday, he was thinking about his death. This may have been secondary to his physical decline because of his loss of sight. There is another reason that may have been the dominant one for his rumination on death. Abraham died on the 100th anniversary of his father's death (Gen. 11:32, 12:1-4). Since Isaac was 37 years old when his mother died at the age of 127, it was the 100th anniversary of her death (Gen. 17:17, 23:1). Isaac was closer to his mother than his father. After her death, he lived in his mother's tent. In addition, Ishmael had died at the age of 137. Isaac had had a good relationship with his half-brother (Gen. 25:17).

People often fear their demise on the anniversary of the death of a family member. Undoubtedly, Isaac was thinking about these significant anniversaries of the deaths of loved ones. Isaac's fears were irrational. He would live 43 more years and attain the age of 180 (Gen. 35:27-29). Isaac had lost his eyesight, possibly due to cataracts. He was depressed and believed he was going to die soon. The LORD determines the length of our days, not our perceptions brought about by our physical and mental infirmities as we age.

Because of his depression, Isaac sought to give a spiritual blessing to his son "before he died." Isaac asked Esau to hunt game and prepare a savory dish for him. He would then give him the blessing of the elder son. Esau had sold his birthright. Traditionally, the elder son received two-thirds of the inheritance and the younger son one-third. There was a connection between the blessing and the birthright (Gen. 25:27-34). Although both were linked, the blessing primarily had spiritual significance and the birthright material significance.

Rebekah's and Jacob's Deceit

Gen. 27:5-24: It is clear that Isaac had never accepted Rebekah's word from *Yahweh* concerning the elder son serving the younger when she was pregnant with the twins. This must have been a subject of disagreement between them throughout their marriage (Gen. 25:22-26).

The fact that Rebekah was listening while Isaac spoke to Esau indicated that she knew his psychological state. As stated above, Isaac had symptoms of depression; he thought that he was going to die (Gen. 27:2). It is possible that Rebekah regularly listened in on

Isaac's conversations with Esau. She wanted to preempt the blessing going to him.

As Isaac experienced physical decline and depression, Rebekah may have taken on more responsibility than she should have. Rebekah took over the leadership role to "outmaneuver" Isaac. This was reminiscent of Eve's effort to lead Adam (Gen. 3:2-6). Rebekah's actions suggest that she was the dominant partner in the marriage. Since her husband disagreed with her on this matter, she wanted to "help" God fulfill the revelation given to her when she was pregnant. Rebekah's actions were a contrast to Sarah's actions. Sarah called her husband her lord (Gen. 18:12).

When Rebekah discussed this with Jacob, she stated that Isaac wanted to bless Esau "in the presence of *Yahweh*" (Gen. 27:7). Isaac did not say that, and it is unlikely that he would have said that to Esau, given his irreligious life style. Rebekah may have spoken these particular words to Jacob to impress upon him the message given to her by *Yahweh* during her pregnancy and her wish that this be the time for its fulfillment. It is likely that she had reminded Jacob of this throughout his 77 years of life.

The ruse included preparing a meal from goat kids, so the meat tasted like savory wild game. The goats would have eaten the grass of the field and would have had meat more typical of wild animals. The spices used would prevent Isaac from discerning that this was not meat from a wild animal; Rebekah was a good cook (Gen. 27:9). She dressed Jacob with Esau's clothes and put goat's skin with its hair on his hands and the smooth part of his neck. Esau had skin "like a hairy garment" (Gen. 25:25).

Jacob was concerned about bringing a curse upon himself for the deception; this suggests some spiritual sensitivity on his part and a reluctance to enter into such a ruse. Deception had been a recurrent sin in the lives of Abraham and Isaac; Jacob had sat at the feet of his grandfather who must have given warning to him about this. Now Jacob worried about his own deceit and his propensity to this sin. Rebekah, as the dominant figure in the household, proclaimed a curse upon herself instead of Jacob. She twice commanded Jacob to obey her (Gen. 27:8, 13). Even though Jacob was 77 years old, at his mother's command, he followed through with his part in the deception. Neither of them prayed to *Yahweh*. They did not seek His way to fulfill the promise given to Rebekah.

Note the evidence of the domineering character of Rebekah. She commanded Jacob and had the "best" (*chamudah,* חמודה) garments of Esau in her home, even though he had been married to his two wives for 37 years (Gen. 27:15 NASB margin). Esau's best garments had been worn in the field and had retained the odor of the same. He was an outdoorsman.

Jacob's statement that "*Yahweh* your *Elohim*" helped him to find the game quickly would not be a typical response from Esau but one expected from Jacob (Gen. 27:20). Jacob may have assumed that Rebekah's description of Isaac's telling Esau of his blessing "in the presence of *Yahweh*" was correct, and thus, he had been misled by her (Gen. 27:7). Such a response would be atypical for Esau. Isaac had not said that to Esau. This prompted him to comment about Jacob's voice, and his wish to feel him and smell his garments to be sure that he was Esau. Like most people who become blind, Isaac's other senses were accentuated. The difference in the skin and voices of Esau and Jacob suggest they may have been fraternal twins, even though they were the same sex.

Jacob continued his deception to his father throughout the rest of the charade. It would have been reasonable for Isaac to call a halt at this time and bring both sons before him to verify their identity. He may have persevered in the blessing of "Esau" (Jacob), because he believed that Rebekah was unaware of the proceedings. The fact that he did not stop suggests that Isaac was determined to carry out the blessing to "Esau" (Jacob) before he got into an argument with Rebekah. As stated previously, this was a bone of contention between them. Still, he may have had a lingering doubt as to whether *Yahweh* had indeed spoken to Rebekah about this matter during her pregnancy with the twins.

THE BLESSING

Gen. 27:25-29: Isaac's transmission of the blessing, only after eating "Esau's (Jacob's) game," suggests that the basis of their relationship was the material things of life. He initiated the blessing based on his smell of Esau's garments. His taste buds and sense of smell were intact; these two senses cross over with each other. He "transmitted" the blessing in the name of *Elohim*, not the name of *Yahweh*, the one who originated the blessing (Gen. 12:1-3; 15:1-21; 17:1-22; 26:1-5, 24). He mentioned *Yahweh's* blessing of the field to try to make the connection between *Yahweh* and *Elohim* in a way that Esau might understand. Isaac was probably trying to convince himself that Esau should receive the blessing and would eventually become a follower of *Yahweh*. Esau believed in *Elohim*, not in the name of the One Triune God, but as the name for many gods. Esau must have adopted polytheism when he married two wives from the surrounding culture. His lifestyle indicated that he did not believe in *Yahweh*. Isaac knew this and tried to bridge the gap:

"So he came close and kissed him; and when he smelled the smell of his garments, he blessed him and said, 'See, the smell of my son is like the smell of a field which the LORD has blessed; now may God give you of the dew of heaven, and of the fatness of the earth, and an abundance of grain and new wine; may peoples serve you, and nations bow down to you; be master of your brothers, and may your mother's sons bow down to you. Cursed be those who curse you, and blessed be those who bless you" (Gen. 27:27-29).

"Brothers" would have included "Jacob" (Esau) and other male relatives. Therefore, the expression, "your mother's sons bow down before you" (וישתחוו לך בני אמך), cannot refer to just "Jacob" (Esau). Since Rebekah had no other sons, this must have referred to the male members of her blood relations.

This prophecy would be fulfilled initially following Jacob's sojourn in Aram, and ultimately, with the triumph of Israel over the seed from Rebekah's family, Laban and his progeny (Gen.

31:29-42). Compare Rebekah's family blessing to this one (Gen. 24:60).

In summary, it is likely that Isaac attempted to convince "Esau" (Jacob) that the blessing of *Yahweh* was one that he could identify with because of *Yahweh*'s blessing on His creation where Esau hunted. Isaac was careful not to ascribe *Yahweh*'s full blessing to "Esau" (Jacob) but invoked the name of *Elohim* instead. Since it demanded a spiritual response by the recipient, Isaac knew that he could not transmit the blessing of *Yahweh* given to Abraham, and subsequently, to him. Only *Yahweh* could transmit that blessing.

Gen. 27:30-40: When Esau returned and Isaac recognized what had happened, Isaac "trembled violently." If this emotional response had been due to anger, he could have summoned Jacob back into his presence and rebuked him. However, the response was due to the tragedy of Isaac's refusal to believe Rebekah about *Yahweh's* revelation to her about their sons. Therefore, he refused to revoke the blessing given to Jacob.

In this sad episode, Esau's bitter cry after losing the blessing illustrated the pathos of one who, at the age of 77, still sought materialism instead of *Yahweh*. Because of his hardness of heart and lack of sensitivity to spiritual matters, he did not repent. He received an epitaph in the Scriptures describing his immoral and godless nature and **inability** to repent, even though he sought it with tears (page 250) (Heb. 12:15-17).

This is a warning to all that live immorally and seek only wealth and reputation. Esau had two wives from godless backgrounds and sought the passing materialistic pleasures of this life. He built his life on godless alliances. Esau mourned the loss of both the birthright and the blessing due to the elder son for the wrong reasons; he had hardened himself.

Esau rightly proclaimed that Jacob had lived up to his name of "grabber." However, he did not accept any personal responsibility in the sale of his birthright for a bowl of stew and the godless lifestyle that kept him from the blessing. Repentance was impossible without acknowledgment of his responsibility in these matters.

Still, the Bible records, "By faith Isaac blessed Jacob and Esau, even regarding things to come" (Heb. 11:20). Isaac blessed Esau by judgment through prophesying the truth that could have led to his repentance, but there is no evidence that he ever repented. Esau's inheritance, based on his breaking away from Jacob to live in a hard country, would lead to Mount Seir and the establishment of his own kingdom, Edom (Gen. 36:1-8).

The danger of continual refusal to obey God is hardening of the heart to the degree that one cannot repent! In Esau's genealogy, there is no record of his death. The Scriptures do not indicate that he was "gathered to his people"; they do indicate a godless outcome (Gen. 36:1-43, Mal. 1:1-4, Heb. 12:15-17).

Esau's blessing was opposite to the one given to Jacob (Gen. 27:27-29, 39-40). The contrast is evident by comparing the two. Jacob received the bountiful inheritance; Esau received a harsh one. Jacob would learn not to "grab" and become Israel, the man of faith. Esau would "grab" his inheritance and suffer spiritually with a downward course.

Yahweh had a perfect plan based on His word to Rebekah. It would have rewarded Jacob's spiritual leanings, instead of Esau's godless ones, without all the subterfuge and deceit engaged in by Rebekah and Jacob. When believers usurp the rightful direction of *Yahweh*, they lose the option of discovering His better, perfect plan.

Enmity in the Family

Gen. 27:41-46: Esau's response was one of anger and threatened violence with no evidence of repentance. He further assumed that his father's talk of death meant that he would die soon. Esau believed he could overrule God and obtain the inheritance by murdering his brother (Gen. 27:41). Rebekah blamed Jacob for Esau's anger and threat; she refused to acknowledge her dominant part in the ruse and her commands to Jacob (Gen. 27:45).

Esau's grudge and death threats prompted Rebekah's request for Isaac to send Jacob back to her relatives to obtain a wife. Her dominance is evident in that she told this to Jacob before she discussed it with Isaac (Gen. 27:42-46). She continued to manipulate expecting that she would be able to call Jacob back a short time after Esau's anger subsided.

Bereavement of both her sons in one day was her major concern. After this event, the animosity between her and Esau must have worsened. Jacob would be gone for about 30 years. There is no evidence that Rebekah ever saw him again. Her self-proclaimed curse did result in bereavement of both sons at one time (Gen. 27:13, 45). Rebekah was around the age of 112 to 117, 20-25 years younger than Isaac; it is unlikely that she would have lived much longer (Gen. 25:20). Her emotional declaration of being tired of living, and the events brought about by her own sin, may have resulted in an unhappy ending to her life (Gen. 27:46).

Rebekah's complaint about the daughters of Heth, "daughters of terror," was accepted by Isaac. Both Rebekah and Isaac were guilty of sin in this matter of the blessing. Rebekah's subterfuge and Isaac's inability to accept the fact that *Yahweh* had spoken to his wife came from the sin of pride. Now they were looking for a resolution to the enmity between their sons in which they had played a major role.

Still, Isaac and Rebekah leave us an example of what to avoid and what to seek by the history of their lives. Their lives provide spiritual benefit to all who will discern the principles of godly living therein and obey them; their life histories are our examples (1 Cor. 10:11).

Isaac Recognizes the Need for *El Shaddai* to Give the Abrahamic Covenant to Jacob Beersheba; Jacob, Age 77

Genesis 28:1-22

Gen. 28:1-5: Isaac called Jacob, and instead of reprimanding him, he blessed him. This action indicated that he had accepted his responsibility for the enmity that had arisen through his sin. He finally accepted that Rebekah's word from *Yahweh* about the elder son serving the younger was correct. He requested that the Abrahamic blessing be given to Jacob by *El Shaddai* (Gen. 28:3-4). *El Shaddai* is the name of God that speaks of His bountiful provision. Perhaps Isaac understood that Jacob's deceit raised questions about receiving the blessing from *Yahweh* until Jacob changed. Jacob left home at the age of 77 to obtain a wife from the daughters of his maternal uncle, Laban (Gen. 24:29).

Esau's Spiritual Dullness

Gen. 28:6-9: It took this incident and 37 years of marriage for Esau to realize that Isaac and Rebekah were dissatisfied with his present wives (Gen. 26:34-35). This suggests a self-centered individual insensitive to spiritual matters and the concerns of others. He finally acknowledged Jacob's obedience to his parents (Gen. 28:6-7).

He now attempted to please them through a marriage to a daughter of Ishmael, Mahalath, not discerning any difference between Ishmael's seed and Rebekah's family. Mahalath was the sister of Nebaioth, the firstborn son of Ishmael; she may have had status in Ishmael's family (Gen. 25:13). Esau still lacked spiritual discernment; he was seeking to increase his acquisitions by an advantageous marital alliance; Ishmael was a partner in the caravan business (pages 242 and 245). Since Ishmael was Abraham's son, he hoped that the marriage would please his parents, but that was a secondary consideration.

CHART 2: ISAAC'S LIFE	
Age	**Event**
Birth	When Abraham was 100 and Sarah 90, Isaac was born at Beersheba.
17?	He was offered and delivered at Mount Moriah.
37	His mother died and was buried at Machpelah.
40	He married Rebekah near *Beer-Lahai-Roi*.
60	The twins were born.
75	Abraham was buried by Ishmael and Isaac at Machpelah.
75-100	He moved to Gerar during the famine and represented Rebekah to Abimelech as his sister; she was protected by God. He reaped a hundredfold during the famine. He re-dug the wells of Abraham. After the move to Beersheba, *Yahweh* appeared to him; he responded by building an altar. He covenanted with Abimelech.
100	Esau married two Hittite women; they brought grief to Isaac and Rebekah.
137	Isaac believed he was going to die on the 100th anniversary of the death of his mother. Abraham had died the 100th year after his father's death. Ishmael died at 137, Isaac's present age. Isaac was depressed. Rebekah and Jacob connived to receive the blessing. Jacob left for Haran.
144-157	Jacob married Leah and Rachel. All of Jacob's children were born, except Benjamin. Jacob became wealthy and left Haran.
157- 164- 167	Jacob procrastinated about his return to Bethel. During this time, Dinah was raped, Deborah died, and Rachel died giving birth to Benjamin, the 12th son of Jacob. Jacob finally returned to Bethel and then to Hebron.
180	Isaac died and was buried at Machpelah by Jacob and Esau.

CHAPTER 10

THE GENERATIONS OF ISAAC

The generations of Isaac are the tenth recorded in the book of Genesis and include the entire lives of Jacob and Esau. Jacob would evolve spiritually to become Israel. His 12 sons would represent the diverse character of the nation of Israel. The transformation of Jacob, "the grabber," into Israel, "the one who strives with God and men and prevails," is an example of the spiritual evolution of all men in their struggles (Isa. 43:1). In a greater sense, the struggle of this man became an example of the spiritual quest of the individual, the family, and the nation (Hos. 12:12-14). That struggle will eventually triumph in the completion of the Israel of God (Gal. 6:15-16).

JACOB'S LIFE

Jacob Leaves Home and Meets *Yahweh*
Bethel; Jacob, Age 77

Gen. 28:10-17: The distance from Beersheba to Bethel was approximately 50 miles. The text suggests that Jacob reached this site in one day. This distance was equivalent to about two marathons. He wanted to put a significant distance between himself and his brother. The phrase, "Jacob lifted up his feet" (*y'saĥ ya'aq̆ob̂ regeliv*, **וישׂא יעקב רגליו**), verifies that Jacob was afoot on this journey (Gen. 29:1 NASB margin). The entire trip was about 500 air miles. Since he was walking or jogging, this is quite a feat for a 77-year-old man who would live 70 more years. The patriarchs were in excellent physical condition due to their extended walking and jogging; theirs was not a sedentary society. Good genes and exercise contributed to their longevity; medical studies are compatible with this observation.

Jacob came to a "certain place" (Gen. 28:11). The subsequent story indicates this was the place where *Yahweh* appeared to Abram. He had built an altar between Bethel on the west and Ai on the east (Gen. 12:7-8).

In his benediction to Jacob, Isaac requested that *El Shaddai* give him the blessing, but it was *Yahweh* who appeared to him in a dream the first night away from home and gave him the blessing of Abraham (Gen. 28:3). The question was not *El Shaddai's* bountiful supply. The question was whether or not Jacob would acknowledge *Yahweh* as his LORD. The ladder had angels ascending and descending upon it, and *Yahweh* at the top of the ladder:

"I am the LORD, the God of your father Abraham, and the God of Isaac" (Gen. 28:13a).

Why did *Yahweh* call Abraham, Jacob's father, instead of Isaac; He did not say "your father Isaac." Isaac had preferred Esau and had neglected Jacob. He had not provided adequate spiritual direction for either of them. Abraham was the model parent for Jacob, the one he should emulate. Jacob had sat at Abraham's feet during the first 15 years of his life. Abraham, his grandfather, was representative of Jacob's true Father, the One who created him, called him, and now took him further on life's journey to develop his relationship with Him. The **dream** that occurred at Bethel was the **first** direct communication between *Yahweh* and Jacob.

Yahweh pronounced the blessing and gave Jacob assurance that he had access to Him and His angels who would protect him on his journey until he returned home (Gen. 32:1-2, Heb. 1:13-14). It was also an assurance that *Yahweh* would protect Jacob during his earthly pilgrimage until he reached his heavenly home. Jacob had waited at home for 77 years to get the blessing previously given to Abraham and Isaac, but he found that he had to venture out on his own, away from his mother, believing God, in order to receive it.

Yahweh's Covenant; Jacob's Altar at Bethel

Gen. 28:18-22: The area between Bethel and Ai is described in Hebrew as "**the** place" (*maq̂ôm̂,* **המקום)** (Gen. 28:11, 19 NASB margin)**.** Details are given concerning the stone Jacob placed at his head when he went to sleep. Abram had built an altar at Bethel and had been there twice in the past, before and after his trip to Egypt

(Gen. 12:8, 13:3-4). Surely, "**the** place" was the same one where Abram built an altar and made sacrifices to *Yahweh*. After building the altar, the famine came and he went down to Egypt. After his misadventure in Egypt, he returned to this altar and called upon *Yahweh*.

Jacob reacted with fear and awe believing the place to be, "The house of *Elohim* and…the gate of heaven" (Gen. 28:17). His early rising suggests inability to get back to sleep after his dream. Following Jacob's experience outside this city of Luz, he christened the place, Bethel ("house of God," *beŷth-'êl*, בית־אל). *El* is the singular form of *Elohim*. Jacob prayed to the One Triune God, *Elohim*. His vow was weak compared to that of *Yahweh's*; he asked only for food, clothing, and a safe return home. If *Yahweh* fulfilled those conditions, then *Yahweh* would be his God. Jacob was negotiating with *Yahweh*. In contrast, *Yahweh* **gave** Jacob the full blessing transmitted to Abraham and Isaac, and now to him. Jacob was not ready to appropriate the breadth of that blessing.

It is likely that the stone that Jacob used as a pillow came from Abram's original altar. He subsequently set the stone up as a pillar and anointed it with oil. Abram's altar became the altar of Jacob. Jacob embarked upon the next stage of his spiritual journey at 77 years of age.

God is not in a hurry! Children do not have to have life's entire journey mapped out by the age of 18 or 22 when they graduate from high school or college, respectively. Life rarely turns out the way parents or children anticipate. Parents must be careful not to push their timetable and aspirations for their children ahead of the LORD's timetable and His design for their lives.

During the first 15 years of their lives, Abraham had been a spiritual mentor for Jacob and Esau (Tables 8 and 9, page 390). Jacob had visited Abraham during those years and heard firsthand the family stories of how *El Shaddai* had guided Abraham throughout his life. Jacob's vow of a tithe is likely to have come from the history communicated directly to him by Abraham about the incident with Melchizedek (Gen. 14:18-20).

In summary, even though God used His name, *Yahweh*, while addressing Jacob, Jacob only acknowledged the One Triune God, *Elohim*. Jacob had not developed in his relationship with God to the point of calling upon Him as *Yahweh*, his LORD. He knew that that would require complete submission to Him. However, he did state that if *Elohim* fulfilled his requests then *Yahweh* would be his God. He knew the difference in the meaning of the names.

Jacob and Rachel at the Well
Haran; Jacob, Age 77

Genesis 29:1-35

Gen. 29:1-13: The phrase, "sons of the east," first occurs here. During the time of the Judges, the Scripture refers to the foes of Israel: the Midianites, the Amalekites, and the "sons of the east" (Jdg. 6:3, 33; 7:12; 8:10). Abraham sent his six sons by Keturah to "the east"; Midian was one of the six (Gen. 25:1-6). The ungodly line settled "east" of Eden. Abraham came out of Ur of the Chaldees in the east and settled temporarily in Haran until *Yahweh* reissued the call to him. Therefore, the intent of this phrase was to indicate that Jacob was going into the geographical area controlled by people in rebellion against God. That would include those living in the top and eastern side of the Fertile Crescent.

The name of the city had reverted from Nahor back to Haran, probably after Nahor's death. Laban, Nahor's grandson, had become the dominant person. Since the departure of Abraham from the area, it continued to be a moral desert.

Jacob was 77 years old; Isaac was 137 years of age. Abraham's servant went to Haran to obtain a wife for Isaac when Isaac was 40 years old (Gen. 25:20). Rebekah had become the wife of Isaac 97 years ago (137 – 40 = 97). She had become the mother of Jacob and Esau 77 years ago.

Yahweh's providence in having Rachel come to the well at the exact time that Jacob inquired about Laban brought back the memory, probably retold in the family many times, of Abraham's servant and Rebekah's appearance at the well as Abraham's servant concluded his prayer (page 235) (Gen. 24:15).

The previous well was a spring outside the city. The current well had a stone over it (Gen. 24:13, 43). Whether someone capped the spring for water rights, or it was a different well, is problematic. It was either the same well or in the same vicinity.

There is no indication in the passage that Jacob was praying at this time as Abraham's servant had done. Jacob met Rachel and reversed what his mother did for Abraham's servant by serving Rachel (Gen. 24:15-22). Jacob was in good physical condition. He rolled the stone from the well and watered the flock, not waiting for all the flocks to be gathered (Gen. 29:8-10). Only after he had watered the sheep, symbolic of the task that his mother had done when she watered the camels of Abraham's servant, did he reveal his identity. The similarity in this circumstance with the prior event was emotionally overwhelming to Jacob; he wept and kissed Rachel.

Since the custom was for women to marry during their teenage years, and Rachel was a shepherdess, she probably was in her early to middle teens. Jacob may have attributed the similarity of his meeting with Rachel to the meeting between Abraham's servant and his mother. He may have believed that it was an indication that Rachel was God's chosen one for him as a bride. His attachment to his mother may have caused him to believe that her story would become his story, not recognizing that God uniquely designs each person's story. He did not inquire of *Yahweh*, as Abraham's servant had done, nor did he attempt to evaluate Rachel's spiritual qualities.

Rachel, like her aunt Rebekah nearly a century earlier, ran to tell her household the news (Gen. 24:28). Laban ran to meet his nephew, just as he had done with Abraham's servant (Gen. 24:29-32). Jacob did not come bearing gifts as Abraham's servant had done, but Laban was aware of the wealth of Abraham. Jacob was naïve in his dealings with Laban; "He related to Laban all these things" (Gen. 29:13). Surely, Laban found out that Jacob, not Esau, was the primary heir to the family fortune.

Jacob's Covenant with Laban

Gen. 29:14-20: Since Laban now knew the story of the friction between Esau and Jacob, and Jacob's need to obtain a wife from Rebekah's relatives, he decided to take advantage of the situation. Jacob naively offered seven years of labor for Rachel's hand in marriage. Why did he suggest such a long period? Rachel may have been a young teenager, not yet physically mature. Her name means "ewe" (*raĉhel̂,* רחל). Fearing the wrath of Esau, Jacob may have decided that it was better to stay away from home for a protracted period. Longevity ran in the family. Jacob would serve seven years for Rachel; he would then be 84 years old. Because of the love he had for her, the time passed quickly.

Jacob and Laban

Gen. 29:21-30: Jacob was a deceiver. The literal translation of Jacob's name, "one who takes by the heel and supplants," was illustrated by his entrance into the world (Gen. 25:26 NASB margin). Jacob had supplanted, i.e., deceived his brother. He took the birthright from Esau by barter at an opportune time and the blessing by deception (Gen. 27:35-36).

Laban deceived Jacob by substituting Leah for Rachel. When believers are guilty of a recurring sin, God often leads them to an unbeliever that is more skilled at the same sin. Laban had many years of service to Satan and his way of doing business. Since Rebekah was 35-40 years older than Jacob, it is probable that Laban was at least 40 years older than Jacob (77 + 40 = 117).

Leah's eyes were weak; she may have had strabismus (cross-eyed) or some other visual abnormality. Her name means "weary" (*le'aĥ,* לאה). She may have been an introvert. In addition, because of the impairment to her countenance, she may have been chronically depressed.

There is no record to indicate whether Leah and Rachel were born from the same mother. The ruse of Laban indicates that polygamy was an accepted norm in his family (Gen. 22:20-24). Isaac and Abraham, except for Abraham's impregnation of his maid Hagar, were monogamous. They were examples to Jacob of God's command for marriage to be a covenant for life between one man and one woman unless parted by death (Gen. 2:24).

There had to be some complicity for Rachel and Leah to participate in this ruse. There can be little question that Laban ordered their cooperation; they obeyed. Since Leah could have been married to someone in another family and potentially enhance Laban's wealth, the only reason for giving her to Jacob must have been the abnormality with her eyes that made her unacceptable "merchandise" for such a match. In support of this is the fact that Leah was older than Rachel and had not married during the seven years that Jacob served Laban.

Leah probably wore a veil in a dark tent that had subdued lighting on their marriage night (Gen. 29:23). Leah must have agreed not to reveal her identity to Jacob. Rachel, on the other hand, had to agree to wait a week to consummate her relationship with Jacob. Rachel could not be sure that Jacob would agree to the deal and may have been unhappy with the arrangement, but her father ruled the home. This must have strained the relationship between Rachel and Leah and their relationship with their father.

Jacob did not use the word for sexual intercourse that means "to know" (*yâda',* ידע). The word used here means "to come into" (*boʼh,* ואבואה). At 84 years of age, Jacob was more concerned about physical sex with the young virgin than "knowing" his wife completely.

The wedding feast was for men only. In such circumstances, the drinking of alcoholic beverages was a possibility. If so, that may have accounted for Jacob's lack of discernment as to whether it was Leah or Rachel with whom he bedded. Leah's physical attributes, other than her eyes, must have been similar to Rachel's (Gen. 29:17). Leah was a virgin. Jacob should have discerned on this first night that there was no deficiency in Leah's ability to "perform" in sexual relations. He thought she was Rachel. Imagine Leah's hurt in being called "Rachel" during the first night of their union, and Rachel's hurt at being deferred because of the "problem" of her older sister.

Laban's excuse for substituting Leah was pure deception. Even if it were true that the practice was to have the older daughter wed first, he should have stated this to Jacob at the time of their original agreement (Gen. 29:15-20). Laban's ruse of substituting Leah provided Jacob the option of accepting her as *Yahweh's* choice for his wife, even though this was done by man's connivance. He never considered this possibility. He accepted the polygamous arrangement, even though it was counter to what he knew was right. Believers often err when they do not ask the LORD the reason for an assumed setback.

Jacob had been deceived. He chose to serve an additional seven years in order to receive Rachel as his wife one week later. Laban gave Zilpah and Bilhah to Leah and Rachel, respectively. Jacob started his polygamous marriage with two competitive sisters and two handmaidens through whom he would produce children. One wife possessed desirable physical attributes and undesirable spiritual attributes; the other wife possessed desirable spiritual attributes and one undesirable physical attribute.

The word for sexual intercourse used in the 21st verse, "come into" (*boʾ̂,* ויבא), is repeated in the 30th verse in the past tense. The emphasis was still on the physical relationship, even with Rachel whom Jacob "loved" (*'âhab,* ויאהב).

Leah, Bilhah, Zilpah, and Rachel: Mothers of the First Twelve Children

Gen. 29:31-35: Jacob did develop in his love for Rachel. He "loved" (*'âhab,* ויאהב) Rachel more than Leah (Gen. 29:30). However, "The LORD saw "that Leah was hated" (*śânêʾ̂ leʾâh,* כי־שׂנואה לאה) (Gen. 29:31a NASB margin). This meant there was active scorn against Leah, not just less love. Rachel was barren;

Leah received *Yahweh*'s blessing of fertility. Jacob and Rachel were to suffer judgment for their attitude to Leah. When *Yahweh* "sees" (*raʾah̑,* ראה), He acts.

There was pathos in Leah's naming of the first four sons. The firstborn's name, Reuben ("see, a son," *re'ub̑en̑,* ראוּבן), reflected her feeling that *Yahweh* saw her present affliction. The word for "my affliction" (*onii,* ענייי) is the same word used by Joseph to describe his alienation in Egypt (*onii,* ענייי) (Gen. 41:52):

"Leah conceived and bore a son and named him Reuben, for she said, because the Lord has seen my affliction, surely now my husband will love me" (Gen. 29:32).

"Then she conceived again and bore a son and said, 'Because the LORD has heard I am unloved He gave this son also,' So she named him Simeon" (Gen. 29:33).

The name Simeon comes from the Hebrew infinitive, "to hear" (*sham̂a',* שמע). *Yahweh* heard Leah's cry that she was hated.

Leah felt the "hate" (*śan̂eʾ,* שׂנא) from her husband, not simply lack of love. Leah invoked the name of *Yahweh* twice with her first two sons as an expression of His active interest in her state and the two sons He gave to her. With her third born, Levi ("attached," *lev̂iŷ,* לוי), she did not invoke the name of *Yahweh* and asked that her husband just "attach" (*lavah,* לוה) himself to her. She was discouraged and was willing to settle for her husband living with her without love.

Finally, with the fourth born son, she returned to faith in *Yahweh* and praised Him and named her son, Judah ("he praises," *yehud̂ah̑,* יהוּדה), but she did not mention her husband. Temporarily, she gave up on Jacob.

Competition Between Rachel and Leah

Genesis 30:1-43

Gen. 30:1-24: Rachel primarily occupied the marriage bed. There are several possible reasons for this. Since it is likely that Jacob believed the meeting at the well was providential, and he believed that Rachel was the one selected by God for him, he saw her as his first choice, his true wife.

Jacob may have been more comfortable with Rachel and her deficient spiritual qualities than with Leah and her devotion to *Yahweh*. Rachel and Leah may have had similar physical attributes, except for Leah's eyes. Rachel may have had the prettier face. As suggested by their names, Rachel may have been an outgoing and vivacious extrovert. Leah may have been a withdrawn introvert. He loved Rachel but hated Leah.

Rachel did not become pregnant with Joseph until the seventh year of marriage, but Leah was often pregnant. None of the physical changes in Leah brought about by her pregnancies would occur in Rachel until her pregnancy with Joseph. Even then, because of her single pregnancy, the physical changes would be of lesser degree. Jacob may have found Rachel's youthful body to be more sexually desirable than Leah's.

From ages 84 to 91, Jacob fathered six sons and a daughter through Leah. He fathered two sons through Rachel's handmaiden, Bilhah, and two sons through Leah's handmaiden, Zilpah. Finally, he fathered Joseph through Rachel. The conflict between the two sisters continued to feature their physical and spiritual attributes. Jacob accepted the handmaidens of Rachel and Leah into the marriage bed without qualms. Abraham had done that with Hagar. More children gave Jacob the potential for more laborers and more wealth (Table 5, page 278).

Leah initially spoke of God as *Yahweh* for the first, second, and fourth sons: Reuben, Simeon, and Judah. She did not speak of God when she bore Levi and when Zilpah, her handmaiden, bore two sons, Gad and Asher. She spoke of *Elohim*, not *Yahweh*, for the birth of her final two sons, Issachar and Zebulun. She then bore Dinah without mentioning any name of God.

By contrast, Rachel first blamed her husband for not getting pregnant. Jacob was angry with her and told her that God controlled "the fruit of the womb." Rachel called upon *Elohim* after the birth of Bilhah's first son, Dan, and did not speak of God for the second son of Bilhah, Naphtali. She spoke initially of God as *Elohim*, the One who took away her reproach when she became pregnant with Joseph (*yôsêph,* יוסף). Then she prayed that *Yahweh* would "add" (*yâsaph,* יסף) [an assonance] another son. The answer to that prayer would result in her death (page 308).

Rachel gave Bilhah to Jacob "to come into her" (בא אליה); it was a sexual transaction to obtain a son (Gen. 30:3). Jacob's interest in sex with Leah and the handmaidens was for bearing children. He enjoyed sex with Rachel, but even then his interests appeared to have been in her physical beauty and her non-demanding spiritual state (Gen. 29:27-20).

The neglected wife, Leah, declined in her spiritual condition. The favored wife, Rachel, showed minimal spiritual progress after the birth of Joseph.

The handmaidens' role was for impregnation and childbearing, not love or "knowing." Rachel had a matter-of-fact attitude toward giving Bilhah to Jacob for this purpose. Rachel saw childbearing as competition with her sister; she did not mind the sexual transaction (Gen. 30:3-8). However, Leah named her fifth son, Issachar, "wages," because she "hired out" Zilpah to Jacob. It hurt Leah to let Jacob have sex with another woman (Gen. 30:18). Rachel was callous; Leah was very sensitive.

During those seven years, the naming of the sons reflected the spiritual status of Leah and Rachel. The interpretation of the names of the sons is meaningful. Additional meaning would evolve in the rest of the Bible as the tribes reflected the character of their respective patriarchs (Rev. 7:5-8).

TABLE 5: THE MEANING OF THE NAMES OF THE TWELVE SONS OF ISRAEL		
SON'S NAME	**MEANING**	**GOD'S NAME**
Reuben (*re'ub̂en̂,* ראוּבן)	"See, a son"	*Yahweh*
Simeon (*shim'ôn̂,* שׁמעון)	"Heard"	*Yahweh*
Levi (*lev̂iŷ,* לוי)	"Attached"	None mentioned
Judah (*yehud̂aĥ,* יהוּדה)	"He Praises"	*Yahweh*
Dan (*dan̂,* דן)	"Judge"	*Elohim*
Naphtali (*naphtal̂iŷ,* נפתלי)	"Wrestling"	None mentioned
Gad (*gad̂,* גּד)	"Good fortune"	None mentioned
Asher (*'asher̂,* אשׁר)	"Happy"	None mentioned
Issachar (*yiśśaŝkar̂,* ישׂשׂכר)	"Recompense/wages"	*Elohim*
Zebulun (*zebul̂un̂,* זבלוּן)	"Dwelling"	*Elohim*
Joseph (*yoŝeph,* יוסף) (*yaŝaph,* יסף)	"Take away reproach" "Addition"	*Elohim* *Yahweh*
Benjamin (*binyam̂iŷn,* בּנימין)	"Son of the Right Hand"	None mentioned

There is divine humor in the incident with the mandrakes (Gen. 30:14-18). The mandrakes were an aphrodisiac that gave a fragrant atmosphere for sexual intimacy (Song 7:13). Rachel received the mandrakes, but *Yahweh* gave conception to Leah. *Yahweh* did not allow conception by the use of plants for their mystical value. He rewarded Leah for trusting in Him.

There was pathos in the fact that Leah, after bearing four sons to Jacob, had to "buy" him for the night with an aphrodisiac. She asked Jacob "to come into me" (אלי תבוא), not "to know me" (ידע אלי). Leah did not invoke the name of God at all. She resorted to purchasing her husband's sexual prowess by bartering the aphrodisiac to Rachel, just so Jacob would go to bed with her (Gen. 30:16)!

Since her husband would not love her, Leah shifted her focus to motherhood. Leah averaged one birth per year, even though she had a brief period of infertility; she was pregnant for 63 out of a possible 84 months. The context suggests that she bore four sons in a row. She ceased bearing and gave her handmaiden, Zilpah, to Jacob; two sons were born through her. Leah did bear two more sons, Issachar and Zebulun, and a daughter, Dinah (Gen. 30:10-13, 18-21).

Leah's six sons are listed in the order of their birth (Gen. 30:9-21). Dan was born first from Bilhah. Gad was born from Zilpah before Leah gave birth to Issachar and Zebulun. The sequence of the births of Asher from Zilpah and Naphtali from Bilhah is not clear. The birth period of the twelve children was 108 months (12 X 9), so there had to be crossover with more than one mother pregnant at a time during the latter part of the seven years (page 380). Leah bore seven children in seven years. Leah's fecundity was a symbol of God's blessing to the "hated one."

Laban's Continued Deceit

Gen. 30:25-36: Joseph's birth occurred in the final year of the agreed upon 14 years of service to Laban for his two wives; Dinah was born through Leah about this same time as her seventh child (Gen. 30:21-22). Jacob was 91 years old. He sought to depart Haran. Since Joseph was the firstborn of Rachel, his chosen wife, Jacob probably rationalized that Joseph would be his heir, even though Reuben was the eldest son born through Leah.

Laban replied that he had "divined" (*naĉhash,* נחש) that Jacob had been used to bring him wealth. In Hebrew, "divined" is from the same root as "serpent" (*nachash*, נחש). Satan indwelt the serpent, when he tempted the woman in the Garden of Eden. Satan directed Laban through his occult practices (Gen. 3:1).

The negotiations between Laban and Jacob were anything but polite. Their strained relationship showed in their conversation. Laban offered to give Jacob "wages." Jacob replied that Laban would not "give" him anything, but he should receive compensation for his labor. Jacob agreed to continue to serve Laban in return for the specified colors and patterns found in the sheep and goats.

TABLE 6: THE CONTRACT BETWEEN JACOB AND LABAN	
JACOB'S BY CONTRACT GEN. 30:32-33	**LABAN'S DECEIT GEN. 30:35**
All speckled sheep	
All spotted sheep	
	All black sheep
All black lambs	All black lambs
All speckled goats	All speckled and spotted female goats
All spotted goats	All striped and spotted male goats

Jacob—"Let me pass through your entire flock today, removing from there every speckled and spotted sheep and every black one among the lambs and the spotted and speckled among the goats; and such shall be my wages. So my honesty will answer for me later, when you come concerning my wages. Every one that is not speckled and spotted among the goats and black among the lambs, if found with me, will be considered stolen" (Gen. 30:32-33).

"Laban said, 'Good, let it be according to your word.' So he removed on that day the striped and spotted male goats and all the speckled and spotted female goats, every one with white in it, and all the black ones among the sheep, and gave them into the care of his sons" (Gen. 30:34-35).

Laban exploited Jacob with his chicanery. Initially, Laban cheated Jacob of all black lambs, all speckled female goats, and all spotted goats. Laban left Jacob with all speckled and spotted sheep and the speckled male goats only. By leaving Jacob some he avoided the appearance of obvious thievery. He dealt via the occult with the aid of Satan; he "divined" (*naĉhash,* נחשׁ) (Gen. 30:27).

Laban believed the striped female and speckled male goats could not produce spotted or speckled goats. He did not think the spotted and speckled sheep could produce black lambs. He thought he was leaving Jacob with spotted and speckled sheep. Laban's lack of understanding of the carryover of genetic traits from generation to generation in his own flocks indicated that he was an ineffective observer of this phenomenon, not personally involved in the raising and care of his flocks. His sons, by their silence, indicated a similar lack of acumen.

Laban gave the stolen goats and lambs to his sons who took them a distance of three days' travel time away from Jacob. Jacob received the remainder of Laban's flocks.

Jacob's Self-Deception

Gen. 30:37-43: The gestation period for goats and sheep is about five months; there are no more than two breeding seasons per year. Laban changed the agreed upon color pattern of the sheep and goats ten times in six years, nearly every breeding season (Gen. 31:7, 41). Since he stole goats and sheep from Jacob before the first breeding season, and the text is not clear about the timing of the last one when Jacob left, it is possible that Laban changed the deal every breeding season.

God revealed to Jacob the colors of the newborn goats in the dream that occurred at the time of the command to return home. Jacob had negotiated his choice of colors of the sheep and goats based on his understanding. In the dream, *Elohim* made clear to Jacob that He had produced the results (Gen. 30:32-33, 31:10-13).

Jacob tried to bring about the color of the lambs and kids by placing colored staves in front of the strongest sheep and goats as they bred (Gen. 31:7-12). Either he was doing this to "direct *Yahweh*" by this method or he thought that such manipulation would produce a physiologic response in the sheep and goats—there is no medical evidence to support his manipulation. Whatever his purpose, he was still in the business of "helping" God, "grabbing," instead of fully trusting God to fulfill His word.

Because Laban kept changing the criteria, God mercifully protected Jacob, blessed him, and overrode his efforts to manipulate the results. He was able to trade for servants, camels, and donkeys. He "broke forth" with wealth (Gen. 30:43 NASB margin). God revealed Himself to the patriarchs as *El Shaddai*, the All-Bountiful One (pages 51-53).

***Yahweh*'s Command; Jacob's Stealth**

Genesis 31:1-55

Gen. 31:1-3: The success that God gave to Jacob produced jealousy and paranoia in Laban and his sons. Like most unbelievers, Laban's sons attributed Jacob's success to his taking away "glory" from their father (Gen. 31:1 NASB margin). They equated wealth with reputation. Jacob's success would diminish the sons' inheritance. Those who lie and steal often attribute their personal motives to others. Because of their own self-centeredness and worship of their occult household gods, Laban and his sons could not conceive of God's gracious blessing of Jacob.

It was at this time that *Yahweh* **spoke** (the **second** direct communication) to Jacob in **a dream** and told him to return to his home and relatives (Gen. 31:3, 10-13). This was one communication, not two (page 283). Since his last interaction with *Yahweh*, 20 years had passed. Once again, He promised that He would be with him. Since Jacob had these specific instructions, how would he respond?

Jacob's Response

Gen. 31:4-21: Jacob was afraid to confront Laban directly. He chose to flee by stealth. In order to do this, he had to have the cooperation of his wives. Since he had mistreated Leah, he needed to know whether she would side with him or her father. Since Rachel was his favorite, he could be sure of her positive response. One suspects that he had already convinced Rachel, the wife of his marriage bed, and expected her presence to influence Leah. Rachel was dominant; Leah was passive. He selected the field for the meeting, so no one could report his plans to Laban. He recounted the following points to his two wives:

1. *Yahweh* had spoken to Jacob, but Jacob only spoke of *Elohim* during the presentation to his wives.

2. Laban was no longer friendly with Jacob.

3. Jacob had served Laban faithfully with all his strength.

4. Laban had changed his wages ten times.

5. *Elohim* had protected him.

6. *Elohim* was the one that had taken their father's livestock (wealth) from him and given them to Jacob.

7. Jacob told them about the communication from God, the *El* of Bethel, but it was *Yahweh* who told Jacob to return to his home and his relatives (Gen. 31:3, 10-13). The angel of *Elohim*, the Creator, was the one that told Jacob of the final selection of the colors of the male goats in a dream. By so doing, he taught Jacob that He had produced the prior nine results also. Jacob had not done it by "his" choices or with the manipulation of the rods when the animals were breeding. *Elohim* had blessed Jacob, even though he had not been aware of *Elohim's* actions on his behalf.

8. *Elohim*, the one whom he had met at Bethel and made a vow on an anointed pillar, had instructed him to leave Haran and return to the land of his birth.

9. Jacob did not say that *Yahweh* guaranteed that He would be with him, and *Yahweh* was the one who appeared to him at Bethel (Gen. 31:3).

10. Thus, Jacob failed to mention that God had spoken to him as *Yahweh* and had instructed him to return to his land **and his relatives**.

It is foolhardy to ignore any part of the LORD's instructions or the name with which He speaks. His name is a revelation of His character applied to the situation. *Yahweh*, the LORD of the covenant who appeared to Jacob at Bethel, was in control. Jacob was willing to return to his land, but not to his relatives and home. This would have dire consequences (Gen. 33:17-20, 34:1-31).

Jacob's presentation to his wives had partial truth but ignored the name of *Yahweh* and His covenantal relationship with Jacob. By taking this approach, he was less than forthright in his witness to his wives. Jacob knew what it meant to submit to *Yahweh* as his LORD; he resisted. When a person will not submit to the LORD, he will not witness to others about God as LORD.

Both Rachel and Leah agreed with Jacob. They felt their father had dealt with them primarily as merchandise and foreigners. They accepted *Elohim*'s instruction to Jacob. One suspects that they were pleased that, through Jacob and by *Elohim*, they would receive the bulk of what would ordinarily have gone to their brothers (Gen. 31:16). Jacob was teaching his wives materialism.

Rachel stole Laban's household idols. This verified that her family still practiced Babylonian polytheism. Rachel was still involved in such worship. She did not trust the One Triune God, *Elohim*; she trusted in *Elohim*, the name used by polytheists for many gods (Gen. 31:32). Therefore, Rachel did not understand Jacob's personal reference to *Elohim* as the One Triune God:

"Then the angel of God said to me in the dream, 'Jacob,' and I said, 'Here I am'" (Gen. 31:11).

When Laban left to shear sheep, Jacob covertly "stole away"; he deceived Laban. The LORD never honors deceit. He crossed the Euphrates River, so it is clear that Laban's property was on the Babylonian side of the Euphrates in Paddan-Aram. Jacob was 97 years old. Joseph and Dinah were each six years old. The other sons ranged from seven to 13 years of age.

Jacob's intent was to return to Canaan (Gen. 31:18). Later, he would procrastinate and delay the return to Bethel to avoid honoring his vow to *Yahweh*. He understood that *Yahweh* was LORD, even if he didn't have full understanding of the meaning of the name. He would not keep his promise to *Yahweh* or return to his father for about a decade.

***Yahweh*'s Protection of Jacob from Laban**
Gilead; Jacob, age 97

Gen. 31:22-29: Even though Jacob had a three-day head start, Laban caught up with Jacob in the hill country of Gilead [map site 15] at the end of a week of pursuit. Laban claimed the right to his daughters, their handmaidens, the children, and the herds.

Elohim warned him in a dream not to speak "either good or bad" to Jacob. That warning recalled to Laban an incident 117 years previously. Laban had used these same words about *Yahweh* to Abraham's servant at the time he came for Rebekah (page 237). Laban avoided confrontation with the *Elohim* of Jacob. Therefore, Laban did understand that *Elohim* was the One Triune God of Jacob, even though he did not worship Him as such.

Jacob was protected by *Yahweh* fulfilling His word to him. He was not commended; he left by stealth and deceit, not confronting Laban and trusting *Yahweh* to protect him during that confrontation.

Laban, the master deceiver, knew what deception really meant. "What have you done by deceiving me." "You have **stolen** my heart" is the literal translation of "by deceiving me" (Gen. 31:26 NASB margin). "Why did you flee secretly and deceive me." "**Steal** me" is the literal translation of "deceive me" (Gen. 31:27 NASB margin). To deceive another is to demean them as a person, to steal their personhood.

Laban accused Jacob of deception; both were guilty of the same. He acknowledged *Elohim's* protection of Jacob. He suggested that he would have sent them off with his blessing. That was not likely, considering his previous behavior. He also stated that he had the power to harm Jacob.

Rachel's Self-Deception—Worship of Idols

Gen. 31:30-35: Laban would not accept that Jacob left because of conflict with him; he wished to "save face." He suggested that Jacob left because he longed for his father's home. Jacob's subsequent delay in his return home indicates that that was not the reason. Jacob was afraid to return to Bethel and keep his vow to *Yahweh*.

In the confrontation about the household idols, there is further evidence of the spiritual status of Laban, Rachel, and Jacob. Laban searched Leah's tent after Jacob's, then the tents of Zilpah and Bilhah, and then reentered Leah's tent before going into Rachel's tent (Gen. 31:33). By reentering Leah's tent, he may have hoped to find the idols in Leah's tent and wanted to make sure he had not missed anything. His prejudice against Leah was obvious; Rachel was still the favorite. Once again Leah was discriminated against by her own father.

Laban must have known the difference in the spiritual natures of Leah and Rachel. It is likely that he suspected Rachel but wanted time to think as to whether he should identify Rachel as the one with his stolen idols. Hence, he may have reentered Leah's tent as a delaying action. Rachel had stolen the household idols of her father but pretended to have her menstrual period, "the manner of women" (Gen. 16:2, 18:11, 31:35). Laban probably saw through her ruse but did not want to press the matter because of Jacob's hasty statement:

"The one with whom you find your gods shall not live" (Gen. 31:32a).

If Laban persisted and identified Rachel as the thief, that may have started a fight; Laban backed off.

The Covenant between Jacob and Laban
The Names of God Invoked by Each

Gen. 31:36-55: Jacob's faithful 20 years of service to Laban and his absorption of all losses during that time resulted in his breaking forth in unleashed anger. He served 14 years for Rachel and Leah and six years for the animals. His closing appeal to the *Elohim* of Abraham and the Fear of Isaac gave ample witness to Laban of Jacob's God.

However, Laban remained selfish and unresponsive to this witness. He again claimed all the family of Jacob and the animals as his own. He did acknowledge that he could do nothing about the situation and asked for a covenant. This suggests that Laban did believe that *Elohim* had blessed Jacob. Laban was afraid to disregard the warning from *Elohim* in the dream the previous night, just as he was afraid to disobey *Yahweh* 117 years previously. Laban was afraid of *Yahweh*, the *Elohim* of Abraham, Isaac, and Jacob.

Jacob, unlike Laban who swore by the gods of Babylon in Aramaic, set up a pillar with stones and swore by the Fear of Isaac in Hebrew. Jacob avoided using the name of *Yahweh*. Unexpectedly, the demand by Laban invoked the name of *Yahweh*. Thus, he introduced this special name of God into the covenant in spite of Jacob's reluctance to do so. He demanded that Jacob not take additional wives or mistreat his present ones. This was a strange request coming from a father who had demeaned his daughters. Laban may have had the remote hope that Esau would murder Jacob. If that happened, Laban may have intended to recover his daughters, the children, and all of Jacob's possessions.

Even though Laban did not believe in *Yahweh*, he knew that Jacob did and made the oath in His name in order to bind Jacob to the oath. The further admonition, not to pass for harm by Galeed ("the witness heap," *galyed̂,* גִּלְעֵד) and Mizpah ("the watchtower," *mitspaĥ,* מִצְפָּה) must have come to mind during Jacob's subsequent wrestling match (Gen. 31:47, 51-52; 32:24-32).

They eventually made a covenant where Laban used the Aramaic language to describe the heap of stones and watchtower that "witnessed" the event and swore by the God of Abraham, Nahor, and Terah. This, taken with the household idols and his history of "divining," confirmed that Laban was still involved with the Babylonian pantheon of Gods as was Rachel (Gen. 30:27). The conflict was between Laban's polytheism and ethnicity, and *Yahweh*'s blessing of Jacob and his family.

Jacob gave further witness by offering a sacrifice to the *Elohim* of his fathers and the Fear of Isaac who protected him from Laban (Gen. 31:29, 42). He then invited his brothers (relatives) to participate in this peace offering. By the grace of God, the blessing by the family of Laban to Rebekah had come true (page 238). The blessing became a judgment to Laban because of his hateful treatment of Jacob (Gen. 24:60).

The sharing of this meal and blessing by Laban of his daughters and grandchildren were signs of peace. Laban then returned to his place with no evidence of turning from his polytheism. Alas, he returned to his former life without accepting the *Elohim* of Jacob who appeared to him in a dream. His eternal destiny was in doubt; he still needed to repent, believe, and learn to know *Yahweh*.

Jacob's example illustrates the fact that witness for the LORD is often half-hearted and associated with strong interpersonal emotions that decrease the effect of the verbal message and/or religious ceremony.

God's Angels; Two Encampments Mahanaim; Jacob, Age 97

Genesis 32:1-32

Gen. 32:1-2: Jacob went forward in obedience to *Yahweh*'s command. As he obeyed, the angels of *Elohim* appeared. This was a reminder to him of his dream 20 years earlier at Bethel where angels ascended and descended the ladder. The meeting with the angels verified *Yahweh*'s recent promise to protect him (Gen. 28:15, 31:3). This occurred prior to the trials that would shortly come to him. God sometimes anticipates our prayers and provides encouragement to us.

If Jacob had trusted *Yahweh* fully, he would have confronted Laban before he left Paddan-Aram. Now he faced a similar confrontation with Esau. No one can run from God's lessons. The angels formed a company to protect and guide Jacob and his company. In recognition of that fact, Jacob named the place, Mahanaim, "two camps" (*machaňayim,* מחנים) [map site 18]. He designated the two camps as his camp and the angels.

Gen. 32:3-5: Having made a covenant of peace with Laban, Jacob now sought peace for the immediate future with Esau because of his deception to him in the remote past. There is no indication that he prayed before sending the messengers to Esau. He acted on his own initiative. Since Isaac was still alive, and Esau had left home, Jacob's inheritance awaited him upon his return home. Isaac had declared that the inheritance would go to Jacob.

Jacob told the messengers to tell Esau that he had servants and herds. It would seem that this announcement of his success during his sojourn with Laban had a twofold purpose. First, he wanted his brother to know that he had acquired wealth and was a successful man. Second, he may have been indicating to Esau that they could negotiate Esau's "losses." Perhaps Jacob was thinking about taking the traditional one-third of the inheritance and giving the two-thirds to Esau. Alternatively, Jacob may have considered giving Esau some of his present possessions to offset what Esau "lost."

Jacob's "Two Companies"

Gen. 32:6-12: The messengers returned with the news that Esau was coming with four hundred men. There are several possible interpretations of Esau coming with his army:

1. Esau, a warlord, would never travel without his personal army for his own protection.

2. Esau could have been coming in wrath with the intention of attacking Jacob and taking all that he possessed.

3. Esau may have wanted to demonstrate his power and wealth to Jacob but without doing him harm.

4. Esau could have been coming with good intentions to provide Jacob an armed escort. He may have desired for Jacob to accompany him back to Mount Seir to introduce him to his family and/or take him home to their father at Hebron.

Jacob's guilty conscience over his previous deception in negotiating the birthright and stealing the blessing allowed him to consider only the worst possible interpretation. He thought that Esau was coming to attack him. Jacob ignored the fact that God had shown him a band of His angels to accompany and protect him.

There was no need for him to have contacted Esau at this time; he could have waited until he was home with his father. Since he had not prayed before contacting Esau, he was now in the position of asking God to bless the action he had already taken.

Jacob, in his fear of an attack, divided his ranks into two companies in hope of preserving one of them. His prayer for protection referred only to his "two" companies. He ignored the company of angels that *Yahweh* had already sent to him. Thus, he now suggested that Mahanaim meant his two companies.

The method for his division into two companies is not stated. In whatever manner he did this, he was sure to offend several members of his family. He finally prayed to the *Elohim* of his grandfather and father and to *Yahweh*, the name God used during his encounters at Bethel and Haran (Gen. 28:13, 31:3). He recognized that his current call was to return to his country and to **his relatives**.

These promises included protection, prosperity, and a numberless progeny. However, he left out the part of the promise that included a blessing through Abraham to all the nations of the earth, which would have included the tribe descended from Esau: "In you and in your seed shall all the families of the earth be blessed" (Gen. 28:14b).

He prayed out of fear with a suggestion to God as to how He should protect him. He made a plea for protection for himself and the mothers; he did not refer to them as his wives. He was appealing to God's compassion for the innocent members of his family, the mothers and children; they had done nothing to Esau. Jacob asked *Yahweh* to deliver him from Esau.

He reminded *Yahweh* of His promise: "I will surely prosper you and make your descendants as the sand of the sea, which is too great to be numbered" (Gen. 32:12). However, that was a promise made to Abraham, not to Jacob, after he had offered up Isaac:

"Indeed I will greatly bless you, and I will greatly multiply your seed as the stars of the heavens and as the sand which is on the seashore; and your seed shall possess the gate of their enemies" (Gen. 22:17).

At Bethel, *Yahweh* told Jacob that he would make his "seed like the dust of the earth" (Gen. 28:14a). Why did Jacob quote the promise given to Abraham (Gen. 22:17)? Protection from his enemies was part of the promise to Abraham. Jacob was concerned about protection from Esau, his assumed enemy. By faith, Jacob had incorporated the promises made to Abraham (page 368).

Jacob was to transitioning from the "dust of the earth" to the "sand of the seashore" (Gen. 22:17). Believers need to change from dust to the tough grit of sand by the continual action of salt water on the dirt and minerals of the soil. If he was to "crystallize" and glisten for *Yahweh*, Jacob was learning that cleansing and spiritual fiber were necessary. He could acquire these qualities by conquering in the spiritual battles of life.

The last stage would be "as the stars of the heavens" (Gen. 15:5, 22:17, 26:4). This would require a lifetime of progressive sanctification that prepared him for graduation to the heavens and life in the presence of the One Triune God to whom the heavenly hosts cry "Holy, Holy, Holy!"

Gifts to Appease Esau

Gen. 32:13-20: After his prayer, Jacob tried to appease Esau by sending him 580 animals in five separate droves at intervals in order to appease Esau with each sequential gift. Five is the number that refers to a princely portion (page 350). Joseph would subsequently treat Benjamin like a prince (Gen. 43:34, 45:22). This was a rich gift. It appears that the least valuable animals were in the front and the most valuable ones in the rear; he wanted to soften Esau the closer he came to Jacob.

Jacob's benefactor and protector was *El Shaddai* (page 51). *Yahweh* had blessed Jacob with the animals and servants obtained in Paddan-Aram (Gen. 30:43). Stewardship sometimes involves losing to those that treat us unfairly. *El Shaddai* had allowed Laban to steal from Jacob. However, He had set boundaries on Laban's thievery and had held Laban in check (Gen. 30:34-36).

Jacob was responsible to *Yahweh* as a steward of the wealth that He had given to him. Jacob had sent several expensive gifts to Esau (Gen. 32:13-21). Esau would hear Jacob's name and his beneficence with each drove. Jacob sought peace with Esau by appealing to his materialism. In his prior deception about the blessing of the firstborn, Esau lost wealth. Therefore, Jacob may have reasoned that he "owed him."

Jacob's Nighttime Ambivalence

Gen. 32:21-23: Sometime during the night, Jacob sent his family and his herds and servants across the Jabbok [map site 17]. Presumably, this was to protect them from Esau, but he may have been concerned about Laban returning. Laban had broken his word to Jacob multiple times in the previous 20 years. If Esau or Laban murdered him, Jacob was considering what would happen to his family.

If he placed them on the north side of the Jabbok, he would have expected them to return to Paddan-Aram. It seems unlikely that he would have placed them on the south side of the Jabbok, which would have required trust in Esau to protect them. If he had decided to do that, it would have been contrary to his prayer request (Gen. 32:11). The Jabbok is thought to have had a loop in this area; he may have placed them on neutral ground toward the Jordan. If so, he was probably relying on his family and servants to try to escape to Hebron, if hostilities broke forth. Deborah knew the way back to Hebron.

Jacob's sons ranged from 6 to 13 years of age. Jacob and Esau were 97 years of age. Laban would have been around 140 years or older. Laban, a polygamist, would have had sons with a considerable age range, possibly from the very young to older than Jacob.

Jacob at the Jabbok—The Wrestling Match

Gen. 32:24-30: Jacob was alone as he anticipated the approach of his "enemy." At the Jabbok, Jacob wrestled with *Elohim* as a man for the entire night. *Elohim*'s touch dislocated Jacob's hip just before daybreak. No person can dislocate an opponent's hip with a single blow ("to strike," *naĝa'*, ויגע) during a wrestling match. Only One with power and supernatural knowledge of physics and anatomy had the ability to do this. This should have raised a question in Jacob's mind about the identity of his "opponent."

Moses asked to see the glory of *Yahweh*. He allowed Moses to see his back, not his face, even though Moses had faithfully served him under trying circumstances (Exod. 33:13-23):

"And He said, 'I Myself will make all My goodness pass before you, and will proclaim the name of the LORD before you; and I will be gracious to whom I will be gracious, and will show compassion on whom I will show compassion.' But He said, 'You cannot see My face, for no man can see Me and live.'" (Exod. 33:19-20).

Sinful man cannot gaze on the purity of holiness in the face of God. When he made his request, Jacob had not attained to Moses' spiritual level. Thus, there was no way Jacob could have been prepared to see the face of God. *Elohim* allowed the match to continue until daybreak to see if Jacob would hold on, but He would not allow him to see His face.

Jacob hung on; he was afraid to let go. He believed that letting go could mean death to him and capture to his family. Jacob's request for a blessing indicates he thought his opponent was a man. In order to unmask the identity of his opponent, Jacob asked for his name. Since Jacob thought that he was wrestling with Laban (or one of Laban's sons) from his recent past, or Esau from his remote past and immediate future, he was surprised when *Elohim* asked Jacob why he wanted to know His name. God's questions to a man are always penetrating. The question revealed to Jacob that he was not fighting with a man from his past, present, or future.

Jacob received the blessing from *Yahweh* of a new name, Israel, the promise of a new character, a new nature. *Elohim* gave the meaning of the name:

"You have striven with God and men and have prevailed" (Gen. 32:28b).

Jacob's history was one of striving with men and prevailing, only through the grace of God. He successfully strove with *Elohim* by not letting go until he received the blessing.

God wrestled with Jacob as *Elohim*, not *Yahweh*. Jacob needed to have a new character, a new name, a new creation, before he could become Israel. Eventually he would submit to *Yahweh* as LORD and seek His glory. God deals with us one step at a time to purify our character and make us right in His sight. Jacob would become Israel. As he evolved into the character of Israel, he would want to know more of *Yahweh*.

Jacob's requested blessing was deliverance from harm. God's blessing was greater, the promise of a new character as exemplified by the new name. God only wrestles with us for our benefit. "The dawn" was breaking upon the beginning of *Elohim*'s new creation. Jacob would become Israel (Gen. 32:26).

Elohim, the Triune Creator, put the dislocated hip back into its place. That action required Jacob's cooperation in allowing his opponent to place him in the correct position for this maneuver, a position where he would have been vulnerable to any hostile action. Jacob had to trust *Elohim*. God was gracious to Jacob.

Jacob named the place Peniel ("face of God," *peniŷ'eĺ,* פניאל). Jacob had wrestled with God "face-to-face," a **Christophany** (the **third** direct communication). Jacob did not see the physical face of the LORD but had "faced Him" in the dark in a wrestling match. His life had been preserved, but he had a chronic limp. Jacob would eventually become Israel and submit to his LORD!

The Son of God became a "man" (*'iŷsh,* איש) to wrestle with Jacob (Gen. 32:24). Adam first used the term, *Ish*, when he saw his bride (Gen. 2:23). *Elohim* came as *Ish*, the Husband of His bride. That bride was represented by Jacob, the man who would engender the nation of Israel. Other Jewish and Gentile believers would join with him to become the church, the bride of Christ. The LORD would wrestle with the church as it evolved to become the Israel of God, just as He wrestled with Jacob during that night:

"But may it never be that I would boast, except in the cross of our Lord Jesus Christ, through which the world has been crucified to me, and I to the world. For neither is circumcision anything, nor uncircumcision, but a new creation. And those who will walk by this rule, peace and mercy be upon them, and upon the Israel of God" (Gal. 6:14-16).

Elohim sees the end from the beginning. It would take years before Jacob would show forth the character of Israel. In the interim, he often manifested the character of Jacob, the old man. However, in the concluding years of his life, he became Israel, the new man (Eph. 4:22-24). Israel would experience a temporary sojourn in Egypt. After that sojourn, his internment would be in the Promised Land. That would be a final act of faith in the promises of *Yahweh* (Gen. 49:28-33, 50:1-13).

The Jabbok River is a tributary that empties into the Jordan River. Jabbok means "emptying" (*yabboq̂,* יבק). Jordan means "to go down" (*yarden̂,* ירדן). Jacob needed to "empty himself of selfishness" at the Jabbok. Then he would be ready to "go down" and cross the Jordan to the Promised Land. If he did not, he would "go down," i.e., regress, in his spiritual walk with the LORD.

Jacob entered the night alone with concern about Esau who represented his remote past and immediate future and Laban and his sons who represented his immediate past. Individuals often think they wrestle with people from their past, present, and/or future. Instead, they find that they have been wrestling with God.

Winning by Losing

Gen. 32:31-32: God blessed Jacob during the wrestling match. Anyone who wrestles with God must remember who He is. The potter forms the clay of His children in His own likeness. He loves us and will perform whatever spiritual or physical surgery necessary to make us in His image (Gen. 1:26-27, Rom. 8:28-30). After losing the wrestling match, Jacob limped across Penuel to rejoin his family.

Those who prevail spiritually are willing to accept the defeat God brings or allows to come their way. If they let Him have control, all such experiences deepen their relationship with Him.

Jacob had a limp that would stay with him and constantly remind him of his momentous wrestling match with the living God. Jacob won by losing!

When helpful for our spiritual development, physical ailments are allowed by the LORD, even when they come from Satan:

"Because of the surpassing greatness of the revelations, for this reason, to keep me from exalting myself, there was given me a thorn in the flesh, a messenger of Satan to torment me—to keep me from exalting myself. Concerning this I implored the Lord three times that it might leave me. And He has said to me, 'My grace is sufficient for you, for power is perfected in weakness.' Most gladly, therefore, I will rather boast about my weaknesses, so that the power of Christ may dwell in me" (2 Cor. 12:7-9).

Reunion with Esau; Jacob, Age 97

Genesis 33:1-20

Gen. 33:1-11: "Then Jacob lifted his eye and looked, and behold, Esau was coming, and four hundred men with him" (Gen. 33:1). After his wrestling match with *Elohim*, Jacob's eyes were initially downcast, perhaps in prayer. Now he was ready to meet his brother, his assumed enemy.

Jacob demonstrated to his family, his brother, and all observers his preferential love by the order in which he had placed his sons, his handmaidens, and his wives. He placed them in reverse preferential order, not the order of their birth. In the front were Zilpah with her sons, Gad and Asher; then Bilhah with her sons, Dan and Naphtali; then Leah with her sons and daughter: Reuben, Simeon, Levi, Judah, Issachar, Zebulun, and Dinah; and in the rear, Rachel with Joseph.

Since Jacob did not have time to do any major change to the two companies from the night before, it appears that one company had the handmaidens and their sons and the other company had Rachel and Leah with their children. The arrangement of wives and children spoke volumes to his family and must have affected their view of their husband and father, respectively, for some time afterwards.

Jacob limped forward to meet Esau in front of his family. They could not have known the reason for Jacob's limp at this time, but the story must have been retold to subsequent generations who did not eat the "sinew" (*ligamentum teres*?) of the hip (Gen. 32:32).

To his credit, Jacob went forward alone to meet Esau. Jacob was humbled before his worldly brother. He made obeisance by bowing seven times to the ground before coming near him. Esau's response was to run and embrace Jacob and fall on his neck. Two 97-year-old twins, having experienced some of the hardships of life, wept together. God answered Jacob's prayer. Esau still had love and concern for his brother. He may have looked forward to this reunion and was not coming with the malice Jacob expected. Jacob's fear came primarily from his own guilt over his past dealings with Esau.

When Esau asked about the family, servants, and animals, Jacob attributed the blessing of them to *Elohim*. He was no longer self-confident but was praising the name of *Elohim*. He took the position of a servant before Esau. When believers sin against unbelievers, God places them in a position of confession and humility in order to experience victory over pride.

He now saw Esau's face "as one who sees the face of God," which had more meaning than Esau could know. Those who pray and trust the LORD for the outcome often find their worst fears are dissipated. Esau was still materialistic and accepted Jacob's gift after his urging. Jacob used the word, blessing, not gift (Gen. 33:11 NASB margin). Jacob had learned to praise God for his material blessings and give freely to others (Gen. 32:7-12). It was fitting that Jacob "lose" some of his possessions in order to understand the meaning of stewardship. Since God is the Possessor of the heavens and the earth, all that we have belongs to the LORD who entrusts us as stewards with His possessions (Gen. 14:22).

Jacob's Continued Deception

Gen. 33:12-16: Esau now offered to go before and protect Jacob with his four hundred men. He was willing to provide Jacob a safe escort (Gen. 33:12). Jacob was still afraid of Esau. Jacob stated he had to go slow because of the herds. He had recently driven them a great distance in an attempt to escape from Laban. This belies the fact that he had just given Esau 580 animals that had the same problem. Esau got the point.

Jacob, still operating with deceit after the wrestling match with *Elohim*, stated that he would proceed to Esau, "his lord," at Seir. Instead, he made a right hand turn and started his journey to the western side of the Jordan. Sometimes spiritual development comes slowly, even after wrestling with God.

Jacob did not see Esau's offer as a provision from *Yahweh* for a safe return to his home. Returning home meant a return to Bethel and obedience to the vow he made with *Yahweh*. It would be close to a decade before Jacob would return to Bethel and his home; it is not clear whether he ever visited Esau at Seir or at Hebron.

Succoth; Jacob, Age 97 plus

Gen. 33:17: *Yahweh* had explicitly told Jacob to return to his land **and his relatives**. Jacob only told his wives that He had told him to return to his land. In his prayer at the Jabbok, he acknowledged to God the command to return to his land and his relatives (Gen. 28:20-21; 31:3, 13; 32:9).

However, he did not proceed to his father's house but built a house on the east side of the Jordan River. In the future, this land would be assigned to the tribe of Gad (Josh. 13:24-28) Jacob still sought to modify the command of *Yahweh*. He stayed at Succoth ("booths," *suk̂kotĥ,* סכתה) [map site 16] for an undetermined period but long enough to build a house and booths for his livestock. He continued to delay his return to Bethel.

The Altar at Shechem; Jacob, Age 97 plus

Gen. 33:18-20: Subsequently, with partial obedience, Jacob crossed the Jordan River and went a few miles further to Shechem ("ridge," *shekem*, שׁכם), the place where Abram first entered the land and built an altar to *Yahweh* (Gen. 12:6-7).

Jacob would most certainly know of Abram's sojourn there through the events described to him by his grandfather during the last 15 years of Abraham's life (Tables 8 and 9, page 390). Now he was willing to enter the land but unwilling to return to Bethel. He would not see his father again until the waning years of Isaac's life (Chart 2, page 266).

Jacob camped in front of the village of Shechem. The Hebrew word for Hivites means "villagers" (*chivviŷ,* חוי). He paid money for the land where he pitched his tent. Buying the land and placing his tent there, without building a house, indicated that he wished to sojourn there temporarily (Josh. 24:32). He again disobeyed *Yahweh*'s command to return to his relatives (Gen. 31:3, 13, 18; 32:9).

However, Jacob had returned to Shechem in safety. *Yahweh* is ever faithful to His word. Jacob built an altar at Shechem and called upon *El-Elohe*-Israel, God, the One Triune God of Israel (*'el 'elohêy yiśra'el,* אל אלהי ישׂראל). By this repetition (singular and plural names of the One Triune God), he was acknowledging *Elohim* as his personal God, *El* (page 50). Jacob had wrestled with *Elohim* at the Jabbok. The location of this altar may have been the same site where Abram built his first altar to *Yahweh* when he entered the land at Shechem (Gen. 12:6-7). Jacob still had not submitted to *Yahweh* as his LORD.

The Price of Delayed Obedience

Genesis 34:1-31

Gen. 34:1-24: Dinah, "judgment" (*"diŷnah,"* דינה), was born to Leah as the last of seven children when Jacob was 91. Rachel also bore Joseph about the same time. It is likely that Dinah and Joseph were the same age (Gen. 30:21-24).

Dinah went out "to see" (*ra'ah̃,* ראה), not "to visit," the daughters of the land. The Hebrew infinitive, "to see," can mean "to act" or "to participate." Dinah may have wished to see for herself and participate in the questionable practices of the teenagers of Shechem who were involved in the worship of Baal. The record suggests that Dinah was a physically mature teenager when she mingled with the daughters of the land. She placed herself in a vulnerable situation that led to rape by Shechem. Subsequent Bible history and archaeological discoveries indicate how immoral the worship of Baal was at Shechem (Jdg. 8:29-35, 9:1-4). Dinah suffered "judgment" (*"diŷnah̃,"* דינה) for her actions.

The fact that the name of the village came from Shechem, not his father, indicates that he was the leader in the village. In addition, Shechem's command to his father to get Dinah for him as a wife indicates that he was the leader of the tribe.

After the rape of Dinah, two Hebrew words describe Shechem's continued interest in her. The first can be translated "deeply attracted" (*dab̃aq,* דבק) and conveys the idea of physical attraction. The second is translated with the usual Hebrew word for "love" (*'ah̃ab,* אהב). Shechem, "spoke to the heart (*leb̃,* לב) of the girl" (Gen. 34:3 NASB margin). Shechem had a sexual attraction for Dinah, mistaken for love, similar to the modern demeaning of the word. Contrast this with *Yahweh*'s definition of sexual love between a husband and his wife, "to know" (*yad̂a',* ידע) each other (Gen. 4:1). Confirmation of this interpretation is the fact that Dinah would not be **the** wife of Shechem, but **a** wife. Dinah would become another addition to his harem (Gen. 34:3-4).

Rape is always a violent act. Dinah represents many from believers' families for whom a first adventure in an evil world has had an horrible outcome. Dinah's rape probably occurred when she was in her early to middle teens, possibly between 13 and 16 years of age. Therefore, Jacob must have delayed his return home for seven to ten years. Levi and Simeon were four and five years older than Dinah, respectively.

Jacob and his sons saw rape for the defilement that it is. Rape affected a young girl's entire life. Dinah would still be single at the age of 39 (23-26 years later). When the family list was compiled in Egypt, her name was on the list; she had not married (Gen. 46:15).

Jacob had changed after his encounter with *Elohim* at the Jabbok. He did not try to act precipitously or to manipulate the event. He waited for his sons to come home and discussed the situation with them. Reuben, the eldest son, abdicated his leadership role among the brothers. Simeon and Levi, the second and third sons of Jacob, took the lead in the matter. They had been raised in a violent and immoral culture for the previous seven to ten years; it had had its effect upon them. Because immoral behavior demeans others, it often becomes violent. Hence, it is not surprising that the two brothers made a violent decision.

The reserve on Jacob's part was commendable, compared to his past aggressiveness, but it was not wise. Jacob's trust in the judgment of young men raised in an evil environment was folly. As could be expected, they reacted with grief and anger over the rape of their "baby sister" and took violent action.

Their father had established a pattern of deceitful behavior in the past and modeled it to his sons. Now they acted with deceit. Jacob abdicated in his role as patriarch of the family. The sons, not Jacob, negotiated with Hamor and Shechem. The negotiated business arrangement, the "bride price" for Dinah, was intermarriage and incorporation into the tribe. The Shechemites believed they would gain wealth through this agreement.

The young sons of Jacob deceitfully proposed circumcision to the Shechemite men. They made mockery of circumcision as simply a physical sign of the covenant of *Yahweh*. This was the sign originally given to Abraham as a symbol of circumcision of the heart, not trusting in one's own potency (Gen. 17:1-27, Ezek.

44:9, Rom. 2:29). The sons of Jacob viewed circumcision as an outward sign only.

The New Testament reveals that the Jewish religious leaders perpetuated this interpretation of the sign of circumcision. With the same view of externalism, Shechem appropriately interpreted the political and religious significance of this act and took it as a sign that they would "become one people" (Gen. 34:22). The merging of the unholy worship of the Baalim with the holy worship of *Yahweh*, if carried to completion, would have been a form of syncretism.

The Deceit of Jacob's Sons
Mayhem and Murder

Gen. 34:25-31: Simeon and Levi, who were between 17 and 20 years of age, approached the village by stealth. They killed the men of Shechem on the third day when they were in pain from their circumcision and did not expect an attack. They were responsible for the sins of murder, the needless maiming of an ox, and pillaging (Gen. 49:5-7). Jacob exposed his children to an evil society without providing spiritual leadership and suffered the consequences.

After Simeon and Levi's "victory," they looted the village. Simeon and Levi now "possessed" the ill-gotten gain of women of questionable character, worshipers of Baal, a religion known for child sacrifice and immorality (Gen. 34:27-29). These Shechemite mothers would raise their children and the children born to these women through Simeon and Levi. It is likely that the children of the captured Shechemite women would become servants, and the women would become concubines. Some of the children and women may have come to faith in *Yahweh* (Gen. 46:10).

It is not certain whether the other sons participated in a share of the "loot." Jacob's condemnation of Simeon and Levi only, and subsequent history, suggests that they were the only perpetrators who shared in their ill-gotten "gain" (Gen. 49:5-7).

The immoral practices of the Shechemite women affected the seed of Simeon and Levi. The tribe of Simeon contributed to Israel's immorality. Levi's tribe became conservative in sexual practices. Jacob deferred judgment of this incident until his deathbed when he prophesied that their progeny would be scattered in Israel (Gen. 49:5-7).

There is always a price to pay for partial and delayed obedience. For Jacob this was the rape of Dinah followed by the murder and pillaging of Shechem and the capture of immoral women by two of Jacob's sons. Delay in the spiritual development of a husband and father may adversely affect the spiritual development of everyone in the family.

Jacob was unaware of the plot of his sons, but he should have been. After their rampage, he reproached Simeon and Levi. The Canaanites and the Perizzites, the inhabitants of the land that remained after the conquest of the Hivites at Shechem, noted the stench of their behavior. An understanding of the Hebrew translation of Canaanites, "merchants" (*kena'aniŷ,* כנעני), and a Canaanite tribe, the Perizzites, "those who live in open country" *perizziŷ,* פרזי), was reflected in Jacob's fear (Gen. 34:30, Hos. 12:7). They had broken a business and religious covenant and offended "the merchants of the lowlands." The spiritual meaning of the two may symbolize the Canaanite merchant as dealing in unscrupulous business practices (page 140) (Zech. 14:21).

Simeon and Levi defended their actions by stating that Shechem had treated Dinah like "a common whore" (*zaĥaĥ,* זנה) (Gen. 34:31, 49:5-7 NASB margin). They did not understand *Yahweh* and his demands for holy living and righteous behavior. Jacob, in his disobedience, was fearful of men. Jacob, Dinah, Simeon, and Levi had placed themselves outside *Yahweh's* "hedge of protection":

"Then Satan answered the LORD, 'Does Job fear God for nothing? 'Have You not made a hedge about him and his house and all that he has, on every side? You have blessed the work of his hands, and his possessions have increased in the land'" (Job 1:9-10).

Jacob later told Joseph that he was giving Shechem to Joseph's sons. He stated that he took the land with his sword and bow (Gen. 48:22). He saw the sovereignty of *Yahweh* in his two sons' inappropriate "war" at Shechem. He also foresaw the conquest by Joshua and his generation that left him with an inheritance from the Amorite nations (page 372) (Gen. 15:16-21). That prophecy's fulfillment would occur after Jacob's departure from this life (Josh. 11:1-15, 21:21, 24:1). When His children repent and obey him, God takes evil and turns it about for good (Gen. 50:20).

Elohim's Repeated Commands; Jacob Obeys

Genesis 35:1-29

Gen. 35:1-6: Jacob was between 104 and 107 years of age. After the rape of Dinah, and the ensuing pillaging of Shechem by Simeon and Levi, *Elohim* **spoke** to Jacob (the **fourth** direct communication) to proceed to Bethel, not to his home. *Elohim* was telling Jacob that his slow return was due to the promise he made at Bethel three decades ago. Jacob was avoiding that meeting with *Yahweh* (Gen. 28:20-22). Jacob, seeing the fruit of his disobedience, was now ready to obey *Elohim's* command. Besides returning to Bethel, Jacob was to build an altar there and dedicate himself anew to *Elohim* who reminded him of how he had, "fled from the face of your brother Esau" (Gen. 35:1 NASB margin). *Yahweh* had not only protected Jacob from Esau according to His covenant, but He also brought about reconciliation with him after the wrestling match at the Jabbok (Gen. 31:3).

Jacob's disobedience at Succoth and Shechem indicated that his way of doing things during the previous three decades was evidence of incomplete submission to *Yahweh*. If *Yahweh* kept covenant with him, Jacob had promised, in his prayer to *Yahweh* in his first experience at Bethel, that *Yahweh* would be his God:

"Then Jacob made a vow, saying, 'If God will be with me and will keep me on this journey that I take, and will give me food to eat and garments to wear, and I return to my father's house in safety, then the LORD will be my God" (Gen. 28:20-21).

The central reason that Jacob had not returned to Bethel was the covenant that he had made with *Yahweh*. He had made a vow at Bethel. If he received necessary maintenance and returned to his home in safety, he would submit to *Yahweh* as his LORD.

Since Jacob had not submitted to God as *Yahweh*, He addressed Jacob with His name, *Elohim*. Jacob also had vowed to tithe to *Yahweh* (Gen. 28:22). There is no definitive evidence that he had tithed to Him. However, he may have done so on the altar that he had built at Shechem (Gen. 28:20-22, 33:20).

Jacob gave testimony to his family of *Elohim*'s faithfulness to him. He demanded that Rachel and others in his family, e.g., Simeon and Levi who had pillaged Shechem, give up their foreign gods and symbols of worship. The household idols and the rings in their ears were emblems of worship of the Baalim at Shechem and the Babylonian pantheon of gods in Paddan-Aram (Gen. 31:19, Hos. 2:13).

If he was to follow *Yahweh*, Jacob knew he had to set a good example. His neglect had fostered unfavorable traits in Rachel, Leah, Reuben, Simeon, Levi, Dinah, and to some degree, his entire household. Jacob further commanded that they bathe and change their garments, symbols of purification for a new life.

He hid the foreign gods under the "oak," the *terebinth*, at Shechem. This was a religious site and the probable place of Abram's first altar (Gen. 12:6-7). Now it was the site of Jacob's repentance. Hiding the idols suggests that Jacob did not want any in his household, or others in the land, to find and use them in the worship of false gods. Abraham had been proactive in his witness at Shechem; Jacob had been reactive due to his sin.

Jacob proceeded to Bethel. In doing so, he retraced the journey of his grandfather (Gen. 12:8). He was now obeying *Elohim* who protected him and his family on the journey by creating "a terror of *Elohim*" (*chittaî 'elohiŷm,* חתת אלהים) in the surrounding area.

The Deaths of Deborah and Rachel
Bethel; Jacob, Age 104-107

Gen. 35:7-15: The rape of Dinah, the pillaging of Shechem, and the deaths of two loved ones forced Jacob to think more seriously about eternal matters and his relationship with God.

Correspondence between Jacob and his parents must have resulted in the sending of Deborah to him sometime during the birth of their children, and most likely, after the death of Rebekah. The first death was Deborah's, the faithful nurse of Rebekah and of Jacob's children. She died south of Bethel at Allon-bacuth ("the oak of weeping," *'allon bakuth,* אלון בכות). Deborah was older than Rebekah. She must have been around 150 years of age at the time of her death (page 238).

God had commanded Jacob to return to Bethel. After he returned from Paddan-Aram, a plateau located in the highland of Syria, God **appeared** to Jacob (the **fifth** direct communication) at Bethel. The time spent at Succoth and Shechem, where Jacob had delayed his return, was a time of disobedience and not further referenced. God carries our sins away, "even as far as the east is from the west" (Psa. 103:12).

God blessed Jacob after the death of Deborah and just before the death of Rachel. He encouraged him during his time of sorrow. He reaffirmed his new name, Israel, and the blessing given to Abraham and Isaac before him. He transitioned from *Elohim* to *El Shaddai*, the name that He had revealed to Abraham (Gen. 17:1). Jacob was to rely solely on *El Shaddai* for his provision (page 51). He had provided for Jacob with His bountiful supply and had kept all the promises made to Jacob during his dream at Bethel three decades earlier.

Jacob obeyed *Elohim* by returning to Bethel, but he still did not address Him as *Yahweh*. The LORD did not force Jacob to acknowledge Him as *Yahweh*. Submission to the LORD is a voluntary act. *Elohim* reaffirmed the name of Israel to Jacob and gave him a creative fresh start in life; He did not give up on him (Gen. 35:10-12). Jacob was between 104 and 107 years old.

Jacob may have tithed by animal sacrifice on the altar at Bethel (Gen. 35:11). When God went up from him, Jacob renewed his vow by anointing the pillar at Bethel with a drink and an oil offering. This may have been the same pillar that he used for his original dedication 27-30 years previously. The drink offering symbolized pouring oneself out for the LORD, and the oil offering symbolized the anointing of God by the Holy Spirit. The offerings were symbols of the necessity of worshiping the LORD in spirit and truth in order to be able to perform service for Him.

This was **the** place where God had appeared to him previously. It was formerly called Luz ("nut tree," *luẑ,* לוּז), a name that reflected its physical produce. Jacob called it Bethel ("house of God," *beŷth' el,* בֵּית־אֵל), a name that reflected its spiritual produce after another transaction between a man and his God (Gen. 28:10-22, 35:1-15).

Gen. 35:16-20: After Bethel and the death of Deborah, Rachel died. Rachel had prayed to *Yahweh* for a second son. She received the answer to that prayer with the completion of her earthly journey (Gen. 30:23-24). Rachel died during childbirth while calling her son Ben-oni ("the son of my sorrow," *ben'oniŷ,* בֶּן־אוֹנִי), but his father called him Benjamin ("the son of the right hand," *binyamiŷn,* בִּנְיָמִין) (Gen. 3:16). The hand symbolized one's power and work.

The midwife's admonition to Rachel, "Do not fear, for now you have another son," spoke of *Yahweh*'s providing the answer to her prayer for a second son (page 277). She gave birth on the road to Ephrath ("fruitfulness," *'ephrathah,* אֶפְרָתָה) [map site 8]. Her last act on earth was one of bearing fruit to the glory of *Yahweh* to whom she had prayed for this son (Gen. 30:24). She need not have feared because her birth into the life where there is no shadow was just beginning (1 Cor. 13:12, James 1:17). She was going to a family reunion.

In the future, Ephrath would be renamed Bethlehem ("house of bread," *beŷth lechem,* בית לחם) where the Bread of Life was born (Gen. 35:19, Luke 2:4-11, John 6:48). A pillar marked Rachel's grave. The most notable references to this event occurred during the time of the deportation to Babylon of Rachel's progeny and after the birth of the Savior when the little babies were killed in Bethlehem (Gen. 35:20, Jer. 31:15, Matt. 2:16-18).

Rachel brought glory to *Yahweh* through the birth of her two sons as testified by their lives. Her son was not *Benoni* ("son of my sorrow," *ben'ônîŷ,* בן־אוני). Jacob's discernment about the name of their son was correct. The name, Benjamin ("the son of the right hand," *binyâmîŷn,* בנימין), looked forward to the birth in Bethlehem of the Messiah, the Savior, the Son who now sits at the right hand of God the Father (Psa. 110:1). Thus, Rachel's death during the **delivery** of Benjamin foreshadowed the Savior who would **deliver** her from her sin (page 368).

Rachel and Leah must have been in their late thirties or early forties. Leah would have been present with her sister when she died in childbirth. Leah assumed the role of mother to Joseph and baby Benjamin following Rachel's death (Gen. 37:10).

God took from Jacob his greatest earthly love to allow him the possibility of fully knowing Him (Luke 14:25-33). Jacob needed to learn to treat Leah with respect and give her all that was due as his wife. She had the right to the marriage bed. She would be Jacob's intimate companion for the rest of her life. This may have helped Jacob to understand that Leah's type of love was more substantial and longsuffering than that of Rachel's. Physical traits wane with time. Spiritual traits, in a woman like Leah, improve with time.

Since Jacob was on his way to the family homestead at Hebron, he could have taken Rachel to the family cave at Machpelah for burial. It was approximately 25 miles from where they were. He must have understood that Leah was the wife chosen by God for him. Jacob would later bury Leah at Machpelah (Gen. 49:30-31). He buried Rachel on the road to Ephrath, Bethlehem.

The *Migdal-Eder*; Lust and Judgment

Gen. 35:21-22: Reuben, who was between 20 and 23 years of age, had intercourse with Bilhah ("timid," *bilhaĥ,* בלהה). She was his father's concubine and Rachel's handmaiden. Bilhah may have been depressed over Rachel's death and concerned about her future. The Hebrew word, "lay" (*shak̂ab,* שׁכב), in the 22nd verse, is the same as the corresponding word for sexual intercourse elsewhere (Gen. 30:16). It is problematic whether Reuben used this act to "get back" at his father for his rejection of him in favor of Joseph for the rights of the firstborn.

The *Migdal-Eder* ("the tower flock," *migdal'eder,* מגדל־עדר) [map site 10] was outside Bethlehem. This was the probable place where the annunciation of the angels to the shepherds of the birth of the newborn King occurred. The shepherds kept the flock for temple sacrifices there throughout the year (Luke 2:4, 8).[70]

Jacob delayed judgment for Reuben until his deathbed during his blessing to his sons (Gen. 49:3-4). Since that judgment would provide opportunity for confession and repentance, which Reuben had not done, it could be a blessing. He suffered the loss of the rights of the firstborn for "defiling his father's bed" (1 Chr. 5:1).

Thus, there is a connection between the *Migdal-Eder* and the "Reubens" of the world. Deliverance from sin is available through the announcement at this site of the sacrifice of the Lamb of God born to die for our sins. If Reuben had confessed to his father, he could have been reconciled to him. If he repented and believed in *Yahweh*, he could have been reconciled to his heavenly Father.

The Twelve Sons of Jacob

Gen. 35:23-26: The names of the 12 sons of Jacob who came back home with him are enumerated once more. Reuben was the firstborn. Jacob never gave him the blessing and the birthright of the firstborn (Gen. 37:3). The episode at the *Migdal-Eder* did not help matters; it solidified his loss of rights as the firstborn (Gen. 49:3-4, 1 Chr. 5:1). This suggests that Reuben had seduced Bilhah at the *Migdal-Eder*. No condemnation was imposed on Bilhah for her part in the sexual transgression. After Rachel's death, Reuben may have taken advantage of her during her reactive depression. As stated above, Bilhah means "timid" (*bilhaĥ*, בלהה); the name suggests a vulnerable woman.

Moses, led by the Holy Spirit, gave a new order to Jacob's 12 sons and listed Leah's sons first. The list of sons followed the death of Rachel. Leah's children came first, Rachel's second, Bilhah's third, and Zilpah's fourth. Bilhah, Rachel's maid, was the first maid to have a son, and thus, came before Zilpah, Leah's maid. Therefore, there is no evidence of condemnation to Bilhah for the episode with Reuben. She did not lose position after Rachel's death. The record states all the children were born in Paddan-Aram, even though Benjamin was born on the road to Ephrath. Perhaps this was recognition of God's appraisal of their birth from mothers obtained in Paddan-Aram.

The Death of Isaac
Hebron; Jacob, Age 120

Gen. 35:27-29: Jacob was 108 years old when the brothers sold Joseph into Egypt; Isaac was 168 years old. Therefore, Jacob was home for 12 years or more before Isaac died. Esau and Jacob were together at the funeral of their father. They buried Isaac in his 180th year, their 120th year. Isaac was "gathered to his people"; he went to his family reunion. Furthermore, he was "satisfied with days" (Gen. 35:29 NASB). Isaac was satisfied with his life and his time of death; he was at peace with his LORD. Jacob's generation now centered on Joseph and, to a lesser degree, on Judah.

CHART 3: JACOB'S LIFE	
AGE	**EVENT**
15	The death of grandfather Abraham occurred at Hebron followed by his burial at Machpelah.
15?	Jacob obtained the birthright from Esau for a meal of bread and red, lentil stew.
Adult	Isaac moved his family to Gerar and then to Beersheba.
40	Esau married two Hittite women.
77	Jacob received the blessing of the elder son by deception and left home. *Yahweh* transmitted the blessing of Abraham and Isaac to Jacob in the dream at Bethel.
77-84	Jacob met Rachel at the well in Haran. He labored seven years for Rachel, but Leah was substituted by Laban's deceit. Rachel was received as his wife one week later in return for another seven years' labor.
84-91	Six sons and one daughter were born through Leah, two sons each through Bilhah and Zilpah, and Joseph through Rachel.
91-97+	Jacob worked six more years for his herds and received God's blessing despite Laban's continual alteration of their covenant. After departing Haran, he argued and covenanted with Laban at Galeed. He wrestled with God at Penuel. He reunited with Esau but settled at Succoth.
104-107?	He then moved to Shechem with the ensuing rape of Dinah. He received God's call to return to Bethel. Deborah died on the way to Bethel. Rachel died during the birth of Benjamin on the road to Ephrath, Bethlehem. He arrived safely back home in Hebron.
108	Joseph was sold in Egypt. Jacob believed that Joseph was dead. Subsequent to this, Judah left home.
120	Jacob and Esau buried their father at Machpelah.
130	Jacob received God's blessing at Beersheba and moved to Egypt with his family. Jacob blessed Pharaoh twice.
147	Israel gave the blessings and prophecies to Ephraim and Manasseh, to his sons, and to their tribes. He died in his bed and was gathered to his people. He was honored with a state funeral in Egypt and a family one at Machpelah.

CHAPTER 11

THE GENERATIONS OF ESAU

The generations of Esau are the 11th recorded in the book of Genesis (Gen. 36:1, 9). Esau became the godless son who sought materialism. His progeny added to the enmity against Israel. There will be a final judgment of Mt. Seir "at the time of the moral perversity of the end." "Moral perversity" (*'avôn*, עון) is translated as "punishment" in the following text (Ezek 35:5):

"Because you have had everlasting enmity and have delivered the sons of Israel to the power of the sword at the time of their calamity, at the time of the punishment of the end, therefore as I live, declares the Lord GOD, 'I will give you over to bloodshed, and bloodshed will pursue you; since you have not hated bloodshed, therefore bloodshed will pursue you. I will make Mount Seir a waste and desolation and I will cut off from it the one who passes through and returns" (Ezek. 35:5-7).

Edom; Esau, Age 40 plus

Genesis 36:1-43

Gen. 36:1-8: The name Esau comes from a Hebrew root that means "rough" and/or "hairy" (*'eśav*, עשו). The name suggests a coarse individual. His name, his character, is compatible with the alliances and military force he used to achieve dominance in Edom. Esau made alliances with the Hittites, the Ishmaelites, and the Seirites through his marriages. Such alliances were made to increase his wealth and status.

Isaac had prophesied to Esau that his dwelling would be away from the "fertility of the earth" in his blessing to him (Gen. 27:39-40). Edom comes from the Hebrew root that means "red" (*'adôm*, אדום). Esau may have had red hair (Gen. 25:25).

There is a division of Esau's genealogy into two parts. The first eight verses describe the first part of his genealogy before moving to Mount Seir. The second part of his genealogy, the rest of the chapter, describes the descendants added in Mt. Seir, the hill country that became Edom. Seir comes from a Hebrew root that means "hairy" (*śeˀiŷr,* שׂעיר). This may have been a reference to this physical trait in both Esau and Seir (Gen. 25:25, 27:11, 36:20).

TABLE 7: ESAU'S WIVES		
NAME	**FATHER**	**MEANING**
Judith (*yehud̂iŷth*)	Beeri the Hittite	"Praised"
Basemath (*bośmath*) Adah (*'adaĥ*)	Elon the Hittite	"Fragrance" "Ornament"
Mahalath (*machal̆ath*) Basemath (*bośmath*)	Ishmael	"Sickness" "Fragrance"
Oholibamah (*'ohol̆iŷbam̂aĥ*)	Anah	"Tent of the high place"

The variance in the names of Esau's wives may be because several individuals had multiple names that could refer to their character, their physical qualities, and/or their personalities. Esau married two Hittite women, daughters of Heth ("terror," *cheṫh,* חת). They were also called Hittites ("descendants of terror," *chittiŷ,* חתי). Esau was 40 years old (Gen. 26:34-35, 27:46). Judith, the daughter of Beeri the Hittite, is absent from the genealogy in this chapter; this suggests either divorce or death. Basemath (a nickname?) and Adah are two different names for the daughter of Elon the Hittite (Gen. 26:34, 36:2). Basemath means "fragrance" (*bośmath,* בשׂמת); Adah means "ornament" (*'adaĥ,* עדה). Similarly, Basemath and Mahalath are names that refer to one woman, the sister of Nebaioth, the firstborn son of Ishmael (Gen. 25:13, 28:9, 36:3). Since the latter name means "sickness" (*machal̆ath,* מחלת), it is possible that Mahalath had a chronic disease.

Oholibamah was a daughter of a Hivite ("villager," *chivviŷ,* חוי) who became a Horite ("cave dweller," *choriŷ,* חרי) in Mount Seir;

she was the daughter of Anah and granddaughter of Zibeon (Gen. 36:2, 5, 25, 29-30). Since Esau married Judith, Adah, Mahalath, and Oholibamah before his departure from Hebron, these marriages were used to establish alliances with Beeri, Elon, Ishmael, Anah, and Zibeon (Gen. 36:2, 5).

The names of the wives and their family backgrounds suggest that Esau placed a premium on tribal alliances, beauty, and idolatry in the high places of Mount Seir. *Bamah* means "high place," and *ohel* means "tent." Hence, Oholibamah means "tent of the high place" (*'oholîybamah,* אהליבמה). The high places were where the hideous worship of the false religions of the land occurred. Esau clearly opted for a sinful life as revealed by his marriages and idolatrous worship in the high places. The final list shows Oholibamah as a chief in Edom. Females were accepted as tribal leaders (Gen. 36:2, 20-25, 41).

Esau moved away from Jacob when the land could no longer sustain the herds of both. This occurred when Jacob was away in Paddan-Aram. When he returned from Paddan-Aram, Jacob knew that Esau was in Edom, Mount Seir (Gen. 27:39-40, 32:3). Family communication continued during Jacob's stay of nearly three decades in Paddan-Aram.

Gen. 36:9-14: This is a list of the progeny of Esau from three of his wives and the concubine of his eldest son, Eliphaz (1 Chr. 1:35-37). Timna, the concubine of Eliphaz and daughter of Seir, became the mother of Amalek (*'amaleq,* אבימלך), the ancestor of the Amalekites who became archenemies of Israel after the Exodus from Egypt (Gen. 36:12, 20-22). In the time of Samuel and in the time of Esther and Mordecai, the progeny of Amalek continued to express their hatred for Israel (Gen. 36:20-22; Exod. 17:8-16; Num. 24:20; Deut. 25:17-19; 1 Sam. 15:1-32; Est. 3:1, 7:10, 8:5-7, 9:1-32).

The marriage of Eliphaz and Timna furthered the alliance between Esau and Seir, the Horite. Timna may mean "restraint" (*timna',* תמנע). She is on the list of chieftains in Edom (Gen. 36:40).

Gen. 36:15-19: Esau's sons became chiefs of their tribes. The summary of the chiefs, and the statement that Esau is synonymous with Edom, indicate that he eventually conquered Mount Seir, which became Edom.

When Israel sought to enter the Promised Land, the Edomites did not let them pass through their territory. They became perpetual enemies of Israel (Num. 20:14-22, 24:18-19; Deut. 2:3-6). Esau transmitted his enmity against Jacob to his progeny. That hateful antagonism continues to this day through the peoples in his bloodline that embrace Islam and detest the Jews.

Gen. 36:20-30: The Horites were mountaineers. *Hor* comes from the Hebrew word that means mountain or hill. The Horites were cave dwellers in the mountains. These verses detail the progeny of Seir the Horite (1 Chr. 1:38-42).

Gen. 36:31-39: This is a list of the kings in Edom before any ruled in Israel. Esau attempted to compete with Jacob by being first to achieve worldly fame (1 Chr. 1:43-50).

Gen. 36:40-43: The list of the Horites and their kings is followed by a different list of eleven chiefs attributed to Esau, the father of the Edomites (1 Chr. 1:51-54). Esau must have been counted as the twelfth chief. The final list includes two women: Timna, Seir's daughter, and Oholibamah, the daughter of Anah and granddaughter of Zibeon the Hivite/Horite. Several other names are different from the previous list of Esau's sons. The list includes leaders from the progeny of Esau, the progeny of Seir, and the two referenced women. This final list indicates that Esau dominated Seir through these alliances.

Twelve is the number given several times in Genesis for the evolution of a family to become a nation: Nahor's seed (Gen. 22:20-24), Ishmael's seed (Gen. 25:12-16), Jacob's seed (Gen. 35:22-27), and Esau's seed through his alliances (Gen. 36:40-43).

In the sovereignty of God, these names foretold the character of these individuals. Since they were named at birth, and only subsequently did their character evolve to reflect that name, God is interested in and foreknows the lives of each individual, even before they are born (Psa. 139:1-18). The same truth has been noted in the names of the righteous and unrighteous lines (Table 2, page 101; Table 3, page 117).

Unlike the accounts of the other patriarchs, there is no mention that Esau was "gathered to his people." Indeed, there is no record of his death. God, who foreknew both Jacob and Esau, stated that He loved Jacob and hated Esau. He knew the final spiritual state of the individuals and the families, tribes, and nations that they engendered, even before they were born (Ezek. 35:5-7, Mal. 1:2-5, Rom. 9:10-13, Heb. 12:16-17).

CHAPTER 12

THE GENERATIONS OF JACOB

The generations of Jacob are the 12th and final genealogy recorded in the book of Genesis. Jacob's life was intermingled with the history of Joseph and Judah. Jacob's generations include the progenitors of the 12 tribes of Israel whose spiritual seed was destined to become the Israel of God (Matt. 21:42-44, Rom. 2:28-29, 1 Pet. 2:6-10, Gal. 6:15-16). The names of the 12 tribes will be recorded in the New Jerusalem on the 12 gates of the city (Rev. 21:12). The Israel of God will continue in heaven.

JOSEPH'S LIFE-I

Hebron and Egypt; Jacob, Age 108; Joseph, Age 17

Genesis 37:1-36

Gen. 37:1-4: Jacob finally returned to the "land where his father had sojourned." He was not an owner but a sojourner in the land of Canaan. The believer's land is the Father's dwelling place. In spite of all the different peoples that dwelled in the land, its name was Canaan, the land of merchants (Hos. 12:7). Surely the name means that striving after prosperity, its worship, is a great threat to all peoples (Gen. 15:16, Luke 16:13, 1 Tim. 6:10).

Joseph was now 17 years old. Jacob was 108. Isaac was 168. The bad report Joseph brought to his father on the sons of Bilhah, Dan and Naphtali, and the sons of Zilpah, Gad and Asher, increased the jealous feelings his brothers already felt due to the preferential treatment given to Joseph by Jacob. Jacob still believed that Joseph, the elder son of Rachel, his first love, had the rights of the firstborn. Reuben, Simeon, and Levi had all committed acts showing their incapacity for leadership in the family (Gen. 34:13-31, 35:22, 49:1-7).

The preferential love of Jacob for Rachel, and their "hate" (*śāne'*, שׂנא) for Leah, had its repercussions (Gen. 29:33). Jacob's preferential love for Joseph resulted in "hate" (*śane'*, שׂנא) directed at Joseph by his brothers (Gen. 37:8). Favoritism within families creates strong emotional responses in the ones who feel left out.

Jacob placed Joseph in a supervisory capacity with a long or varicolored robe that signified leadership and royalty (2 Sam. 13:18). The sequence in the account suggests that he did this after Joseph had brought the report on his brothers. Jacob may have interpreted Joseph's report as demonstrating the ability to exercise authority over his brothers. The brothers may have perceived that Joseph obtained this favored position by such means.

The preferential love shown by Jacob to Joseph so inflamed his brothers that they hated him and could not address him with the traditional greeting of "peace" (*shalôm*, שׁלם) (Gen. 37:4 NASB margin). The sin of Jacob's continual favoritism contributed to, but was not solely responsible for, the sins of the brothers (James 1:14).

Joseph's Dreams

Gen. 37:5-11: It was in this context that Joseph, the preferred son, younger than all his brothers except Benjamin, had his dreams. God chose the time and circumstances. The first dream of the sheaves involved only Joseph and his brothers. He related this to them, but not to anyone else, and did not interpret the dream. They bristled at the obvious interpretation.

Joseph first recounted the second dream with the sun, moon, and stars to his brothers. There is no record of their response; they ignored him (Gen. 37:9-10). Since it involved his parents, and he did not receive a response from his brothers, he then recounted the dream to his father when his brothers were present. Since Rachel was dead, Joseph may have been asking his father if "the moon" referred to Rachel or to Leah. Jacob gave his interpretation and referred to Leah as Joseph's mother. Whether this was further reflection on the probability that Leah was God's chosen wife for him, or he was merely noting Leah's role after Rachel's death, is problematic. This latter dream provides information important in interpreting the symbols of the nation of Israel in prophecy about the end times (Rev. 12:1).

These dreams, and the thought of bowing down to Joseph, increased the brothers' jealousy. In reciting the dreams to his family members, Joseph may have been proud and wanting to justify his position in the family. Alternatively, he may have felt the need to relate what God had revealed to him. His subsequent actions and character suggest the latter as the dominant motive. Joseph was undoubtedly aware of his father's dreams in the remote past. The fact that he related the dreams to the ones involved, and did not state a personal interpretation, suggests that he wanted confirmation of the interpretation from those involved.

Jacob's pondering of Joseph's dreams may have been due to the fact that God had previously spoken to him through dreams (Gen. 28:12, 31:10-13). He may have interpreted Joseph's dreams as confirmation of God's choice of Joseph to have the rights of the firstborn. Israel, not Jacob, spoke twice in this narrative (Gen. 37:3, 13). Perhaps this was due to the prophetic role he assumed when he elevated Joseph over his brothers.

Gen. 37:12-17: Joseph went in a supervisory role to check on his brothers at Shechem. The man who directed Joseph to Dathan [map site 3] from Shechem ensured that Joseph kept his date with God's destiny for him. The special role of this individual raises the question of whether this was God's directions through a man or an angel (Heb. 13:2).

Dothan; Joseph, Age 17

Gen. 37:18-36: In Hebrew, Dothan means "two wells." The brothers had moved the flocks to Dothan to further graze and water them. It placed them near the east to southwest trade route between Mesopotamia and Egypt.

When the brothers saw Joseph in the distance, they plotted to murder him. This plot may have originated with the sons of Bilhah and Zilpah about whom he had given a negative report (Gen. 37:2).

They planned to blame his death on a wild beast. Reuben, the eldest, attempted to save Joseph without having to stand alone against his brothers. At his suggestion, they temporarily aborted the murder plot. They cast Joseph into a pit without any water in it. Reuben left expecting to come back and rescue Joseph later.

While they listened to the cries of Joseph, cries that continued in their souls for 22 years afterwards, they sat down to eat:

"Then they said to one another, 'Truly we are guilty concerning our brother, because we saw the distress of his soul when he pleaded with us, yet we would not listen; therefore this distress has come upon us.' Reuben answered them, saying, 'Did I not tell you, 'Do not sin against the boy'; and you would not listen? Now comes the reckoning for his blood'" (Gen. 42:21-22).

A caravan from the progeny of Abraham approached. After Abraham sent Ishmael, Midian, and Medan to the land of the east, they formed a business alliance. Ishmael's contacts in Egypt, through his mother and his wife, would have helped in forming such a trade route (pages 242 and 329) (Gen. 21:21; 25:1-6; 37:25, 28, 36). The translation of Midianites (מדינים) in the 36th verse should be Medanites (מדנים) (NASB margin).

Judah converted the plot from murder to the sale of Joseph as a slave. The Midianites bought Joseph after lifting him out of "the pit" (*bor,* בור) (Gen. 37:28). His price was 20 shekels of silver, the price subsequently given in the law for the social value (productivity) placed on a male between five and 20 years of age (Lev. 27:5). Since Benjamin was not present, and Joseph was the one sold, each of the ten brothers received two shekels of silver.

Reuben returned to the pit but did not find Joseph whom he referred to as a "boy" (*yeled,* ילד). At 17 years of age, Joseph was viewed as a boy, not a "lad" (*na'ar,* נער), the youngest of the eleven (excluding Benjamin) (page 223). Reuben was 23-24 years old. He took responsibility for the loss with his brothers, but not at the time they reported to their father (Gen. 37:29-30).

They sacrificed a male goat to put its blood on Joseph's robe (Lev. 4:22-23). They continued the travesty of the lie about Joseph's death having been due to a wild animal. Note that they spoke of Joseph to Jacob as "your son," instead of "our brother." They were still angry with him.

Jacob initially accepted that Joseph was dead and mourned, swearing to mourn until his own death. He refused comfort from his sons and daughters. Part of Jacob's remorse may have been perceived guilt related to his sending Joseph alone to find his brothers. The brothers punished their father for his favoritism by the emotional toll they exacted from him. Jacob's life was intertwined with Joseph's life. As he mourned for Joseph, Jacob's thoughts were about dying. Jacob believed that he was destined for the place of the unrepentant dead, Sheol, a sign of depression.

Sheol (*she'ol̂,* שְׁאֹלָה) is the same as Hades (*hades̄,* ᾅδης), the place of the unrepentant dead who refuse their redemption and await their final judgment (page 19) (Deut. 32:22, Luke 16:23). The LORD Jesus Christ indicated that those who believed Him under the Old Testament dispensation went to Abraham's bosom, the equivalent of Paradise in the New Testament dispensation (Luke 16:23, 23:43).

Abaddon, "the place of destruction" (*'ab̆addon̂,* אבדון), is the Old Testament name for Hell; Gehenna (*geenna,* γέεννα*)* is the equivalent in the New Testament (page 19) (Job 26:6, Matt. 5:22). Gehenna is derived from *Ge-Hennom*, "the valley of Hennon," the place of child sacrifice in Jerusalem that became emblematic of Hell (2 Kin. 23:10). God hates abuse and murder of children so much so that He called the place of such practices, Hell. Abaddon is personalized in Revelation as Satan, the destroyer; Hell was created for him and his angels (Matt. 25:41, Rev. 9:11).

The Medanites in the caravan sold Joseph to Potiphar, "an eunuch" (*sar̂iŷs,* סריס), and Pharaoh's "officer" (*śar,* שׂר), the captain of his bodyguard. This last verse serves as a bridge from the 37th chapter to the 39th chapter where it continues the narrative on Joseph's life.

Judah's Rebellion

Adullam; Judah, age 20 to 40 plus

The insertion of the story of Judah at this stage is most instructive. The events therein continue until the time of the famine. Judah, the fourth son, was born when Jacob was 87-88 years old. Joseph, who was born when Jacob was 91 years old, was three or four years younger than Judah. Therefore, Judah was about 20 or 21 years old at the beginning of the chapter and over 40 years of age at its end. Joseph would be 39 and Judah 42 or 43 when the family of Israel would go down to Egypt (Gen. 41:46-47, 45:6).

Judah, the Prodigal Son of the Old Testament

Genesis 38:1-30

Gen. 38:1-10: The Hebrew names depict a story within a story; a person skilled in the Hebrew language should recognize this immediately. It is helpful to remember this principle when searching for meaning throughout the Scriptures. The student of the Bible must try to understand what the message meant to those who originally received it. The interested Bible student can learn the basic meaning of words in the original languages with helps like "e-Sword."[71]

Judah's suggestion that they sell Joseph to the caravan of traders resulted in inner turmoil. Soon thereafter, he decided to leave home and seek a life based on materialism. He left home and "went down" from his brothers and "turned aside to" Hirah (splendor," *chiŷraĥ,* חירה) who was an Adullamite ("justice of the people," *'ăduĺlamîŷ,* עדלמי) from a city in the lowlands of Canaan [map site 9], subsequently, in the lowlands of Judah (Josh. 15:21, 35). He turned aside from his family and went down to the lowlands of Canaan to dwell near a foreigner of splendor, a person of means and position, possibly a judge.

He "took" (*laq̂ach,* לקח) Shua ("wealth," *shuâ',* שׁוּע), the daughter of a Canaanite, "a merchant" (*kenaani,* כנעני) (Hos. 12:7).

The prefix, "bath" (*bath,* בת), means "daughter." Thus, *Bath-Shua* means "the daughter of wealth."

The chronicler also gave this name, *Bath-Shua*, to the wife of Uriah the Hittite whom David connived to murder, because of his illicit sexual union with her. This indicates she was a person of wealth. Her other name was Bathsheba, "the daughter of seven" (*bath-sheba',* בת־שׁבע). Bathsheba's name suggests a "perfect" daughter, possibly possessing "perfect" physical attributes. Her grandfather was Ahithophel, King David's adviser who helped Absalom in his revolt against King David. He must have done this to seek revenge for King David's adultery with Bathsheba and murder of Uriah (2 Sam. 11:3, 23:34; 1 Chr. 2:3, 3:5). Ahithophel, as King David's adviser, would have been wealthy. *Bath-Shua's* name could have reflected her grandfather's and her father's wealth. In the Old Testament, father, son, and brother can refer to the name of any "father," "son," or "brother" in the ancestry (father, grandfather, great-grandfather, etc.) (page 359).

It is problematic whether Judah's union was a marital covenant, or this was a "common-law" arrangement. It is clear that *Bath-Shua* became his wife (Gen. 38:12).

The Hebrew words, "go" (*haȋak,* הלך) and "come" (*boȋ,* בוא), have different meanings but are often translated as equivalent. "Come" has the idea of proximity, to come towards or into something; "go" has the idea of distance, to go or walk away from something.

For example, Joseph commanded his brothers to go to Canaan and come back to Egypt. These two words are contiguous in the Hebrew construct in the following verses, "go-come" (*hâlak bô',* לכו־באו); they are not synonyms:

"'If you are honest men, let one of your brothers be confined in your prison; but as for the rest of you, go, carry grain for the famine of your households, and bring your youngest brother to me, so your words may be verified, and you will not die.' And they did so" (Gen. 42:19-20).

The same contiguous wording of "go-come" (*halak bo'*, לכו־באו) was used by the Pharaoh, when he commanded Joseph to send for his family and bring them to Egypt (Gen. 45:17-20).

"He took her and came into her." This means that Judah "took" (*laqach*, לקח) *Bath-Shua* in order to "come" (*bo'*, בוא) into her, i.e., used her for sexual purposes. Satan delights to twist Biblical terms into slang that distorts the impact of the original meaning. This must not interfere with the translation of Scripture as given in the original text. The original meanings must be renewed "in the spirit of our minds" (Eph. 4:23). This description of sexual intercourse is different from the one originally designated for the union of a couple in marriage. Rather, "to know" (*yada'*, ידע) each other through sexual intercourse, sanctified by the marriage covenant, is the relationship hallowed by God (Gen. 4:1). Judah wanted sex and money without personal involvement.

He named his firstborn son, Er ("to awaken," *'er*, ער), and the second son, Onan ("strong," *'onan*, אונן). The third son, Shelah ("request," *shelah*, שלה), was born at Chezib ("false," *keziyb*, כזיב).

Onan used his "strength," whenever he had sexual intercourse with Tamar, to repeatedly practice *coitus interruptus*, rather than raise up an heir for his brother's estate. *Yahweh's* judgment, on Er for his evil "awakening," and Onan for his sexual use of Er's wife and wish to inherit the elder son's portion, resulted in death to both.

The sovereign LORD judges each individual during this life. The evil of the two brothers' was such that the just course was to grant them death. Otherwise they would have continued to perpetuate evil in their lives that would have affected others. They had hardened themselves beyond redemption in the eyes of the LORD, the only one who can make such a determination.

The use of the name of God, *Yahweh*, was evidence of God's faithful covenant to Judah by disciplining him. Judah was not faithful to *Yahweh* and unaware of His concern for him.

Judah's Deceit

Gen. 38:11: After the death of his two sons, Judah feared for the death of his third son, Shelah. Judah had promised Shelah to Tamar ("palm tree," *tam̂ar̂,* תמר) when he became old enough to marry. Palms are trees with two major characteristics, beauty and roots that spread out in the soil. They are able to withstand many of the storms of life. Judah misinterpreted *Yahweh's* judgment of him and his sons for their godless lifestyle and blamed the death of his first two sons on Tamar. Young adults often die of a febrile illness. Judah may have believed that Tamar had a sexually transmitted disease that infected his first two sons and was responsible for their deaths, e.g., syphilis. He feared for the life of his third son and did not give him to her as promised. Furthermore, he refused to have Tamar in his home and sent her to her father's house.

Tamar's Deceit

Gen. 38:12-26: Thus, these three sons were born to Judah and *Bath-Shua*. Subsequently, *Bath-Shua* died. Since there was a maximum of a little over two decades for the events in this chapter, the remaining episodes occurred near the end of that time.

Judah lied to Tamar. He did not allow the fulfillment of her "request" for Shelah to be her husband. Shelah had been born at Chezib, the place of "falsehood," the forecast of "the lie" that would be told to Tamar concerning him.

Tamar's resolution to her problem suggests that incest may have been common in the culture. The masquerade of Tamar as a prostitute at the gateway of Enaim ("two springs," *enayim,* עינים) occurred during the time of sheep shearing at Timnah ("a portion," *timnaĥ,* תמנה).

The word used for prostitute here means "a common whore" (*zan̂aĥ,* זנה), not a temple prostitute. Temple prostitutes were thought to be "holy" (*qad̂eŝhah,* קדשה) and to have a holy occupation. The distorted religion of the Canaanites sanctioned sexual intercourse with temple prostitutes as a fertility rite to promote the fertility of the people, their animals, and the produce of the land. Both male and female prostitutes were available for this purpose at their worship sites.

The worship of Baal around a palm tree, Baal-Tamar, was observed during the time of the Judges (Jdg. 20:33). However, the current text does not suggest that Tamar was near a worship site. Because Tamar covered her face, Judah believed her to be "a common whore" (*zan̂aĥ,* זנה) (Gen. 38:15). Judah pledged a kid from the goats as payment for her sexual favors. She requested a pledge of his seal, cord, and staff. These were items that represented his wealth and authority.

Judah must have reinterpreted that the *zanah* was a *qadeshah* at a worship site when He sent his friend, Hirah, to pay the prostitute. Thus, Hirah believed that Judah had had sexual intercourse with a temple prostitute ("holy," *qad̂eŝhah,* קדשה) and inquired about the same. The men of the place confirmed that no temple prostitute was in the area. When Judah discovered that the *qadeshah* could not be found, his main concern was that they would be ridiculed, presumably for his having had sexual intercourse with a *zanah*, not a *qadeshah*. He failed in his attempt to "sanctify" his actions; Judah was a proud man.

Tamar, a primigravida (first pregnancy), began to show at three months. This indicates that she was of normal body proportions and may have been an attractive woman ("palm tree," *tam̂ar̂,* תמר). Judah discovered his own sin at the time he condemned Tamar to burning as a *zanah* (Gen. 38:24). Even though he had sent her back to her father's house, Judah pronounced the death sentence.

When Judah found out that he had impregnated his daughter-in-law, he admitted that she exhibited a greater righteousness than he did because of his "lie" (*chezib*) about the "request" of Shelah to be her husband. His "justice" (*adullam*) and "portion" (*timnah*) came from the Supreme Judge who rules over the affairs of men.

Judah never had sexual intercourse with Tamar again. He was ashamed; he was her father-in-law. In addition, he was concerned that she may have been responsible for the death of their first two sons, and thus, may have been capable of spreading a sexually transmitted disease. It is unclear whether either of them remarried. Nevertheless, Judah took full responsibility for her and their twins.

The Hebrew translation of the names and places reveals that Judah had opted to run from "the lie" told about Joseph to a life of wealth, sexual freedom, and ease. As with all of Satan's lies and deceptions, Judah ran from one lie to a greater one with its associated sin and misfortune (Gen. 3:4-5).

Judah was an Old Testament prodigal son. When the LORD Jesus Christ related the story of the younger son, the prodigal, He may have had some elements of this story in mind (Luke 15:11-32).

Contribution to the Ancestry of the Messiah

Gen. 38:27-30: Judah departed from his home for a life of materialism. This was terminated by a famine in the land and probable financial devastation. He returned home with Shelah (Gen. 46:12), Tamar, their twins, and the story of his misfortunes. In spite of all that had happened, the family received them during a time of famine.

The twins represented the opening of "two springs" (*enayim,* עינים) that came forth from Judah and Tamar. Zerah ("a dawning," *zerach,* זרח) continued as a separate family in Judah (Num. 26:20). Achan ("troubler," *'ak̂an̂,* עכן), Zerah's seed, troubled Israel during the conquest of the Promised Land (Josh. 7:1-26).

The other twin, Perez ("breach," *perets,* פרץ), "broke forth" with his hand at birth and then broke with Zerah's line to continue the righteous line from which the Messiah would be born. Judah, Tamar, and Perez were all included in the genealogy of the LORD Jesus Christ (Matt. 1:3). Abraham's seed continued to reach out to the *Goyim*. The redemption Judah experienced may have softened his approach to Tamar, which would have helped in her redemption through faith in *Yahweh*. After all, she was the mother of his twin sons (Gen. 46:12). Thus, it is likely that Tamar came to faith in *Yahweh* during her sojourn with the family of Israel.

The people and events in this history illustrate the grace of God in providing redemption for all of mankind, Hebrew and Gentile alike. Tamar, the Canaanite, was welcomed into the family of Israel with Judah, the prodigal son. She was also welcomed into the family of God and the genealogy of the LORD.

JOSEPH'S LIFE-II

Joseph's Obedience—*Yahweh's* Blessing Egypt; Joseph, Age 17 to 30

Genesis 39:1-23

Gen. 39:1-6: The Ishmaelites sold Joseph in Egypt. As previously discussed, the Ishmaelites, Medanites, and Midianites were partners in the caravan business (pages 242 and 321) (Gen. 37:23, 28, 36; 39:1). Potiphar was "an eunuch" (*sar̂iŷs,* סריס) and Pharaoh's "officer" (*śar,* שׂר) over the bodyguard. Since he was married, one presumes castration occurred after his marriage, perhaps by trauma related to his occupation.

If he had been promoted to the position of captain of the bodyguard in Pharaoh's palace, castration may have been a requirement for his promotion. Pharaoh's chief wine steward and chief baker, who were in his household, were eunuchs (Gen. 40:2). The chief jailer, who was not in his household, was not an eunuch (Gen. 30:22). Castration of many officials that had intimate access to a ruler's household was a usual requirement in many ancient cultures. Castrated men do not seek the women of the harem or the household. In addition, they become less aggressive, which might decrease the possibility of an assassination attempt, but not always (Gen. 40:1-23).

Joseph learned the Egyptian language. *Yahweh* caused all that Joseph did to prosper, even though he was a slave. It is possible that Potiphar's former overseer and other servants were defrauding

Potiphar for their own benefit. Whether this was so or not, *Yahweh* blessed the house and fields of Potiphar for Joseph's sake. He became the personal servant of Potiphar who made him overseer of everything in his possession, except his meals. *Yahweh* gave Joseph the ability to perform well in his managerial role. He was a trusted servant.

Gen. 39:7-15: Joseph was "handsome in form and appearance" (*yap̂heh toʾar yap̂heh mar'eh,* יפה־תאר ויפה מראה). The same words were used to describe his mother's physical attributes (*yap̂heh toʾar yap̂heh mar'eh,* יפה־תאר ויפה מראה) (Gen. 29:27). Rachel used her beauty to enhance herself and demean Leah. Joseph avoided using his physical traits in a manner unworthy of the name of *Elohim* (Gen. 39:6-9).

In spite of being young, handsome, alone, and a young man in his twenties, Joseph successfully resisted repeated temptation to sexual sin by Potiphar's wife. When Potiphar's wife found him alone in the house and grabbed his robe, Joseph fled. Joseph becomes an example to all men and women tempted to sexual sin. When temptation arises and others are around, resist; when no witnesses are present, flee.

Although the record indicates that she did not scream when Joseph fled and left his outer garment in her hand, the male servants of the household still verified her story. Potiphar's wife called to the men of the household, not the women (Gen. 39:14). She did not scream. The fact that Potiphar was an eunuch, and Potiphar's wife condemned Joseph by a lie that was verified only by the male servants of the household, suggests previous sexual liaisons with some of them. Thus, they were unlikely to cross her. They were to back her claim that she "called with a great voice" when Joseph "accosted her" (Gen. 39:14 NASB margin).

Potiphar's wife knew the male servants would not believe her insinuation about Joseph's sexual assault because of her reputation with them. The derision with which she referred to Joseph, a Hebrew, indicates that Egyptians discriminated against Hebrews. She said that Joseph came "to make sport" ("laugh," *tsaĉhaq,* צחק),

of us (page 252). Besides sexual sport with her, she inferred that Joseph was laughing at the male servants of the household under his supervision. If the male servants had practiced fraud in the past, and no longer received "favors" from Potiphar's wife, they would be happy to help remove Joseph from his position. She manipulated their anti-Semitic prejudice and their jealousy of a Hebrew slave that had become their overseer. He may have deprived them of "profit."

Gen. 39:16-20: If rape had occurred, it is incomprehensible that she did not send for her husband immediately after the event. She did not relate her story to him until after he came home from his routine workday. Since her only credible evidence was Joseph's outer garment, Potiphar's wife kept the article of clothing with her until her husband came home. She referred to Joseph as a Hebrew slave who tried to rape her, i.e., was "sporting" with her, and referenced her scream.

Since the normal penalty for this accusation against Joseph would have been death, Potiphar's anger was directed against his wife for causing him to lose a choice, personal servant and overseer, not against Joseph. The fact that Potiphar was an eunuch suggests his expectation that his wife would seek sexual pleasure elsewhere. However, he would have expected her to be discreet. Clearly, he did not believe her. He did not take any action against her; his wife may have had "status" in the royal household.

Indeed, instead of receiving the death penalty, Joseph was not confined in the prison for commoners but "in his master's house" (Gen. 39:20; 40:3-4, 7). It is probable that Potiphar gave a positive recommendation to the chief jailer about Joseph's ability and honesty (Gen. 39:2-6, 21-23). Potiphar put Joseph in charge of the chief wine steward and the chief baker (Gen. 40:4). Thus, Potiphar continued to hold Joseph in high esteem, and Joseph continued to relate well to Potiphar, even after he was imprisoned.

It is worth noting that after Joseph's elevation from prison by Pharaoh to his position as governor of the land, he did not seek revenge against Potiphar or his wife, even though he had the power to do so. Joseph knew that God did not sanction grudges; he trusted the LORD's ultimate, righteous judgment (Rom. 12:19).

Continued Obedience—Continued Blessing

Gen. 39:21-23: In prison, Joseph rose to the top again. *Yahweh* extended kindness to him and gave him favor with the chief jailer who committed all oversight of the prisoners into Joseph's care. Note that the chief jailer was "an official" (*śar,* שׂר), but not "an eunuch" (*saȓiŷs,* סריס); he did not serve in Pharaoh's household. *Yahweh,* mentioned three times in these verses, gave success to Joseph. Joseph was an obedient servant of *Yahweh* throughout the time of his affliction. Joseph came to the same place of responsibility and respect in Potiphar's jail as that given to him in Potiphar's household.

Interpreter of Dreams

Genesis 40:1-23

Gen. 40:1-4: After Joseph had been elevated to a position of responsibility in "the house of the captain of the bodyguard," Pharaoh imprisoned the chief wine steward and chief baker "where the king's prisoners were confined" (Gen. 39:20, 40:3). The Hebrew word translated into English as "officials" should be translated as "eunuchs" (*saȓiŷsim,* סריסים) (Gen. 40:7).

God placed Joseph in a prison where he could have contact with the royal household, and where he could use the unique gifts God had given to him in management and dream interpretation. Adverse circumstances can be the key God uses to bring about a mighty victory. He did so for Joseph who was faithful during his entire stay in the prison.

Gen. 40:5-7: Since these two prisoners were in charge of Pharaoh's wine and food, it is probable that there had been an attempt to poison him. A less likely interpretation would have been that he had suffered a bout of food poisoning, but in that situation, several would have succumbed, not just the Pharaoh. The guilt of the chief baker, revealed by his dream, also makes that unlikely. While an investigation ensued to ascertain who was guilty, Joseph faithfully took care of the two prisoners for an undetermined period.

Gen. 40:8-15: In the providence of God, the two officials had a dream the very same night that depressed them in the morning. They discussed the dreams with each other, and upon Joseph's inquiry, stated, "We have had **a** dream and there is no one to interpret it." This suggests that they had discussed the dreams and thought them to be one dream with the same essence and meaning. They would assume that Joseph's interpretation of the first dream would apply to the second one.

Joseph did not say that he had the ability to interpret dreams; he ascribed the interpretation of dreams to *Elohim*. Joseph was careful to give God glory for all the ability that He gave to him.

Since he was innocent, the chief wine steward led off. He related his dream about the vine with its three branches and the buds from which the blossoms rapidly shot forth to reveal clusters of ripe grapes. He took the ripe grapes and squeezed them, placed them into Pharaoh's cup, and gave it to him. The rapidity of the evolution from buds to grapes to wine indicated a brief period. The three branches indicated that the time was three days. The fact that he squeezed the grapes from his hand would mean his restoration to his work. In the culture of the time, the "hand" referred to one's work (Gen. 39:4, 6, 8, 22-23 NASB margin).

Joseph's favorable interpretation to the chief wine steward was that Pharaoh would "lift up your head," an apparent idiom that was a *double entendre*. The wine steward's restoration would occur three days later. Joseph declared his own innocence to the chief wine steward, not the chief baker, suggesting that he accepted the dream as evidence that the chief wine steward was innocent.

Joseph described his departure from his homeland as a kidnapping. This was compatible with the Midianite traders pulling Joseph out of the pit, not his brothers (Gen. 37:28). Joseph may not have witnessed his brothers' sale of him to the traders in the caravan. They may have been ashamed to make such an arrangement where he could overhear them. Joseph gave his brothers the benefit of the doubt and believed that they had left him in the pit as a prank and would return for him. Indeed, Reuben attempted to do so. Joseph would not find out the truth for another decade (Gen. 42:21-22).

Joseph asked the chief wine steward to mention his case when Pharaoh restored him to his position. Since the chief baker was guilty, it would have been futile to make this plea to him. The chief baker did not have the insight to recognize the meaning of Joseph's request to the chief wine steward and not to both of them. After his restoration, the chief wine steward promptly forgot about Joseph until Pharaoh's dreams two years later (Gen. 41:9-13).

The literal description of the dungeon by Joseph was the "pit" (*bor̂,* בּוֹר) (Gen. 40:15 NASB margin). Joseph had been thrown into the pit by his brothers and now was in a pit again (Gen. 37:28). Since he stated this in the discussion about his "kidnapping," he certainly saw himself as going from "pit to pit." Two robes and two pits led to his present circumstances. However, a third robe, a royal one, was awaiting him, and the awarding of that robe would give him understanding of the reason for these trials (Gen. 41:42). In the meantime, he still could trust that God would fulfill the dreams given to him when he was 17 years old (Gen. 37:5-11).

He hoped that the chief cupbearer would be the agent used to effect his rescue from this second pit. Indeed he would, but Joseph had to wait two more years. What was the purpose of this delay? The seven years of plenty would start two years later. It was important that Joseph interpret the dreams of Pharaoh on his birthday, just before the start of the prophesied 14 years.

Gen. 40:16-19: There was reluctance on the part of the chief baker to tell his dream first, probably due to his guilt. Only after the favorable interpretation of the chief wine steward did he relate his dream. Since they had presented their dreams as one, he probably expected a favorable interpretation. He expected his head to be "lifted up" in the same manner as the wine steward. In his dream, the three baskets of white bread were not in his hand (his work) but on his head where the thoughts of his conspiracy occurred. He had rebelled against Pharaoh and tried to poison him. The top basket differed in that the birds ate the baked goods.

In the interpretation given to Joseph, the top basket with its baked goods represented the consumption of the baker's produce and the destruction of his own flesh by the birds. The three baskets indicated three days. On the third day, "Pharaoh will lift up your head from you." The second part of the *double entendre* of the idiom indicated that he would hang on a tree followed by the destruction of his flesh by birds of prey. The baker would die, because he was guilty.

Gen. 40:20-23: Joseph must have known, as he gave the interpretation of the dreams, that Pharaoh's birthday would be three days hence (Gen. 41:1). The interpretation of dreams for the chief wine steward and the chief baker, and their fulfillment on Pharaoh's birthday, demonstrated God's continued gift to Joseph of the interpretation of dreams relative to the circumstances that were prevalent at the time.

For these eunuchs, the next three days in the pit would bring either redemption or condemnation to death. The recording of this incident, the specification that the fulfillment of the dreams would occur in three days on Pharaoh's birthday, the subsequent period of two years, and the fact that Joseph would confine his brothers in prison for three days suggest that Joseph spent three years in prison from the ages of 27 to 30 (page 344) (Gen. 41:46, 42:17).

Joseph remained faithful to *Yahweh* during those years in prison. He had the opportunity to learn more about the political decisions made by Pharaoh through the confinement of various officials and his conversations with them during that time (Gen. 39:20, 40:3). Joseph not only honed his management skills but also became conversant with the political and cultural operation of Pharaoh and his court. The time was not wasted.

Pharaoh's Birthday Dreams

Genesis 41:1-57

Gen. 41:1-8: It was "at the end of two full years" i.e., from the day of judgment for the chief wine steward and the chief baker. The Hebrew phrase is "two years of days" (שנתים ימים) (Gen. 41:1). The meaning of the text is exactly two years later on the birthday of Pharaoh. Pharaoh would believe that dreams given to him on his birthday had special meaning.

God gave the dreams to Pharaoh; He gave the interpretation to Joseph. God selected Joseph to preserve the family of Israel and the nation of Egypt. Joseph would have made the connection between Pharaoh's dreams on his birthday and his judgment rendered to the chief wine steward and chief baker two years prior on Pharaoh's birthday (Gen. 40:20).

Pharaoh's soothsayer priests and wise men could not interpret the dreams. The fact that the soothsayer priests and wise men were present indicates that Pharaoh was looking for an understanding of the dreams either from God or from men. Even if Egypt was monotheistic at this time, it does not mean that they knew about *Yahweh* and His concern for people during the prophesied famine.

Two dreams came to Pharaoh that provided details concerning the future of Egypt. One, the dream of the cows, represented animal husbandry; the other, the dream of the ears of corn, represented the agricultural produce of the land.

In Hebrew, the cows are described as "evil" (*raot,* רעות) and "lean" (*daqot,* דקות), instead of "ugly" and "gaunt," respectively. "Gaunt" and "lean" were appropriate descriptions of their physical appearance. "Evil" better represents the circumstances described than does "ugly." God is sovereign and rules over Satan and his evil activity. By His permissive will, He allows evil to reign only for the period He determines. God gave Egypt warning and the potential for blessing, if they listened to His servant, about how to prepare for the evil of the famine. The LORD often forewarns about evil times (Dan. 9:27). The Judge of all the earth always does right (Gen. 18:25).

The cows grazed in the marshlands at the edge of the Nile, the source of fertility for the soil in Egypt. At the time of Moses, worship of the Nile was prevalent. However, there is data to indicate that monotheism was the basic religion of most ancient cultures, if not all.[72] Egypt may have been monotheistic at this time.

Providential Recall

Gen. 41:9-13: The chief wine steward, overhearing the discussion and the lack of response by Pharaoh's advisers, remembered Joseph. He introduced the subject by telling of his past "sins" (*cheṭ̂'i,* את־חטאי), even though he had been adjudicated as innocent (Gen. 41:9 NASB margin). He was careful not to offend Pharaoh for confining him to prison two years earlier. Pharaoh had the power of life and death over those around him, according to his whim or fancy (Gen. 40:22).

He then authenticated the Hebrew "youth" (*na'ar,* נער), possibly a depreciative term, a foreign servant who was "a boy." When the wine steward was in prison, Joseph was about 28 years old. Joseph had interpreted his and the chief baker's dreams with the outcome exactly as per the interpretation. He said nothing about Joseph's ascription of his skill in interpretation of dreams to God (Gen. 40:8b). He did mention that Joseph was in a position of responsibility as "a servant of the captain of the bodyguard." He did not indicate that Joseph was a prisoner. His description lauded Joseph as a servant of one of Pharaoh's officials with a positive recommendation from Potiphar for his managerial abilities. Thus, when Pharaoh sent for Joseph, he did not view him as a despised foreigner and prisoner, but as one who had the ability to interpret dreams and had demonstrated leadership under adverse conditions.

Gen. 41:14-32: Joseph had to shave and dress appropriately for his appearance before Pharaoh. During that time, he must have prayed for wisdom. It is likely that Joseph became a man of prayer during the previous 13 years, particularly the previous three years of his confinement in a prison in a foreign land where "heads could roll" with little or no justification.

When he came before Pharaoh, Joseph did not grovel, show bitterness, or complain about the unfair events of his life. Pharaoh said to Joseph that no one could interpret his dreams. Pharaoh did not mention the wise men at this time, only the soothsayer priests (Gen. 41:8, 24). This suggests that he was now looking for an answer from God, not from men. He then said that he had heard that Joseph could interpret dreams.

Joseph Interprets Pharaoh's Dreams

Joseph denied such ability and faithfully attributed the interpretation of dreams to *Elohim*. Joseph used a singular pronoun for He, *hu* (*hu,̂* הוּא), with the plural noun, *Elohim* (the equivalent in the Egyptian language). He gave witness that *Elohim* was the One Triune God (Gen. 41:25, 28). Joseph's witness through language would have suggested the Trinity to Pharaoh.[73] If Egypt was monotheistic at this time, Pharaoh may have understood that *Elohim* was the One Triune God.

The subject matter had to do with the preservation of part of the creation by the Creator, Egypt and the Middle Eastern region that extended beyond its borders (Gen. 41:57). God had the option of using another Middle Eastern nation for the prophecy about the seven good years followed by the seven years of famine. Why did He choose Egypt and send Joseph to that nation? It is possible that God sent Joseph to Pharaoh because he was "a seeker" who wanted to know more about the living God.

Pharaoh repeated his account of the dreams with added detail (Gen. 41:21). He emphasized how "evil-(רע)-looking" the cows were. They were more evil than anything he had seen in all of Egypt. He again exclaimed that no one could explain the dreams for him (Gen. 41:24). Joseph began to interpret the dreams immediately upon hearing them. God had answered his prayer. He declared the dreams to be one message, not two. The repetition was due to the fact that God would quickly bring about the seven years of plenty with the seven years of famine to follow.

The selection of the seven years as a time for the famine may have foreshadowed the final seven years of the reign of evil by the Antichrist, backed by Satan and the False Prophet, at the end of the present age. It will be a time of physical and spiritual famine (Rev. 6:1-8). God has forewarned believers about this coming evil time, just as he used Joseph to forewarn Egypt and the family of Israel about the seven years of famine (Dan. 9:24-27). Those who hear must prepare. The tribulation of those times will be followed by the righteous reign of the LORD Jesus Christ.

Joseph's Administrative Advice to Pharaoh

Gen. 41:33-36: Joseph's experience and sagacity, learned during the 13 years of administration and observation of the political nature of the monarchy while in Potiphar's house and prison, was propitious for his recommendations to Pharaoh regarding the character of the person needed to oversee the collection and sale of the agricultural produce. Excellent character, discernment, and wisdom are necessary for all in authority who are qualified according to Biblical standards.

Joseph did not recommend himself or another Hebrew. He emphasized the need to store the grain under Pharaoh's authority as a reserve for the land during the time of famine. Joseph's suggestion of a 20 percent tax on the produce during the years of plenty continued after the end of the famine (Gen. 47:24).

Gen. 41:37-44: Pharaoh accepted the interpretation of the dreams without further question. Pharaoh and his servants responded favorably to Joseph's suggestion of a person with discernment and wisdom. Pharaoh gauged that Joseph had those attributes. He acknowledged that Joseph's ability was due to "a Spirit of *Elohim*" (אלהים רוח) in him (Gen. 41:38). Indeed, the Hebrew verb indicates that Pharaoh attributed Joseph's abilities to the fact that *Elohim* had made "known" (*hȗdia'*, הודיע) to Joseph the interpretation of the dreams (Gen. 41:39). Pharaoh believed

Joseph had a personal relationship with *Elohim* (John 17:3). He was right. Whether or not Pharaoh subsequently became a believer in *Yahweh Elohim* is problematic.

Joseph had dealt with the officials of Pharaoh, the people of the land, and the political system during the previous 13 years. Joseph had demonstrated loyalty, honesty, managerial ability, and faithfulness to God in a foreign land. Joseph was trained by the LORD through the adversity that he experienced. It was *Elohim* who elevated Joseph to become the chief operating officer, the "governor" (*hēgeomai,* ἡγέομαι) of the land (Acts 7:10). Pharaoh was merely the instrument He used. Joseph received the Egyptian garments, neckpiece, chariot of the number two leader, and the signet ring of authority from Pharaoh for all operational matters in the land. He now received the third robe, a royal one (page 334)!

Joseph, Missionary to Egypt

Gen. 41:45: Joseph received an additional title, *Zaphenath-paneah*, "God speaks, He lives" (NASB margin, probable translation of this Egyptian name). The name confirmed the fact that God spoke through Joseph. Note that this name speaks of God, not "gods." This demonstration of faith in a God who speaks and is alive lends credence to the possibility that Egypt was monotheistic at this time.

The new name, *Zaphenath-paneah*, and Joseph's marriage to Asenath, the daughter of Potiphera, priest of On (Heliopolis), suggest that the Egyptians also viewed Joseph as a priest. This was an accolade related to the acknowledgment that *Elohim* gave to Joseph wisdom and interpretation of the future through dreams.

The hierarchy of Egypt accepted Joseph as both a religious and political leader. While serving as governor of the country, Joseph was a missionary to Egypt who learned their cultural, political, and religious systems and became a witness to *Yahweh*. Joseph became a model leader of fair and balanced government for all citizens of any land, believers and unbelievers alike. Joseph was an honest politician.

Seven Years of Plenty; Seven Years of Famine

Gen. 41:46-49: When he became governor, Joseph was 30 years old; he would be 37 years of age when the seven years of plenty ended. During that time, he carried out the plan presented to Pharaoh and approved by him. It is noteworthy that he did not attempt to communicate with his family during the first seven years of his reign as governor in Egypt, even though he had the power to do so. He waited upon God for His time and method for restoration to his family. He had the assurance of the dreams God had given to him as a teenager that still awaited their fulfillment.

Gen. 41:50-52: Joseph, unlike his father, accepted the choice of his wife, sight unseen. Joseph was faithful in following God's prescription for the restriction of sexual intercourse to marriage. At the age of 30, he received a wife selected by *Elohim* from the priestly hierarchy. One suspects that God, in His faithfulness, provided an ideal wife for Joseph. Another Gentile, an Egyptian, was introduced to the family of God. Asenath bore two children during the seven years of plenty. Since *Elohim* made him "forget" all his trouble and his father's household, his firstborn was named Manesseh, "making to forget" (*menashsheh*, מנשׁה). Since *Elohim* made him fruitful in the land of his affliction, his second son was named Ephraim, "fruitfulness" (*'ephrayim*, אפרים).

After his elevation as governor in Egypt, he still called Egypt the land of his affliction. This suggests that he still longed to return to the land of his birth with the associated promises given to Abraham, Isaac, and Jacob. Hebrews suffered discrimination from the Egyptians. Joseph knew that from his prior experience (Gen. 43:32).

Gen. 41:53-57: Pharaoh must have observed Joseph closely during the seven years of plenty and waited to see if the famine would start at the predicted time. He would have observed the marked increase in produce during the seven years. When the famine came and the people asked for food, he told them to go to Joseph. He now had explicit as well as implicit trust in Joseph.

During the seven years of plenty, it is noteworthy that the people of the land did not accept Joseph's prediction. Otherwise they would have saved grain for themselves during that time. During those seven years, Joseph must have suffered ridicule by the hierarchy and the common people of Egypt who were prejudiced against Hebrews. It is likely that they joked about the prediction, until the famine came.

Joseph sold grain to the people of Egypt. He also sold grain to people from other countries. The original interpretation of Joseph to Pharaoh did not state the boundaries of the famine, but it was a reasonable inference to believe that bordering countries would be affected (Gen. 41:36, 57).

Joseph received additional favor and authority from Pharaoh. *Yahweh* was fulfilling through Joseph, Abraham's seed, the promise given to Abraham to bring blessing to all the earth through those that blessed Abraham and his seed, even as Pharaoh had blessed Joseph by believing the interpretations he gave to Pharaoh's dreams (Gen. 12:3). True believers have ever blessed unbelievers in social good, e.g., responsible government and the development of schools and hospitals.

Jacob's Affect and Decision

Genesis 42:1-38

Gen. 42:1-5: The first year of famine affected "all the face of the earth" (Gen. 41:56). Because of the severity of the famine, Jacob must have observed that Canaanites were going to Egypt (Gen. 42:1-5). He would have remembered the history of the famines during the lives of Abraham and Isaac. Abraham went to Egypt without God's direction and suffered the consequences (Gen. 12:10-20). God told Isaac not to go down to Egypt and blessed him during the time of famine because he obeyed His command (Gen. 26:2-6, 12-14). It is to Jacob's credit that he did not move to Egypt until directed by *Yahweh*.

Jacob's sons must have known this family history and the fact that there was grain in Egypt. They were waiting for their father's instructions. Famine brings stress. Jacob must have weighed carefully what he was to do. He had become sullen and sarcastic with his sons as evidenced by the manner in which he ordered them (Gen. 42:1-2). Finally, he sent his ten sons to Egypt to buy grain. He still favored Benjamin, the only known remaining son of Rachel, and refused to allow him to go on the trip (Gen. 42:3-4).

Joseph's Patience—the Dreams Come True

Gen. 42:6-15: Since each city had its own grain (Gen. 41:48), Joseph must have selected the place (On [Heliopolis] in Upper Egypt) where foreigners came to buy grain (Gen. 41:45 NASB margin). His wife was the daughter of the priest of On. On must have been Joseph's home.

Joseph, governor over all the land, sold to all the people who came to buy grain in On. Someone else could have done this perfunctory job under his supervision. Joseph may have been concerned that Egyptians would cheat any foreigners who came to buy grain. In addition, Joseph may have taken this responsibility, because of his belief in God who had given him the dreams when he was a teenager. He had waited 21 years for their fulfillment. When the brothers finally came, Joseph had mixed emotions. He wanted to see his father and Benjamin, and he wanted to be reconciled with his brothers. How could he accomplish this considering all that had happened in the past?

When the brothers came and bowed down before him, it reminded Joseph of the dreams that he had related to them over two decades ago. He must have thought of those dreams often during the 21 years he had been Egypt. His brothers did not recognize Joseph who was clean-shaven, spoke the Egyptian language, and used a Hebrew interpreter (Gen. 42:23).

Joseph was dressed as befitted the governor of Egypt. The brothers probably had beards and wore shepherds' garb. Joseph was minimally bilingual. The fact that he did not reveal his knowledge of the Hebrew language, and his accusation of his brothers as spies, suggest that Joseph had long beforehand developed a plan to assess their spiritual state. If there was to be a lasting reconciliation, he needed a plan that could produce redemption from past sin and guilt. Joseph had to implement that plan and patiently carry it out, regardless of his feelings. First, he needed to ascertain the facts as to what happened 21 years ago.

Guilty Consciences

Gen. 42:16-24: After hearing their declaration of honesty, and obtaining necessary details about his father and Benjamin, Joseph instituted his plan to provide redemption for their nefarious deed in selling him as a slave. Joseph spoke harshly to his brothers. He put all of them in prison for three days. This is congruent with the probability that he may have been in prison for three years (page 335). After bringing them from the prison, he listened in order to obtain more information as to how he was sold as a slave to the caravan that brought him to Egypt.

Note that the first expression is "three days," but he released them on the third day (Gen. 42:17-18). In the Bible, it does not take a full night and a full day to count as a day. This is helpful in interpretation of subsequent Scripture: "The Son of Man will be three days and three nights in the heart of the earth" (Matt. 12:40a). The time between the LORD's crucifixion on Friday afternoon and resurrection on Sunday morning, "the third day," was counted as three days and three nights. Albeit, the risen LORD was omnipresent and may have spent the three days and three nights in Hades while He made visits to the disciples in His body on the earth (page 203) (Gen. 18:21-22, Luke 24:38-45, 1 Peter 3:18-20).

On the third day, Joseph appealed to their declaration of honesty and asked them to go and return with Benjamin upon penalty of death for failure to accept the mission (Gen. 42:20). Initially, he gave evidence of some anger in that he was going to keep all but one brother. He first swore "by the life of Pharaoh" (Gen. 42:16). He relented because he "feared *Elohim*" and kept only Simeon, the second eldest, after hearing of Reuben's attempt to save him. His brothers failed to recognize the significance of this expression of Joseph's faith in *Elohim*. It is possible that they thought that Joseph used the name of *Elohim* as a polytheist. They were probably unaware of the religion that was dominant in Egypt at the time.

The pathos of their guilt for selling Joseph as a slave, and years of anticipating retribution for their sin, was more than Joseph could bear. He went out and wept. Still he knew that it was necessary to follow through with his plan. "Cheap grace," by revealing himself at that time, would not have had the potential for a lasting, redemptive restoration.

Joseph's Compassion

Gen. 42:25-28: The return of the money to the men's sacks and the provisions for the journey were well intentioned. When one brother discovered the money in his sack, the others did not bother to check to see if the same thing had happened to them.

Instead of viewing the provisions and money as a kind act from Joseph, and speculating as to why he had done this, the brothers assumed the worst. Guilt often drives paranoid thinking. They attributed their misfortune of appearing to be thieves to *Elohim*, but their guilty consciences were the problem. They blamed God at a time He was working through Joseph to bring redemption to them for their sin and guilt for selling Joseph (Gen. 42:28). Such is the tendency of all who walk through life's maze.

Gen. 42:29-36: In relating the story to Jacob, they described themselves as honest three different times. It was even more embarrassing, as they emptied their sacks, to find their money in each sack. Jacob must have thought that they were anything but honest and did not believe their story. His statement that they had bereaved him of "my children" indicates that he never completely believed their original story about Joseph's death. Jacob blamed his sons for the "loss" of Joseph and Simeon and the potential loss of Benjamin. When Judah left home shortly after Joseph's disappearance, it may have reinforced his suspicion about their role in Joseph's disappearance and presumed death.

Gen. 42:37-38: Reuben showed his deficiency in character by offering his sons as atonement, if Jacob placed Benjamin in his care, and he did not return with him. Since he knew about the bedding with Bilhah, and Reuben's other deficiencies, Jacob did not trust Reuben and refused to let Benjamin go. Jacob was 129 years old. He had experienced the assumed death of Joseph 21 years previously. He feared for Benjamin's life; he believed Benjamin to be the only living son of Rachel.

Jacob's Reluctance Overcome; Judah's Character Shines Forth

Genesis 43:1-34

Gen. 43:1-2: God wanted Jacob and his family in Egypt. The famine continued. They finished the grain brought from Egypt. If they were to live, they needed food. God sometimes uses physical and spiritual famines to get his servants to the place where He wants them.

Gen. 43:3-10: When the grain was gone, Judah interceded and became the representative leader for the brothers. Reuben had lost the leadership by his present and past displays of deficient character. Simeon and Levi were in disrepute for their deeds at Shechem (Gen. 49:5-7).

Judah was concerned about the little children (Gen. 43:8). His and Tamar's twin sons would be around eight years of age. Judah gave his word to Jacob that he would be personal warranty "all the days" (*kol̂ h'yom̂im,* כל־הימים), i.e., the rest of his life, for the return of Benjamin. After accepting their need to reveal to the governor of Egypt the details about Benjamin and the family, still pitying himself, Jacob relented.

Often the prodigal that returns home after suffering some of the woes of this life becomes more mature than other children who never leave home and show little evidence of development. Judah foreshadowed the seed that would become his spiritual heirs. After the exile of the tribe of Judah, the remnant would learn from their disobedience (Appendix III, page 396).

Gen. 43:11-15: Only after Judah became surety for Benjamin did their father change his mind. Now he was willing to accept the possible outcome for this decision, even to the point of losing Benjamin. He alluded to the possibility that his sons' story may have been true and asked them to take double the amount of money with them upon their return to Egypt.

Jacob was still miffed at Simeon, possibly related to the events at Shechem more than two decades earlier (Gen. 34:25-31). Thus, Simeon's character appears to have waned in the eyes of Jacob. He did not use Simeon's name; he referred to "your other brother" (Gen. 43:14). Jacob would give a prophetic judgment to Simeon on his deathbed (Gen. 49:5-7).

His appeal was to *El Shaddai*, the one who supplied all their needs. Since God progressively revealed His different names in specific circumstances, it is helpful to use the name of God in prayer that relates to our circumstances. It builds an understanding of the nature of God. It is instructive to note how Israel, by the Holy Spirit, used the names of God, and how the Holy Spirit used Moses to pen the names of Jacob, Israel, and the names of God!

Until he made the decision to let Benjamin return with Judah and his brothers, the name of Jacob appears in the text. With his expression of faith in *El Shaddai* to care for Benjamin, regardless of the outcome, the name changes to Israel, the one who strives with God and wins by holding on, even in adverse circumstances.

Gifts from Home

Israel brought nostalgic joy to Joseph by the special foods sent from home, even though he was unaware that Joseph was alive. God gives the small gifts of love, gifts that have special meaning, to each of his children. The fact that these items were still available indicates that they had a reservoir of food. However, their supply would diminish as the famine progressed.

Joseph's Brothers Return Egypt; Joseph, Age 39; Jacob, Age 130

Gen. 43:16-17: Joseph patiently awaited the return of his brothers. It was now the second year of famine. Jacob was 130 years old, Joseph was 39, Benjamin was between 23 and 26, and the other brothers ranged from 40 to 45 years of age. Only after Joseph saw that they brought Benjamin with them did he instruct his house steward to take them to his home and prepare a midday meal.

Was Joseph's House Steward a Believer?

Gen. 43:18-25: The guilty consciences of the brothers resulted in irrational comments. The invitation to Joseph's house raised fears that they would be accused as thieves, and they would become slaves and their donkeys taken. If Joseph had wanted to keep them as slaves, he could have done it long before this and would not have invited them to his private home. It is beyond comprehension that the governor of Egypt would need their donkeys. They stood at the entrance of the house and pled with the house steward to take their money. The house steward's reassurances eased their apprehension, and they entered the home. He stated, "Your money had come to me" (Gen. 43:23 NASB margin). The house steward must have been Joseph's manager.

The brothers were treated according to the Middle Eastern customs for guests. Their feet were washed, and their donkeys were provided with grain. After having served a year in prison, while he awaited their return, Simeon received his release. Joseph apparently refrained from visiting Simeon during that year. He undoubtedly made sure that Simeon was protected and received proper care. Joseph trusted that God would honor the plan for redemption that he had put in place.

The house steward's use of "your God" (*'eloheqem,* אלהיכם), and his use of the God of "your father" (*'elohe 'abiv,* לאלהי אביו), suggest that he was a believer in *Elohim*. He intimated that he understood the meaning of the name, even as they understood it. He may have been a Gentile who became a believer through Joseph's witness to him or a displaced Hebrew living in the land of Egypt. Regardless of his background, he believed in *Elohim*, the One Triune God. He attributed the "treasure in your sacks" to be a gift from *Elohim*. He believed *Elohim* to be gracious and providential in His bounty. What did they believe?

Joseph's Love for Benjamin, His Brother

Gen. 43:26-31: When Joseph appeared, the brothers bowed to the ground twice in homage (reference Joseph's dreams). Joseph's continued concern for his father prompted his initial inquiry about his welfare. Joseph was 13-16 years older than Benjamin who was born when their mother died: "May God be gracious to you, my son" (Gen. 43:29b). He was overwhelmed with emotion at the sight of his brother and hurried to his chamber to weep. Benjamin would have reminded him of his mother. After washing away the tears, he controlled himself and was able to carry out the plan given to him by *Yahweh*. The next step was to place Benjamin in the favored position that Joseph held when he was younger.

Joseph's Brothers Lack Cultural Discernment

Gen. 43:32-34: The pattern of the meal had several cultural nuances concerning the identity of Joseph that the brothers did not recognize. Joseph, dressed as an Egyptian ruler, did not sit with the other Egyptians because of his position. In addition, Egyptians viewed Hebrews as "an abomination" (Gen. 43:32).

They noted the seating arrangement in order of their ages with amazement. One suspects that Joseph had a twinkle in his eyes as he seated them. Guilt and apprehension can wipe away all discernment; they were clueless. Joseph demonstrated the heart of a servant, not that of an autocratic ruler of Egypt. Joseph served his brothers their food from his table instead of having a servant do it, thereby indicating that he could not be an Egyptian (Gen. 43:32 NASB margin).

Joseph continued his plan for their repentance and the relief of their guilt due to their trespass against him. By placing Benjamin in a position similar to Joseph's when he was sold into slavery, it allowed him to see if there was any residual jealousy on their part. Benjamin received a princely portion, five times larger than the other brothers.[74] They did not comprehend the reason for this favoritism for their youngest brother by the governor of Egypt.

Joseph's Plan Brought to Fulfillment

Genesis 44:1-34

Gen. 44:1-13: Joseph had the house steward place a "silver cup of divination" in Benjamin's sack, as much food and grain as they could carry, and their money in the mouth of each of their sacks (Gen. 44:1-2). The food should have prompted them to consider why Joseph gave them this kind provision; they "purchased" only the grain. Presumably, the purpose of stealing the cup would be in its value in silver or its religious significance. He waited until they had left the city and then sent his house steward after them.

The angry accusation, "Why have you repaid evil for good?" would raise feelings of guilt over their treatment of Joseph years earlier (Gen. 44:4b). This statement would resonate when Joseph taught them about the One who took their evil act against him and turned it about for good:

"As for you, you meant evil against me, but God meant it for good in order to bring about this present result, to preserve many people alive" (Gen. 50:20).

After having previously told the house steward of their honesty in returning the money to him, they were disheartened to find the money in the mouth of each sack as the house steward searched each one. Because of the money in their sacks, he could have arrested them all as thieves. They did not appreciate the fact that only the silver cup was allegedly stolen, not the money.

If the cup was found in anyone's baggage, they vowed for all to become slaves. If they were to return with the loss of Benjamin, they were afraid to face their father. They did not appreciate the change in the house steward's reply to take back only the one with the cup. The house steward started with the eldest brother and finished with Benjamin, the youngest; he remembered the seating arrangement by Joseph. Did Joseph suggest this, or did the house steward create additional drama? Alas, the silver cup was in Benjamin's sack (Gen. 43:20-23, 44:8-12).

If the diviner's cup was part of the priesthood's symbols, it is an argument against pure monotheism at the time of Joseph (Gen. 44:5). Since many foreigners would have sought refuge from the famine, it is probable that there was a mixture of religious practices in the land of Egypt. Joseph may have obtained the silver cup as payment for grain from one of the buyers from Canaan. Joseph was able to understand and use religious symbols and still be faithful to *Yahweh*.

The ruse with the silver cup triggered the intended response. The suggestion that Joseph used the cup for divination gave the impression that Joseph had unusual powers that were similar to the dreams given to him years earlier. The brothers did not leave Benjamin behind but rent their clothes in despair, loaded their donkeys again, and returned to the city.

Judah, the Intercessor

Gen. 44:14-17: They had bowed three times to Joseph on previous occasions; this time they fell to the ground and prostrated themselves before him (Gen. 42:6; 43:26, 28; 44:14). Judah continued as the leader of the brothers. Joseph was a good actor; Judah pleaded for Joseph's "anger" to abate. He acknowledged that Joseph's authority as governor was equal to Pharaoh's.

Joseph still spoke through an interpreter. He claimed the ability to "divine" their stealing the cup, even though he did not have the cup of divination with him at the time (Gen. 44:15)! The Hebrew word for "divination" (*nâchash,* נחש) is the same as the word for the Serpent (*nâchash,* נחש) in the Garden of Eden (Gen. 3:1). They knew the history of the Fall and the role of the Serpent in the Garden of Eden. They needed to decide whether Joseph was the type of person who would practice such evil divination. Before they embarked on their return journey, he had served them as guests in his home, returned their money to them, and gave them food for their journey. Was this the behavior of a servant of Satan?

Suffering from their guilt over their participation in the sale of Joseph to the traders, Judah stated that *Elohim* had found out their "iniquity" ("moral perversity," *'âvôn,* עוון) as he referred to their past sin against Joseph, not the thievery of the silver cup (Gen. 42:21-22). Judah did not attribute Joseph's discernment about the incident to divination, thereby indicating that he had an understanding of the spiritual implications of Joseph's statement. Judah offered for all of them to serve as slaves, not just Benjamin. They did not wish to face their father without Benjamin. Joseph, persisting with his plan, rejected their plea. He told them they could leave in peace, but Benjamin would have to become a slave.

Gen. 44:18-34: Judah then recounted the details of their father's situation. There are several noteworthy points:

1. After the presumed death of Joseph, their father showed preferential love to Benjamin. Judah expressed no jealousy.

2. He referred to Rachel as the mother of Joseph and Benjamin without comparing her to Leah, Bilhah, or Zilpah. There was no evidence of continued family strife and jealousy between the sons.

3. He gave a direct quote from their father who referred to Rachel as his wife with no reference to Leah and the handmaidens.

4. He expressed the reluctance of their father to let Benjamin go with them.

5. If Benjamin did not return with them, he stated that Jacob was depressed to the point of death.

6. Judah's compassion expressed his genuine fear that the loss of Benjamin would bring Jacob to his grave.

Two different Hebrew words translated as "sorrow" in two verses have a different impact in their meaning. In the 29th verse, he spoke of the "evil" (*raah,* רעה) that would come to his father. In the 31st verse, Judah said that the loss of Benjamin would bring his father down to Sheol in "sorrow" (*yağoñ,* יגון). Judah was stating that the evil of the loss of Benjamin would bring Jacob to his grave by the grief that he would experience (Gen. 44:29, 31, 44).

7. Judah, true to his word to his father, offered himself as warranty for Benjamin.

The rivalry within the family was gone. Their concern and love for their father was genuine. They were repentant for their sin of selling Joseph and lying to their father. They implied that their father's depressed state might have been due to their action against Joseph. They felt responsible for Jacob's fragile health.

While reciting this narrative, Judah referred to Benjamin as a "lad" (*na'ar,* נער) and their father's "little child of his old age" (*yeled zaqunim qatan,* וילד זקנים קטן) (Gen. 44:20, 22). Benjamin was somewhere between 23 and 26 years of age. Since Judah and the brothers were around a couple of decades older, they treated Benjamin as the beloved kid brother. Their father believed him to be Rachel's only living child. The brothers may have felt disproportionate love for him because of their guilt over what they had done to Joseph.

Restoration in the Family

Genesis 45:1-28

Gen. 45:1-4: The brothers had stood the test. Joseph could no longer contain himself and wept openly. Imagine the surprise of

Joseph's brothers. Relief from all the restrained emotions of the previous two years, and even more so, the previous two decades plus, came like a flood. Since he was a foreigner in Egypt, one suspects the normal affect of Joseph was one of guarded restraint. When the Egyptians and the household of Pharaoh heard Joseph's loud weeping, they would have marveled at his emotional outburst.

At the time of revelation, he requested all his servants to leave, so he could be alone with his brothers. He was dressed as a ruler in Egypt, was clean-shaven, and had communicated in the Egyptian language. He now spoke to them in Hebrew and asked that they come closer. He wanted them to recognize him; he wanted to be close to them.

Joseph's Testimony of the Sovereignty of God

Gen. 45:5-8: In revealing himself to them, Joseph explained that *Elohim* sent him to preserve life, the lives of the remnant of Israel. A remnant is "an escaped company" (*peleŷtaĥ,* פליטה), an excellent description of those whom the LORD delivers (Gen. 45:7 NASB margin).

The LORD had made Joseph "a father to Pharaoh and lord of all his household and ruler over all the land of Egypt" (Gen. 45:8b). God overrules in the affairs of men and turns evil about for good (Gen. 50:20). *Elohim* sent Joseph to Egypt; their action was simply the mechanism.

He told them of the five years of famine to come. Now they could recognize and accept God's special, direct communication through him by dreams and their interpretation.

Bring My Father Down with the Rest of the Family

Gen. 45:9-15: The admonition that they must hurry and tell his father to "come down to me" spoke volumes about his love and concern for his father. Judah's speech suggested that Jacob was near death; there was urgency in Joseph's voice (Gen. 44:29-34).

Joseph's words and affect were those of a person with pent-up emotion. He fell upon the necks of his brothers and kissed them one at a time, starting with Benjamin. By so doing, each brother who had betrayed him experienced his love and forgiveness. Only after this emotional release were they able to talk together.

Joseph was confident the family would live in Goshen, even though he had not cleared that with the Pharaoh yet (Gen. 45:10, 47:1-6). Joseph may not have known the prophecy given to Abraham about a sojourn for four generations in a foreign land (Gen. 15:13-16). He did not relate the prophecy to Egypt at this time, but he did so at the time of his death (Gen. 50:24-26). Perhaps Jacob would give Joseph further instruction about this, after Jacob's vision at Beersheba (Gen. 46:1-4).

Twice he asked them to hurry and bring his father down. He repeated that the famine would last for five more years. They needed to trust his word about this. The evidence of what God had done with Joseph during the previous 22 years could refurbish their faith. *El Shaddai* would providentially provide for them, their children, their herds, and all their possessions. He placed emphasis on his splendor in Egypt and the need to tell his father of the same. He wanted his father to be proud of him.

Gen. 45:16-20: Joseph did not directly intercede with Pharaoh for his family. He was careful to demonstrate his subservience as a Hebrew in a foreign culture, even after nine years in his position. Pharaoh's response indicated the favor that Joseph still had with him. Pharaoh twice offered the best of the land of Egypt. It is doubtful that he would have considered Goshen as such. He was probably thinking about one of the major cities. He ordered wagons for transport and samples of the best produce from the land of Egypt to be sent as provision for the journey of Joseph's family. Pharaoh's actions demonstrated his desire to bless the family of Israel because of his delight in Joseph.

Gen. 45:21-24: Joseph willingly carried out his order. He provided ten male donkeys loaded with the best of Egypt and ten female donkeys with grain, bread, and other sustenance for the journey. The provisions were sent from earth's royalty to heaven's royalty; Israel was the royal heir of the promises of God.

Joseph may have given Egyptian clothing to his brothers to prepare for their sojourn in Egypt and appearance before the Pharaoh. He gave the princely portion of five changes of garments and three hundred pieces of silver to Benjamin but less to his other brothers. He had the right to favor his younger brother. Joseph's favoritism of Benjamin was again a test to his brothers and was depicted in his final words to them: "Do not quarrel on the journey" (Gen. 45:24b). They had learned their lesson; there was no expression of further jealousy.

Jacob's Heart Disease and Depression

Gen. 45:25-28: When Jacob heard about Joseph and the recent events in Egypt, "His heart grew numb" (*puĝ leb̂o,* ויפג לבו) (Gen. 45:26b NASB margin). He had a period of partial responsiveness followed a short time later by a return to his normal status. This suggests a cardiac (heart) condition with a brief episode of poor circulation to the brain secondary to decreased cardiac output, perhaps due to an arrhythmia (irregular heartbeat). This was secondary to the stress of the moment. After seeing the wagons sent by Joseph, Jacob's "spirit came back to life" (*tachay ruâch,* ותחי רוח). This suggests that he continued in a state of partial responsiveness until he was convinced of the truth of their story.

The name shifts again to Israel. He believed his sons, accepted their message, and agreed to go to Egypt to see Joseph. Besides probable cardiac disease, Jacob still had symptoms of depression that was reminiscent of Isaac when he was 137 years old. When people have been disappointed after the loss of loved ones, and undergo physical decline near the end of their lives, they often become depressed. Jacob spoke of his soon demise: "I will go and see him before I die" (Gen. 45:28b), even though he would live an additional 17 years.

When Joseph was believed dead, Jacob's reactive depression was appropriate. It was not appropriate to be depressed 22 years later. Sometimes, not always, depression is secondary to a spiritual problem. Regardless of the etiology (cause) of the depression, it will contribute to physical decline. Depression from a spiritual problem is more common than people think. Many physicians do not believe that man has a spirit, so they may not include this in their differential diagnosis. Even if they recognize the spiritual dimension, they rarely receive training to deal with the same. In the times in which we live, pastors and physicians need to work together to cover this deficit in medical training.

For most people, dying will be a protracted process. Personal losses of loved ones, and waning of strength and dysfunction in different body parts, provide an opportunity for weaning from the things of earth in preparation for the greater life to come. Many believers become depressed at this time of life instead of using the time to prepare for their better future. Studying the Scriptures, praying, expressing gratitude for the positive ventures in life, and concentrating on the needs of others can lift a person from depression. It is the last chance to honor the LORD in this life.

After he went down to Egypt, Jacob would realize that truth and would reestablish his relationship with Joseph and his family, his sons and their families, and the rest of his household. In addition, he would renew his relationship with his LORD.

Jacob's Lack of Faith; Israel's Faith

Genesis 46:1-34

Gen. 46:1-3: It was Israel, the man of faith, who set out on the journey and stopped at Beersheba, the well of the sevenfold oath, with its significant history in the patriarchs' lives. There Abraham had christened the well and planted a tamarisk tree (an evergreen) and called on the name of the Everlasting God; there Isaac had re-dug Abraham's well and built an altar to *Yahweh* (Gen. 2:22-33; 26:23-25, 32-33).

Part of Jacob's reluctance to go down to Egypt may have been *Yahweh's* word to Isaac not to go down to Egypt during the time of that previous famine. Therefore, he addressed God as "the God of his father (*'elohe 'abiv,* אלהי אביו)." God responded to him as "God (*el*), the God of your father" (*'elohe 'abiq,* ואלהי אביך), and spoke to him in **visions of the night** (the **sixth** direct communication). After Jacob became convinced that Joseph was dead, he had become chronically depressed. His faith had weakened. Therefore, God spoke to Israel, but He called him by his old name, "Jacob, Jacob."

The Promised Birth of a Nation

Gen. 46:4: *Elohim* confirmed that Israel would become a great nation. Joseph would preside at his death. "I will surely bring you up again" might better be translated, "And I, I will watch over you and bring you up" (*annaki 'alak gam 'alah,* ואנכי אעלך גם־עלה). Besides referring to the return of his body to Machpelah, God may have been referring to Jacob's resurrection after his death. God would never leave him or forsake him. He would bring Israel **up to Him** (page 386) (Deut. 31:6, Heb. 13:5).

Elohim spoke to Jacob with words of comfort and a renewal of the covenant passed down from Abraham to Isaac to him. God is compassionate in our times of depression. He did not browbeat Jacob for his lack of faith; He encouraged him. Friends and counselors need to recognize God's gentle dealing with His own children and treat needy people in the same manner.

Elohim would make of Israel a great nation. God revealed to Abram that enslavement and oppression for four generations would come to his seed from another nation (Gen. 15:12-14). Jacob now knew that that other nation was Egypt, even though the time of slavery was not yet upon them.

The Family—Seed of a Nation

Gen. 46:5-27: Since he now had the guidance of *Elohim*, and knew about the fulfillment of the historical promise to Abraham, Jacob left Beersheba and went down to Egypt with confidence. He relocated with all that he had (Gen. 15:13-16, 46:5-7).

Seventy individuals are included in Jacob's family in the Hebrew manuscript of the Old Testament. Stephen referred to 75 in his speech when he quoted the Greek manuscript of the Old Testament, the Septuagint (Gen. 46:27, Acts 7:14). Five additional individuals from the seed of Joseph, progeny of Manasseh and Ephraim, are on the list in the Greek manuscript. Those five account for the difference. During his defense before the religious leaders, Stephen discussed the evolution of the family of Israel to become a nation (Acts 7:19-15).

Sons and daughters can refer to the extended progeny of Jacob, e.g., grandsons and granddaughters, etc. (page 324) (Gen. 46:7).

The list is in quantitative numerical order. Jacob is included first as one of the 33 listed with his progeny through Leah. This further suggests that Leah was God's intended wife for Jacob. The other wives accounted for 37 of Jacob's progeny: Zilpah—16, Rachel—14, and Bilhah—seven.

The four wives of Jacob—Leah, Zilpah, Rachel, and Bilhah—are not counted in the 70. Presumably, all had died prior to the journey to Egypt (Gen. 35:18, 49:31). The wives of the sons are not on the list. Asenath, the wife of Joseph, is on the list but not counted in the 70. It is likely that she became a believer in *Yahweh* through Joseph's witness to her.

Shaul, the son of Simeon, had a Canaanite mother (Gen. 46:10). He would become the head of a family of the Simeonites (Exod. 6:15). His mother may have been one of the Shechemite women that Simeon obtained after the rape of Dinah and the pillaging of Shechem (Gen. 34:25-29). His inclusion indicates the outreach to Canaan by Israel (Num. 1:23; 25:9, 14; 26:14). The Shaulites would continue as a family after the episode at Baal-Peor. This suggests that the family did not participate in that orgy (Num. 26:13). Er and Onan were not counted in the 70; they died in the land of Canaan due to their sin.

Dinah, the daughter of Leah, is included in the 70. There is no indication that she married following her rape as a teenager. She may have become a leader in Israel and participated in the inheritance with her brothers.

Zilpah's granddaughter, Serah, is one of the 70; the reason for this is not clear. Serah's name is recorded in two other genealogies (Num. 26:46, 1 Chr. 7:30). Since she is listed as one of the leaders of the tribe of Asher, she may have participated in the inheritance with her brothers (1 Chr. 7:30, 40).

Since Benjamin was in his early to mid-twenties at the time of the entrance into Egypt, it is improbable that he had had ten sons by that time. Thus, the 70 extends beyond the time of Israel's entrance into Egypt. It may represent the leaders that came to the fore during the early part of their sojourn in Egypt.

The 70 included male progeny and selected females and excluded wives and those who had died before the event. The emphasis was on 68 men and two women who contributed to the nation of Israel, probably as significant leaders within the 12 tribes. Note that God did select two of the women to leadership positions. Seven is a number of perfection in the Bible (Gen. 2:2-3). Here the 70 illustrates the promise of *Yahweh* to perfect His chosen people and the foreigners who became part of that family, the Israel of God (Gal. 6:15-16).

Gen. 46:28-30: Israel now accepted Judah as the leader of the other sons. He sent him ahead to meet Joseph in the land of Goshen. Joseph arrived in his chariot. He wanted to demonstrate to his father his position and accomplishments. When they met, Joseph wept on the neck of his father for a long time. Israel, at the age of 130, stated that he was prepared to die after seeing Joseph's face once again. He took the promise given by *Elohim* for Joseph to close his eyes as being in the near future. His interpretation suggests continued symptoms of depression.

Joseph's Judicious Advice

Gen. 46:31-34: Joseph coached his brothers to prepare them for their appearance before Pharaoh, so they could obtain permission to dwell in the land of Goshen. He took advantage of the fact that Hebrews were discriminated against, because of their occupation as shepherds. Shepherds took care of all livestock, not just sheep (Gen. 46:32, 34). This was land suitable for their occupation and in close proximity to the Promised Land. Since it was the best pastoral land, Goshen was "the best" land in Egypt for the family of Israel.

The land of Rameses is synonymous with the land of Goshen. Some scholars believe that the name Rameses comes from an Egyptian word that designates pastoral land. The Torah, the Pentateuch, written by Moses, would refer to this place more than four centuries later (Exod. 12:37). This would be the place where the Exodus would start.

God sometimes uses the things that this world disparages to fulfill His will for His people. The family of Israel could avoid assimilation into the Egyptian culture and stay close to the land of their inheritance. One of the strongest arguments for God's care of His chosen people, the Jews, is the observation that many have not assimilated into the cultures where they have scattered throughout the world; they have retained their cultural identity.

Five Brothers Selected by Joseph

Genesis 47:1-31

Gen. 47:1-6: Joseph knew the character of his brothers and weighed their past behavior and his recent observation of them before selecting five to appear before Pharaoh. It is speculative as to which five he selected. Those likely excluded were the four about whom he had previously given a negative report to his father—Dan, Naphtali, Gad, and Asher (Gen. 37:2). Simeon and Levi were responsible for the murder and pillaging at Shechem and possibly excluded for that reason (Gen. 34:25). The probable five selected were Reuben, who had interceded for Joseph; Judah, who diverted his brothers from murder to selling Joseph and had become the recent intercessor; Benjamin, Joseph's brother; and the two remaining sons of Leah, Issachar and Zebulun.

Joseph met with Pharaoh first and reported that he had carried out his orders (Gen. 45:19-20). He indicated that his family was in the land of Goshen with their flocks and herds. Pharaoh had offered the "best" of all the land of Egypt. As previously stated, he may have interpreted this to be in and around the major cities. Joseph, by referring to the flocks and herds, was emphasizing that his relatives were shepherds, an occupation that was "an abomination" to the Egyptians. The land of Goshen was best suited for their occupation (Gen. 43:32, 46:34 NASB margin). Pharaoh accepted Joseph's suggestion. It would solve the problem of the cultural differences that existed between Hebrews and Egyptians.

Pharaoh followed Joseph's recommendations. He repeated the offer for the "best" land in Egypt but now selected Goshen as that land. He trusted Joseph's opinion as to which of his brothers were capable and put them in charge of his livestock. Since they disdained this occupation, the Egyptian shepherds may not have been as capable as the brothers of Joseph (Gen. 46:34). Pharaoh knew a good thing when he saw it.

Joseph was an astute governor with insight into his brothers whom he coached by direction, and insight into Pharaoh, his superior, whom he coached by suggestion. Pharaoh and his brothers followed the format Joseph laid out for them (Gen. 45:10, 46:31-34, 47:1). Joseph was an adroit executive.

The Twofold Blessing of Pharaoh by the Man of Faith

Gen. 47:7-12: The Hebrew text indicates that Joseph "set" Jacob before Pharaoh (Gen. 47:7 NASB margin). The phrase, "set him before" (*'yamadhu,* ויעמדהו), suggests that Jacob may have been unable to walk. As previously noted, he had evidence of cardiac (heart) disease (Gen. 45:26-27).

One of the most dramatic scenes in all history then occurred. Jacob, the nomadic foreigner who had come to settle in the land of plenty at Pharaoh's invitation, standing, or sitting in a chair due to disability, did not offer obeisance to Pharaoh. Instead, he blessed Pharaoh. When Pharaoh accepted the blessing and inquired about his age of 130, Jacob blessed Pharaoh again. These were actions of faith. Israel recognized God's blessing to Pharaoh by sending Joseph to him.

However, the words he expressed to Pharaoh about his pilgrimage were in the negative. He spoke of his years as "few and evil" (*me'aṭ̂ raim,* מעט ורעים) (Gen. 47:9 NASB margin). Hence, reference is to the name of Jacob, "the old man." Surely, a man who was 130 years old had not lived "a few years." Even though he had suffered many hardships, it was inappropriate to call his entire life evil. These are the words of a depressed man. God uses all the years of our lives to develop us and bring us to oneness with Him.

Jacob's twofold blessing to Pharaoh, and his testimony that he and his fathers were "sojourning" on the earth, was a positive witness to him. All people need to understand the transitory nature of this present life. The blessed people are those who turn their lives over to the living God by faith in His Son, the LORD-Jesus-Christ/*YHWH-Yeshua-Mashiach*. They recognize that they are sojourners on the earth.

Joseph provided food for the family "according to their little ones." When they are hungry, babies and young children develop contractions, i.e., pain, in their stomachs. The number and hunger of the children determined the necessary food during a time of famine. No child went hungry in the family of Israel. God did deliver the family of Israel, the Egyptians, and the Canaanites from devastation and possible extinction.

God Used Joseph to Bless the Family of Israel, the Egyptians, and the Canaanites

Gen. 47:13-15: The time sequence in the depletion of the Egyptians' resources is not entirely clear. A possible sequence follows based on the certainty that the famine must have been secondary to a drought, and there would have been no use in giving the people grain to sow until the seventh year. When the famine was over, the rain would come and a crop would be produced in the eighth year.

During the first five years of the famine, the Egyptians and the Canaanites bought grain from Joseph in Egypt until their money was gone (Gen. 47:14-15). After depleting their financial resources, it is not clear what the Canaanites did. Many may have migrated to Egypt for the duration of the famine. The record only tells the outcome for the nation of Egypt and the family of Israel.

Gen. 47:16-17: In the sixth year, the Egyptians rendered their livestock as payment for the grain. Since the children of Israel were in charge of Pharaoh's livestock, this enhanced their income. Joseph, with his usual foresight, anticipated this probability. He turned the occupation that the Egyptians looked down upon into the most prosperous one in the land.

Gen. 47:18-19: The Egyptians offered themselves and their land as payment for food during the seventh year. Joseph moved the people to the cities. Besides the request for food, the people asked for seed to plant again. They finally realized that Joseph's interpretation of the dreams were true. Joseph accepted their offer.

Pharaoh had gained all the money of Canaan and Egypt and all the livestock, land, and servitude of the people of Egypt (Gen. 47:14-21). Since Pharaoh was now the landlord of all Egypt, and all the people were indentured servants, Joseph gave them grain to sow and work the land during the remaining year of the famine and thereafter. Joseph showed special concern for the Egyptian children:

"Then Joseph said to the people, 'Behold, I have today bought you and your land for Pharaoh; now, here is seed for you, and you may sow the land. At the harvest you shall give a fifth to Pharaoh, and four-fifths shall be your own for seed of the field and for your food and for those of your households and as food for your little ones'" (Gen. 47:23-24).

Gen. 47:20-26: Joseph submitted himself to the LORD for His direction for the future. The people were assessed a 20 percent tax on the produce during the harvest. Israel was in charge of the animals, so they were not taxed (Matt. 17:25-27). He exempted the land of the priests; they had an allotment from Pharaoh. Joseph may have had land in that area (Gen. 41:45). Joseph, with foresight, saw the need to protect those who serve the LORD. The provision for the priests would eventually become law in Israel for the Levites and priests (Deut. 18:1-8). The 20 percent tax became a statute in the land of Egypt (Gen. 47:26). A 20 percent tax on the majority of workers is still sound advice for countries today.

Joseph, Administrator *Par Excellence*

Gen. 47:27: Joseph excelled as an administrator in finding a way to bless the people of God and the Egyptians. History does not make the man, and man does not make history. Rather, God raises up leaders to accomplish His sovereign will, either to preserve or to allow the destruction of individual nations on the earth. The LORD is the designer of history and the central determinant of it.

Besides the oversight of the livestock of Egypt, the children of Israel were able to purchase land in Goshen (Gen. 47:27). They multiplied; the family was evolving to become a nation. Joseph became a type of the LORD-Jesus-Christ/*YHWH-Yeshua-Mashiach* who would bring ultimate salvation to the faithful remnant from Israel and to all other people who would receive it by faith (Rom. 2:28-29, 11:25-27).

Gen. 47:28: Israel, at age 147, was ready to die. *Yahweh* had revealed to him that the time for his departure was at hand. He had lived 17 years in Egypt. *Yahweh* graciously gave him these 17 additional years with Joseph. This was the same number as the initial 17 years of Joseph's life that they had had together.

The Oath of Faith—Bury Me at Macpelah

Gen. 47:29-31: In anticipation of his return to the Promised Land, Israel requested the intimate swearing of an oath by Joseph to return his body to Machpelah (Gen. 46:4, 49:29-30). Israel thought about lying down with his fathers, and *Yahweh's* covenant that he had heard from his grandfather during the first 15 years of his life (Tables 8 and 9, page 390). That covenant was transmitted to his father and then to him (Gen. 15:16, 26:2-5, 28:13-15). It was testimony to the fact that he believed the promises of *Yahweh* to be more reliable than the riches of Egypt. Israel bowed in worship to *Yahweh* for this blessing at the end of his life. He was at the head of his bed, apparently too weak to be out of bed.

Holy Memories at the End of Life

Genesis 48:1-22

Gen. 48:1-4: The LORD never designed illness; there was no sickness in Eden. After the Fall, illness came through the design of Satan. Illness, authored by Satan and allowed by the LORD in a fallen world, is often the means used to transition from this life to the next (Job 2:5-7). Israel embarked upon his terminal illness. Most people will die from an illness. Elisha, whom God used to heal others, died from an illness and still was used by Him to heal a person from the grave (2 Kin. 13:14-21).

Believers need to discern when to pray for healing from an illness versus praying for the transition from this life to one where there is no disease. As a physician, I have observed several patients who lived beyond all medical prognostication, i.e., they should have died sooner. However, some held on until they had restored a damaged relationship with loved ones. Alternatively, I have seen patients hold on until a loved one could accept their departure. Ideally, all need to be prepared for their personal exit and have their loved ones ready for the same.

As Israel reappeared on the scene, he had become a man of faith. He exhibited no symptoms of depression. His healing had allowed him to live longer and not die prematurely. He looked forward to his transition. The LORD wants the best for each of us and will do whatever is necessary to develop us. God is not in a hurry. Old age can be a precious time to sit at the feet of the LORD and learn from Him. Only **one** thing is necessary—choose the good part, particularly during the waning years of life:

"Now as they were traveling along, He entered a village; and a woman named Martha welcomed Him into her home. She had a sister called Mary, who was seated at the Lord's feet, listening to His word. But Martha was distracted with all her preparations; and she came up to Him and said, 'Lord, do You not care that my sister has left me to do all the serving alone? Then tell her to help me.' But the Lord answered and said to her, 'Martha, Martha, you are worried and bothered about so many things; But only one thing is necessary, for Mary has chosen the good part, which shall not be taken away from her'" (Luke 10:38-42).

Joseph knew his father was frail. He took his two sons to see him in order to receive the blessing. Joseph knew that this blessing must be a private one to avoid a jealous response in the other brothers. Long ago he had learned from their jealous response to his dreams.

Israel was so weak that he had to strengthen himself to sit up in bed. Jacob, not Israel, recounted his prior experiences with God. He referred to God as *El Shaddai* who appeared to him at Luz and blessed him when he returned from Paddan-Aram. *El Shaddai* is the name of God that reflects His bountiful provision (page 51). The patriarchs needed such provision as they evolved from an individual family to a nation.

God appeared to Jacob as *Yahweh* on the first occasion at Luz, not as *El Shaddai* (Gen. 28:12-15). Upon his return to Luz, now called Bethel, God appeared to him as *El Shaddai* and specified at that time that Jacob would become "a company of nations" (Gen. 35:6-13). Jacob emphasized the second visit. This may have been his acknowledgment of the fulfillment of the promises of God to him during the intervening years of nearly three decades between the two visits to Bethel. Older people sometimes merge significant spiritual events into one because of the singular impact on their lives. Soon after the return to Bethel, Joseph left home. Jacob may have reflected on this time to indicate to Joseph the start of his spiritual depression that had continued for 22 years until *El Shaddai* reunited them 17 years ago. Reminiscent thoughts are often multivariate.

Since that initial direct communication by *Yahweh* at age 77, *Yahweh* had given Israel 70 more years. The 70 years represented a full life span (Psa. 90:10). Although all the years of life are important, the acceleration of one's spiritual journey often begins in the second half of the years allotted by the LORD.

By faith, Israel demonstrated that what *Yahweh El Shaddai* had promised, He would do. Jacob spoke of the Promised Land at this time of blessing his grandsons. The promise extends to the new heaven and earth (Rev. 21:1). The Israel of God will continue forever (Gal. 6:15-16). He again merged the promise given to Abraham (that the land would be an everlasting possession) with the promise given to him (page 291) (Gen. 17:8, 35:11, 48:4):

"I will make you fruitful and numerous, and I will make you a company of peoples, and will give this land to your descendants after you for an everlasting possession" (Gen. 48:4).

Gen. 48:5: The double portion that would go to the elder son went to Joseph through Ephraim and Manasseh. Their share would equal the inheritance of Reuben and Simeon, the two eldest sons of Leah. The subsequent progeny of Joseph would receive their inheritance through either Ephraim or Manasseh.

Gen. 48:6-7: Jacob than recounted how Rachel died "upon me" (*'ali,* עלי) on the road to Ephrath while giving birth to Benjamin (Gen. 48:7 NASB margin). Jacob retained this poignant, sorrowful memory. Jacob was reminiscing of the time that Rachel, Joseph's mother, Ephraim and Manasseh's grandmother, died in his arms. He loved her. Israel was about to die. He reflected on the fact that Rachel's gravesite was not at Machpelah but on the way to Ephrath (pages 308-309).

Ephrath would become Bethlehem. Bethlehem is a composite of two Hebrew words meaning "house" (*beŷth,* בית) and "bread" (*lechem,* לחם), i.e., "house of bread." When the Messiah, the Bread of Life, was born in Bethlehem, "the House of Bread," He produced the "fruit" (*'ephrathah,* אפרתה) of the people He saved and prepared for eternal habitations with Him (John 14:1-3).

Manasseh means "making to forget" (*menashsheh,* מנשה). Ephrath (sg. noun, *'ephrathah,* אפרתה) and Ephraim (pl. noun, *'ephrayim,* אפרים) are from the same Hebrew root that means "fruitfulness." Joseph forgot the troubles of his earlier life and became fruitful in the land of Egypt (Gen. 41:51-52). Jacob forgot the troubles of his earlier life and spoke by faith of the fulfillment of *Yahweh El Shaddai's* promises. His depression had dissipated long ago; God healed him. Those who have suffered from depression know that such a healing is their private miracle.

Ephraim before Manasseh

Gen. 48:8-20: The more common causes of Israel's poor vision would have been cataracts or cardiovascular (heart and blood vessel) disease with vascular disease of the retina (back of the eye) (Gen. 48:10). Since he could not see adequately, he asked for Joseph's verification that these were his sons.

It is unlikely that he would have believed that Joseph would have deceived him as Jacob had deceived his father (Gen. 27:21-24). Since *Yahweh* had given him a revelation, Israel, not Jacob, wanted to be sure of transmitting the blessing to the younger son. Thus, there must have been a **seventh** direct communication between God and Israel about his death and the blessings to his seed. God had visited him at least **seven** times in **seven** decades.

Even though his vision was nearly gone, he spoke of *Elohim* letting him "see your seed" (*ra'ah zeraq,* ראה זרעך). Blind people develop increased touch sensitivity; he may have felt the features of their faces. He saw with the eyes of faith their physiognomy and future (Gen. 47:10-11).

Joseph attributed the blessing of his sons to *Elohim*. Both sons had been born prior to Israel's coming to Egypt. They were in their early to mid-twenties (Gen. 41:50-52). Israel kissed them and embraced them. They were at Israel's knees. Thus, they were on their knees and bowed before their grandfather (Gen. 48:11-12). The family patriarch's age and authority were respected by his son and grandsons. Joseph took his sons from between Israel's knees and bowed to his father with his face to the ground.

Joseph guided his sons to his father with Ephraim toward Israel's left hand and Manasseh toward his right hand. Presumably, Israel was sitting on the edge of the bed (Gen. 48:2). Joseph believed that the blessing of *Yahweh*, through his father, was more important than the blessing of Pharaoh. There was no thought of permanent abode in the land of Egypt.

To the displeasure of Joseph, Israel's right hand was crossed over to the head of Ephraim with his left hand on the head of Manasseh. Israel prophetically placed the younger grandson before the elder one. He granted them his blessing. Israel recognized that, "The gifts and calling of God are irrevocable," and placed Ephraim before Manasseh (Rom. 11:29, Heb. 11:21). Ephraim would eventually represent the northern tribes in Israel (Hos. 14:1-9).

This prophecy from Israel, spiritual elder statesman of the family, was a contrast to the history of Jacob and his mother when they tried to obtain the blessing of the elder son for Jacob by deception (Gen. 25:23, 27:1-29). Here the LORD provided the message of the blessing through His servant, Israel. The way of the LORD is always best. His wisdom comes from above and brings peace with it (James 1:5-8, 3:13-18).

Israel's blessing of Joseph's sons was a blessing to Joseph (Gen. 48:15) His blessing was invoked in the name of the *Elohim* of Abraham and Isaac and Israel's Shepherd, "The Angel who has redeemed me from all evil" (Gen. 48:16a).

Israel personally knew his Redeemer. The Angel (*h'mal'ak̂,* המלאך) was *Yahweh* who first appeared to him at the top of the ladder that extended from earth to heaven (Gen. 28:12-15). He had nearly completed his earthly journey. He was ready to ascend to the Angel of *Yahweh* at the top of the ladder, to ascend to heaven.

Note the contrast between his speech to Pharaoh 17 years previously concerning a life of "few and evil" years and his present statements (Gen. 47:9). To repeat, his depression was gone! Old age can be a time of healing. He had submitted to *Yahweh*; his outlook was that of a man walking close to his LORD! He anticipated a family reunion in his heavenly home.

Israel then blessed Ephraim and Manasseh (Heb. 11:21). The blessing was in the name of the God of Abraham, Isaac, and Israel, the one who had been his Shepherd all his life (page 51) and had redeemed him from all evil. Jacob had become Israel. The final 17 years were necessary and productive!

The prayer was for the names of Abraham, Isaac, and Israel (their character) to live on in them. Manasseh would become a great people. Ephraim would become "a fullness of nations" (*meloʾ goŷim*, מלא־הגוים) (Gen. 48:19 NASB margin). Israel was invoking the blessing for character development in his two grandsons that *Yahweh* had wrought in his life and the lives of his fathers (Gen. 48:16).

How would Ephraim become "a fullness of (Gentile) nations" (*meloʾ* ***goŷim***, מלא־הגוים)? Ephraim's numbers would decline during the 40 years in the wilderness; Manasseh's numbers would increase (Num. 2:18-21, 26:28-37). Manasseh would become a great people. Most of the book of Hosea tells of the horrendous spiritual adultery of Ephraim's tribe throughout most of its history. Ephraim would become the symbol of the northern kingdom of Israel with its apostasy and exile to Assyria (Isa. 7:17-18). There is no visible evidence that Ephraim ever became "a fullness of nations." Still, the prophets tell of the future kingdom of Israel where Ephraim will be blessed by God (Isa. 11:1-16, Jer. 31:1-40, Hos. 14:1-9, Zech. 10:6-12).

Today it is difficult to define a Jew. What percent of blood makes one a genetic Jew? If the Jew is defined by religious adherence, which are intended—Hasidic, conservative, liberal, reformed, other? Perhaps the true Jew can only be defined as the Apostle Paul gave the definition—one who has accepted his Messiah. Christ, the Messiah, responds to anyone who turns to Him in faith (Rom. 2:28-29, 9:23-25, 11:17-27; Gal. 6:15-16).

"Sing for joy and be glad, O daughter of Zion; for behold I am coming and I will dwell in your midst, declares the LORD. 'Many nations will join themselves to the LORD in that day and will become My people. Then I will dwell in your midst, and you will know that the LORD of hosts has sent Me to you'" (Zech. 2:10-11).

Whenever the Jews believed and obeyed *Yahweh*, they blessed the nations where God sent them. Might this mean that Ephraim would become a multitude of nations through its alliances and spiritual "fruit" produced among the Gentile nations where the ten tribes would be exiled (page 382)? If so, the completion of the prophecy about Ephraim will happen in the future when the Israel of God becomes one body of Jewish and Gentile believers from all the nations (Zech. 2:11, Gal. 6:15-16). The prophecy may come to further fulfillment during the future millennial reign of the LORD Jesus Christ (Ezek. 37:1-28, Rev. 20:4).

Gen. 48:21-22: Israel prophetically spoke of his upcoming death. *Elohim* would take Joseph's progeny back to the land of his fathers; they would receive two portions of the land. There is no record of Israel himself taking the land from the Amorite with his sword and bow. It is likely that he was speaking prophetically of the time his seed would conquer the Amorite nations and historically of the time his sons pillaged Shechem with the sword (page 305) (Gen. 15:16-21, 34:1-31; Josh. 11:1-15).

Israel Assembles His Sons

Genesis 49:1-33

Gen. 49:1-2: "Then," i.e., after pronouncing the double portion of inheritance to Joseph through his two sons, Jacob summoned the rest of his sons. His intent was prophetic, to tell them what would be the future "days of their posterity" (*'achariŷth hayomim,* אחרית הימים), not "the end of days" (*qets yomim,* קץ ימים) (Gen. 49:1).

The prophecy referenced each individual's past behavior and character development that contributed to the future of their seed, the tribes of Israel. Jacob gathered his sons, but Israel gave the prophetic word about each of them and their seed. They knew him before as Jacob, the old man. In this final family meeting, they would know him as Israel, the new man, the prophet of *Yahweh*.

It was not too late for them to experience a change similar to Jacob's becoming Israel. Judgment followed by repentance could initiate change in their character. They were still in their middle years. Their names would be registered on the gates of the New Jerusalem; each of the 12 would come to full spiritual development before their transition (Rev. 21:12). After each person's earthly sojourn is over, judgment comes from the LORD (Heb. 9:27).

Judgment Can Result in Punishment or Redemption

Gen. 49:3-7: Judgment had the potential for redemption in the lives of Jacob's sons who had not confessed their sins and deceit, i.e., Reuben with Bilhah and Simeon and Levi's actions at Shechem. It is remarkable that Israel waited until his deathbed to deal with them. Perhaps he waited over the years in the hope that his sons would come to him voluntarily and confess their sins and seek restoration and fellowship with him. Our heavenly Father ever waits for His children to do the same.

Reuben is related to a Hebrew root meaning "see, a son" (*re'uben,* ראובן). What did Reuben see? The character of Reuben was exemplified by his life. Reuben was the firstborn who had the preeminence and power of the same. He failed, because of his inability to control himself. He was as uncontrolled as "boiling water" (*pachaz,* פחז) (Gen. 49:4 NASB margin). The example that Israel used to illustrate this was the time Reuben had sexual intercourse with Bilhah in his early twenties, soon after the death of Rachel (Gen. 35:22). There is judgment for all who cannot control their sexual drive. Reuben was 63 years old at the time of this judgment and had failed to confess his sin in four decades. By refusing to admit his sin, he had lost years of a potential loving relationship with his father to the detriment of his own spiritual development. Reuben lost the birthright. The birthright went to Joseph, the one spiritually qualified to have the rights of the firstborn (1 Chr. 5:1-2).

Dathan and Abiram, the seed of Reuben, would die when they demonstrated godless leadership by joining with Korah in rebellion against God as they contended with Moses and Aaron (Num. 16:1-35, Deut. 11:6). The tribe of Reuben would receive only one portion of land on the west side of the Jordan (Josh. 13:15-23). Ephraim and Manasseh would receive the two portions of the firstborn given to Joseph (Josh. 17:1-18, 1 Chr. 5:1-2). Those in the family of Israel, and the kingdom of God, gain acceptance by faith that produces godly deeds, not by position and claim to inheritance on a genetic basis (James 2:17-26).

Simeon comes from a Hebrew root that means "to hear" (*shim'ôn,* שמעון). What did Simeon hear? His deeds sounded forth his character. The Hebrew root of Levi means "attached" (*lêvîŷ,* לוי). To what was Levi "attached" as demonstrated by the example of his life?

Simeon and Levi were 62 and 61 years old, respectively, at the time of this judgment. They received judgment for their counsel that led to violent behavior at Shechem in their late teens or early twenties; they deceived and killed the men of Shechem on the third day after their circumcision (Gen. 34:25-31). They obtained wives from an immoral culture (Gen. 34:29). Their cruelty extended to the laming of an innocent ox (sg. noun, Gen. 49:6 NASB margin). Note God's and Israel's concern for cruelty to a single ox.

The Simeonites and the Levites at Baal-Peor

The comparison between the initial 59,300 tribal warriors of Simeon near the beginning of the wandering in the wilderness and the 22,200 at the time of their entrance into the Promised Land reveals a decrease of 37,100 warriors, nearly a 63 percent decline (Num. 1:22-23, 26:14).

Near the end of the 40 years of wandering in the wilderness, the titular perpetrator of sexual sin at Baal-Peor was Zimri, the son of Salu, a leader from the tribe of Simeon (Num. 25:14). The decline in numbers was not from Baal-Peor alone with its 24,000 deaths, but the event suggests significant participation in that sexual orgy by the tribe of Simeon. They may have taken part in the first sexual orgy at the beginning of the wilderness journey when Moses was up on the mountain (Exod. 32:1-35).

Their sinful attitude about sex, perhaps initiated at the time Simeon and Levi captured the women and children of Shechem, contributed to this result. These women had been involved in the worship of Baal-Berith, an odious worship that involved the same types of sexual practices and child sacrifice associated with Baal-Peor. Intimate sexual relations always affect the participants for good or for ill (Gen. 34:1-31; Jdg. 8:28-35, 9:1-4; Psa. 106:28-29).

At Baal-Peor, in which tent did the sexual travesty occur? The tribe of Simeon was one of the three tribes encamping on the south side of the tent of meeting "at a distance" (Num. 2:2, 10-17). The ark was kept a thousand yards in front of the children of Israel at the time they crossed the Jordan. This suggests that the distance of the encamped tribes from the tent of meeting may have been a thousand yards (Josh. 3:4). Therefore, the only tent that was supposed to be in this vicinity was the tent of meeting. The leaders and congregation were weeping at the "tent" (*'ohel,* אהל) of meeting (Gen. 25:6).

However, the Hebrew word for the tent where the sexual transgression occurred is not the usual one. It does not refer to the tent of meeting. Instead, it indicates "a very large vaulted tent" (*haqubbah,* אל־הקבה) that the Talmud references as the type where prostitutes practiced their trade (Num. 25:8). The equivalent of a bordello, placed in proximity to the tent of meeting, was the structure in question where the couple, the Simeonite prince and the Midianite princess, entered. This large tent, this bordello, was an invitation to Israel to join in the fertility rites of the surrounding nations. They were trying to introduce these "religious" rites into the worship of *Yahweh*, an attempt at syncretism.

Moses, Eleazar, and the judges disobeyed the LORD and took no action against the leaders. Moses wanted to kill the participants, just as had been done at Mt. Sinai (Exod. 32:27-28, Num. 25:4-5).

Phinehas, the son of Eleazar, did take action. Phinehas is an Egyptian name that means "Nubian." Eleazar, his father, married a daughter of Putiel when he was in Egypt, and Phinehas was a son from that union (Exod. 6:25). His Egyptian name indicates that he was a black man born from an international, interracial marriage.

The construction of the Hebrew sentence and the single noun for **"belly" (*qeb̂aĥ*, קבה)** indicates the "two" (את־שׁניהם), the Simeonite prince and the Midianite princess, were engaged in sexual intercourse in the **"bordello" (*qub̂baĥ*, קבה)** tent. Note the similarity between the word for belly and the word for the bordello tent that verifies that this was a place for sexual congress. This is not apparent in the NASB's translation of "tent" and "body":

"And he went after the man of Israel into the tent and pierced both of them through, the man of Israel and the woman, through the body. So the plague on the sons of Israel was checked" (Num. 25:8).

Phinehas' action stopped the plague when he thrust a spear or a javelin through the belly of both the prince, i.e., leader (Num. 25:3) of Simeon and the princess of Midian while they were coupled in sexual intercourse. Phinehas, from the tribe of Levi, received a commendation from *Yahweh* for his action at Baal-Peor because he experienced a jealousy similar to that which *Yahweh* had over His adulterous children (Num. 25:11).

The Levites were instrumental in stopping the first plague at Mt. Sinai, and Phinehas, as a representative of the priests, was instrumental in stopping the one at Baal-Peor (Exod. 32:1-35, Num. 25:1-18). God gave Phinehas His covenant of peace and a perpetual priesthood (Num. 25:7-18). The details of this event at Baal-Peor, and praise for Phinehas' exploits, are part of the spiritual lore of Israel (Psa. 106:28-31).

Phinehas was the priest in charge of the ark during the punishment of Midian instead of his father, Eleazar, who did not take action at Baal-Peor (Num. 31:1-6). He was the High Priest who supervised the punishment of the tribe of Benjamin for their sexual sin during the early period of the Judges as recorded in an appendix to that book (Jdg. 20:28). He was the priest sent to settle the matter of possible apostasy with the altar built by the Reubenites, Gadites, and the eastern Manassites (Josh. 22:13-14).

Phinehas inherited land in the hill country of Ephraim near Gibeah where his father was buried (Josh. 24:33). He contributed to a "perpetual priesthood"; his heritage extends beyond this life (Num. 25:12-13).

Compared to the other tribes, Levi was the smallest. This may have been due to Levi's repentance from the episode at Shechem with less proclivity to sexual activity and sexual sin in his progeny (Num. 3:39-43). The response to Levi's participation in the sin at Shechem was the opposite of that of Simeon and his progeny.

Israel reserved judgment on their activity until his deathbed when he condemned Simeon and Levi for their sin. His prophetic word would be fulfilled:

"I will disperse them in Jacob, and scatter them in Israel" (Gen. 49:7b).

Eventually the tribe of Simeon would receive an inheritance of only 17 cities in the south of Judah. They would require help from the tribe of Judah to gain control over these (Josh. 19:1-9, Jdg. 1:3). David later would transfer one of these cities to the tribe of Judah after he had regained it from its Philistine captors (1 Sam. 27:6). Simeon would decline numerically and spiritually and be scattered about in southern Israel.

The redemption of the tribe of Levi would occur through the actions of Moses and the Levites at Mount Sinai with the episode of the golden calf and the action of Phinehas during the episode at the *qubbah* at Baal-Peor (Exod. 32:26-28, Num. 25:6-12). Levi and the progeny of Aaron would receive honor by inheriting the cities occupied by the Levites and priests that would be scattered throughout Israel (Josh. 21:1-42).

Although the prophecy would come true, it bore opposite results. Judgment has the potential to bring about repentance and renewal. The LORD's mercies are great for those who turn to him. The tribe of Simeon would take a downward spiral into further sexual sin, and the tribe of Levi would repent from their sin and practice sexual conservatism. Israel's prophecy would come true over four centuries in the future with condemnation for the tribe of Simeon and restoration for the tribe of Levi.

Judah Earned the Right of Leadership

Gen. 49:8-12: Judah comes from a Hebrew root that means "he praises" (*yehûdâh,* יהודה). Judah was the son who would praise *Yahweh*. He was the one who left home as a prodigal son for two decades (Gen. 38:1-30). After his return home, Judah became the leader of his brothers (1 Chr. 5:2). He was lion-like; the lion became the standard for the tribe of Judah (Gen. 49:9).

The translation of Shiloh (*shîylôh,* שׁילה) may mean, "He to whom it belongs," an epithet for the Messiah. Both the staff and scepter are articles of authority for "the One to whom it belongs," the Messiah. Note the contrast with Judah's historical use of his staff and other symbols of authority during his prodigal days (page 327). Redemption and restoration are marvelous!

The Messiah would come from the tribe of Judah and would bring salvation to the world (Gen. 49:10, Heb. 7:14). The Messiah will return in triumph over His enemies with blood-red apparel like wine (Gen. 49:11-12):

"Who is this who comes from Edom, with garments of glowing colors from Bozrah, this One who is majestic in His apparel, marching in the greatness of His strength? 'It is I who speak in righteousness, mighty to save. Why is Your apparel red, and Your garments like the one who treads in the wine press? I have trodden the wine trough alone, and from the peoples there was no man with Me. I also trod them in My anger and trampled them in My wrath; and their lifeblood is sprinkled on My garments, and I stained all My raiment. For the day of vengeance was in My heart, and My year of redemption has come'" (Isa. 63:1-4).

Gen. 49:13-21: The prophetic statements of these first four sons have to do with their individual character, illustrated by their names, and the conviction that their character would influence the tribes generated from them. There would be a choice for each individual and tribe between a downward spiral into sin (Simeon and his progeny) or repentance and restoration (Levi and his progeny). By the grace of God, a remnant from the tribes would spiritually evolve to become part of the Israel of God (Gal. 6:15-16, Rev. 21:12).

The prophecy of the first four sons of Leah is sequential by age. Since Issachar was born before Zebulun, the next two sons of Leah are not listed in order of their birth (Gen. 30:18-20). Zebulun comes from the Hebrew word, "dwelling" (*zebuluͮn,* זבלון). The tribe's territory never reached the sea, but it was near the sea (Josh. 19:10-26). Part of the fulfillment of this prophecy would occur through the One who would come "by way of the sea" to make the land glorious (Isa. 9:1). Future fulfillment will occur during the millennium when its landmass reaches the sea (Ezek. 48:1, 27).

Issachar comes from the Hebrew root for "recompense" (*yiśśaŝkar̂,* יששכר); the spiritual wages of Issachar would be received (Gen. 49:14-15). At the time of the kings, the tribe of Issachar would come to David with their chiefs during the civil unrest. Out of this tribe would come, "Men who understood the times, with knowledge of what Israel should do" (1 Chr. 12:32a).

Israel came next to the prophecy for the sons of Bilhah, Dan ("judge," *dan̂,* דָּן) and Naphtali ("wrestlings," *naphtal̂iŷ,* נַפְתָּלִי) and the sons of Zilpah, Gad ("good fortune," *gad̂,* גָּד) and Asher ("happiness," *'asher̂,* אָשֵׁר). Dan was born prior to the other three; the birth sequence of the remaining three relative to each other and to Zebulun is not clear (page 279) (Gen. 30:6-13).

Chiefs from the tribe of Gad would join David during the civil unrest (1 Chr. 12:14-15). Thus, they also would reap a spiritual harvest during a time of conflict.

The prophetess, Anna, would come from the tribe of Asher and would prophesy at the announcement of the baby Jesus, the Messiah (Luke 2:36).

The tribes of Zebulun and Naphtali would conquer during the time of Deborah, one of the Judges, when several other tribes would be delinquent in their response to war (Jdg. 5:12, 18).

Dan means "judge"; he received two distinct prophecies. The first prophecy was as a judge of his people, which may have referred to the future time of Samson, one of the judges (Gen. 49:16, Jdg. 16:30-31). The second prophecy may have referred to the future minority group from the tribe who would murder the undefended occupants of a village in the north of Israel. Like the Serpent, they would take possession of a territory not allotted to them and would take an apostate priest to be their spiritual advisor (Gen 49:17, Josh. 19:47-48, Jdg. 18:1-31). That minority group will undergo judgment for their actions at the Great White Throne (Rev. 20:11-12).

Their inglorious action may be prophetic of the tribe's participation in the final apostasy during the Antichrist's reign, which will be aided by the False Prophet and the power of Satan (Jdg. 18:27, Jer. 8:16-17, Ezek. 38:8-12, Matt. 27:35-37, Rev. 20:7-10). This may be the reason that the tribe of Dan is absent from the record of the tribes in Revelation (Rev. 7:4-8). However, the righteous majority from the tribe of Dan will be restored during the millennial reign of the LORD (Ezek. 48:2).

The "horned serpent" may refer to a poisonous adder, the *cerastes*, which is the color of sand and can camouflage itself and strike victims who are unaware of its presence. Perhaps the False Prophet will be a Jew from the tribe of Dan (like the apostate priest), a snake camouflaged as a true prophet (Rev. 13:11-12). In those future days, the LORD will know his tribal derivation. Salvation will come through *Yahweh Tza'vot* who will judge and condemn the Antichrist and the False Prophet (Rev. 19:20-21).

Gen. 49:22-27: Some insight into the remaining tribes can be gained by comparing the prophecy of Moses at the end of his life with Israel's at the end of his life (Deut. 33:1-29).

In the 49th chapter of Genesis, the blessing went to Joseph, not to Ephraim and Manasseh. The private session with Joseph, Ephraim, and Manasseh avoided provoking jealousy among the rest of the brothers (Gen. 48:1-22). Both Moses and Israel described Joseph as having "the crown of the head of the one distinguished among his brothers" (Gen 49:26b, Deut. 33:16). This statement authenticated Joseph as the one who received the blessing of the firstborn. The imagery of these verses indicates that the seed of Joseph would be great and fruitful. The blessing of *El Shaddai* would include "blessings of the breasts" (*shaddim,* שׁדים) and the womb (pages 52-53).

Ephraim would not live up to the expectations of the tribe; it would decline from 40,500 to 32,500 warriors during the wanderings in the wilderness; Manasseh would grow from 32,200 to 52,700 warriors (Num. 1:32-35; 26:34, 37). This would result in a larger portion of land allotted to the tribe of Manasseh than to Ephraim (Josh. 16:1-17:18).

After the wandering in the wilderness, Moses would pronounce a blessing on "the ten thousands of Ephraim" compared to "the thousands of Manasseh" (Deut. 33:17). After the future civil war in Israel, Ephraim would become the dominant tribe in northern Israel, and Judah would become the dominant tribe in the south.

Joshua, a major Ephraimite, would be the leader of Israel that would succeed Moses. Israel would be faithful all his days (Num. 27:15-23, Josh. 24:31). Joshua would bring spiritual glory to the tribe of Ephraim. This may have been the time of Israel's greatest generation:

"All that generation also was gathered to their fathers" (Jdg. 2:10).

Joseph's progeny would receive blessings from the Mighty One of Jacob, the Shepherd, the Stone of Israel (page 51), the *Elohim* of your fathers, and *Shaddai*. There would be blessings from heaven above and blessings of the deep that lies beneath (Gen 49:24-26). Fruitfulness would come to Ephraim in the future (Hos. 14:8). Since the northern kingdom would be dispersed among the Gentile nations, the blessing would come through the spiritual fruit produced through the individuals in those nations that accept their Messiah and spread His message abroad (pages 371-372).

Benjamin, "the son of the right hand" (*binyam̂iŷn,* בנימין), would develop the behavior of a wild carnivore, a wolf. The tribe of Benjamin rebelled in hideous sin and nearly came to extinction (Jdg. 21:3). King Saul and his namesake, Saul, who became the Apostle Paul, would come from the tribe of Benjamin. The former would demonstrate spiritual inadequacy; the latter would bring honor to the tribe and the kingdom of God (1 Sam. 9:15-16, Acts 9:4, Rom. 11:1).

Israel Was Gathered to His People

Gen. 49:28-33: The blessings given by Jacob were to the "twelve tribes of Israel," not simply to his sons (Gen. 49:28). Each blessing was appropriate to each individual and tribe. Sin, without repentance and redemption, can carry over for three to four generations to those who hate God, but blessing can carry over for those who love God and keep His commandments to a thousand generations (Exod. 20:5-6, Deut. 7:9-10).

Israel was "gathered to his people"; he was going to a family reunion. He specified his burial place, the cave in the field of Machpelah before Mamre. The details he gave about the site and his forebears indicate that he had been thinking about the place and longed to go there.

Even though he expressed to Joseph his sorrow over losing Rachel, it was at Machpelah that he buried Leah. He had come to understand that Leah was the primary one chosen by God to be his wife and mother of his children, even though he loved and favored Rachel. Leah earned the right of burial at Machpelah. He would soon see both of them again without competition or rancor.

The charge to his sons was the last act of Jacob: "He drew his feet into the bed and breathed his last, and was gathered to his people" (Gen. 49:33b).

Israel glorified God in the dying process with the prophetic blessings to his sons and his witness to return his body to the Promised Land after his death. Believers need to remember that their death is a potential seed that they can sow to glorify God with their last breath and leave a productive witness behind them. If one does not live daily for the LORD, dying will not be a time of effective witness for Him (Luke 9:23, John 12:24).

The beauty of the patriarch's death, after charging his sons, is lost in today's society where most people die in medical facilities, instead of their homes. There is a need to appreciate the spiritual inadequacy of modern medicine and make plans for one's final days. If adequate care is available, some will choose to die at home without undue expense as opposed to dying expensively in a medical facility. Whatever the choice, believers should consider praying for a return to using one's final moments to bless their family and witness for their LORD.

Since he preferred burial in the Promised Land, Israel's death was a testimony to the Egyptians. The burial bore witness to the Canaanites and the Egyptian burial party that returned Israel's body to Machpelah. It was a witness to Joseph and the family; they were to look forward to their return to the Promised Land.

The Funeral at Machpelah

Genesis 50:1-26

Gen. 50:1-14: This is the first mention of physicians in the Bible. They were servants of Joseph. Subsequently, *Yahweh* would reveal Himself as the "LORD your Healer" (*Yahweh raphakh,* יהוה רפאך) (Exod. 15:26). Therefore, "physicians" (*raphim,* את־הרפאים) should be servants of the living LORD and those placed in authority over them.

In order to fulfill the promise that Joseph made to his father, the physicians embalmed Israel's body over a period of 40 days.[75] It is probable that this process included spices and resins used for mummification. The body of the departed saint received respect. This is an object lesson for those who care for dead bodies today, those in the health care professions and those who serve as undertakers.

Medicine was once a servant profession; for many physicians it has evolved to become a self-serving one. There is a need to return to medicine as a servant profession honoring *Yahweh Rapha*. In Hebrew, "healers" (*raphim*) and "physicians" (*raphim*) are the same word. Physicians are meant to be healers of body, mind, and spirit. Physicians should deem it an honor to be entrusted with the care of their patients. They are called to be an extension of the Great Physician, *Yahweh Rapha*.

Medicine was designed as a godly profession. Its original assignment was to the priests in Israel and in most, if not all, ancient cultures (Leviticus 13-15). The spiritual component and administration by the priesthood were the foundations of the profession. Sadly, those emphases are almost absent today. Many of today's physicians withdraw from the patient and family at the time of death, a time when they can render the greatest care and healing to the living. There is little emphasis in the medical curriculum for training physicians on the care of dying patients and their families.

At the time of death of a loved one, many seek the spiritual solace that can only come from the One who created them. At this crucial time, **care** should go to those who grieve and continue their earthly journey. Physicians have the distinct privilege of telling about the One who bids them come to Him for that care and solace:

"Come to Me, all who are weary and heavy-laden, and I will give you rest. Take My yoke upon you and learn from Me, for I am gentle and humble in heart, and YOU WILL FIND REST FOR YOUR SOULS. For My yoke is easy and My burden is light" (Matt. 11:28-30).

Joseph fell on his father, wept, and kissed him (Gen. 50:1). It is unclear whether the other brothers were similarly demonstrative. Grief is a proper and Scriptural necessity at the time of the death of a loved one. Joseph, by his position, and with the blessing of the Pharaoh, declared a national time of mourning for his father. The Egyptians wept for Israel for 70 days (Gen. 2:2-3). Respect for the greater age of Israel (147 years) compared to the ideal Egyptian age (110 years), and respect for Joseph, may have influenced their willingness to mourn for a foreigner (Gen 47:8-9).

In spite of his position, Joseph spoke to the appropriate officials in the household of Pharaoh to seek permission from him to return his father to Canaan for burial. Joseph was still a servant of Pharaoh. The basis of Joseph's plea was the oath sworn to his father. The reply and permission by Pharaoh revealed that old age and oaths deserved respect. Joseph was still a trusted servant.

Joseph may have spoken often of his father and the Promised Land. Pharaoh may have been concerned that Joseph would depart and not return. In addition to his own relatives, Joseph took with him all the servants of Pharaoh, the elders of Pharaoh's household, and all the elders of Egypt. Joseph was careful to give evidence that they would return to Egypt after the funeral by leaving behind their children and animals. The prophecy of four generations in a foreign land still awaited fulfillment (Gen. 15:13-16).

Machpelah, "a double portion" (*makpelah,* מכפלה), is here described as "possession of a burial place" (Gen. 50:13 NASB margin). The only possession the patriarchs received in the Promised Land during their lifetimes was a gravesite. By faith, they would receive their "double portion," the Promised Land of Israel in the future and the Promised Land of the Israel of God during the millennium. Eventually, they would dwell in **the** Promised Land, i.e., the new heaven and earth.

Another seven days of mourning occurred in a meadow that was "beyond the Jordan" (Gen. 50:10-11). The Egyptian company was on the east side of the Jordan and north of the region of the Dead Sea. Hebron was on the west side of the Jordan and west of the Dead Sea. The Egyptians were several miles distant from the burial site at Machpelah (Gen. 23:19). The cave at Machpelah had spiritual significance to Israel. It was hallowed ground, not to be viewed by unbelievers. Joseph and his brothers took Israel's body on the final stage of the journey to the land of Canaan and buried him in private.

The mourning totaled 70 days in Egypt and seven in Canaan. Seven and its multiples represent the perfection of unending time. Israel had left the arena of this life and continued in eternity (Gen. 2:2-3). God did bring Israel up from Egypt and up from the earth (page 358) (Gen 46:4). After he had buried his father, Joseph returned to Egypt with the burial party.

Joseph's Brothers Still Do Not Get It

Gen. 50:15-17: Joseph was now 56 years old. Benjamin was 40-43 years old. Joseph's other brothers ranged from 57-63 years of age. After the burial of Israel at Machpelah, Joseph's brothers demonstrated the guilt that still haunted them regarding their past evil deed to him, even though they had been with him in Egypt for 17 years. They feared for their lives. They had seen Joseph's love for their father. They concocted a "charge" from Israel before his death for Joseph to forgive them for their sin 39 years ago. They never received the forgiveness that Joseph freely gave to them. One person can genuinely forgive another without the second person accepting the forgiveness. Many times people do not accept the forgiveness God so freely gives to them after they turn to Him.

Elohim Turns Evil about for Good

Gen. 50:18-21: For the fifth time, the brothers bowed before Joseph as in his dreams nearly four decades ago. Joseph's actions had not relieved them of their guilt. His selection of only five to appear before Pharaoh 17 years earlier may have festered in the consciences of the six not selected. They continued to experience the guilt of their sin. Joseph wept out of love for them and for their lack of belief in the gracious working of God.

Joseph then enunciated to them a great principle in the life of a believer—all that they had done by their evil act God had turned about for good. Joseph did not view himself in his exalted position in Egypt as being in the place of God. All in authority need this understanding. *Elohim* had brought about a marvelous deliverance for the family of Israel, Egypt, and the surrounding nations. Joseph then reassured and comforted his brothers.

Any past evil in our lives can be turned about for good by the gracious working of the LORD. All believers should rejoice and appropriate this truth.

Gen. 50:22-23: Joseph lived to the ideal age for an Egyptian, 110 years. Perhaps God gave him 110 years because of his faithful service to Him in Egypt. He became a great-great-grandfather to Ephraim's children and a great-grandfather to Manasseh's children. He saw Israel begin its evolution from a family to a nation.

As part of the promise to Abraham to bless all the nations of the earth through his seed, *Yahweh* brought Joseph to Egypt, elevated and protected him in his position, and brought deliverance to Israel and many other people. Joseph also brought some into the fold of believers and helped his brothers grow in their faith in *Yahweh*.

Joseph's Faith—Return My Bones to the Promised Land

Gen. 50:24-26: Near the time of his departure, Joseph used his death as a stimulant to faith for the children of Israel. His sarcophagus was a continual reminder to the Israelites that Egypt was not their home. He charged them to carry his bones back to the Promised Land (Heb. 11:22). Moses and Joshua would fulfill that charge (Exod. 13:19, Josh. 24:32). Joseph's example is still a stimulant to faith for all the children of God.

Joseph renounced Egypt, as his father before him had done, and expressed his wish to return for burial in the land of Israel. That would occur 430 years after Joseph's entrance into Egypt, followed by 40 years of wandering in the wilderness after the Exodus, and the first seven years of the conquest of the Promised Land. Thus, his sarcophagus would be carried for nearly a half-century after the Exodus. It would be placed in the inheritance of the tribe of Ephraim by Joshua, an Ephraimite, and leader of all Israel at the time of the conquest of the Promised Land (Josh. 24:29-32).

Like Abel before him, Joseph offered up his life as a sacrifice that was a fragrance to his LORD. Although he is dead, Joseph still speaks:

"By faith Abel offered to God a better sacrifice than Cain, through which he obtained the testimony that he was righteous, God testifying about his gifts, and through faith, though he is dead, he still speaks" (Heb. 11:4).

CHART 4: JOSEPH'S LIFE	
AGE	EVENT
6	Joseph left Haran with his family.
13-16?	Dinah, who was the same age as Joseph, was raped at Shechem.
17	Joseph left Hebron and was sold as a slave to a caravan by his brothers. They sold him to Potiphar in Egypt.
27-30?	Joseph was accused of rape by Potiphar's wife and put in charge of Potiphar's prison.
30	Joseph ascended from prison to become governor of Egypt. He received priestly status and Asenath as his wife.
30-37	Manasseh and Ephraim were born during the seven years of plenty.
37-44	During the seven years of famine, Pharaoh was made wealthy by Joseph's reforms. Joseph instituted a 20 percent tax that continued after the famine.
38	Joseph's brothers came to Egypt during the first year of famine.
39	After the second visit by his brothers, his father and the rest of his family came to settle in Egypt.
56	Israel blessed Joseph's two sons, Ephraim and Manasseh. He gave a specific blessing and prophecy to all of his sons and their tribes. Israel died and was honored in Egypt, then followed a family burial at Machpelah. Joseph renewed his promise to his brothers and enunciated the principle of God taking evil and turning it about for good.
110	Joseph died at the ideal Egyptian age of 110. His sarcophagus became a stimulant to faith for the children of Israel who awaited their deliverance and return to the Promised Land with Joseph's body.

TABLE 8: AGE OF THE PATRIARCHS WHEN EVENTS TOOK PLACE			
ABRAHAM	**ISAAC**	**JACOB**	**JOSEPH**
100	Birth		
160	60	Birth	
175—Death	75	15	
	151	91	Birth
	168	108	17
	180—Death	120	29
		130—Egypt	39
		147—Death	56
			110—Death

Method for Interpretation of This Table:

When Abraham was 100 years old, Isaac was born.
When Isaac was 60 years old, Jacob was born.
When Abraham was 175 years old, Jacob was 15 years old, etc.

TABLE 9: PATRIARCH CONTEMPORARIES					
NAME & AGE AT DEATH	**ISAAC**	**ESAU & JACOB**	**LEVI**	**JOSEPH**	**EPHRAIM & MANASSEH**
Abraham—175	75	15			
Isaac—180		120	33	29	
Jacob—147			60	56	19-25

Explanation: This table is a comparison of the crossover in the lives of selected progeny of Abraham, Isaac, and Jacob.

APPENDIX I

THE WORD OF GOD

Some who read this book may have difficulty understanding the meaning of the phrase, "the Word of God."

The Bible gives its own definition of this phrase in several places; a few examples follow.

1. God gave specific words to individuals to transmit to others:

"As they were going down to the edge of the city, Samuel said to Saul, 'Say to the servant that he might go ahead of us and pass on, but you remain standing now, that I may proclaim the word of God to you'" (1 Sam. 9:27).

The oral words communicated from God to the writers of the Bible became the written text that eventually made up its content.

2. The LORD Jesus Christ and the apostles authenticated the *Tanakh*, the Old Testament:

"If he called them gods, to whom the word of God came (and the Scripture cannot be broken), do you say of Him, whom the Father sanctified and sent into the world, 'You are blaspheming,' because I said, 'I am the Son of God?'" (John 10:35-36).

"But know this first of all, that no prophecy of Scripture is a matter of one's own interpretation, for no prophecy was ever made by an act of human will, but men moved by the Holy Spirit spoke from God" (2 Pet. 1:20-21).

3. In addition, there were commands that God gave:

"Then God said, 'Let there be light'; and there was light" (Gen. 1:3).

"For when they maintain this, it escapes their notice that by the word of God the heavens existed long ago and the earth was formed out of water and by water" (2 Pet. 3:5).

4. Finally, God expressed Himself and called Himself the Word. The Apostle John begins his gospel by writing about the *Logos* (*log'-os,* λόγος), the Greek word that encompasses the expression of God to mankind in the person of the LORD Jesus Christ as the living Word:

"In the beginning was the Word and the Word was with God, and the Word was God. He was in the beginning with God. All things came into being through Him, and apart From Him, nothing came into being that has come into being. In Him was life, and the life was the Light of men. The Light shines in the darkness, and the darkness did not comprehend it" (John 1:1-5).

When the LORD Jesus Christ returns to the earth, He will be called "the Word of God":

"He is clothed with a robe dipped in blood, and His name is called The Word of God" (Rev. 19:13).

In the ultimate sense, God is the Word. However, He speaks through men who have recorded His spoken words. The Bible is the written record of the Word of God.

Nevertheless, the Bible can be a sterile book to some readers. The LORD Jesus Christ told the Samaritan woman that certain qualifications are necessary for knowing God and His truth:

"But an hour is coming, and now is, when the true worshipers will worship the Father in spirit and truth; for such people the Father seeks to be His worshipers. God is spirit, and those who worship Him must worship in spirit and truth" (John 4:23-24).

The person who wishes to become enlightened by studying the Bible must consider the aforementioned. The first qualification is a desire to know God. If one wishes to know His truth, it is helpful to speak a simple, honest prayer prior to initiating the study of the Bible and ask God to give enlightenment. God always responds to those who seek Him “in spirit and truth.”

APPENDIX II

SCRIPTURAL PRINCIPLES OF INTERPRETATION

1. In Scripture, a day = 24 hours, a month = 30 days, a year = 12 months containing 360 days (Gen. 7:11, 8:3-4; Rev. 11:2-3). As discussed in the text, numbers may have literal and/or symbolic meaning.

2. A Biblical day starts in the evening at sundown and finishes in the evening 24 hours later. The Hebrew word for "day" (*yom̂,* יום) can mean a period of 24 hours or an extended time (Gen. 2:4).

3. The names of people and places in the original Hebrew may give literal and symbolic understanding to the text (Gen. 38:1-30).

4. Hebrew is the basic Old Testament language. The original manuscript of the Gospel of Matthew was in Hebrew. There is evidence that the LORD dictated the book of Revelation in Hebrew; the Apostle John then transcribed a direct translation into Greek, the most widely used language of that day.

5. A large portion of the New Testament contains quotations from the Old Testament with commentary on the same. A difficult text may require translation from English to Greek and from Greek to Hebrew to gain full understanding of its meaning.

6. It is more accurate to learn the original meaning of a word, phrase, idiom, or sentence in the ancient culture of the people who originally received the message. This is more reliable than using the linguistic idiom and transient cultural mores of the West.

7. An understanding of the last book of the Bible, Revelation, depends on an understanding of the prior books of the Bible. This is particularly true of the foundational truths found in Genesis. The writings of the prophets depict many of the symbols and the prophecy necessary to understand much of the message of the Revelation (Rev. 10:7, 22:6).

APPENDIX III

BIBLICAL TIMELINES FROM ADAM TO CHRIST[76]

The tables that follow utilize the Biblical method of 360 days in a year to complete the analysis of the timelines recorded in the Old Testament. These tables depict the timelines from Adam to the birth of Christ. The first table depicts the period from the creation of Adam until the time of Joshua and the conquest of the Promised Land (Table 10, page 397).

The ages of individuals are taken at face value. The first humans lived nearly a millennium. Instead of posing the question as to whether men really lived that long, one should ask why they died. Man was not created to die; death came after the rebellion, the Fall, of man. As discussed in the text, because of man's propensity to sin, the life span was shortened. A long life span of evil actions would have resulted in such an accumulation of evil that the world would become subject to an early demise through the mutual destruction of war (Genesis 6-8).

Biblical Years from Adam to the Birth of the Christ

The Jewish system of lunar months has been fraught with difficulties in determining the exact time of the new moon. The basis of 360 days in a Biblical year is stated at the time of the flood and in the prophecy of the end of the present age (Gen. 7:11, 8:3-4; Rev. 11:3, 12: 6, 13:5). This corroborates the prophecy of 70 weeks of Biblical years for the nation of Israel (490 years) and the Sabbath-year (Lev. 25:8; Dan. 9:24-27, 12:7; Rev. 12:14). The tables detail Biblical years for both AA (After Adam's creation) and BC (Before Christ's birth).

It is difficult to ascertain specific dates as related to the Julian calendar that was in use until October, 1582, when the Gregorian calendar came into use. Gregorian years are not applicable to Biblical times. A Biblical year and a Julian year are not the same. Julian years average 365.25 days. As stated above, Biblical years are 360 days each (Gen. 7:11, 8:3-4; Rev. 11:2-3). In order to convert from Julian years to Biblical years, it is necessary to multiply by 1.01458 (365.25/360 = 1.01458). In order to convert from Biblical years to Julian years, it is necessary to multiply by 0.98563 (360/365.25). One can produce minor variations in results based on the number of decimal spaces used in the multiplier, but this does not affect the major dates.

There were 3,626 Biblical years from the creation of Adam until the exile of Judah. The final exile of Judah occurred in 594 Biblical years BC (594 Biblical years = 586 BC in Julian years, the known historical date of the final exile of Judah) (Table 12, page 407). Adam was created 4220 Biblical years BC (3626 + 594 = 4220) (Table 10, page 397).

Therefore, 4220 Biblical years AA minus any time AA = Biblical years BC. For example, 4220 – 930 (age of Adam at his death) = 3290 Biblical years BC. Adam's creation occurred around 4,160 Julian years (4220 X 0.98563 = 4160) before the dividing line between BC and AD (Table 10, page 397).

The LORD was born near the end of five BC, or early in four BC, based on evidence that Herod the Great died in March or April of four BC. There was a lunar eclipse documented close to the time of Herod's death that also occurred near the known date of Passover that spring.[77] The creation of Adam was 4,216 Biblical years BC (4220 – 4 = 4216). The birth of Isaac in 2108 AA was halfway between the creation of Adam and the birth of Christ (2108 X 2 = 4216) (Gen. 21:1-7). Therefore, the birth of the promised son, Isaac, was equidistant between the creation of Adam and the birth of the promised Son of God, the Messiah (Table 10, page 397).

TABLE 10: THE LINE FROM ADAM TO THE JUDGES							
ADAM'S CREATION WAS 4220 YEARS BC							
#	**Father**	**Birth**	**Initial[1]**	**Plus[2]**	**Total**	**AA[3]**	**BC[4]**
1	Adam	Adult	130	800	930	930	3290
2	Seth	130	105	807	912	1042	3178
3	Enosh	235	90	815	905	1140	3080
4	Kenan	325	70	840	910	1235	2985
5	Mahalalel	395	65	830	895	1290	2930
6	Jared	460	162	800	962	1422	2798
7	Enoch	622	65	300	365	987	3233
8	Methuselah	687	187	782	969	1656	2564
9	Lamech	874	182	595	777	1651	2569
10	Noah-1	1056	500	-	-	-	-
	Flood	1656	-	100	-	-	-
	Noah-2	-	-	350	950	2006	2214
11	Shem	1558	100	500	600	2158	2062
12	Arpachshad	1658	35	403	438	2096	2124
13	Shelah	1693	30	403	433	2126	2094
14	Eber	1723	34	430	464	2187	2033
15	Peleg	1757	30	209	239	1996	2224
16	Reu	1787	32	207	239	2026	2194
17	Serug	1819	30	200	230	2049	2171
18	Nahor	1849	29	119	148	1997	2223
19	Terah	1878	70	135	205	2083	2137
20	Abraham	2008	100	75	175	2183	2037
21	Isaac	2108	60	120	180	2288	1932
22	Jacob	2168	84	63	147	2315	1905
23a	Joseph	2259	30+	80	110	2369	1851
23b	Levi	2255	-	-	137	2392	1828
24	Kohath	-	-	-	133	-	-
25	Amram	-	-	-	137	-	-
26	Moses	2626	-	-	120	2746	1474

[1]Initial = Age of father in the left column when the next son in the righteous line was born. [2]Plus = additional years of life of the father. [3]AA = After Adam's creation. [4]BC = Before Christ's birth.

Comments on the Timelines

There was a significant decline in the ages of individuals after Noah. The changes in the diet that contributed to the decline in age in a post-flood environment have already been discussed. The more hostile environment outside the Garden of Eden, disease, and the violence of murder and war made their contributions to the decrease in the average age (pages 138 and 147).

Noah was the tenth generation AA; Abraham was the 20th. Joseph and Levi were brothers in the 23rd generation; Moses was the 26th generation.

Calculation of the 430 Years in Egypt

The calculation of the entry date into Egypt may start with Joseph's entrance or the time of Jacob's entrance. Joseph was 17 and Jacob was 130 years old at their respective times of entry into Egypt. Since the 70 years of exile in Babylon is calculated from the time of the first exiles (pages 409-410), the 430 years in Egypt is calculated from Joseph's entrance (Table 9, page 390).

The Four Generations in Egypt

At the time of the census at Mount Sinai, the tribe of Levi had a lower numbers of males, even though the numbering was started at the age of one month and above compared to the other tribes where it started at 20 years old and above. In addition, the number of Levites who served in the tabernacle from ages 30 to 50 was much less than expected for that age group compared to the other tribes (Num. 1:1-2, 2:1-34, 3:15-43, 4:22-49). The lesser numbers may be due to several factors: late onset marriages, sexual conservatism within marriage, and the possibility that the Levite leaders may have had young wives late in their lives that bore their children by whom the stay in Egypt can be calculated.

Moses was born 350 years into the 430 years of Egyptian exile (Exod. 7:7, 12:40-41). Moses' father Amram married his Aunt Jochebed, sister of Amram's father, Kohath, the son of Levi (Exod.

6:20). Thus, Jochebed was the daughter of Levi. Levi entered Egypt at age 43, when Joseph was 39; Levi spent 94 years in Egypt before his death at age 137. The cumulative years of Levi, Kohath, Amram, and Moses in Egypt were 444 years (94 + 133 + 137 + 80 = 444) (Gen. 41:46, 45:6; Exod. 6:16-20, 7:7). This gives 14 years for the crossover of these four generations (444 - 14 = 430). Thus, the birth of these leaders was late in the lives of their fathers.

The Time of the Exodus

The 480 years from the Exodus to the fourth year of Solomon's reign (3186 AA - 2706 AA = 480) is concordant with starting the sojourn in Egypt with Joseph's entrance (Table 10, page 397; Table 12, page 403):

"Now it came about in the four hundred and eightieth year after the sons of Israel came out of the land of Egypt, in the fourth year of Solomon's reign over Israel, in the month of Ziv which is the second month, that he began to build the house of the LORD" (1 Kin. 6:1).

The Exodus occurred in the year 2706 AA/1514 BC in Biblical years. There were 1514 Biblical years from the time of the Exodus until the dividing line between BC and AD (4220 AA - 2706 AA = 1514). The Exodus occurred in 1492 BC according to the Julian calendar (1514 X 0.98563 = 1492).

Calculation of the Period of the Conquest

Caleb was 85 years old, when he received the area around Hebron from Joshua. He was 40 years old at the time of the spies, the second year after leaving Egypt. Israel wandered in the desert an additional 38 years (40 + 38 = 78 years) (85 years of age - 78 years = 7 years) (Josh. 14:6-15). Thus, there were seven years of conquest up until the time of the allotment of the land to the tribes by Joshua.

However, the tribes had not completed the occupation of the land at the time of Joshua's death (Jdg. 1:1-36, 2:1-10). Seven years are missing in the 480 years from the Exodus to the fourth year of the reign of Solomon (Table 10, page 397; Table 12, page 403) (1 Kin. 6:1). Therefore, the total time of the conquest of the Promised Land by Joshua's generation until the first judge, Othniel (2760 AA/1460 BC), occupied 14 years, not seven years (Table 11, page 402) (Jdg. 2:16, 3:9).

The Time of the Judges

Jephthah argued that Israel had occupied an area east of the Jordan for three hundred years (Jdg. 11:26). The end of the 40 years in the desert and the beginning of the conquest of Canaan was 2746 AA/1474 BC. Jephthah began his rule in 3079 AA/1141 BC, 333 years (3079 – 2746 = 333) after the completion of the wandering in the wilderness (Table 11, page 402). Therefore, the time of the Judges was greater than three hundred years.

The defeat of the Philistines by King David and the return of the ark after consolidation of the kingdom effectively date the end of the period of the Judges. Eli died when the ark was taken in 3130 AA (1 Sam. 4:17-18). The ark was initially in the land of the Philistines for seven months and later was kept for 20 years at Kiriath-jearim (1 Sam. 6:1, 7:1-2). King David brought the ark back in the first year of his consolidated reign over Israel in 3150 AA/1070 BC, 20 years after Eli's death (1 Chr. 12:38-40, 13:1-14).

During the time of the judges, King Saul was on the throne for 40 years and King David came to the throne of Judah for seven and one-half years. The end of the Philistine rule was 3150 AA. King Saul's reign was 40 years from 3102-3142 AA (Acts 13:21). The reign of King David was from 3143-3150 AA over Judah and 3150-3183 AA over the consolidated kingdom of Israel and Judah (Table 11, page 402; Table 12, page 403).

The total time of the Judges, including the crossover with King Saul and King David, was 390 years (Table 11, page 402; Table 12, page 403). Note that the Israeli Judges, shown in italics, accounted for 296 of the 390 years (76 percent) (Table 11, page 402). Even in a very bleak period of Israel's history, God brought forth a predominance of Hebrew Judges.

Other Contemporary Judges

Shamgar, the son of Anath, was a local judge contemporary with Deborah (Jdg. 3:31, 5:6).

Samson was born soon after the start of the 40 years that the Philistines ruled (Jdg. 13:1-25). He was a local judge in the western part of the country during the last 20 of the 40 years of Philistine rule; he crossed over with King Saul and King David in the east (Jdg. 13:1, 15:20, 16:31).

Eli, a descendant of Ithamar, served as High Priest (Num. 4:1-3; 1 Sam. 1:3, 2:27-35; 1 Kin. 2:26-27; 1 Chr. 6:3, 24:6). He also served as a judge of Israel for 40 years from 3090-3130 AA (1 Sam. 4:15-18). He died at the age of 98 when the ark was taken; therefore, he was born in 3032 AA.

Perhaps the most significant spiritual leader of the period was Samuel who held the offices of judge and prophet during the time of Eli, King Saul, and King David. He was from the seed of Korah, the son of Izhar, the son of Kohath, the son of Levi. He lived to a great age (Exod. 6:18-21; 1 Sam. 1:25-28; 3:20; 7:15; 12:2, 11; 25:1; 28:14; 1 Chr. 6:22-38).

TABLE 11: THE TIME OF THE JUDGES[1]			
NAME OF JUDGE WHO RULED OVER ISRAEL	DURATION OF RULE (IN YEARS)	LAST YEAR[2] OF JUDGE'S RULE, AA[3]	LAST YEAR[2] OF JUDGE'S RULE, BC[4]
Cushan-rishathaim of Aram-naharaim	8	2768	1452
Othniel[5]	40	2808	1412
Eglon of Moab	18	2826	1394
Ehud	80	2906	1314
Jabin of Canaan	20	2926	1294
Deborah and Shamgar	40	2966	1254
Midian	7	2973	1247
Gideon	40	3013	1207
Abimelech of Shechem	3	3016	1204
Tola	23	3039	1181
Jair	22	3061	1159
Philistines/Ammon	18	3079	1141
Jephthah	6	3085	1135
Ibzan	7	3092	1128
Elon	10	3102	1118
Abdon	8	3110	1110
Philistines *Samson*-20 years	40	3150	1070

[1]The period of the Judges started in 2760 AA/1460 BC.
[2]Note that the last two columns denote the **last year** of the rule of a particular judge.
[3]AA = After Adam's creation in Biblical years.
[4]BC = Before Christ's birth in Biblical years.
[5]Italicized names indicate Israeli judges.

TABLE 12: THE TIME OF THE KINGS
PAGES 403-407

PART I: ISRAEL'S UNITED KINGDOM	
NAME OF THE KING	**YEARS OF REIGN AA/BC[1]**
Saul	3102-3142 AA 1118-1078 BC
David[2]	3150-3183 AA 1070-1037 BC
Solomon	3182-3222 AA 1038-998 BC

[1]In this section and the subsequent sections of this table—AA = After Adam's creation/BC = Before Christ's birth.

[2]King David assumed the throne of Judah for seven and one-half years from 3142 AA/1078 BC to 3150 AA/1070 BC before he became King of all Israel (2 Sam. 5:5, 1 Chr. 26:31).

In subsequent sections of this table, the year of Judah's king is compared to the corresponding year of the king of Israel and *vice versa*. The length of each king's reign is taken from the books of 1 and 2 Kings, and 2 Chronicles.

PART II-A: ISRAEL'S DIVIDED KINGDOM			
JUDAH'S KING	AA/BC	ISRAEL'S KING	AA/BC
Rehoboam	3222-3239 AA 998-981 BC	Jeroboam I	3222-3244 AA 998-976 BC
Abijam- Year 18 of Jeroboam I	3240-3242 AA 980-978 BC		
Asa- Year 20 of Jeroboam I	3242-3283 AA 978-937 BC	Nadab- Year 2 of Asa	3244-3245 AA 976-975 BC
		Baasha- Year 3 of Asa	3245-3268 AA 975-952 BC
		Elah- Year 26 of Asa	3268-3269 AA 952-951 BC
		Zimri- Year 27 of Asa	3269 AA (7 days) 951 BC
		Tibni/Omri- Year 27 of Asa	3269-3273 AA 951-947 BC
		Omri- Year 31 of Asa	3273-3280 AA 947-940 BC
Jehoshaphat- Year 4 of Ahab	3284-3309 AA 936-911 BC	Ahab- Year 38 of Asa	3280-3302 AA 940-918 BC

Part II-B: Israel's Divided Kingdom			
Judah's King	AA/BC	Israel's King	AA /BC
		Ahaziah- Year 17 of Jehoshaphat	3301-3302 AA 919-918 BC
Jehoram- Year 5 of Joram	3307-3314 AA 913-906 BC	Joram- Year 18 of Jehoshaphat	3302-3314 AA 918-906 BC
Ahaziah- Year 12 of Joram	3314 AA 906 BC		
Queen Athaliah- Year 12 of Joram	3314-3320 AA 906-900 BC	Jehu- Year 1 of Athaliah	3314-3342 AA 906-878 BC
Joash- Year 7 of Jehu	3321-3361 AA 899-859 BC	Jehoahaz- Year 23 of Joash	3343-3360 AA 877-860 BC
Amaziah- Year 2 of Jehoash	3360-3389 AA 860-831 BC	Jehoash of Israel- Year 37 of Joash	3358-3374 AA 862-846 BC
Interregnum	3390-3400 AA 830-820 BC	Jeroboam II- Year 15 of Amaziah	3375-3415 AA 845-805 BC
Uzziah (Azariah)- Year 27 of Jeroboam II	3401-3452 AA 819-768 BC	Interregnum	3416-3437 AA 804-783 BC

Part II-C: Israel's Divided Kingdom			
Judah's King	**AA/BC**	**Israel's King**	**AA /BC**
		Zechariah- Year 38 of Uzziah	3438 AA (6 months) 782 BC
		Shallum- Year 39 of Uzziah	3439 AA (one month) 781 BC
		Menahem- Year 39 of Uzziah	3439-3449 AA 781-771 BC
		Pekahiah- Year 50 of Uzziah	3450-3451 AA 770-769 BC
Jotham- Year 2 of Pekah	3453-3468 AA 767-752 BC	Pekah- Year 52 of Uzziah	3452-3471 AA 768-749 BC
Ahaz- Year 17 of Pekah	3468-3483 AA 752-737 BC	Hoshea- Year 20 of Jotham Year 12 of Ahaz	3472-3480 AA 748-740 BC 3480-3488 AA 740-732 BC

PART II-D: THE EXILES OF ISRAEL AND JUDAH			
JUDAH'S KING	**AA/BC**	**ISRAEL'S KING**	**AA /BC**
Hezekiah- Year 3 of Hoshea	3483-3512 AA 737-708 BC	Israel's exile occurred in the sixth year of Hezekiah- 3488 AA/732 BC[1] (2 Kin. 18:9-10)	
Manasseh	3512-3567 AA 708-653 BC		
Amon	3568-3569 AA 652-651 BC		
Josiah	3570-3601 AA 650-619 BC		
Jehoahaz	3602 AA (3 months) 618 BC		
Jehoiakim	3603-3614 AA 617-606 BC	Judah's initial exile occurred in the third year of Jehoiakim- 3606 AA/614 BC (see text)[2]	
Jehoiachin	3615 AA (3 months) 605 BC	Jehoiachin went into exile in the eighth year of Nebuchadnezzar in 605 BC in Biblical years/597 BC in Julian years.	
Zedekiah	3615-3626 AA 605-594 BC[3]		
[1]732 BC in Biblical years = 722 BC in Julian years, Israel's exile. [2]614 BC in Biblical years = 605 BC in Julian years, Judah's first exile. [3]594 BC in Biblical years = 586 BC in Julian years, Judah's final exile.			

The Kings to the Exile of Israel and the Exile of Judah

There was an interregnum in Judah from 3390-3400 AA/830-820 BC. Uzziah (Azariah) was 16 years old when he became king in 3401 AA/819 BC. He would have been about four years old at the time of the death of his father, Amaziah, in 3389 AA/831 BC.

There was an interregnum in Israel for 21 years after the death of Jeroboam II from 3416-3437 AA/804-783 BC. Zechariah may have been too young to ascend the throne at his father's death; his age is not given. It is unclear as to why it took 21 years for him to become king; no reason is given.

It is likely that the priests controlled the respective kingdoms any time the thrones were vacant and when a young king was on the throne (2 Chr. 23:1-24:27).

Many of the kings died at an early age and the cause of death is not given; disease would be the most likely explanation. Apparent discrepancies in the years of reign recorded in different verses for several kings can be explained by a period of co-regency between the father and son. A terminal illness in the father may have been the reason for several co-regencies. In addition, the king's reign may have been calculated from the start of a new calendar year (2 Chr. 29:3, 17; 30:2-3).

The most confusing time in the kings is during the reign of Jotham, king of Judah, and Hoshea, king of Israel. Hoshea conspired against Pekah and put him to death in the 20th year of Jotham, 3471 AA/749 BC, **nine** years before Hoshea officially became king. Jotham became king in the second year of Pekah, king of Israel, for **16** years.

The likely explanation is that Jotham was co-regent for two years with his father Uzziah (Azariah) from 3451-3452 AA/769-768 BC who died with a contagious skin disease after trying to assume the duties of the priesthood. The Hebrew word, *tsara* [*tsar̂a'*, צרע], simply means "a skin disease," not "leprosy." Since Pekah was murdered in 3471 AA/749 BC, these calculations also indicate that Jotham continued with a co-regency of three years with Ahaz from 3468-3471 AA/752-749 BC (2 Kin. 15:27-16:2).

Hoshea officially became king in the 12th year of the reign of Ahaz, king of Judah, from 3480 AA/740 BC for nine years. Therefore, he was reigning the previous nine years without title. No reason is given; it may have been related to the fact that he assassinated Pekah at the time Assyria was gaining control in Israel (2 Kin. 15:29-30, 17:1). His conspiracy against Assyria was the final act that resulted in the LORD allowing Assyria to take Israel into exile (2 Kin. 17:3-6). Israel went into exile in 3488 AA/732 BC, the sixth year of Hezekiah's reign in Judah, the same as Hoshea's final year (2 Kin. 18:9-10).

The Exile of Israel and the Exile of Judah

The Biblical record gives comparison details between the kings of Israel and the kings of Judah until the time of the exile of Israel. Israel's exile occurred in 722 Julian years BC according to documentation in extra-Biblical historical sources (722 X 1.01458 [365.25/360] = 732 Biblical years BC) (Table 12, page 407).

The book of Daniel records the **first** year of King Nebuchadnezzar, 606-605 Julian years BC, as the **third** year of Jehoiakim (Dan. 1:1). Biblical writers sometimes referred to either Jewish civil years or Jewish religious years. Daniel, living in Babylon, may have been referring to the Jewish civil year that started in the fall (our September or October) as it related to Jehoiakim's reign. According to Jeremiah, the **first** year of King Nebuchadnezzar was the **fourth** year of Jehoiakim (Jer. 25:1). Jeremiah, living in Israel, may have referred to the Jewish religious year starting with the month of Abib that became the month of Nisan after the exile (March or April, the time of Passover) (Exod. 12:2, 13:4; Esther 3:7).

Thus, the first deportation of Judah occurred in the first year of King Nebuchadnezzar in 606-605 Julian years BC. The 70 years when the land lay fallow lasted from 606-605 BC to 536-535 Julian years BC (2 Chr. 36:20-21; Ezra 3:8, 5:13; Jer. 25:11,

29:10). Cyrus's decree resulted in the resettlement of the land at the time the prophesied 70 years was completed in 536-535 Julian years BC (Ezra 1:1, 5:13, 6:3; Jer. 25:1-12; Dan. 1:1, 9:1-2).

The final deportation of Judah occurred in the 11th year of Zedekiah and the 19th year of Nebuchadnezzar, 594 Biblical years BC, i.e., 586 Julian years BC (2 Kin. 25:8-11, Jer. 39:1-2). The 70 years of the desolation of the temple until its rebuilding went from 586 BC to 516 BC in Julian years (Ezra 6:15, Jer. 39:2, 2 Chr. 36:19-21).

The LORD counted the Sabbaths that were not kept after the commandment was given at Mount Sinai in Biblical year 2706 AA/1514 BC. Judah disobeyed the commandment for 70 years of Sabbaths, an equivalent of 490 Biblical years (70 X 360 = 25,200 Sabbaths divided by an average of 51.4286 Sabbaths per year [360/7 = 51.4286] = 490 Biblical years) (Lev. 26:34, 2 Chr. 36:21, Jer. 25:11).

If we apply this number of 490 Biblical years to the time of the exile of Judah, we can glean the following insight. There were 920 Biblical years from the Exodus until the exile of Judah (1514 BC – 594 BC = 920). Judah kept the Sabbath just 430 of a possible 920 Biblical years, 47 percent of the time (920 - 490 = 430).

The LORD has His method of keeping time. We must analyze time in the Scriptures according to His system. He kept specific records of the period of apostasy in Judah and their disobedience of the law as reflected by their failure to keep the Sabbath.

Interestingly, the 490 Biblical years where Judah failed to keep the Sabbath, is the same as the prophetic period of 70 weeks of years (7 X 70 = 490 Biblical years) for the nation of Israel before the LORD's return to the earth (Dan. 9:24-27). The theme of both of these periods is judgment to Judah and the nation of Israel followed by redemption. The final week (seven years) of Daniel's prophecy will involve the church, the Israel of God.

EPILOGUE

The LORD has the history of His people recorded by generations. Herein we have studied the 12 generations recorded in the book of Genesis. It is worth looking beyond Genesis to what may have been the greatest generation recorded in the Old Testament.

The Scriptures tell of an entire generation that was "gathered to their fathers." That generation lived through a time of war and conquest. They served *Yahweh* all the days of Joshua and were honored with this wonderful epitaph:

"All that generation also was gathered to their fathers" (Jdg. 2:10a).

Their family reunion was a marvelous one. Unfortunately, today there is no nation on earth seeking to serve the LORD as ancient Israel did during the days of Joshua and his generation. Nevertheless, let us seek to tell our relatives and acquaintances about the LORD-Jesus-Christ/*YHWH-Yeshua-Mashiach*, so that we may experience a glorious family reunion like that generation.

The LORD uses the events of each person's life at different ages, places, and circumstances to shape that person. The lives of the patriarchs described in the book of Genesis are instructive to all of us. The stories of individuals throughout the Bible are literal histories. They are as real as our lives and the circumstances we face. Let us learn from them:

"Now these things happened to them as an example, and they were written for our instruction, upon whom the ends of the ages have come" (1 Cor. 10:11).

Let us look forward to the time that we will recline at table with our relatives in the family of God and our blessed LORD. The invitation is open to all who will submit their lives to the LORD Jesus Christ:

"And someone said to Him, 'Lord, are there just a few who are being saved?' And He said to them, 'Strive to enter through the narrow door; for many, I tell you, will seek to enter and will not be able. Once the head of the house gets up and shuts the door, and you begin to stand outside and knock on the door, saying, 'Lord, open up to us!' then He will answer and say to you, 'I do not know where you are from.' Then you will begin to say, 'We ate and drank in Your presence, and You taught in our streets'; and He will say, 'I tell you, I do not know where you are from; DEPART FROM ME ALL YOU EVILDOERS.' In that place there will be weeping and gnashing of teeth when you see Abraham and Isaac and Jacob and all the prophets in the kingdom of God, but yourselves being thrown out. And they will come from east and west and from north and south, and will recline at the table in the kingdom of God. And behold, some are last who will be first and some are first who will be last" (Luke 13:23-30).

REFERENCES

[1] A.W. Tozer, *The Knowledge of the Holy; the Attributes of God: Their Meaning in the Christian Life* (New York: Harper and Row, 1961), 27-28.

[2] Paul Davies, *God and the New Physics* (New York: Simon & Schuster, 1983), 13.

[3] William Dembski, *Intelligent Design: The Bridge Between Science & Theology* (Downers Grove IL: InterVarsity Press, 1999), 203-205.

[4] Davies, *God and the New Physics,* 21.

[5] Ibid., 51.

[6] Ibid., 51.

[7] Ibid., 121-122.

[8] Ibid., 121-122.

[9] Ibid., 199-213.

[10] William C. Ho, *Evolution? Degeneration? Creation?* (Paradise PA: Ambassadors for Christ, 2003), 43-46.

[11] Ibid., 33-36.

[12] Dembski, *Intelligent Design*, 211-236.

[13] John D. Sanford, *Genetic Entropy & The Mystery of the Genome* (Lima NY: Ivan Press, 2005), 20-21.

[14] Davies, *God and the New Physics,* 174.

[15] Ibid., 179-180.

REFERENCES—CONTINUED

[16] Ibid., 180.

[17] Ho, *Evolution? Degeneration? Creation?* 47-52.

[18] Sanford, *Genetic Entropy & The Mystery of the Genome,* 15-32.

[19] R.J. Britten, Divergence between samples of chimpanzee and human DNA sequences is 5% counting indels. *Proceedings National Academy of Science,* 99:13633-13635.

[20] Sanford, *Genetic Entropy & The Mystery of the Genome,* 20-21.

[21] Eugene Linden and Francine Patterson, *The Education of Koko* (Emeryville CA: Alibris, 1981).

[22] James P. Gills and Thomas E. Woodward, *Darwinism under the Microscope* (Lake Mary FL: Charisma House, 2002), 97-109.

[23] Charles Darwin, *The Origin of the Species, Ch. 6: Difficulties with the Theory* (London: John Murray, Albermarle Street, November 24, 1859).

[24] Michael J. Behe, *Darwin's Black Box* (Free Press, A Division of Simon & Schuster, Inc. Rockefeller Center, New York, NY 2006), 51-73.

[25] Gills, *Darwinism under the Microscope,* 153-162.

[26] Dembski, *Intelligent Design*, 82-85.

[27] Ho, *Evolution? Degeneration? Creation?* 69-72.

[28] Mary H. Schweitzer, et al. "Soft-Tissue Vessels and Cellular Preservation in Tyrannosaurus Rex," *Science*, 3005:1952-1955, March 25, 2005.

REFERENCES—CONTINUED

[29] Don Richardson, *Eternity in Their Hearts* (Ventura CA: Regal Books, 3rd ed., 2005), 9-63.

[30] Don Richardson, *Secrets of the Koran* (Ventura CA: Regal Books, 2003), 73-86, 160-175.

[31] Robert M. Hutchins, ed., *Great Books of the Western World, Vol. 16: Ptolemy, Copernicus, Kepler* (Chicago: The University of Chicago1952), 1005-1085.

[32] Geoffrey W. Bromiley, gen. ed., *The International Standard Bible Encyclopedia*, *Vol. 3: Music,* and *Vol. 4: Religions of the Biblical World* (Grand Rapids: Wm. B. Eerdmans, 1986), 436-437 and 85-100.

[33] DK Peneny, The History of Rock 'n' Roll (3/98, Last update 3/26/06), http://www.history-of-rock.com/

[34] Chuck Israels, Aspen no. 1, item 2: Jazz: A Cool Duel, http://www.ubu.com/aspen/siteIndex.html

[35] A. W. Tozer, *The Set of the Sail* (Camp Hill, PA: Wingspread Publishers), 155.

[36] Alfred E. Edersheim, *The Temple: Its Ministry and Services* (Peabody MA: Hendrickson Publishers, 1994), 49-54, 131-133.

[37] A. W. Tozer, *Of God and Men* (Camp Hill, PA: Wingspread Publishers), 35-37.

[38] A. W. Tozer, *That Incredible Christian* (Camp Hill, PA: Wingspread Publishers), 129-130.

[39] Ho, *Evolution? Degeneration? Creation?* 79-82.

[40] Richardson, *Secrets of the Koran*, 52-63.

REFERENCES—CONTINUED

[41] Ho, *Evolution? Degeneration? Creation?* 89-93.

[42] Ibid., 69-72.

[43] Ibid., 95-100.

[44] Ibid., 95-100.

[45] Ibid., 101-106.

[46] Gills, *Darwinism under the Microscope,* 97-109.

[47] Ho, *Evolution? Degeneration? Creation?* 107-113.

[48] Ibid., 107-113.

[49] David Edwin Harrell Jr., *Oral Roberts: An American Life* (Bloomington IN: Indiana University Press, 1985), 460-463.

[50] Oral Roberts, *Expect a Miracle: My Life and Ministry* (Nashville, TN: Thomas Nelson, 1995), 52-63.

[51] Alfred Edersheim, *Bible History: Old Testament, Book 1* (Peabody MA: Hendrickson Publishers, 1995), 41-45.

[52] Bromiley, gen. ed., *The International Standard Bible Encyclopedia, Vol. 1: Tower of Babel* and *Vol. 3: Moon,* 382-384 and 410-411.

[53] Gene Addison, *Who Is Allah? The Terrorists' God; Additional Facts about Islam* (Tampa FL: private printing, 2002), 50-53.

[54] Richardson, *Eternity in Their Hearts*, 9-63.

[55] Ibid., 65-116.

[56] Ibid., 9-63.

REFERENCES—CONTINUED

[57] Ho, *Evolution? Degeneration? Creation?* 83-87.

[58] William Varner, *The Messiah: Revealed, Rejected, Received, The Second Testament, Melchizedek and Messiah* (Bloomington IN: AuthorHouse, 2004), 215.

[59] Edersheim, *Bible History: Old Testament, Book 1,* 52-57.

[60] Richardson, *Secrets of the Koran*, 237-252.

[61] Richardson, *Eternity in Their Hearts*, 149-174.

[62] Ibid., 65-116.

[63] Richardson, *Secrets of the Koran*, 87-115.

[64] Jonathan D. Burnham, *A Story of Conflict—The Controversial Relationship between Benjamin Wills Newton and John Nelson Darby* (Waynesboro GA: Paternoster, 2004).

[65] John F. Walvoord, *The Revelation of Jesus Christ* (Chicago: Moody Press, 1966), 142.

[66] Alfred Edersheim, *Prophecy and History in Relation to the Messiah (The Barburton Lectures for 1880-1884)* (Eugene OR: Wipf and Stock Publishers, 2005), 2, 315.

[67] Lambert Dolphin, "Mount Moriah, Site of the Temple Mount in Jerusalem," The Temple Mount in Jerusalem, April 8, 1996, http://www.templemount.org/moriah2.html.

[68] Ibid.

[69] Richardson, *Secrets of the Koran*, 87-115.

[70] Alfred Edersheim, *The Life and Times of Jesus the Messiah, Book II* (Grand Rapids: Wm. B. Eerdmans, 1981), 186-190.

REFERENCES—CONTINUED

[71] Rick Meyers, *e-Sword*®, Copyright © 2000-2007, All rights reserved worldwide. www.e-sword.net

[72] Richardson, *Eternity in Their Hearts*, 9-63, 117-133.

[73] Ibid.

[74] Edersheim, *Bible History: Old Testament, Book 1,* 118.

[75] Edersheim, *Bible History: Old Testament, Book 1,* 130-131.

[76] Larry D. Edwards, M.D., *Family Reunion with Old Testament Patriarchs—and Old Testament Timelines* (Odessa FL: BBI Publications, 2003).

[77] Edersheim, *The Life and Times of Jesus the Messiah*, *Appendix VII,* 704-705.

ACKNOWLEDGMENTS

Reference 1 is from *The Knowledge of the Holy; the Attributes of God: Their Meaning in the Christian Life* by A. W. Tozer, copyright © 1961 by Aiden Wilson Tozer. Reprinted by permission of HarperCollins Publishers.

Reference 35 is reprinted from *The Set of the Sail* by A. W. Tozer, copyright © 1986 by Zur Ltd. Used by permission of WingSpread Publishers, a division of Zur, Ltd., 800.233.4443.

Reference 37 is reprinted from *Of God and Men* by A. W. Tozer, copyright © 1960, 1988 by the Tozer Family. Used by permission of WingSpread Publishers, a division of Zur, Ltd., 800.233.4443.

Reference 38 is reprinted from *That Incredible Christian* by A. W. Tozer, copyright © 1964 by Zur Ltd. Used by permission of WingSpread Publishers, a division of Zur, Ltd., 800.233.4443.

Printed in the United States
84231LV00004B/73-510/A

9 781600 349133